The Cinematic Mode of Production

INTERFACES: STUDIES IN VISUAL CULTURE
Editors: Mark J. Williams & Adrian W. B. Randolph, Dartmouth College

This series, sponsored by Dartmouth College Press, develops and promotes the study of visual culture from a variety of critical and methodological perspectives. Its impetus derives from the increasing importance of visual signs in everyday life, and from the rapid expansion of what are termed "new media." The broad cultural and social dynamics attendant to these developments present new challenges and opportunities across and within the disciplines. These have resulted in a trans-disciplinary fascination with all things visual, from "high" to "low," and from esoteric to popular. This series brings together approaches to visual culture—broadly conceived—that assess these dynamics critically and that break new ground in understanding their effects and implications.

Jonathan Beller, *The Cinematic Mode of Production: Attention Economy and the Society of the Spectacle*

Ann B. Shteir and Bernard Lightman, eds., *Figuring It Out: Science, Gender, and Visual Culture*

Anna Munster, *Materializing New Media: Body, Image, and Interface in Information Aesthetics*

Luc Pauwels, ed., *Visual Cultures of Science: Rethinking Representational Practices in Knowledge Building and Science Communication*

Lisa Saltzman and Eric Rosenberg, eds., *Trauma and Visuality in Modernity*

DARTMOUTH COLLEGE PRESS

HANOVER, NEW HAMPSHIRE

PUBLISHED BY

UNIVERSITY PRESS OF

NEW ENGLAND

HANOVER AND LONDON

The Cinematic Mode of Production

Attention Economy and the Society of the Spectacle

Jonathan Beller

DARTMOUTH COLLEGE PRESS

Published by

University Press of New England,

One Court Street, Lebanon, NH 03766

www.upne.com

© 2006 by Jonathan Beller

Printed in the United States of America

5 4 3 2 1

Library of Congress Cataloging-in-Publication Data

Beller, Jonathan.

   The cinematic mode of production : attention economy
and the society of the spectacle / Jonathan Beller.

      p.   cm.

Includes bibliographical references and index.

ISBN-13: 978-1-58465-582-4 (cloth : alk. paper)

ISBN-10: 1-58465-582-8 (cloth : alk. paper)

ISBN-13: 978-1-58465-583-1 (pbk. : alk. paper)

ISBN-10: 1-58465-583-6 (pbk. : alk. paper)

1. Motion pictures—Philosophy. I. Title.

PN1995.B336 2006

791.4301—dc22   2006024629

For Neferti,

Who inspires more than words

CONTENTS

ACKNOWLEDGMENTS

Thanks, many of them belated, to the following people for helping to make this book: Fredric Jameson, Barbara Herrnstein-Smith, Kenneth Surin, Cathy Davidson, Ariel Dorfman, George Yudice, Edward Said, Ramón Saldivar, Jay Schecter, Denis Wood, Michael Diamond, Lucho Marcial, Kevin Dalton, Valerie Beller, Carlo Tadiar, David "3000GT VR-4" Thompson, Eva-Lynn Jagoe, Sara Danius, Stefan Jonsson, Cesare Cesarino, Saree Makdisi, Xudong Zhang, Richard Dienst, Mark Simpson, Michael Hardt, Rebecca Karl, Eleanor Kaufman (tee-hee), Renu Bora, Imre Szeman, Sandy Swanson, Priscilla Lane, Joan McNay, Gail Hammer, Sandy Mills, Jose Muñoz, and Brian Selskey. Also to Vicente Rafael, Sean Cubitt (thank you, Sean!), Christopher Connery, Gopal Balakrishnan, Gail Hershatter, Jennifer Gonzalez, Warren Sack, Jody Greene, Anjali Arondekar, Lucy Burns, Gina Dent, Angela Davis, Jim Clifford, Nobi Nagasawa, Carla Freccero, Rob Wilson, Paul Bové, Donald Pease, Jonathan Arac, Meg Havran, Wimal Dissanayake, Brian Massumi, Michael Hardt, Eyal Amiran, John Unsworth, Steven Shaviro, Sheila Peuse, Nicholas Rhombes, Hugh Culik, Wayne Lesser, Lisa Parks, Jon Simons, W.J.T. Mitchell, James Elkins, Chip Lord, Maggie Morse, Cathy Soussloff, Bill Nichols, Judith Butler, Toni Oliviero, May Joseph, Jim Elledge, Paul Narkunas, Ethan Spigland, Suzie Verderber, Sameetha Agha, Amy Lesen, Miriam Greenberg, Ann Holder, Amy Guggenheim, Edel Garcellano, Manny Garibay, Elmer Borlongan, Ellen Paglinauan, Ivan Zatz-Diaz, Roland Tolentino, Hugh Raffels, Seth Goldstein, Coco Fusco, John Landrigan, Gloriana Russell, Sina Najafi, Edy Mcwilliams, Linda Holiday, Hal Lehrman, mom and dad.

My heartfelt and eternal gratitude to Nicholas Mirzoeff, without whose support this project would not have seen the light of day. And my thanks to Luna and Neferti, who not only inspire but bring joy to my days on Earth.

ABBREVIATIONS

MM   Regis Debray, *Media Manifestos,* trans. Eric Rauth
(London and New York: Verso, 1996)

FFCP   Jacques Lacan, *The Four Fundamental Concepts of Psychoanalysis,* ed. Jacques-Alain Miller, trans.
Alan Sheridan (New York: W.W. Norton, 1981)

Vertov   Dziga Vertov, *Kino-Eye: The Writings of Dziga Vertov,*
ed. Annette Michelson, trans. Kevin O'Brien (Berkeley and
Los Angeles: University of California Press, 1984)

Grundrisse   Karl Marx, *Grundrisse,* in *Karl Marx and Frederick Engels Collected Works,* vol. 28 (Moscow: Progress, 1986)

Wurzer   Wilhelm S. Wurzer, *Filming and Judgment: Between Heidegger and Adorno* (Atlantic Highlands, N.J.: Humanities Press, 1990)

Writings   Sergei Eisenstein, *Selected Works: Writings 1922–1934,* vol. 1,
ed. and trans. Richard Taylor (London: BFI Publishing, 1988)

CR   Ivan Petrovich Pavlov, *Conditioned Reflexes,* ed. and trans.
G.V. Anrep (New York: Dover Publications, 1960)

SM   Frederick Winslow Taylor, *The Principles of Scientific Management* (New York: Norton Library, 1967)

The
Cinematic
Mode of
Production

Introduction
The Political Economy
of the Postmodern

But all the story of the night told over,
And their minds transfigured so together,
More witnesseth than fancies images,
And grows to something of great constancy;
But, howsoever, strange and admirable.
—A Midsummer Night's Dream *(the movie)*

The Cinematic Mode of Production

The Cinematic Mode of Production remands to the reader the following idea: Cinema and its succeeding (if still simultaneous), formations, particularly television, video, computers, and the internet, are deterritorialized factories in which spectators work, that is, in which we perform value-productive labor. It is in and through the cinematic image and its legacy, the gossamer imaginary arising out of a matrix of socio-psycho-material relations, that we make our lives. This claim suggests that not only do we confront the image at the scene of the screen, but we confront the logistics of the image wherever we turn—imaginal functions are today imbricated in perception itself. Not only do the denizens of capital labor to maintain ourselves as image, we labor in the image. The image, which pervades all appearing, is the mise-en-scène of the new work.

What is immediately suggested by the cinematic mode of production (CMP), properly understood, is that a social relation that emerged as "the cinema" is today characteristic of sociality generally. As Pierre Boulez says, "Art transforms the improbable into the inevitable."[1] Although it first appeared in the late nineteenth century as the built-in response to a technological oddity, cinematic spectatorship (emerging in conjunction with the clumsily cobbled together image-production mechanisms necessary to that situation), surreptitiously became the formal paradigm and structural template for social organization generally. By some technological sleight of hand, machine-mediated perception now is inextricable from your psychological, economic, visceral, and ideological dispensations. Spectatorship, as the fusion and development of the cultural, industrial, economic, and psychological, quickly gained a handhold on human fate and then became decisive. Now, visuality reigns and social theory needs become film theory.

At the moment, in principle at least, that is, in accord with the principles of late capitalism, to look is to labor. This is not to say that all looking is necessarily productive for capital, but looking first was posited as productive by capital early in the twentieth century, and currently is being presupposed as such. The cinematicization of the visual, the fusion of the visual with a set of socio-technical institutions and apparatuses, gives rise to the advanced forms of networked expropriation characteristic of the present period. Capitalized machinic interfaces prey on visuality. As Raul Ruiz remarked, "Cinema in its industrial form is a predator. It is a machine for copying the visible world and a book for people who can't read."[2] Noting the power exercised through a process of normalization, Ruiz writes:

> I gradually came to understand that every spectator of the movies today is really a "connoisseur," that is, the opposite of a spectator. I take the expression "connoisseur" in Benjamin's sense: in cinema as in sports, the spectators understand what's going on, to the point where they can anticipate what happens next, because they know the rules, by learning or by intuition (the rules of a cinematographic narration are verisimilar, that is, made to be believed, easily legible, because they must be identical to those of the dominant social structure). That's why commercial cinema presupposes an international community of connoisseurs and a shared set of rules for the game of social life. In that sense, commercial cinema is the totalitarian social space par excellance."[3]

We might want to add here that this totalitarian social space is not only a scene of representation, but of production. The cinema is in dialectical relation to the social; in learning the codes of commercial cinema, spectators also learn the rules of dominant social structure—indeed, they become experts.

Noel Burch, in a chapter of *Theory of Film Practice* called "Spatial and Temporal Articulations" elucidates what he calls "the fifteen different types of shot transitions and the parameters that define them," adding that they are all capable of "rigorous development through such devices as rhythmic alteration, recapitulation, retrogression, gradual elimination, cyclical repetition, and serial variation, thus creating structures similar to those of twelve-tone music."[4] While one is free to wonder if there are indeed precisely fifteen, this work serves as a kind of catalogue of and testament to the cinematic codification of space and time. It details the organization of perception by a cinema that renders and depends upon a new plasticity of space and time. This plasticity not only creates new worlds but makes them articulate. Spectators (along with filmmakers) must confront and process new orders of spatiality and temporality that are technologically enabled and were previously impossible.

Others have also noted the exhortation in the cinema to foster a kind of directed creation. Cinema has been understood as providing the space, the stimulation, and the impetus, for the re-organization of desire itself. As Dana Polan writes:

> The cinema has been one of the most important kingdoms of our century. Complete with its own royalty—its constellation of stars—and its legal system of rules and prohibitions, the cinema has exhorted and received massive investments—economic (in its "Golden" years, Hollywood was one of the 10 largest industries in the world) as well as psychical. Any number of anecdotes stand as symptoms of these investments—some verging on the pathological, as the many cases of star worship that Edgar Morin describes in his book, *The Stars,* attest. Morin quotes the testimony of movie-goers—worshippers—who experience the cinema not in terms of the standards of their own experiential reality, but in terms determined by the flickers on the screen which come to be the basis of reality. People learn to kiss, to talk, to live, according to shadows that they make, and need to make, into a kingdom.[5]

While we will encounter numerous other examples of world-making at the behest of cinema, cinematic technologies, and cinematic social organization in *The Cinematic Mode of Production,* it is today possible to mark clearly, at the outset (a luxury not available when I began this work), that the industrialization of vision has shifted gears. With the rise of internet grows the recognition of the value-productive dimensions of sensual labor in the visual register. Perception is increasingly bound to production.

The emergence of the industrialization of the visual, of visuality, was not a sudden or even a singular event. Rather, it has a long, multiplex trajectory. As Jonathan Crary has shown, "The production of the observer in the nineteenth century coincided with the new procedures of discipline and regulation. . . . [I]t is a question of a body aligned with and operating an assemblage of turning and regularly moving wheeled parts. The imperatives that generated a rational organization of time and movement in production simultaneously pervaded diverse spheres of social activity. A need for knowledge of the capacities of the eye and its regimentation dominated many of them."[6]

This notion of corporeal practices welded to visual technologies raises the whole question of industrialization and its protocols. It might raise the additional question of the political-economy of visuality. Interestingly, Crary also notes that "photography and money become homologous forms of social power in the nineteenth century. They are equally totalizing systems for binding and unifying all subjects within a single global network of valuation and desire. As Marx said of money, photography is also a great leveler, a democratizer, a 'mere symbol,' a fiction 'sanctioned by the so-called universal consent of mankind.'"[7] This connection between photography and money, a connection intimately related to the transformation of—and to an increasing extent not simply the overdetermination but the capture of—the sensorium from the period of industrialization onward is the subject of *The Cinematic Mode of Production*.

Recently, corporations such as FreePC—which during the NASDAQ glory days of the late 1990s gave out "free" computers in exchange for recipients' agreement to supply extensive personal information and to spend a certain amount of time online—strove to demonstrate in practice that looking at a screen can produce value. For more than a decade, I have argued that the historical moment has arrived that allows us to grasp that looking is posited by capital as labor. If, in the early 1990s, the idea was difficult for academics to fathom, corporations have been faster on the uptake. What I will call "the attention theory of value" finds in the notion of "labor," elaborated in Marx's labor theory of value, the prototype of the newest source of value production under capitalism today: value-producing human attention. The cinematic organization of attention yields a situation in which attention, in all forms imaginable and yet to be imagined (from assembly-line work to spectatorship to internet-working and beyond), is that necessary cybernetic relation to the *socius*—the totality of the social—for the production of value for late capital. At once the means and archetype for the transfer of attentional biopower (its conversion into value and surplus value) to capital, what is meant today by "the image" is a cryptic synonym for these relations of production. The history of the cinema, its development from an industrial to an electronic form, is the open book in which may be read the history of the image as the emergent technology for the leveraged interface of biopower and the social mechanism.

The world-historical restructuring of the image as the paradigmatic social relation currently is being acted upon in practice by large corporations. In the epilogue to this volume, I discuss the latest business plans for what is quickly becoming known as "the attention economy." However seductive the appearance and however devastating the consequences of the capitalization and expropriation of the image relation (of the imaginary) may be for the vast majority of people on the planet, this exploitation is in keeping with the developmental logic of capital and therefore must be understood as the development of business as usual. For the new thing that is "the image" and its attendant attentional productivity sustains the perpetuation of extant gendered, nationalized, waged, and enslaved labor. That fact that extraordinary innovation goes hand in glove (or better, tongue in cheek), with the intensification of world oppression may be understood conveniently in Guiseppe Lampedusa's assessment of the dialectics of domination: "Things must change in order to stay the same."[8] The image structures the visible and the invisible, absorbs freeing power, and sucks up solidarity time. The mode of domination shifts in order to maintain hierarchical society. As spectators begin to value their attention, corporations struggle to get more of what they previously got for nothing. In 1999, for example, Mypoints.com advertised in the *San Jose Mercury News* with the copy, "We'll pay you to read this ad." At the same moment, another website banner displayed disembodied roving eyes with the caption, "We'll pay you for your attention." It should come as no surprise that "bellwether" internet company Yahoo, which always has considered itself a media company, recently hired Terry Semel, former chief of Warner Brothers studio, to head its operations.

The failure of some of these dotcom corporations should not lead us to believe that this new era of corporate designs on our attention was a temporary speculative error. As Jeff Bezos, founder of Amazon.com, is (understandably) fond of pointing out, just because 2,700 automobile manufacturers folded in the early twentieth century doesn't mean that the car was a bad idea [*sic*, it was]." Besides, mass media corporations long have given out "free" content over the airways in exchange for viewer attention that already has been marketed to advertisers. Remember TV? Additionally, as Benedict Anderson in *Imagined Communities* has suggested forcefully with respect to print media, even those contents (news stories) for which we paid a delivery surcharge in coin had a productive effect, and therefore something like a production agenda, far in excess of the single instance of consumption. Imagine, communities, nay, nations, being produced (simply?) through reading the newspapers! In contradistinction to Anderson, Rey Chow places not print technology but rather visuality at the center of emergent nationalism, and suggests that modern literature is a consequence of the blow dealt to language and the imagination by the technological onslaught of images.[9] In Chow's brilliant and at times only implicit critique of Anderson in *Primitive Passions*, it is Lu Xun's traumatic encounter with the cinematic image that marks both his literary work and therefore the founding moment of Chinese Literary Modernism. The shock of "the image" of seeing oneself being seen precipitates a new sense of China, of audience, of self, and therefore of literary style. Thus in Chow's work, not just modernism, but the entire history of modernity stands ready for a thorough reconceptualization as the consequence of the trauma of filmic practice. Stated differently, because of the transformation of sociality by and as visuality, film theory today is confronted with the task of writing a political economy of cinematic culture as a mode of production.

Nowadays, as it enlists viewers to build the pathways for its infrastructure, both as fixed capital and in themselves, Corporate America consciously recognizes that ramifying the sensual pathways to the body can produce value, even if the mechanisms of value production have not been theorized fully. Sensuo-perceptual contact between body and social mechanism, what Sean Cubitt refers to as "cybertime," provides opportunities for value extraction for capital.[10] That gap between the actually existing practice of stealing human attention and a radical theory of this practice exists in part because until very recently there has been no money in theorizing the mechanisms of value production as a dialectical relation, just as for Marx there was money neither in the labor theory of value nor in Marxism. Put another way, the generalized blindness with respect to the economicization of the senses is a constitutive element of hegemony. This leveraged theft of sensual labor is the postmodern version of capital's dirty secret; the spectator is the Lukacsian subject-object of history. What might be the consequences of reconceptualizing "passive" spectatorship as active production, production currently inextricable from imperialism and militarization?

The history of advertising, with its utilization of psychoanalysis and statistical methods to sell product elucidates the uses that capital makes of cultural theory. At the level of engagement with the body (as desiring subject, as unit of the mass market) there are plenty of theories, but at the level of profit-taking, pragmatics provides the bottom line. Advertising power houses use psychoanalytic techniques under the rubric of "theater of the mind," and only the marginalized think to argue with success. Thus the logistics of social production in general, and the conceptualizations thereof, remain difficult to grasp, profitably buried as they are under the surface of simulation. One of the most eloquent and realistic figures for the current situation of social production via the image as the preeminent social relation, is to be found in the late-capitalist social-realist film *The Matrix* (1999). That film depicts a situation in which the computerized (incorporated) control of the sensual pathways to our body have reduced us, from the point of view of the system, to sheer biopower, the dry-cells enlisted by the omnipresent spectacle to fuel an anti-human artificial intelligence. Whatever life-energy we put into the world is converted into the energy to run the image-world and its illusory logic, while we unknowingly remain imprisoned in a malevolent bathosphere, intuiting our situation only through glitches in the program. Our desires for deviance, our bouts with psychopathology, even our fantasies of wealth and power represent such glitches, but (as is well known to advertisers, media-moguls, and cold-war policymakers alike), these mini-revolutions also can be made readily to turn a profit for Big Capital.

Such a relation of the senses and particularly of the visual to production did not emerge overnight. One principle purpose of my theory of cinema is to provide a theoretical and historical account. To repeat, looking has long been posited as labor by capital: In the present moment, it is being presupposed as such. That a critical theory of the mode of exploitation should lag behind the practice of exploitation is no longer tenable, if it ever was. Overcoming this epistemic lag-time is another aim here, one bound up in the revolutionary potential contained in understanding how the world goes on as it does, and in whose interests. The transformative saturation of the visual realm, which gives rise to the term "virtual reality," and the increasing incidence of the term "visuality," was itself produced—and instrumentally so.

The transformation of the visual from a zone of unalienated creative practice to one of alienated labor is the result of capital accumulation, that is, the historical agglomeration of exploited labor. By the "alienation of vision," I do not mean that there have not existed prior scopic regimes that structured sight.[11] Rather, I have in mind the Marxist notions of separation and expropriation endemic to commodification. The separation and expropriation of labor from the laborer, the alienation of labor, is a precursor to the separation and expropriation of vision from the spectator. This alienation of vision, in which vision is captured to produce worlds that confront spectators as something hostile and alien, depends upon a kind of disembedding of the commons—the expropriation of a communal province (nature) that was heretofore an inalienable characteristic (possession) of humanity. This estrangement of the visual, its new qualities of "not belonging to me," as Lacan puts it, characteristic of the cinema and its dissociation from "natural language," is simultaneous with the semi-autonomization of the visual—what we call "visuality."[12] In a brilliant essay entitled "On Visuality," Nicholas Mirzeoff points out that the term visuality is used first by Thomas Carlyle in "On Heroes and Hero Worship" to figure the reactionary hero's broad historical vision in contradistinction to the shortsighted views of, for Carlyle, the degraded (and racialized) masses.[13] In my own view, it would not be incorrect to retain this original reactionary inflection of the term. Furthermore, the maintenance and intensification of the transformed situation of "visuality" (transformed by industrialization and capitalization) remains essential to capital's expansion and valorization.

However, despite what I might be tempted to call the world-historical truth of this claim regarding both the productive and reactionary character of visuality, it remains difficult to write sentences written in the key of Marx: "Communism is the riddle of history solved and knows itself to be this solution."[14] Given that the expropriation of the visual is leading up to a generalized expropriation of attention, and that this attention is becoming productive of value for capital, the flexiblized, scaled back, postmodernized equivalent reads, The attention theory of value is the riddle of post-global capitalism properly posed, and has a germinal contribution to make to counter-hegemonic struggle. At the most basic level, grasping mediation as the extraction of productive labor (value) from the body radically alters the question of visual pleasure by contaminating it with the question of murder.

The dialectic between pleasure and murder that underpins the society of the spectacle brings into relation the Freudian parameters for psychoanalysis—specifically the struggle between the pleasure and reality principles—and Negri's idea of participatory social production theorized under the category of "social cooperation," and resolves it as a dynamic best grasped in the logistics of the image.[15] For it is both pleasure and murder, indeed the (mass) pleasures of (systematic) murder, as worked out in the calculus of the image that sustain the reality of hierarchical society. A corollary to this deduction is that pleasure and murder do not have to be conceived in terms of individuals and their responsibilities or fates, but rather these are precipitated along the lines of force perpetuated by bureaucracies, such as the CIA, in which many participate but no one is accountable. Thus we can see that often as not, people neither work nor are murdered in discreet units: fractions of us work, fractions of us are killed both at the level of the concrete individual and at the level of the collective. The deep meaning of flexible production/accumulation includes not only the vertiginous movements of factories and markets, it is also that the shattered subject of the postmodern is a result of an organization of labor that produces value and takes life in inorganic units, units that do not respect, or better, have transcended the unity and indeed the singularity not only of locales, communities, and families but of the human individual. Whether we kill part of ourselves while watching TV or whether 8,598 viewers of Fox news are responsible for the death of one Iraqi child, value and exploitation are, like the shares in your pension plans, worked out to the nth decimal place in capital's brutal calculus.

As we shall see, the organizational role of visuality, and the transformation of the mode of production arise directly out of industrial production. The ramification and organization of the visible by visual technologies is part of the emergent calculus of the visible. Materially speaking, industrialization enters the visual as follows: Early cinematic montage extended the logic of the assembly-line (the sequencing of discreet, programmatic machine-orchestrated human operations) to the sensorium and brought the industrial revolution to the eye. Cinema welds human sensual activity, what Marx called "sensual labor," in the context of commodity production, to celluloid. Instead of striking a blow to sheet metal wrapped around a mold or tightening a bolt, we sutured one image to the next (and, like workers who disappeared in the commodities they produced, we sutured ourselves into the image). We manufactured the new commodities by intensifying an aspect of the old ones, their image-component. Cinema was to a large extent the hyper-development of commodity fetishism, that is, of the peeled-away, semi-autonomous, psychically charged image from the materiality of the commodity. The fetish character of the commodity drew its energy from the enthalpy of repression—the famous non-appearing of the larger totality of social relations. With important modifications, the situation of workers on a factory assembly line foreshadows the situation of spectators in the cinema. "The cut," already implicit in the piece-meal production of assembly-line work, became a technique for the organization and production of the fetish character of the commodity and then part of a qualitatively new production regime long misnamed consumerism. Consumers produced their fetishes in the deterritorialized factory of the cinema, but factories and markets already contained the seeds of cinema, circulating their image-commodities to the furthest reaches of society. As in the history of factory production, in the movie theater we make and remake the world and ourselves along with it.

The interiorization of the dynamics of the mode of production is a lot more complex than the sketch above might allow and it is the purpose of this book to begin an inquiry into this process. But there are some fundamental principles here. Cinema took the formal properties of the assembly line and introjected them as consciousness. This introjection inaugurated huge shifts in language function. Additionally, the shift in industrial relations that is cinema indicates a general shift in the organization of political economy, and this change does not occur because of a single technology. The development of cinema marks deep structural shifts and accommodations in a complex and variegated world. Indeed, I use the term cinema not only to refer to the set of institutions traditionally configured as "the cinema," in popular usage, but to refer to the manner in which production generally becomes organized in such a way that one of its moments *necessarily* passes through the visual, that is, that it creates an image that (while the tip of the iceberg) is essential to the general management, organization, and movement of the economy.

Additionally, this world-historical role for cinema, and the dependence upon the organization of the visible world (as visuality) demands a total reconceptualization of the imaginary. The imaginary, both as the faculty of imagination and in Althusser's sense of it as ideology—the constitutive mediation between the subject and the real as "the imaginary relation to the real"[16]—must be grasped not as a transhistorical category but as a work in progress, provided, of course, that one sees the development of capitalism as progress.[17] Numerous works on what usefully could be considered as the mediatic organization of the Western imaginary already exist and the scale of its restructuring by technology is becoming more and more clearly grasped. Vast swaths of the formerly organic world are being subjected to capital's *techné* of enclosure. Martin Heidegger's works on technology and the world picture could be read this way, as could the work of someone like Jean Baudrillard. It would be an important project to historicize the work of these thinkers alongside that of figures such as Cornelius Castoriadis and Jean-Joseph Goux.

In Christian Metz's *The Imaginary Signifier: Psychoanalysis and the Cin-*

ema, Metz speaks of the three machines of cinema—the outer machine (the cinema industry), the inner machine (the spectator's psychology), and the third machine (the cinematic writer)—and proposes that "the institution [the coordination of the three machines] has filmic pleasure alone as its aim."[18] Metz argues that "cinema is a technique of the imaginary" (3) and indeed modifies spectators through a system of "financial feedback" (91). These claims are appropriate to the moment of psychoanalytic theories of the cinema in which the cinema is believed to engage the dynamics of an existing psyche. However, the scope of today's (counter)revolution— a revolution that at first glance might appear merely as a technological shift—emerges from a reversal of these very terms: *the imaginary is a technique (a technology) of cinema,* or rather, of mediation generally. Such a reversal de-ontologizes the unconscious and further suggests that the unconscious is cinema's product: its functions, which is to say, existence of the unconscious as such, emerge out of a dynamic relation to technocapital (technology being understood here as sedimented, alienated species being). Thus Metz's sense of what the spectator does in the cinema, "I watch, and I help" (93), can be grasped as an intuition about the labor required for the modification of a cybernetic body organized through financial feedback. This labor is human attention building a new form of sociality: hardware, software, and wetware. At nearly the same moment of the Metzian shift, albeit with different purposes in mind than my own, Jean-Louis Commoli, in his canonical essay "Machines of the Visible," comes out and, in an echo of the Althusserian theory of the subject, says explicitly that "the spectator . . . works."[19] However, while the participatory and even contestatory roles of spectators in the 1970s and 1980s were understood as artifacts of the technology, the mode of engagement with a commercially available pleasure was understood as being at once particular to the cinema, and as something like a cultural option, rather than as comprising a structural shift in the organizational protocols of globalizing capital.

More recently, Regis Debray, in *Media Manifestos,* gives an account of the fundamental shifts in the social logic of mediation wrought by the emergence of the current "mediasphere," what he calls "the videosphere."[20] The videosphere, which Debray dates from the mid-nineteenth century, succeeds the logosphere and the graphosphere. For Debray:

The sphere extends the visible system of mediation to the invisible macrosystem that gives it meaning. We see the microwave oven but not the immense grid of electric power that it is plugged into. We see the automobile but not the highway system, gasoline storage facilities, refineries, petroleum tankers, no more than we see the factories and research installations upstream and all the maintenance and safety equipment downstream. The wide-bodied jet hides from view the planetary spider's web of the international civil aviation organization, of which it is but one strictly teleglided element. To speak of the videosphere is to be reminded that the screen of the television receiving signals is the head of a pin buried in one home out of millions, or a homing device, part of a huge organization without real organizers—of a character at once social, economic, technological, scientific, political—much more in any event than a network of corporate controlled production and programming of electronic images. (*MM*, 33)

Debray, for whom "'ideology' could be defined as the play of ideas in the silence of technologies" (*MM*, 31), invokes the term "'medium' in the strong sense [of] *apparatus-support-procedure*" (*MM*, 13, italics in original) to foreground the technological basis of mediation and, I would say, to denature consciousness. He writes, "Our history of visual efficacies needs to be written in two columns: the one that takes account of the material equipment or 'tool kit' enabling the fabrication, display, and distribution of objects of sight, and the other which chronicles the belief systems in which they were inscribed" (*MM*, 136). "The mediological approach . . . would consist in *multiplying the bridges that can be thrown up between the aesthetic and technological*" (*MM*, 137). *Media Manifestos* makes explicit that what has been at stake in mediation has been the mode of inscription and the functionality of signs—their organizing force.[21] My own work specifically addresses the cinematic image as machinic interface with the *socius* emerging as a response to the crisis for capital known as "the falling rate of profit." I continue to see the commodity-form, the money-system, and capital's violent hierarchical domination as the limit questions faced by our species. In my own view, the ongoing crisis that drives capital to continual, infinite expansion—specifically, the falling rate of profit—also drives the century-long fusing of culture and industry inaugurated by and as cinema. The expansion of capital, once markedly geographical and now increasingly cultural (corporeal, psychological, visceral), deepens, to borrow Stephen Heath's words, the relation of "the technical and the social *as cinema*."[22] Cinema becomes a means to extend the range and effect of capitalized machinery and the logic of capitalization. The cinematic mode of production becomes the necessary means of extending the work day while reducing real wages on a global scale. "Elevating" commodity production to the visual realm, cinema extracts human labor and pays in fun (know-how, anesthesia, acquired stupidity, fashionability, enjoy[n]ment). Cultural pathways, including those mapped under the categories of race, gender, sexuality, and nationality, are thus being subsumed as media of capitalist domination—zones of oppression that capital exploits for its own purposes.[23] Thus in an act mimetic of the relation between cinema and culture, where cinema subsumes culture and renders it productive for capitalism, the concept of the cinematic mode of production would organize the major theoretical contributions of the works cited above, as well as many others here overlooked, under its own rubric. In what follows, I highlight some of cinema's horizons of transformation, while suggesting that "theory" as the critical thought that follows on the heels of philosophy's demise was film theory all along.

So Not Just Psychoanalytic Film Theory but Psychoanalysis as Proto-Film Theory

In this book, I argue that cinema is, in the twentieth century, the emerging paradigm for the total reorganization of society and (therefore) of the subject. From a systemic point of view, cinema arises out of a need for the intensification of the extraction of value from human bodies beyond normal physical and spatial limits and beyond normal working hours—it is an innovation that will combat the generalized falling rate of profit. It realizes capitalist tendencies toward the extension of the work day (via entertainment, email), the deterritorialization of the factory (through cottage industry, TV), the marketing of attention (to advertisers), the building of media pathways (formerly roads), and the retooling of subjects. Understood as a precursor to television, computing, email, and the World Wide Web, cinema can be seen as part of an emerging cybernetic complex, which, from the standpoint of an emergent global labor force, functions as a technology for the capture and redirection of global labor's revolutionary social agency and potentiality.

Utilizing vision and later sound, industrial capital develops a new, visceral, and complex machinery capable of interfacing with bodies and establishing an altogether (counter)revolutionary cybernesis. This increasing incorporation of bodies by capital co-opts the ever-increasing abilities of the masses to organize themselves. As a deterritorialized factory running on a new order of socially productive labor—attention—cinema as a sociological complex inaugurates a new order of production along with new terms of social organization, and thus of domination. "Cinema" is a new social logic, the film theater the tip of the iceberg, the "head of the pin." The mystery that is the image announces a new symptom for analysis by contemporary political economy. Production enters the visual and the virtual enters reality. Labor as dissymmetrical exchange with capital is transacted across the image.

Under the rubric of the cinematic mode of production, "cinema" refers not only to what one sees on the screen or even to the institutions and apparatuses that generate film but to that totality of relations that generates the myriad appearances of the world on the six billion screens of "consciousness." "Cinema" means the production of instrumental images through the organization of animated materials. These materials include everything from actors to landscapes, to populations, to widgets, to fighterplanes, to electrons. "Cinema" is a material practice of global scope, the movement of capital in, through, and as image. "Cinema" marks the changeover to a mode of production in which images, working in concert, form the organizational principles for the production of reality. The whole regime of classical value production extends itself into the visual. While Warren Sack rightly muses that "Children born now will wonder how previous generations just sat in front of the screen without anything to do," something was being done.[24] What may be recognized first in its mature form in the cinema is media's *capitalization* of the aesthetic faculties and imaginary practices of viewers. Social practices were converted into mediations of capital. These were not simply harnessed, but like land under the regime of ground rent, water under the regime of privitization, and genetic code under the regime of international patent law, utterly reconfigured, that is, constituted as media for the production of capital. Below, I will indicate the co-extensive world-historical determinants for the simultaneous socio-technological articulation of consciousness and cinema, and further suggest that not only are consciousness and cinema mutually overdetermined by the constraints of capitalist production, but that they increasingly function on a continuum.[25]

For a first-order approximation of the cinematization of social relations, one might turn to the cinematic dynamics of social production implicit in (posited by) the shifting terms of the interpellation of subjects by an increasing number of institutions and apparatuses (the state, multinational corporations, politicians, "the media," boards, offices, etc.) variously invested in the expansion of capital. Take, for example, the observation common during the last couple of decades that everyone is concerned with his or her "image." The term is no mere figure of speech, but rather a "condensation," in Freud's sense, a matrix of partially unconscious forces that means something else. What is meant by this condensed metaphor, produced and utilized by contemporary consciousness neurotically and now psychotically pursuing the conditions for its own perpetuation, can only be fully elaborated if we understand consciousness itself to have become a desperate measure to account for the dreams dreamt by, in, through, and as the contemporary world-system. In saying this, I am in no way endeavoring to delimit the variations of consciousness that are possible from the outset, nor to patronize what can be thought and felt. Rather, in the context of the production and reproduction of society under capitalist domination, I am trying to register the shifting terms of language function and subject formation in the emerging media environment. Tracing the increasing marginalization of language by images in his "Language, Images and the Postmodern Predicament," Wlad Godzich, probably borrowing from Roger Munier's pamphlet *Against Images,* puts it thus: "Where with language we have a discourse on the world, with human beings facing the world in order to name it, photography substitutes the simple appearance of things; it is a discourse of the world. . . . Images now allow for the paradox that the world states itself before human language."[26] To register the crisis that the proliferation of images poses for language and thus for the conscious mind would be to agree with Godzich that today language is outpaced by images. "Images are scrambling the function of language which must operate out of the imaginary to function optimally."[27] The overall effect of an ever-increasing quantity of images is the radical alienation of consciousness, its isolation and separation, its inability to convincingly "language" reality and thus its reduction to something on the order of a free-floating hallucination, cut away as it is from all ground.

When linked to the rise of image technologies, this demotion of language and of its capacity to slow down the movement of reality suggests, that the radical alienation of language, that is, the alienation of the subject and its principle means of self-expression and self-understanding, is a structural effect of the intensification of capitalism and therefore, an instrumental strategy of domination. In addition to Marx's description of the four-fold alienation produced by wage-labor (from the object, the self, other people, and the species), bodies become deprived of the *power* of speech. This image-consciousness, or better, image/consciousness in which consciousness is an afterthought of the spectacle, participates in the rendering of an intensified auratic component, theorized as "simulation" or "the simulacrum," to nearly every aspect of social existence in the technologically permeated world. Beyond all reckoning, the objective world is newly regnant with an excess of sign value, or rather, with values exceeding the capacities of the sign. Frenzied attempts to language "reality" (what appears) become hysterical because everything is a symptom of something else. Such a promiscuity of signification, what Baudrillard called "the ecstasy of communication," implies, in short, a devaluation of signification— a radical instability, unanchoredness, and inconsistency of consciousness to such an extent that consciousness becomes unconsciousness by other means.[28] In the onslaught of the spectacle, consciousness cannot take hold, it does not "take," but rather roams and sputters in fits and starts. Although the critique of metaphysics, under the sign of "deconstruction," imputes a certain transhistoricity to these excesses and depletions of the sign, and generates deconstruction's *jouissance* through the truth effect produced by its analytical vanishing of the metaphysical securities of ground and presence, we must now recognize deconstruction as an historical phenomenon of the late 1960s, 1970s, and 1980s and pose the question of the very historicity of its critique. In light of the cinematic mode of production, deconstruction appears not as an advance in intellectual history, which reveals the misapprehended truth (under erasure) of all previous eras, but as a philisophico-linguistic turn brought about in response to a socio-technological transformation in political economy. The cinematic mode of production's account of the crisis of metaphysics might assert that all that is solid melts into cinema. It is the visual economy and the transformation of labor that liquidates being. Deconstruction's crisis management of the sign, which could be grasped as a coming to terms with the withering away of the state of being under the analysis of the econometrics of the signifier, finds its historical conditions of possibility for its linguistic neurosis in the intensifying delimitation of the province of language by the image. Language just can't process all that visuality—it's like trying to eat your way out of a whale, which, of course, is somewhere you don't belong in the first place. That's why "you" is such a hard thing "to be."

Thus to "win the imaginary for the symbolic," as Metz described the task of film theory, today means codifying the cinematicity of domination for consciousness.[29] A rendering that reveals cinema as a new paradigm of socio-material organization would answer Fredric Jameson's thoughtful imperative: "Perhaps today, where the triumph of more utopian theories of mass culture seems complete and virtually hegemonic, we need the corrective of some new theory of manipulation, and of a properly postmodern commodification," with an analysis of the image as the cutting edge of capital, and "media-ocracy" as the highest stage of capitalism (to date).[30] To rethink the paradigm that is the cinema means to inscribe the material basis of visuality in the unthought of the image and to disrupt its affect of immediacy, plenitude, and truth. This inscription of the materiality of the virtual must traverse not just technology as it is ordinarily understood, but social relations: psychology, migration, the masses. Though not everything is an image, nearly everything is con(s)t®ained by them.

In considering the retooling of human thinking that, along with industrial and technological transformations, led up to cinema as it came to be during our century, let me pursue my reversal of the assumption that cinema and cinematic form emerge historically out of the unconscious (creating, for example, images "cut to the measure of [male] desire," as Laura Mulvey says of film images of women), by saying that *the unconscious emerges out of cinema* (male desire is cut to the measure of cinema and therefore of cinematic capital).[31] This reversal restores a lost dimension of the dialectical development of both desire and cinema. The coincidence of Freud's theory of the unconscious (1895) with the Lumiere brother's first film (1895) is no mere coincidence. Theorists of suture, sexuality, and more recently Hitchcock (Zizek) assert that cinema engages the architecture of the unconscious in a kind of play.[32] This engagement with an actually existing unconscious is not unlike what Sartre in "Why Write?" called, somewhat filmically, the "directed creation" engaged in by a perceiver but with somewhat fewer degrees of freedom.[33] To the situation of Sartre's technologically embedded perceiver as *"director* of being" (italics mine), in which "our car or our airplane . . . organizes the great masses of the earth," Stephen Heath asserts that cinema adds the following delimitations: "The passage from views [early French films were listed in catalogues as views] to the process of vision [in cinema] is essentially that of the coding of relations of mobility and continuity."[34] In other words, cinema *codifies* technological movement and juxtaposition for and as consciousness—it induces semiotic effects via technical means. But at the same time (with the notable exceptions of Dziga Vertov and his like), the plenitude of the image obscures the social conditions and politico-economic trajectories underpinning its production of signification. Thus, in the simultaneous processes of delimiting the significance of movement and developing conventions for the production of continuity, what is often referred to by the misleading term "film-language" is created. (The term is correct if one revives the indexicality of the hyphen: film (as film) amalgamated to language (as language)—film does not have a language, it operates on language—thus film *and* language, film-language.) But perhaps, following my suggestion that it is the unconscious that emerges out of cinema, it is just as illuminating here to think of the cinematic apparatus not as a late-blooming technology for imaginary titillation through an industrial interface with the unconscious, but indeed as the precursor of and model for the unconscious as it is has been theorized during the course of the twentieth century. The cinematic movement of images instantiates the modern unconscious. Cinema "speaks" in the silence of techno-capitalism, its image, as Benjamin so astutely noted, an "orchid in the land of technology." If cinema speaks, it is because it does its talking through us, demanding the production of cinema's second and third machines (the spectator's psychology and the cinematic writer). As the circulation of programmatic images increases, there's more and more unconscious around—as well as more cinematic speech/writing. Increasingly, we are all cinematic writers.

One could take Adorno's observation about the culture industry being "psychoanalysis in reverse" as a thesis on the history of consciousness—in which industrial culture produces not just the modern psyche (cinema's second machine), but psychoanalysis itself (cinema's third machine, the expanded version).[35] Thus in chapter 3 of this volume, "The Unconscious of the Unconscious, or, The Work of Consciousness in the Age of Technological Imagination," I use this approach to consciousness as besieged by the rising imaginary as I work my way through a rather specialized form of consciousness, specifically, a theory of consciousness—the one given voice in Jacques Lacan's famed Seminar XI, *The Four Fundamental Concepts of Psychoanalysis*.[36] Writ large and too briefly, my argument is that if, as Lacan says, the unconscious, in a most cinematic fashion, first appears "through the structure of the gap," that is, in the cut between words, then the unconscious of the unconscious is cinema (*FFCP*, 29). The unconscious, in Lacan, appears through the breakdown of the symbolic order (parapraxis in Freud), but is theorized in Lacan as being inaugurated scopically (the *objet petit a* is, after all, an image). On the whole, this situation of linguistic breakdown conforms to Godzich's description of language confronted by images. Lacan's figures for the unconscious often involve technologies of visual reproduction, including montage, painting, photograpy, and the cinema—the technological is the repressed of the theory of the unconscious. Noting the appearance of cinema and things cinematic in Lacan would build an analysis of psychoanalysis that functions in accord with the principles of psychoanalysis while leading beyond them. The process of such an approach would at once allow the claims of psychoanalysis regarding the structuring of the subject to stand while retroactively showing that cinema is, to play on a formulation of Lacan, "in it more than it"; in other words, that it is, finally, *psychoanalysis itself that is the symptom*—of cinema.

Visual Economy

To understand the material history of the spectacle, one must show (1) the emergence of cinema out of industrial capitalism, (2) the reorganization of the *socius*, the subject, and the built environment by the image in circulation, and (3) the utter reconfiguration of capital-logic and hence of labor and accumulation in and as visuality. If the spectacular, the simulated, and the virtual are not somehow eminently productive of culture, and if culture is not, again, somehow, eminently productive of capital (in the strict sense of "productive" as utilized by political economy) then all the hoopla over postmodernism is simply wrong.

Let me then add a few periodizing markers in order to show the general fit of cinema with cultural shifts. What I call the "Cinematic Mode of Production" begins with the codification of early cinema and psychoanalysis (but also behaviorism), and culminates, as it were, in the postmodern and the advance of new media. Thus the cinematic mode of production begins with the historical moment in which the concrete technology of cinema is codified simultaneously with the abstract, socio-subjective, and bureaucratic technologies of monopoly capital (Edison) and continues into the present.[37] The argument in this book spans the three fundamental movements in capitalism as specified by Ernest Mandel, beginning with the shift from steam-driven motors to electric and combustion engines, and continuing through the changeover to electronic and nuclear-powered apparatuses that is still occurring. Cinema spans the three great machine ages, each one marking, for capital, a dialectical expansion over the previous stage. These stages, associated with market capitalism, are the monopoly stage or the stage of imperialism, postmodernity or the stage of neo-imperialism, and what one might call neo-totalitarianism, respectively.[38] Somewhat crudely put, it could be said that cinema has its origins in the shift from market to monopoly capital and reconstitutes itself in the shift from monopoly to multinational capitalism. Another useful index to the character of these transformations in the evolving logics of capitalized production and circulation is the mode of image making itself: the indexicality of the photograph, the analogue electronic signal, and the digital image.

In the first two chapters, I argue that both cinema and capital employ the same abstract or formal structures to realize their functions. The becoming-image of the world, or rather the increasing dematerialization of the commodity is also necessary for capital development. Capital's fundamental transformation during the twentieth century is cinematic, that is, it becomes visual. Surprisingly, perhaps, these insights are derived from two of the great revolutionary soviet filmmakers, Dziga Vertov and Sergei Eisenstein. If cinema indeed opened up a whole new domain of capitalist domination, if its very structure was an extension of the capitalist organization of production, then it was in the anti-capitalist cinema of the early Soviet that this domain of organization and control received its most strident negative articulation and therefore attained its highest degree of denaturalized visibility. By going directly against the grain of capitalist culture, early Soviet cinema allows us to grasp the means by which capitalism slated its extension into the human viscera and psyche. In a first chapter on Dziga Vertov and a second on Sergei Eisenstein, I show that cinema and its circulation of the image provide the archetype for the new order of capital production and circulation generally. My analysis of the structure and dynamics of the cinematic apparatus is nothing less than an exploration of the industrial extension of capital's "re-mediation" and reconfiguration of the functioning of the body through the historically achieved interface with machinery known as the image. The mining of human bodies of their power always has been the goal of capital. While revolutionary Soviet cinema endeavored to liberate bodies from the domination of capital by utilizing the emergent productive force that inheres in the relation called cinema, for capital, the continuing "liberation" of these same productive forces depends upon the non-liberation of the value-producers.

This tendency toward the dematerialization of social relations (meaning abstraction, codification through visuality, the increasing leverage of exchange-value over use-value) is accelerated by this self-same cinematic technology, which anchors itself in place through ever more rigid material constraints (poverty, international dependence, materially produced psychosis). The mediation and modulation of appearance becomes an essential dimension of social organization, structuring the beliefs, desires, and proprioception of image-consumers in ways productive for capital expansion. Much of this social programming (for that is what it is, even if the results are somewhat indeterminate) occurs outside of the current (possible?) purview of semiotics, in zones that elude or exceed meaning even as they structure practice.

Already in the nineteenth century, the commodity had a pronounced visual-libidinal component—a fetish character. If in Freud the fetish arouses and cancels the knowledge of castration, in Marx it arouses and cancels the knowledge of alienated production. In the commodity, this beacon of quashed subjectivity ("the feminine?") scintillated in the material, making overtures toward becoming animate. Such a beckoning presence of impacted subjectivity in the commodity-form underlies the modernist theories of collecting as redemption as well as Hollywood narratives of chivalric love—both messianic endeavors to remove objects from commodity circulation and revive them in a more benevolent setting.[39] Cinema, which is technologically on a continuum with industry, latches onto a nascent aspect of the commodity in circulation—the productive potential of its fetish character—and circulates it through the sensorium with a new intensity: the objects "speak."[40] In other words, the affective dimension of the commodity is emphasized and rendered more eloquent, capturing the imagination and calling upon the desire of spectators. If one views the mechanically reproduced image as a new order of reification, a qualitative shift in the shine as well as in the materiality of the commodity-form, then cinema as an industry is the productive orchestration of images and therefore, necessarily, the consequent extraction and management of human subjective potential.

Both the fetish character of the commodity and what Baudrillard calls simulation, two perceptual phenomenon that are predominantly visual in the first instance, have been theorized to a greater or lesser extent as artifacts of reification under the capitalist regime of dissymmetrical exchange. In brief, these arguments can be grasped as follows: The ascendancy of exchange-value over use-value (the domination and tendency toward liquidation of the latter by the former) warps the visuo-perceptual field in and as an expression of the psycho-libidinal dimensions of alienation. In the classical four-fold account of alienation from the *Economic and Philosophic Manuscripts of 1844*, humans are alienated from their products, from the work process, from each other, and from the species.[41] The alienation of sensual labor leads to an alienation of the senses. The very effacement and naturalization of the historical production of alienation leaves its auratic or phantasmagoric impress on the sensorium. Objects have a new pyrotechnics.

When, in capitalist production, a worker's product confronts him or her as "something alien," a new order of perceptuo-imaginary pyrotechnics is inaugurated, the order that leads Marx to introduce the category of fetish-ism. This consequence of alienation is precisely the phantasmagoria of the object, the part that stands out in place of the whole as a totality of process, the supplemental excesses of a history rendered invisible yet smoldering within the material. The commodified object is the residue of a whole net-work of subjective (human) activity. The fetish is precisely the severance of community *appearing* as an object. It is the activity that the object under-takes as a medium for severing consumer from community. It is violated subjective and intersubjective activity. It is essential to recall here that the experience of this phenomenon is not without its pleasures, its ecstasy. As a compulsion to repeat a traumatic condition of primordial loss, the fetish arouses desire and invites imaginary reunification. It is the partial and imaginary pratice of community. One might see in commodity fetishism a kind of severance pay, a pleasure in the mode of Platonic longing for a lost wholeness, in which commodity as missing piece promises wholeness, completion, repletion. This relation between human beings that first ap-pears on a massive scale during the industrial revolution as a thing, finds its higher articulation in the spectacle that Debord describes as "the pseudo-community" of the commodity.[42]

If one wanted to trace the cultural logic of the spectacle, the place to look for a formal precursor is in the operations and movements of money. I trace out these relationships in more detail in chapters 4 and 5. According to Georg Simmel in *The Philosophy of Money*, law, intellectuality, and money "have the power to lay down forms and directions for contents to which they are indifferent."[43] So it is with film. It might be said here that money, as an evolving medium that leaves its imprint on all aspects of cerebral ac-tivity, and which is an empty form that can take on any contents, assumes film-form, while capital as an evolving system of organization, production, and *exploitation*, becomes cinematic. Historically, capital precedes cinema as we commonly understand the term. Money is the medium for regulat-ing wage-labor (the spread and development of the money-form coincides with the putting in place of a global working class), while capital denotes the *system* of dissymmetrical exchange. "Film" can be understood as the so-cial relation that separates the visual component of human subjective ac-tivity from the body in its immediate environment, while "cinema" is the systemic organization of this productive separation.

If the commodity-object is an impacted social relation in which the sub-jective contribution of the human worker is effaced, so much the more for the image. Andy Warhol registers this change in much of his work, but perhaps never more elegantly than in the Campbell's Soup silk-screens. These soups are indeed condensed: objects formed by the condensation of farming technologies, migrant labor, canning process, trucking, warehousing, and supermarketing. Warhol grasps the mass-produced object as an icon of reification, effectively peeling the label from the can, and allowing it to circulate unencumbered. This free-floating signifier of an already reified condensation dramatizes the mode of appearance for the soup, a soup that as long as it is to remain a commodity also must remain invisibly locked in a hermetic tin. In increasing the distance between the label and the use-value, Warhol registers the ascendance of image over materiality, distancing yet further whatever human subjective elements comprise the soup proper while dramatizing the subjective pyrotechnics of the image-commodity itself. Where once a portrait would have been displayed, there hangs an image of a commodity, itself a higher order of commodity.

Warhol underscores the ascendant dimension of the commodity-image by *reproducing* it, not as an anonymous designer, but as an artist. By inscribing the image at a distance, he also inscribes its social effects; he becomes the representative of a representation. Like previous art icons, Warhol is an author of an imagistic relation, but unlike others he is an author who does not immediately appear to create an original text, he only grasps it through reproduction. In the postmodern, the image always occurs twice, the first time as commodity, the second as art.

As importantly as the subjective labor that goes into the production of images—in both the objectification that becomes the referent and the imagification that becomes the image in circulation—*human subjectivity is bound to the image in its very circulation,* and that in two very different ways. First, our gazes accrete on the image and intensify its power. Take, for example, the case of a work of Vincent Van Gogh. The fifty-million-dollar fetish character is an index of visual accretion, that is, of alienated sensual labor resultant from the mass mediation of the unique work of art. All that looking sticks to the canvas and increases its value. To develop that relation has been the job of the painter, and remains the strategy of producers of unique works of art. The traditional labor theory of value cannot explain this hysterical production of value; only a theory that accounts for the systemic alienation of the labor of looking can. Second, and equally significant, in viewing the image, we simultaneously and micrologically modify ourselves in relation to the image as we "consume" it—a misnomer if there ever was one, since images equally, or almost entirely, consume us.[44] If this production of both value and self (as worker, as consumer, as fecund perceiver) through looking is indeed the case, then the emergence of visual culture must be set in relation to the development and intensification of commodity fetishism. Capital must be grasped not only as an engine of exploitation, but an image-engine of exploitation—a cinematic apparatus.

Globalization, Affect, and Negation

The assertion that global production is coordinated through the screen of capital (the screens of the many capitals) is operationally correct, and, if one considers the role of CNN, international cable stations, computers, Hollywood film, advertising, and the like, may perhaps seem intuitively obvious. The development of a new order of visuality and of a visual *economy* is signaled here by a qualitative shift in the character of capital. This shift is colloquially known as postmodernism. It is arguable that even in its early stages capital was already cinematic. For example, "capital," in the work of Marx, was the screen of appearance for all politico-economic and therefore social metamorphosis. In Marx's representation (*darstellung*) of capital process, all that is solid melts into air precisely on the screen of capital; each moment of production as well as of world history is marched across the frame that capital provides. In short, like Vertov's *Man with a Movie Camera*, Marx's "capital" films social practice, and in fact (that is, in practice), it was precisely through the framework of capital that the social was grasped. Cinema is first posited by capital, and then presupposed.

As noted, photography and the cinematic apparatus are no mere perks or spin-offs of industry as Tang was to the space program. Visual technologies developed the key pathways for capital expansion, increasing as they do the speed and intensity of commodity circulation, as well as historically modifying the visual pathway itself, transforming the character of sight—opening and filling it, ramifying space and time. The visual, captured as a productive relation for capital, clears the way for the institution of what Fredric Jameson identifies as "constitutive features of postmodernism": "a new depthlessness," "a weakening of historicity," "a whole new type of emotional ground tone" under the heading of "intensities," "the deep constitutive relationships of all this to a whole new technology which is itself a figure for a whole new economic world system," and "mutations in the lived experience of built space itself."[45] This cultural sea change known as postmodernism may be defined as the subsumption of a formerly semi-autonomous cultural sphere by capital. This subsumption of culture registers the change of state necessary to "economic growth," or simply "development" (neo-imperialism) in the latter twentieth century. Culture became a scene, and is fast becoming the principle scene (the mise-en-scène) of economic production. Without the reorganization of the visual (and thus of the affective) the massive, global immiseration currently in existence could not be effected. The postmodern distortions, which are actually spatial, temporal, and corporeal *transformations,* and hence new forms of social relations, are created and sustained through a generalized extension of the capacity to mediate vision and to prolong the interface between human beings and social machines.

The new order of visuality marks a transformation of that relationship between bodies and machines previously epitomized by the assembly line. Visual images of cybernetics such as those found in *Robocop* or *Terminator* are actually the interfaces themselves. The hypothesis here is that the principle locus of capital's dissymmetrical exchange (exploitation) characteristic of M-C-M (Money-Commodity-Money) where the second M is larger than the first is increasingly the imaginary. Labor is done in what Althusser calls "an imaginary relation to the real," but in an utterly transformed because massively mediated imaginary and with effects that are no less material for all that. The large-scale technological mediation of the imaginary is a practical-material shift.[46]

Jean-Joseph Goux positions what might be recognized as the imaginary in relation to economic production thus: "Consciousness (social or individual) . . . [i]s *constituted* in its very form, in its *mode of reflection,* by and in the process of social exchange."[47] Goux's work delineates the homologous structures of psychoanalysis and political economy. However, for all of its undeniable brilliance, it lacks a materialist theory of mediation. Goux lacks an answer to the question "how do you get capitalism into the psyche, and how do you get the psyche into capital?"[48] They are isomorphic, but why? Goux argues that "the affective mode of exchange," meaning the symbolic, is a function of "the dominant form of exchange," meaning capital. The expression of the imaginary is therefore a function of the dominant mode of exchange. While Goux's statement is accurate, what is left out is that it requires the history of twentieth-century visuality to make it so. The twentieth century is the cinematic century, in which capital aspires to the image and the image corrodes traditional language function and creates the conceptual conformation, that is the very form, of the psyche as limned by psychoanalysis. The cinematic image, as paradigmatic mediator between these two orders of production (political economy and the psycho-symbolic) better describes the historically necessary, mutual articulation of consciousness and capital expansion than does Goux's provocative but too-abstract idea of the "socio-genetic process" in which social forms mysteriously influence one another or take on analogical similarities. Goux's theory of *mediations* itself lacks a general theory of mediation. It is only by tracing the trajectory of the capitalized image and the introjection of its logic into the sensorium that we may observe the full consequences of the dominant mode of production (assembly-line capitalism) becoming "the dominant mode of representation" (cinema). Cinema implies the tendency toward the automation of the "subject" by the laws of exchange. This transformed situation of the subject (which has been registered via its breakdown products in psychoanalysis, deconstruction, and post-structuralism), demands a thoroughly new epistemology almost as urgently as it demands new forms of transcendence. Indeed, the former is a necessary if not sufficient condition of the latter.

If we combine such a thesis regarding the cinematization of the subject with Guy Debord's insight that "the spectacle is the guardian of sleep," then it becomes clear that the terrain of cinematics is at once macro- and microscopic, that is, world-systemic, economic, and historical, as well as individual, perceptual, and psychological.[49] What was already true for Lacan, albeit ontologically, here takes on its world-historical character: The dominant mode of representation induces unconsciousness. The mode of production is one with the repressed. Cinema is an orchestration of the unconscious and the unconscious is a scene of production. Dreamwork turns out to be real work. It is important to remember here that the category "cinema" is now detached from the film industry and its array of institutions and provides *a figure for the orchestration of material production by images.* With even greater range and significance than war or the automobile (albeit on a continuum with both), as the predominantly visual mediation of material relations *cinema ceaselessly coordinates global economic forces with the extremely local* (meaning regional, but also interior to particular individuals) *productions of affect, trajectories of desire, and proprioception.*[50]

How does this cybernesis function? Antonio Negri describes postmodernism as the "'real subsumption' of society in capital" and affirms that the "form of value is the very 'communication' which develops among productive forces."[51] He then raises the following question:

> If "communication" constitutes the fabric of production and the substance of the form of value, if capital has become therefore so permeable

that it can filter every relation through the material thicknesses of production, if the laboring processes extend equally as far as the social extends, what then are the consequences that we can draw with respect to the law of value?[52]

Negri's stunning "Twenty Theses on Marx," from which this passage was taken, ultimately answers the question of value by calling for the radical wresting of "social cooperation" (labor) from "productive command" (capital). These extremely promising categories and the work that informs their constitution demand significant attention. Indeed, *The Cinematic Mode of Production* struggles to provide a materialist history of this very subsumption that is postmodernism. In addition, it aims to show that however encouraging Negri's assertion is—that the history of the proletarian power is asymmetrical with the history of capitalist power and that what he calls "the proletariat" has therefore never been in lockstep with capitalist exploitation—Adorno and Horkheimer's critique of the culture industry is not dispensed with adequately in Negri's model. Thus the question of the role of critical negation and of negative dialectics remains open.

Adorno and Horkheimer's critique, in which human interiority effectively has been liquidated and replaced by the culture industry, has been criticized for an inadequate account of different modes of reception and use of mass-mediated cultural production by the incredible variety of consumers extant. Statements like, "the inflection on the telephone or in the most intimate situation, the choice of words in conversation, and the whole inner life . . . bear witness to man's attempt to make himself a proficient apparatus, similar (even in emotions) to the model served up by the culture industry," seem to negate the creative aspects of fandom and performativity, but Negri himself almost inadvertently proposes a grim addendum to the Frankfurt school architectonic that "Amusement under late capitalism is the prolongation of work."[53] In his words, with respect to the development of capital, "every innovation is the secularization of revolution."[54] This statement, meant to underscore the creative and liberatory power of workers, strikes me as also providing the appropriate negative dialectic for thinking about image-culture as a system: The extra-economic creativity of the masses, their quests for empowerment, fulfillment, and why not say it, "freedom," are absorbed and rendered productive for capital. What a century ago I. P. Pavlov observed as "the freedom reflex" (in dogs) is harnessed by capital for alienated production. New affects, aspirations, and forms of interiority are experiments in capitalist productivity. It seems that it is precisely here, in the capture of humanity's quests for freedom by capital's myriad strategies of exploitation, that intellectuals (if you will pardon the term) must today make their interventions.

With this recuperative aspect of capital in mind, its ability to turn the struggle for freedom into domination, along with the rise of the emergence of visuality as I have described it thus far, it is important not to abandon the dialectics of negation. Thus far, only the negative dialectic allows us to think the political economy of the visual and hence the paradigm of a global dominant. Negation, however, has very serious limits that ultimately may include it as among the psychopathological strategies modulated by Hollywood. In conceiving the cinematicity of production, the fabrication of affect as well as the valorization of images by watching them, we are able to grasp a new order of production slated by the emerging visual economy. The cinematicity of capital dialectically re-ordains the categories of political economy, meaning that it leaves its older forms extant (wage-labor, circulation, capital, use-value, exchange-value, etc.) while bringing them to a higher level of articulation and abstraction. Also, in ways that for the most part exceed the scope of the current work, it re-ordains the key operators of race, gender, sexuality, and nationality.

The commodified object tends toward the image, money tends toward film, and capital tends toward cinema. People are slotted in accordingly as value-producing media for the new visual economy—as if living in accord with preordained scripts or programs. Thus, as I have only suggested here, the labor theory of value that has been in Marxism the basis on which capital was valorized during the production process and also the basis on which revolutionary action was predicated, must be reformulated as the attention theory of value, that is, as *the productive value of human attention*. This reformulation leaves labor as a subset of value-productive attention while positing the development of a new order for cementing of the *socius*. Furthermore, it accounts for the capitalization of forms of interstitial human activity ("women's" work, "desiring-production," experience, survival) that previously fell beyond the purview of the formal scene of value production, meaning the workplace. Additionally, as I discuss in more detail in chapter 4, such a new order of production not only extends the working day and therefore combats the falling rate of profit, it instantiates new orders of commodities such as air-time and vision itself, whose values are measured, for example, by a statistical estimate of the size and now the "quality" of an audience.[55]

Visual, psychological, visceral, and haptic events are the pathways for new kinds of work, new kinds of machine-body interfaces, which simultaneously instantiate an effective reality or media-environment for the subject-form (and its fragments) as a context for its action, and valorize capital investment. As I show in chapter 6, when appearance itself is production, the ostensible immediacy of the world always already passes through the production-system. Cinema is a deterritorialized factory that extends the working day in space and time while introjecting the system's language of capital into the sensorium. "Cinema" means a fully mediated mise-en-scène that provides humans with the contexts and options for response that are productive for capital. Yet we must remember that it is humanity who made the cinema, despite the masters of global appearance's claims to the contrary. The star is not out there, but s/he is of ourselves. Cinema is the secularization of a world-historical revolution in human interaction that contains in *potentia* the material realization of a universal disaffection with capitalist domination and oppression. As it stands, cinema is the leveraged management and expropriation of humanity's "freedom reflex," the de-sacralization of human communion. In solidarity with all those who have fought and continue to fight against the racism, sexism, homophobia, fascistic nationalism, and developmental ideologies that have justified the dirty work of capitalist accumulation, we must organize ourselves and the parts of ourselves that aspire not for justification of things as they are but for the justice still to come.

NOTES

1. Quoted in Zygmunt Bauman, *The Individualized Society* (Cambridge, Mass.: Polity Press, 2001), 32.

2. Raul Ruiz, *Poeties of Cinema,* trans. Brian Holmes (Paris: Editions Dis Voir, 2005), 73.

3. Ibid., 58.

4. Noel Burch, Theory of Film Practice, trans. Helen R. Lane (Princeton: Princeton University Press, 1981 [1969]), 14.

5. Dana Polan, "'Above All Else to Make You See': Cinéma and the Ideology of Spectacle," *boundary* 2, 11:1/2, fall 1982–winter 1983, pp. 129–44, 131–32.

6. Jonathan Crary, *Techniques of the Observer: On Vision and Moderity in the Nineteenth Century* (Campbridge, Mass.: MIT Press, 1990) 112.

7. Ibid., 13.

8. This is the most famous line from Guiseppe di Lampedusa, *The Leopard,* Pantheon, 1991 [1958].

9. Rey Chow, *Primitive Passions: Visuality, Sexuality, Ethnography, and Contemporary Chinese Cinema* (New York: Columbia University Press, 1995).

10. Cubitt, Sean. "Cybertime: Towards an Aesthetics of Mutation and Evolution." in *Differential Aesthetics: Art Practices, Philosophy and Feminist Understandings.* ed. Penny Florence and Nicola Foster (Aldershot, UK: Ashgate, 2000).

11. See Martin Jay, "Scopic Regimes of Modernity," in *Vision and Visuality*, ed. Hal Foster (Seattle: Bay Press, 1988).

12. See Hal Foster's preface to *Vision and Visuality*, op. Cit.

13. Nicholas Mirzoeff, On Visuality, unpublished manuscript.

14. Karl Marx, *Economic and Philosophic Manuscripts of 1844*, in *The Marx-Engels Reader*, ed. Robert C. Tucker (New York and London: W. W. Norton and Company, 1978), 84.

15. "By social we understand the co-operation of several individuals, no matter under what conditions, in what manner and to what end. It follows from this that a certain mode of production, or industrial stage, is always combined with a certain mode of co-operation, or social stage, and this mode of co-operation is itself a 'productive force,'" Karl Marx, *The German Ideology*, in *The Marx-Engels Reader*, 157, op. Cit. Antonio Negri develops this idea in "Twenty Theses on Marx," in *Polygraph 5: Contesting the New World Order*, trans. Michael Hardt (Durham: 1992), 136–70 and in his later work as well.

16. "What is represented in ideology is therefore not the system of the real relations which govern the existence of individuals, but the imaginary relation of those individuals to the real relations in which they live," Louis Althusser, "Ideology and Ideological State Apparatuses (Notes Towards an Investigation)" in *Lenin and Philosophy and Other Essays* (New York and London: Monthly Review Press, 1971), 165.

17. Ibid., 165.

18. Christian Metz, *The Imaginary Signifier: Psychoanalysis and the Cinema*, trans. Celia Britton et al. (Bloomington: Indiana University Press, 1982).

19. Jean-Louis Commoli, "Machines of the Visible," in *The Cinematic Apparatus*, ed. Teresa de Lauretis and Stephen Heath (New York: St. Martins Press, 1980) 140. See also the following essays from the same volume: Stephen Heath, "The Cinematic Apparatus: Technology as Historical and Cultural Form," and Teresa de Lauretis, "Through the Looking Glass." For a broader theory of the social organization of the imaginary, see Cornelius Castoriadis, *The Imaginary Institution of Society*, trans. Kathleen Blamey (Cambridge: MIT Press, 1998).

20. See Regis Debray, *Media Manifestos*, trans. Eric Rauth (London and New York: Verso, 1996). Hereafter cited parenthetically as *MM*.

21. Although Debray is committed to thinking "'the becoming-material' forces of symbolic forms" (*MM*, 8) and retains a sense of the violence inherent in mediation ("transmission's rhyme with submission," *MM*, 46), and is further aware that technol-

ogy is the repressed of the history of consciousness, he is no longer interested in production per se. This weakness, consistent with his devolving relation to Marxism, renders the passages on ethics in this work lame, and very nearly posits technology as fully autonomous ("A good politics can no more prevent a mass medium from functioning according to its own economy than it can prevent a severe drought," *MM*, 124). Without the standpoint of production, in which mass media and even droughts are seen as the product of human activity, the new order of consciousness, even when understood as such, cannot be challenged adequately.

22. Heath, "The Cinematic Apparatus," 6.

23. See George Yudice, *The Expediency of Culture: Uses of Culture in the Global Era,* Durham: Duke University Press, 2004.

24. Warren Sack, private conversation in the Pogonip.

25. By "consciousness," I am referring to modern(ist) consciousness, that is modern subjectivity—a mode of knowing vis-à-vis a way of being presently in decline.

26. Wlad Godzich, "Language, Images and the Postmodern Predicament," in *Materialities of Communication,* ed. Hans Ulrich Gumbrecht and K. Ludwig Pfeiffer (Stanford: Stanford University Press, 1994), 367–68. Raul Ruiz, in *Poetics of Cinema,* trans. Brian Holmes (Paris: Editions Dis Voir, 1995), cites Munier's pamphlet, paraphrasing as follows: "Langue is discourse *about* the world, photography and cinema are languages *of* the world. The world speaks through its images in an inarticulate way, and each sequence of moving icons is either illusory or stripped of all meaning (because devoid of all discourse)" (32).

27. Godzich, "Language, Images and the Postmodern Predicament," 369.

28. Jean Baudrillard, *The Ecstasy of Communication* (New York: Semiotext(e), 1988).

29. Metz, *The Imaginary Signifier,* 3.

30. Fredric Jameson, *Late Marxism: Adorno, or, the Persistence of the Dialectic* (London and New York: Verso, 1990).

31. Laura Mulvey, "Visual Pleasure and Narrative Cinema," *Issues in Feminist Film Criticism,* ed. Patricia Evans, (Bloomington and Indianapolis: Indiana University Press, 1990), 39.

32. Slavoj Zizek, *Everything You Always Wanted to Know About Lacan (but Were Afraid to Ask Hitchcock)* (London: Verso, 1992).

33. Jean Paul Sartre, "Why Write?" in *Critical Theory Since Plato,* ed. Hazard Adams (New York: Harcourt Brace Jovanovich, 1971), 1059.

34. Stephen Heath, *Questions of Cinema* (Bloomington Indiana: Indiana University Press, 1981) 26.

35. See Max Horkheimer and Theodor Adorno, "The Culture Industry: Enlightenment as Mass Deception," in *Dialectic of Enlightenment,* trans. John Cumming (New York: Continuum, 1976).

36. Jacques Lacan, *The Four Fundamental Concepts of Psychoanalysis*, ed. Jacques-Alain Miller, trans. Alan Sheridan (New York: W.W. Norton, 1981). Hereafter cited parenthetically as *FFCP*. My essay is as yet unpublished.

37. The institutional history of Hollywood provides fertile ground for thinking further about the relationship between vertical and horizontal integration at the level of film production and distribution (capital in the traditional sense) on the one hand, and the (always incomplete) codification of the image-system called cinema on the other. See, for example, Charles Musser, *Before the Nickelodeon: Edwin S. Porter and the Edison Manufacturing Company* (Berkeley: University of California Press, 1991); and David Bordwell, Janet Staiger, and Kristin Thompson, *The Classical Hollywood Cinema: Film Style and Mode of Production to 1960* (New York: Columbia University Press, 1985). In another vein, see Terry Ramsaye, *A Million and One Nights: A History of the Motion Picture through 1925* (New York: Simon and Schuster, 1926). See also Thomas Schatz, *The Genius of the System* (New York: Pantheon, 1988).

38. Ernest Mandel, *Late Capitalism* (London: Verso, 1978), 118, cited in Fredric Jameson, *Postmodernism or, the Cultural Logic of Late Capitalism* (Durham: Duke, 1991), 35.

39. See Walter Benjamin, "Unpacking My Library," in *Illuminations* (New York: Schocken Books, 1969), or "Eduard Fuchs: Collector and Historian," in *The Essential Frankfurt School Reader*, ed. Andrew Arato and Eike Gebhardt (New York: Continuum, 1987).

40. This is more true in the silent era, that is, in the early modern. With talkies, the visual objects are spoken for more properly.

41. Alienated labor estranged people from 1. objects (nature); 2. self (labor-process); 3. species (objectified humanity, the general social wealth); 4. one another. See the section entitled "Estranged Labor" particularly pps. 72–77 in Marx, *Economic and Philosophic Manuscripts of 1844*, op Cit.

42. See Guy Debord, *The Society of the Spectacle*, trans. Donald Nicholson-Smith (Cambridge, Mass.: Zone Books, 1995), 172.

43. George Simmel, *The Philosophy of Money*, (London: Routledge, 1986), 441–42.

44. Arjun Appadurai correctly takes issue with the "optical illusion . . . fostered by neoclassical economics of the last century or so . . . that consumption is the end of the road for goods and services, a terminus for their social life, a conclusion of some sort of material cycle," in "Consumption, Duration and History," in *Streams of Cultural Capital*, ed. David Palumbo-Liu and Hans Ulrich Gumbrecht (Stanford: Stanford University Press, 1997), 23. Appadurai is correct to note that commodities have an afterlife following their material consumption, and further correct to figure these misapprehensions regarding this consuming productivity as optical.

45. Fredric Jameson, *Postmodernism* (Durham, N.C.: Duke University Press, 1992), 6.

46. See "Ideology and Ideological State Apparatuses," op cit.

47. Jean-Joseph Goux, *Symbolic Economies: After Marx and Freud,* trans. Jennifer Curtiss Gage (Ithaca: Cornell University Press, 1990), 86.

48. "Just as the genesis of the money form is the construction that accounts for the enigmatic disjunction between money and the commodity (a disjunction, moreover, which is required for the capitalist mode of production to be established), so the psychic apparatus is the construction that accounts for the distance between nonlinguistic forms of consciousness and linguistic forms of consciousness" (ibid., 77).

49. Guy Debord, *Society of the Spectacle* (Detroit: Black and Red, 1977), 21.

50. The three things that in "The Culture Industry: Enlightenment as Mass Deception" "keep the whole thing together." The passage reads: "No mention is made of the fact that the basis on which technology acquires power over society is the power of those whose economic hold over society is the greatest. A technological rationale is the rationale of domination itself. It is the coercive nature of society alienated from itself. Automobiles, bombs and movies keep the whole thing together until their leveling element shows its strength in the very wrong which it furthered. It has made the technology of the culture industry no more that the achievement of standardization and mass production, sacrificing whatever involved a distinction between the logic of the work and that of the social system. This is the result not of a law of movement in technology as such but of its function in today's economy." Theodore Adorno and Max Horkheimer, *Dialectic of Enlightenment,* (New York: Continuum, 1991), 121. See also Elaine Scarry, *The Body in Pain,* (Oxford: Oxford University Press, 1985), especially the chapter entitled "War as Injuring." See also Kristin Ross, *Fast Cars, Clean Bodies: Decolonization and the Reordering of French Culture* (Cambridge: MIT Press, 1995), in which Ross argues that "the car is the commodity form as such in the twentieth century" (6). Additionally, see Paul Virilio, *War and Cinema* (London: Verso, 1989), and Virilio, *The Vision Machine* (Bloomington: Indiana University Press, 1994).

51. Antonio Negri, "Twenty Theses on Marx," trans. Michael Hardt, in *Polygraph 5: Contesting the New World Order,* (Durham: [private], 1992), 139.

52. Ibid. Note Negri's own periodization of the three moments of class struggle.

53. Adorno and Horkheimer, *Dialectic of Enlightenment,* 137. See also the passage on 124 on *Gesamtkunstwerk.*

54. Negri, "Twenty Theses," 146–7.

55. See Robin Anderson, *Consumer Culture and TV Programming* (Boulder: Westview Press, 1995).

I

Chapter 1
Circulation
Dziga Vertov and the Film of Money

The spectacle is the other side of money: it is the general abstract equivalent of all commodities. —*Guy Debord,* Society of the Spectacle

---

1. Seeing through Matter. De-reification. Cinema— the Fusion of the Objective and Subjective Dimensions of Production. Practical Activity as Thought-Forms.

The opening sequence in Dziga Vertov's 1929 film manifesto *Man with a Movie Camera* invites the audience into the theater. Magically, empty chairs fold open their seats, inviting us to sit. As we shall soon witness, the movie theater would be, for Vertov, the public sphere, a place for collective and democratic consciousness and hence democratic representation, and film would be the medium for such a possibility. The postulating of a significant role for cinema during the 1920s correctly suggests that the twenties was a period of radical transformation in both the nature and the function of the image. For Vertov, film is the technology that will provide the utopian inspiration and practical means for the arrival of socialism. For those of us on the other side (historically speaking) of the Soviet experiment, Vertov's film must take on a different significance. This significance is, in part, Vertov's provisions for the groundwork of a political economy of the visual.

Before turning to the possibility of a political economy of the visual suggested by Vertov's *Man with a Movie Camera,* let us examine the film closely. With this film, the audience experiences a journey through a day in the life of the city (an assemblage of Moscow, Odessa, and Kiev), but an unprecedented one made possible by the advent of cinema. This visual journey through the varied moments and activities comprising complex metropol-

itan life is very precisely a journey through the production and reproduction of social life in general. What's more, it is a materialist vision—a way
of seeing through matter.

Enabling the journey through the city's self-production are a variety of
cinematic techniques: acceleration, deceleration, double exposure, rapid
montage, optical printing of single frames, shots of celluloid undergoing
the editing process that are then intercut with that celluloid, and the use of
still and mobile cameras. These techniques are regarded by Vertov's group,
the *kinoks*, not as special effects but as necessary means for the representation of reality. In a technological extension of the senses, in the cinema
the new capacities of film are fused to the eye, hence the name "kino-eye"
or "film-eye."[1] Kino-eye marks a cybernetic suturing of human and machine, of corporeality and industrialized perception. The organicity of machines, as well as the machinic organization of human beings, will be rendered in and as cinema.

Vertov uses the cinematic machine to assemble the movement of matter
in such a way that this movement becomes precisely the consciousness of
material relations. As Annette Michelson has suggested in her invaluable
introduction to Vertov's *Kino-Eye*, this journey through matter is the cinematic equivalent of Marx's *The German Ideology*. She deftly argues that in
Man with a Movie Camera, Vertov "take[s] or reinvent[s] *The German Ideology* as his text, for he situates the production of film in direct and telling
juxtaposition to that other particular sector, the textile industry, which has
for Marx and Engels a status that is paradigmatic within the history of material production." She continues:

> Now it is Vertov's positioning of film-as-production within the cyclical
> and parallel structure of his cinematic discourse and his insistence on
> the simultaneous and related revolutions of the wheels of industry and
> transportation and of the cranks and spindles of the filmmaking appa-
> ratus that establishes . . . the general relation of film production to other
> sectors of labor. (Vertov, xxxvii–xxxviii).

Cinema is a product—part of the emergent consciousness of industrial
society.

Using cinematic techniques to show myriad places and temporalities
consecutively or even simultaneously in order to find "the resultant force
amongst the million phenomena related to [a] given theme" (Vertov, 88),
Vertov foregrounds the movie camera as the condition of possibility for the
production of a new moment in the history of the understanding of social

relations and thus for the *production* of a new moment in the history of social relations. The materiality of visuality achieves a form of self-consciousness. Later we shall see how the kino-eye (machine-body) interface is posited as a site of production itself, and therefore that perception and consciousness are posited as such as well. This understanding of cinema's emergent role in the dialectic of social organization is a result of the extension of industrial processes to the senses—an implicit development of Marx's labor theory of value as a theory of montage. For Vertov, "montage means organizing film fragments (shots) into a film-object" (Vertov, 88); moreover, for him and for other Soviet filmmakers of his time, the consciousness characteristic of montage is the consciousness endemic to modernity's assemblage process, from the assembly line to constructivism.[2] Through the rationalization, routinization, and standardization of certain aspects of industrial production, montage achieves new orders of particularity and expressivity in the visual. Montage as fragmentation and montage as the connecting of fragments are at once the condition of modern life and the condition for the production of meaning in modern life. In short, all objects, from trains to concepts, are combined and combining; the rationalization of combinatory processes joins function and expression in a manner realized as cinema. As we shall see, Vertov represents both film technology and montage itself (what he theorized under the musical category of "the interval")—the concrete and abstract machines of cinema—as on a developmental/conceptual continuum with other productive technologies and operations of the period.[3] Cinema is seen as an extension and indeed as a completion of the general logic of socio-industrial production. The cinematicity of production in general is realized as cinema and it is cinema that confers self-awareness upon a humanity embroiled in and scaled by industrialization.

The structure of *Man with a Movie Camera* is on one level very simple. However, the film's articulation of the structure and function of the image is extraordinarily complex. The simple structure of *Man with a Movie Camera*, then, is as follows: Bracketed at the beginning by the images of the empty theater, and at the end by shots of the theater, now full, in which an audience watches the same film that we have been watching, *Man with a Movie Camera* begins in the morning with the city waking up, moves on to the working day, and then to recreation. By depicting a day in the life of the city framed by the experience of cinema—made conscious by the experience of cinema—the film announces the new role of cinema in society. Cinema is the becoming self-conscious of social relations—literally, the relations of production.

Although the theoretical sophistication and historico-materiality visible in the images put forth in the work of Vertov will disappear after Vertov from easy imaginal legibility by fading back into the unthought of the image, the terrain of production that Vertov stakes out for the image will not disappear. The image, just as Vertov so clearly shows in *Man with a Movie Camera*, still will be built like a commodity and still will be generative of the consciousness of material relations—but not the same type of consciousness, not a dialectically self-aware consciousness. The critical theory of the image as historico-material mediation will disappear, that is, become unconscious and even become The Unconscious, despite the intensification of the image's historico-material effects (see chapter 3).

Because film is understood by Vertov as being on a technological continuum with the rest of industrial society and as the means in which a society at a certain level of development achieves a higher level of self-articulation, *Man with a Movie Camera* is necessarily about its own conditions of production. During the production of a day, the camera draws analogies among the actions of the individual, the city, and its own operation. Indeed, the parallels among tools and structures operating in different social formations or utilized at different levels or moments in the production process (for example, the train wheels, the wheels of industry and of the great weaving machines, and the film crank of the camera) are less analogies than particular instantiations or embodiments of abstract industrial possibilities. The parallels drawn between cinematic production and social production are extensions of the forms of social production into the visual field. They mark the abstraction and intellectualization of a social practice—a making of the senses theoretical. A procedure or a tool is not just a dead thing but a form of consciousness with numerous possibilities and applications. As George Simmel writes, "For even where the mind is tied to matter, as in tools, works of art and books, it is never identical with that part of them that is perceptible to our senses. The mind lives in them in a hardly definable potential form which the individual consciousness is able to actualize. Objective culture is the historical presentation or more or less perfect condensation of an objectively valid truth which is reproduced by our cognition."[4] Vertov's cinema makes objective culture, specifically objects and material practices, directly representational and therefore cognitive in order that society can understand the interdependence of its myriad practices and achieve its higher, that is, democratic autopoesis.

Vertovian cinema releases what Simmel sees as the condensed accretion of historical cognition in matter. This cinema provides cognitive enrichment of what Simmel calls "an objectively valid truth." All the tools and operations represented in *Man with a Movie Camera* are embodied structures produced and producing at a particular moment in social and technological development. They all occupy various niches in the cycle of production, and all are necessary for, on the one hand (as production), the objectification of human beings in their materials and, on the other hand (as cinema), the subjective understanding of this social process as such. Cinema is the fusion of the objective and subjective dimensions of production. The film shows that the same technologies are at work at all levels of society and that, at each level, activity can simultaneously be cognition. The levels presented may be distinguished as those that directly involve the production of society as a whole, "(s)"; the individual, "(i)"; and consciousness, "(c)." Each of these different levels of production embodies forms of movement, that is, patterns of repetition and circulation, that are repeated throughout these levels of social production. Because these levels all are shown to be on a continuum, "the blade," for example, functioning as an ax (s), a razor (i), and a film splicer (c), or "the wheel," functioning as a train (s), an automobile (i), and the crank of the camera (c), index particular technological forms or abstract machines (cutting and rolling) in multiple applications that characterize production in this industrial period. Thus, "the cut," whether of an axe or a film-splice and "spatio-temporal translation," whether of a railroad car or sprockets in a movie projector, constitute at once abstract and historical forms, themselves the accretions of the inventive labor and consciousness of humanity. The similar forms of tools and procedures shown in operation at all levels of society establish not merely the interrelationship of different undertakings to one another but also the historicity and collective aspect of these undertakings. Their differentiation and their unity testify that technology is the collective historical achievement of humanity.

By showing that particular technological forms (such as the machine-driven wheel) run through all aspects of industrial society, *Man with a Movie Camera* countermands the fragmentation and reification that is ordinarily the immediate experience of the individual alienated in the workplace. The abstract form is utilized in specific contexts by specific people. Vertov (and the viewer) builds the abstraction from the specifics, and then the abstractions inform the specifics. This collective creation of an image of society is not accomplished all at once but is built painstakingly by passing through different moments of the *socius*, different realms of human activity separate in place and time. This image recapitulates and extends in-

dividual and historical learning processes while dramatizing the possibilities of their synthesis. The filmic result is an extraordinary vision of integration in the complex and finely tuned music of collective life. The interdependence of each event on all is at once made present and historical. The
making of all things, from cloth to knowledge to history, appears as the integrated collective activity it is in practice.

In one crescendo of this visual symphony, an aerial shot of a city plaza
shows in fast motion the movement of thousands of pedestrians, street-
cars, bicycles, automobiles, and horse-drawn carts. Extraordinarily, despite
the speed and intensity of modern circulation, there are no collisions.
Against all odds, the city is a coordinated and functioning organism. Vertov takes the movie camera as an essential element of future coordinations
because social complexity is resolved intelligibly by cinema. Though the
revolutionary dictatorship of the proletariat for which Vertov worked never
materialized, he saw the "organization of the visible world" as its precondition (Vertov, 72). In ways that escaped him, but that did not entirely escape Stalin, Hitler, or, for that matter, Ted Turner and Bill Gates, the organization of the visual world would be decisive.[5]

At the climactic moment of the visual understanding of teeming urban
activity mentioned above, Vertov freezes a frame and, in effect, presents us
with a still of the frenetic city. This still, like the others in the film (the ar-
rested galloping horse, for example), announces not only the difference between still photography and cinema but also the difference between
reification and a vision of process, that is, vision as process. Through cinema, the frozen products of photography (and of pre-Marxist societies) are
made eloquent. They speak their own process and complexity, revealing
themselves as assemblages of social relationships ordinarily laminated by
reification. In taking practical activity as thought, Vertov shows the integration of every aspect of society into this frenzied but rational circulation
of people, images, and objects. He depicts processes as diverse as haircuts,
mining, fire fighting, birth, marriage, divorce, death, cigarette packing,
cloth spinning, and athletic endeavor. The common theme, however, is
the collectivity in all its interdependent and productive complexity—and
the possibility of the collectivity seeing itself. This is why, when the photograph of the crowd is reanimated—that is, allowed to flow again in
time—Vertov uses optical printing to split the image in two. In the cinema, the metropolis faces itself and we are presented with an image of
self-consciousness. The self-consciousness of the city emerges here because the eye circulates through the city's very materiality.

2. Political Economy as the Unconscious of the Object World. The Camera as Political Economist. Image as a Necessary Moment in the Development of Circulation. Image as a Developmental Consequence of the Relations of Production. The Becoming-Image of the Commodified Object. The Image/Commodity.

"Kino-Eye," according to Vertov, is "the documentary cinematic de-coding of both the visible world and that which is invisible to the naked eye" (Vertov, 87). The manifesto from which this phrase is drawn has affinities with the filmic aspirations—inspired in part by Vertov—in the surgical cinema discussed by Walter Benjamin.[6] "Our taverns and our metropoli-tan streets, our offices and furnished rooms, our railroad stations and our factories appeared to have us locked up hopelessly. Then came the film and burst this prison-world asunder by the dynamite of the tenth of a second, so that now, in the midst of its far-flung ruins and debris, we calmly and adventurously go traveling. With the close-up, space expands; with slow motion, movement is extended." Benjamin continues, "The camera inter-venes with the resources of its lowerings and liftings . . . its enlargements and reductions. The camera introduces us to an unconscious optics as does psychoanalysis to unconscious impulses."[7] For Vertov, the unconscious of objects that can be revealed optically is precisely the relations of production that ordinarily are repressed or invisible. It was because the acted cinema mystified the relations of production—leaving them in the obscure world of the director's fantasy—that Vertov detested it so profoundly. Political economy, as a set of necessarily unthought relations, is the unconscious of the objective world dominated by capital. Like the political economist, the psychoanalyst, and the author in modernist literature, the camera breaks apart the objective world and enters into it in order to bring forth the re-pressed or the unconscious elements and bring them to the level of con-sciousness. Such investigative processes engender the new forms and modes of analysis associated with modernity. In Vertovian cinema, the ob-jective world is revealed as frozen subjectivity; it is seen to be composed of historically sedimented, subjective practices and activated by subjective ap-plication. Thus, as Benjamin notes, "By close-ups of the things around us, by focusing on hidden details of familiar objects, by exploring common-place milieus under the ingenious guidance of the camera, the film, on the one hand, extends our comprehension of the necessities which rule our lives; on the other hand, it manages to assure us of an immense and unexpected field of action."[8] With Benjamin, Vertov's film theory utilizes scientific precision and "the dynamite of the tenth of a second" in an effort to liquidate the aura or, what in mass production will evolve intensively as the fetish character that accompanies objects in modern bourgeois society, despite his Vertov's efforts.

In a series of observations that corroborate Vertov's "communist decoding of reality," Georg Lukács's reification theory, and the transformations noted by Benjamin in aesthetic objects, Simmel shows in *The Philosophy of Money* that, under the regime of mechanical reproduction mediated by a money economy, a transformation is manifest in objects in general. The sense of being oppressed by the externalities of modern life is not only the consequence but also the cause of the fact that objects confront us as *autonomous* objects.

> What is distressing is that we are basically indifferent to those numerous objects that swarm around us, and this indifference [emerges] for reasons specific to a money economy: their impersonal origins and easy replaceability. The fact that large industrial concerns are the breeding ground for socialist ideas is due not only to the social conditions of the workers, but also to the objective quality of their products. Modern man is so surrounded by nothing but impersonal objects that he becomes more and more conditioned into accepting the idea of an anti-individualistic social order—though, of course, he may also oppose it. Cultural objects increasingly evolve into an interconnected enclosed world that has increasingly fewer points at which the subjective soul can interpose its will and feelings.[9]

Thus the general circulation of objects creates a system of perceptions and affects that are of an altogether new character.

For Marx, the social conditions of wage workers and the objective quality of their products are not two distinct features of the social as they seem to be for Simmel; rather, they follow one from the other in alienated labor—impersonal objects are so because they embody workers' severed, that is, alienated, subjectivity, or labor-time, which then confronts workers as a power over them, as something alien.[10] Simmel seems to consider reification and the anti-individualistic character of socialism as being of a piece—not a contradiction but a confirmation—of the autonomy of objects and thus seems to find in the relation between the social conditions of industrial wage workers and the objective quality of their products a lamentable but inexorable anti-individualist condition rather than a fully legitimate scene of contestation aspiring toward the collectivization of production. In spite of this nostalgia, he nonetheless, as a phenomenologist of money, provides a brilliant account of the character of assembly-line-produced objects produced and circulating in capital.

With the anti-individualistic character of objects themselves in mind, we can see that Vertov works to combine the idea of an anti-individualistic social order with *an increase* in the number of "points at which the subjective soul can interpose its will and feelings" and can therefore intervene in the "immense and unexpected field of action" that Benjamin sees as being opened up by cinema.[11] What Vertov calls the interval, that is, the negative space between the montage fragments, emphasizes not so much the shock or the conflict between elements, as in Sergei M. Eisenstein's "montage of attractions," but rather, the connections between elements. Thus the interval creates what we might call a montage of abstractions, in as much as we are to understand that the logic of the social totality is iterated in each and every sequence. This unconscious scene of formation, emerging through the structure of the gap that Vertov calls the interval, is made of connections that dismantle the phenomenological (reificatory) effects of capital circulation and create a new relation to the social product at once collective and personal. With the proper discernment of the resultant vector of a given theme, the objectively repressed content of social interaction appears. To counter the mediation of objects by money, cinema endeavors to remediate their relations.

In positioning cinema as that which remediates social relations, the image is posited as a necessary moment in the circulation of social materials (though not yet as a relation of production that demands work). Just as Vertov allows concrete material practices to become modes of cognition through a repetition of instances (the concept emerges as the link between two distinct processes), the concept of the social totality appears as the summation of the intervals between the various social moments. "Totality" posits the connective human tissue in object(ive) relations in a way not visible when viewing the circulation of objects from the standpoint of money. This central point suggests that Vertovian cinema works both with and against money. *Man with a Movie Camera* emerges directly out of industrial technologies and takes industrial modes of operation as a means as well as an end for expression. In this sense, film is like money—an eloquent, highly nuanced, highly differentiated, multivalent, organizing form for giving expression to the forces of social mediation that develop out of capitalist industrialization. Like money, film covers the entire scene of the socius and is the other side of the circulation of objects; it is fragmentary in its distribution and use and yet unified as a medium—it extends equally as far as the social extends. And yet Vertovian cinema works directly against the phenomenology of money; it is a strategy of remediation.

Although Vertovian cinema makes explicit the (world-historical) transformation of the status of objects in industrialization (their becoming-image) and articulates what we can begin to discern as the commodity structure of the image, the affect of circulation conferred on objects by Vertovian cinema precisely opposes the effect of circulation that advances commodity reification. The presentation of the consciousness of matter, a consciousness that is lost to the worker/consumer in alienated production, constitutes Vertov's dialectics of seeing.[12] Under capital, the human processing that constitutes an object is sealed off from view through expropriation and the resultant sheen of the commodity-form. Money as the vanishing mediator and the labor process itself are disappeared in a universe of objects. By unpacking the object and revealing it as an assemblage of individuated processes, the subjectivity impacted in its form comes to life. The visual analysis that is tantamount to the de-reification of the object and therefore of the objective world is the unique content of Vertov's phrase "I see."[13] Vertov discovers an "art" in which there is no irresolvable contradiction between technology and the body, materiality and consciousness, base and superstructure. Instead, these generally opposing moments are conceived by him as nodes in a coextensive cybernetic system that finally, through full creative utilization, can be made self-conscious. The cinema represents a dialectical convergence of men and machines—a genuine materialization of thought. By making social practice cognitive, cinema was to oppose the logic of reification by creating a circulatory form alongside capital circulation. Vertov shows humanity on a continuum with mechanization—machines are human, the historical product of human sensuous labor, and potentially function in accord with, rather than in contradiction to, human potentiality. Vision of the kind Vertov produces, via the cinema of kino-eye, registers and results from the flow of industrial production/circulation, yet opposes its capital logic. Thus kino-eye locks vision into a struggle with capital over the phenomenological appearance of the commodity. It is precisely here, in the field of objective appearance, that revolutionary cinema images its combat with capital. And it is precisely in the mediate, the sensual, and predominantly the visual that this struggle is waged most intently.[14] We must therefore deduce that it was also the realm of the visual that capitalist organization was laying claim to most intensively, first through reification and the phenomenology of objects, and later, as advertising, propaganda, and a generalized expropriation of the senses.

Vertov attempts to demystify the commodity by showing the social relations embedded in the reified object. Consequently, the relations of production are shown to be internal to the image. Images are consequences of the development of the relations of production and are constituted precisely by passing through these relations. Though these relations are explicitly visible in the film of Vertov (images are assembled like commodities and appear as processes), they nonetheless inhere in other kinds of cinematic images in which these relations again become invisible. What we learn from Vertov is that the image is constituted like an object—it is assembled piece by piece like a commodity moving through the intervals of production—and it is a (technological and economic) development of the relations of production capable of materializing consciousness.

Within the space of capital logic, the social object takes on the commodity form. It is constituted as a use-value and an exchange-value, and exhibits a fetish character that is derived in part from this internal contradiction manifest both as its indifference to us and its power over us. These qualities derive from its autonomized excess as exchange-value and its irreducibility as a signifier of our general relation to social production where we are ourselves annihilated in the object and socially visible only as exchange-value. These characteristics of the commodity are instituted by design in the case of industrial objects, but they generally are conferred upon any and all objects taken up by capitalist circulation. In a capitalist social space in which objects circulate as commodities, images come to exhibit precisely these same properties.[15] The task is to show why. Though Vertov's images do not exactly exist with the characteristics of commodities—since they induce a (self-)consciousness of existing practice—the endeavor to de-reify the commodity necessarily reveals the general commodity-structure of the image. Vertov articulates from a Marxist standpoint an implicit relationship between images and objects under modern capital, a relationship that, like the primal scene, does not have to be witnessed in order to be deduced. In capital, the object and the image, both resulting from the relations of mechanical reproduction and the affective dimensions thereof, are on a convergence course. The image as a social relation is a direct consequence of advances in the industrial production of objects. At present, the object has a tendency to become the image (think, for example, of a Mercedes-Benz or a television set), and the image, assembled like a commodity, elaborates and intensifies the character of the commodified object, taking on and indeed often surpassing the inductive agency of conventional material objects. I will call these emergent forms image-objects, object-images, or image/commodities, depending on which aspect of these circulating entities is to be emphasized in a given situation.

To grasp how deeply the logic of production infuses objects and images, recall that, in *Man with a Movie Camera*, perception's journey circulates through and is made possible by the material and technological resources of a particular historical juncture. Objects and images are formed by the same means. Vertov's trains, with their wheels, cranks, and tracks, are understood to be at once assembled by a society from and for its own conditions, and to embody the same technology (both abstract and concrete) as that of cinema, with its corresponding gears, cranks, and perforated film. The image runs through the sprockets as the train runs through the track. Each functions as a sign of the other. Both are objects and images simultaneously; both are media. However, cinema is the higher media form here because, like money, it has the greater capacity (greater even than trains) to put all objects into circulation.[16] With its capacity for self-consciousness in the hands of Vertov, but more importantly because of its capacity to induce consciousness instrumentally by converting industrial process to sensory affect, cinema is the greater mobilizing force.

---

3. Image as Use-Value/Exchange-Value. Visible as Materialized Subjectivity. Cinema as the Organization of the Visible World, That Is, of the Materialized Subjective World. The Dialectical Materialism of the Image. Dialectical Vision. The Emergent Visual Economy.

Vertov's most important film, when read as an analysis of the composition and a critique of the phenomenology of the image, stands as one of the intellectual triumphs of the twentieth century. A political economy of the spectacle must show its achievements and limits. According to Marx, "Each form of production produces its own legal relations, forms of government, etc."[17] In the Vertovian dialectic, the production of consciousness through kino-eye was predicted to have its effects on these realms.

One of the revolutionary aspects of *Man with a Movie Camera* is that, in the film's construction of an image of social life, concrete social relations take on an abstract significance not because they are concrete iterations of abstract-labor that are taken up by capital as exchange-value, but because of their dialectical presentation; through the fabric of vision, particular moments in social life and social production are understood as having a definite relationship to the totality of social production. It is production rather than exchange-value that is the animating abstraction in each concrete object. Each shot in Vertov has a literal and an abstract dimension; it is a sign of itself (one of the various "film-facts"), and it signifies a moment in the totality of social production. This is why, for Vertov, it is not the montage fragments themselves that alone carry the significance of a particular shot but the spaces between the fragments, the abstract links. "Intervals (the transition from one movement to another) are the material, the elements of the art of movement, and by no means the movements themselves. It is they (the intervals) which draw the movement to a kinetic resolution" (Vertov, 8).[18] The question of the intervals between movements here is precisely the question of the circulation of production, the connective tissue of each filmed instance that cumulatively constitutes the totality of social relations. It is the image in circulation that gives the image its dual character, its specific content, and its general significance, or, to make a point that I shall return to, its use-value and its exchange-value.

The quintessential image of the Vertovian manifesto, the seeing eye reflected in the camera lens and projected on the screen, is a dialectical image that contains a vision of the conjunction of humanity and the machine in a circulatory system that produces consciousness precisely by passing through materiality. This image presupposes the history of humanity. It is the intervals between the eye and the camera, and between the camera and the screen—society in its entirety—that Vertov wishes to account for. Each journey through a particular strand of social production to the screen of consciousness, like the threads teased out on the film's great spinning machines, can be woven into the production of the social fabric. Society becomes visible as materialized subjectivity or subjective agency. At the broadest level, this analysis of materialized subjectivity is an investigation into the conditions of possibility of cinema and for the cinematic production of the future.

For Vertov, showing objects and states as processes creates sites of potential action. He depicts all moments of social production as both part of a conscious process and part of a process becoming conscious. The consciousness specific to a particular process—say, the packing of cigarettes—is, through montage, put in relation to other processes, such as the switching of phone lines or of train tracks. The glaze of the commodity form of cigarettes, media, transport, and so forth is revealed to be the hidden integration of bodies and machines—an amalgamation of labor, conscious-ness, and materials. In Vertov, we see the labor in the object as we see the labor in the image, because we are made aware of the process of integra-tion, the integral of the commodity and its calculus. Thus are previously in-dividualized consciousnesses—the people who work on their products and who formerly disappeared into them, as well as the people who enjoy the use of aspects of the social product—seen in the theater by the audience and producers alike in their collective interdependence.

In the unprecedented technology of cinematic representation lies, for Vertov, the potential solution to the problem of self-conscious democracy. Since the films were meant to be renewed every day (Vertov envisioned teams and resources that would multiply his efforts a hundredfold—quite a different concept of the evening news), they were intended to achieve a new order of autopoesis, the emerging Soviet's form of self-consciousness. Properly utilized, cinema was, for Vertov, the perceptual apparatus that ex-tended the range of the senses through space and time.[19] Though in a way quite different from his primary competitor, Eisenstein, who believed that cinema was "the organisation of the audience through organised mate-rial," for Vertov cinema was "the organization of the visible world" (Vertov, 72).[20] As we shall see in chapter 2, Eisenstein had an avant-gardist ap-proach to social organization, in which ideology outpaced materiality, while here we may see that Vertov worked from what he considered to be the truth told by materials.[21] By means of the historico-technological ex-tension of the senses, society, for Vertov, became potentially transparent.[22] In the Vertovian logic, such transparency was itself the necessary instru-ment of democratic social action.

Without going into the insidious side of transparency, let me explore further the utopian strains of Vertov's work in the endeavor of seeing.[23] Vertov sets out to demonstrate that each moment of the real is informed by a logic of totality that encompasses all moments of social existence. "Noth-ing is accidental," writes Vertov. "Everything is explicable and governed by law" (Vertov, 287). The basic figure of this law is circulation. As noted, Ver-tov makes each image in *Man with a Movie Camera* both a signifier of its object (what he calls a "material document") and a linked moment in the larger flux of totality (an "interval"). An alternative mediation between use-value (quality) and exchange-value (circulativity) induces revolutionary consciousness. Here, the exchange-value system manifest in the abstrac-tion of Vertov's images has its gold standard in the concept of totality. It is the concept of totality that allows the spectral recuperation of capital's fragments by the people. The film traces the complexly mediated multiple relationships of individuals to each other and to the totality of social life. The film makes individuality and social relations self-consciously dialectical by producing each visual moment (image) from an object or an objective relation. This objective relation is, in the last, abstract instance, exchange-value, the system of exchange-values that actively constitutes the totality of capital/society. The concept of totality is the specter of capital, its antithesis. Therefore, each object as an image becomes a medium, a mediator; that is, each object expresses its concrete (object) existence as well as its dynamic (and impacted) relations to totality. This is the dialectical materialism of the image, the (re)mediation of use-value and exchange-value, that, like other Marxisms before it, endeavors to remediate the very form of the commodity, meaning the relations that constitute capital itself.[24]

Lukács, who could well have been commenting on Vertov's visual destruction of reification, notes that the goal of Marxism in relation to quotidian reality

> is not a condition which can be happily forgotten in the stress of daily life and recalled only in Sunday sermons as a stirring contrast to workaday cares. Nor is it a "duty," an "idea" designed to regulate the "real" process. The ultimate goal is rather that relation to the totality (to the whole of society seen as a process), through which every aspect of the struggle acquires its revolutionary significance. This relation informs every aspect in its simple and sober ordinariness, but only consciousness makes it real and so confers reality on the day-to-day struggle by manifesting its relation to the whole. Thus it [consciousness] elevates mere existence to reality.[25]

The interval, as the consciousness that "elevates mere existence to reality," utilizes the dialectical structure of the commodity in order to make the commodity self-conscious.

In Vertov's words, "*Man with a Movie Camera* represents not only a practical result; it is, as well, a theoretical manifestation on the screen" (Vertov, 83). In Vertov, dialectical consciousness is achieved through vision: The eye becomes theoretical.[26] Vertov situates his camera along the lines of sight specified by Marx: "The premises from which we begin are not arbitrary ones, not dogmas, but real premises from which abstraction can only be made in the imagination. They are the real individuals, their activity and the material conditions under which they live, both those which they find already existing and those produced by their activity. These premises can be verified in an empirical way."[27] The abstraction made in the imagination of Vertov's viewers is a dialectical vision of the dialectical structure of the commodity generated by the empirical observation of production.

The relation between the production of the image (of consciousness) and social production in general will take on greater importance for us as we deepen our exploration of the relationship between the image and the commodity. Though dialectical vision will not become de rigueur, the image as a media byte with its obverse in its content and its reverse in global circulation will grow to express nondialectical, yet nonetheless instrumental, affects of totality (the omnipresent world-system as nature itself). These cinematic affects remain dialectically functional (for capital) though not dialectically perceived (for socialism). However, it is apparent that in the age of mechanical reproduction a confluence occurs in the techniques for the production of the image and the object, and, furthermore, that all the social relations that inhere in the object also inhere in the image. Vertov's brilliant articulation of the relationship between the formation of the image and the formation of what will, despite his best efforts, remain the commodity foretells not the end of prehistory and the historical victory of communism but the emergence of new laws of exchange. The image in circulation will indeed carry the logic of exchange-value, but for capital.

---

4. Capital Circulation as the Abstract Machine of Cinema. Meshing the Nonsynchronous. The Montage of Capital. The Cinematic Industrial Complex. Material Concepts Made Visible. Circulation of Capital in and as Consciousness Is Cinema. Cinema Extends the Logistics of Capital to the Senses.

Because the underpinnings of a historical phenomenon often are grasped more easily from the artifacts produced during its formation than from those produced during its more fully realized form, we may discern from Vertov, who was working in a society that was not yet fully capitalized and, in retrospect, was undergoing the vertiginous process of modernization, that certain technology needed to be available before cinema could come into being. Also, it was not until capital circulation had developed to a certain point (both via technologies of circulation and as technologies in circulation) that cinema was possible as an abstraction (and as a calculus of abstraction). Before this moment in the developmental trajectory of capital, cinema's particular form of movement and time had not yet arrived. It is well known that cinematic technology preexists the cinema.[28] But just as the Roman steam engine (of little use in a precapitalist slave economy) was a mere mechanical curiosity until the industrial revolution, capital circulation (churning out ever more complex pathways under the sway of exchange) had to develop to a certain point—as an industrial form (routinized mass production) and as a visual phenomenon (fetishism)—before cinema was possible. Capital circulation is, in Gilles Deleuze's vocabulary, the "abstract machine" of cinema; circulation itself genetically engenders cinema's form of abstraction.

Likewise, *Man with a Movie Camera* demonstrates, in its resistance to the visual effects of capital circulation, through its decodification process, the fact that cinema is an extension of capital's circulation. By filming various moments of production, Vertov shows that cinema, like capital, implies the coordination of nonsynchronous temporalities and the montage of space. In the present situation of multinational capital, modes of production in Latin America, Asia, and Africa are coordinated with those of the United States and Europe, despite the radically differing ways in which the local economies articulate space and modulate time. This is also true at the local or national level of the economy, where the coordination of temporalities becomes necessary for the coordination of labor in various factories, in agriculture, and in the production of crafts (each of which might be understood as groups of shots in the multiform fabric of the total film of capital). As Ernst Bloch eloquently describes the phenomenon of nonsynchronicity, "Not all people exist in the same Now."[29] Such nonsynchronicity does not necessarily posit a temporal continuum, that is, a necessary process of social evolution through various temporalities of increasing speed, but rather the introduction—in technologically advanced societies—of a gear system for the differential coordination of various temporal speeds. In Marx's analysis of economics, this gear system is capital itself, or, rather, the circulation of money against exchange-value; in Vertov, it is film—the circulation of film against object codification. This parallel does not limit itself to the fact that in cinema different scenes are shot at different times, nor does it limit itself to the fact that temporal flow—what Andrey Tarkovsky later called "time-pressure"—is different from scene to scene in Vertov and must be coordinated into a production that is the film.[30] Rather, it can be generalized to read that film, at the level of form, is the most articulate iteration of the basic relations of nonsynchronicity and fragmentation that inhere in capitalist production. Cinema raises the montage of capital to a new level of expressivity. This is true of cinema qua technology and occurs precisely because the moving image arises out of the logic of capital circulation. As Vertov's work eloquently reveals: (1) cinema arises out of industry and industrial processes; (2) in industrial society, the construction of the image recapitulates the construction of the object/commodity; (3) the confrontation among times running at different speeds is nowhere more directly expressed than in the cinema; (4) spatial contiguity can be manufactured; and (5) the resultant effects of the combinatory logic of matter in circulation creates a panoply of affects, utopian and otherwise. It is just such a battle with nonsynchronicity, along with a similar struggle over the contiguity of space, that engages both capital and Vertov. Vertov wages a battle with capital over the logistical question of how to organize the fragments of social life to produce an object, an image, a civilization.

If it is true that *Man with a Movie Camera* expresses the material relations with a camera that is "an eye in matter," and that matter is in circulation, it is equally true that capital circulation is precisely the montage of capital.[31] The process of capital is itself cinematic. Material in an assembly-line process is transmogrified at each station: Materials pass through an editing process to become a car; money, in its endless exchange, takes on the form of the commodities it passes through. Capital as exchange-value passes through all things; in cinema, capital logic addresses the eye. Material and money circulate in an endless metamorphosis. This metamorphosis produces and is produced by the myriad temporalities, movements, objects, and now images of and for social production and reproduction. Capital, then, as abstract value with concrete instantiations, serves as the paradigm of cinema as abstract representation with particular images composing particular elements in particular films.

This idea, it should be noted, goes far beyond the fact that film, like capital, is itself a commodity that must circulate and be valorized through the extraction of surplus-value (from somewhere—it will be necessary to show from where). In chapter 2, I will have more to say about how the cinematic image as a new technology of social production is also a new technology of exploitation (value-extraction) under capitalism. The idea that capital serves as the paradigm for cinema also goes beyond the idea that film provides a return on investment in many separate instances spread out over space and time. Clearly, the returns given to cinema cannot be only money paid, given the interest in form and content taken in cinema by audiences, corporations, and the state. Although these latter two shadow institutions (corporations and the state) for securing concrete bodies for spectatorship presently lack an economic theory that explains their existence with respect to cinema, their effects are no doubt at the cutting edge of capitalist economics. The film, in some way or another, has been required to produce its own audiences, its own markets, and, explicitly in Soviet and Nazi cinema but implicitly in "free-market" cinema, the state. All the psychoanalytic, ideological, Third World, ethnic, feminist, and queer criticism of Hollywood testifies to the fact of the production of audiences by the cinema, precisely through this criticism's interrogations and indictments of the role of film in the production of hegemony and, in some cases, of its role in the production of the resistance to hegemony. These audiences, with their new capacities, require new modes of management if they are not to rise up and smash the state that conspires to cheat and impoverish them, but rather to continue to be kept subservient. What films did (and continue to do) was to provide a vehicle, a cinematic industrial complex, through which workers (or, more precisely, spectators) could produce the practices of the socius and of the state both objectively and within themselves. Indeed, an increasingly precise coordination of interiority with the requisites of production is, from an economistic point of view the raison d'être of the cinema.

Cinema as an abstract figure, as a conceptual possibility, represents, for Vertov's period, the concrete limit of the period's ability to think its mode of production, that is, the unconscious limits of the period to figure the workings of capital in the dynamics of its production process. The conceptual figure of cinema was already the conceptual figure of capital. The rise of commercial cinema means the subsumption of these conceptualizations by capital. In Vertov's case, the film is at once analogous to capital circulation and alternative to it, since it retains the trace of the flow of its objects in a manner ordinarily "known" only to capital itself and necessarily invisible to labor under capitalism. We see in Vertov the flow of capital from the standpoint of Marx. Put in vulgar terms that we will have to revise immediately, cinema in general is the superstructural form of basic global organization. A revision of this statement is necessary because, as Vertov's cinema proves, cinema as a form of consciousness is simultaneously a material practice—the consciousness of material relations—that was to affect social-material organization. Material in organized motion has a visual effect; cinematic vision, however immaterial it may be in appearance, is a material practice with material effects. It depends for its very existence on the historical development of a complex material infrastructure. The abstract machine of capital drives itself through the visual field to become the abstract machine of cinema; cinema is the abstraction and intensification of the general socioeconomic process.

Cinema in its fully capitalized form moves capital through the two ostensibly distinct but dialectically related realms that have been hypostasized utilizing the false dichotomy "base and superstructure." In Vertov, we apprehend directly that the movement of capital through the "base" circulates as consciousness in the "superstructure." In other words, the circulation of capital in and as consciousness *is* cinema. This isomorphism of capital circulation as material and capital circulation as consciousness is no mere echo or analogy—it is the materialization of the consciousness of capital through an ostensibly immaterial, affective medium. The image is a cybernetic interface. Cinema as the organized flow of image/commodities means the productive coordination of human perception and material process.

In general, capital is edited at each moment in its circulation, that is, it is made to take one route rather than another, and is constantly creating new pathways. Vertov makes perceptible the extension of the form of capital circulation to the visual arena. Thus, cinema as a potential set of new pathways through the senses also must be understood as an extension of the logistics of capital at once across space, through time, and into the sensorium.

These new pathways result in new commodities, new needs, and, of course, new images. They also produce multiple temporalities—times running at different speeds—and different spatial conjunctures. In addition, they produce functional relationships to these disjunctive perceptual shocks, intensities, and spiritualities. Capital's orchestration of the relationships among space, time, images, and finally bodies, in a flexible yet systemic coordination of the *productive* movement of exchange-value (this productive aspect has yet to be demonstrated here), strives to reorganize and control the new capacities of technological bodies struggling against domination. This shift from industrial capital with its commodities, factory discipline, and bourgeois culture to cinematic capital with its images, desires, and consumer culture, defines a period in which all relations tend toward the cinematic and in which the relation between capital and value-producers inscribes itself as the cinematic mode of production.

Vertov's choice to intervene directly in the dialectic, in the materiality of history, shows that the image has become a necessary site of regulation (and production) in the capitalized flow of value. Furthermore, the image—which is always moving, if at highly differentiated speeds—becomes the paradigmatic social relation. Consequently, capital, as the standpoint from which to interrogate, understand, or regulate human reproduction and world history, functions as the aperture/screen through/on which the machinations of human reproduction and world history become visible.

With Vertov, capital as an analytic standpoint becomes the equivalent of the movie screen. In the circulating frame, all that is solid melts into air. Thus, we could say that Vertov grasps cinema as the standpoint of capital and assembles it dialectically, while cinema in general is assembled from the standpoint of the capitalist. Thus, viewers of Vertov are enjoined to understand what appears from the perspective of Marxism, while viewers of commercial cinema see from the hegemonic standpoint of capital.

Because I will have to defer the analysis of how value is transacted across the image (hypothesis: the image-commodity bypasses the direct mediation of money as wage in the extraction of necessary labor and pays the viewer in a combination of pleasure and *techné*), the following claim cannot at this time be substantiated fully: The logistics of cinematic production (the production of society via cinema and cinematic technologies and effects) embodies the logistics of capitalist production but raises it to a higher level of abstraction; cinema is, in effect, the very form of late capital, the highest stage of twentieth-century capitalism. This assertion would place cinema on par with imperialism in its world-historical significance and suggests that the two are intertwined inexorably. Although the productive dimensions of this assertion's general outlines have not yet been proven here, they nonetheless are visible already. The present consideration of Vertov and of *Man with a Movie Camera* accounts only for the production and circulation of object-images, not explicitly for their productivity. A further account, which I will provide in the next chapter, must discuss their valorization. As we know, Vertov failed; the images weren't valorized. It is for this reason (kino-eye's failure to reproduce its conditions of production) that the rest of my discussion here confines itself primarily to film and money rather than to cinema and capital.

---

5. Film : Money :: Cinema : Capital. Film as Measure; Price as Proto-Image. Film as Medium of Exchange. Judgment of Wilhelm Wurzer's "Filming." Toward a Materialism of Dematerialization.

The mediation that occurs between commodity and commodity in Marx's description is performed by money:

> At first sight, circulation appears to be simply a never-ending process. The commodity is exchanged for money; money is exchanged for the commodity, and this is repeated ad infinitum. This constant renewal of

an identical process does indeed constitute an essential feature of circulation. But on closer examination, it reveals other phenomena as well: the phenomena of closing the circle or the return of the point of departure into itself. The commodity is exchanged for money; money is exchanged for the commodity. So, commodity is exchanged for commodity, except that this exchange is a mediated one. (*Grundrisse*, 132)

The commodified contents of general cinematic circulation, however, are not, materially speaking, objects but images; the mediation between "objects" by which a film constitutes itself is between abstractions from objects. In *Man with a Movie Camera*, the mediation between the interval of image-commodity and image-commodity is film. It is the film frame (the screen) that allows the images to circulate; film is the money of cinema (and the frame is the unit). The affective dimensions of capital circulation are distilled and experienced in their most purified form in the cinema—in the enchanted registration of everything by money. This spectacularity, which is the mark of achievement in American films, is what Guy Debord refers to as "the epic poem" of the commodity.[32]

That film is the money of cinema is true in at least two senses. First, it posits objects as images. This parallels Marx's idea of the notional function of money, what he refers to as the first determination of money, "money as measure" (*Grundrisse*, 123). The frame seizes an object and transforms it into an image. But the mere existence of the frame marks, and indeed makes, the notional transformation of an object into an image without actually filming it. Consonant with Vertov's kino-eye project, the frame becomes built into perception itself. Money also posits objects as images of themselves, as prices—the money-image of their exchange-value. As is well known, the fetishistic excess of the commodity, its alien allure, is a necessary component of this act. Price, then, appears as a proto-image—the abstracted silhouette of a commodity. In this way, both the film frame and money capture a ghost of the object—abstract, ethereal, and metaphysical, certainly, but nonetheless real for all that. Indeed, one could say that the specter of the object that results from traditional capital circulation (the tidal attractions of the exchange-values lurking in use-values) decrees that the object is already becoming an image, and that cinema is immanent in the flow of objects existing in the field of exchange. The circulation of industrial capital along with its perceptual pyrotechnics (objectification, fetishism) is the general form of cinema. The development of the cinematic apparatus is thus the technological articulation of an immanent material practice. The proprietorship that always earmarks exchange-value in the commodity will become the perspective of the object: the Lacanian economy of the shot.

Second, not only does film posit objects as images, but it converts them into images; fetishistic capture induces a displaced flow. Once converted, film allows these converted objects (images) to circulate, just as money allows objects themselves to circulate. This circulation corresponds to Marx's second determination of money, "money as a means of circulation" (*Grundrisse*, 128) or money as a medium of exchange. "For circulation, two things above all are necessary: firstly, the premise of commodities as prices; secondly, a circuit of exchanges, rather than isolated acts of exchange; a totality of exchanges in constant flow and taking place over the whole surface of society; a system of acts of exchange" (*Grundrisse*, 123). Here, analogous to the premise of commodities as prices, with Vertov we have the premise of objects as images (the whole project of kino-eye) and the effort to construct a viable circuit of exchanges. The "vanishing mediator"—in Vertov's case, film, not money—subjects visual objects to the laws of cinematic exchange by abstracting them into the medium of exchange and putting them into circulation. In Vertov, the proprietorship that founds exchange-value through the negation of the producer is attacked because other relations of production are made visible—the shadows of objects are the shadows of their makers and all are equally present. But it is the general case that the abstraction of things (qualities) as monetary quantity or as cinematic image introduces new orders of indeterminacy and flow.

This act of filming, which is already immanent in the logic of the circulation of commodities, is the historical condition of possibility for Wilhelm S. Wurzer's claim, in his startling book *Filming and Judgment,* that "the entire history of metaphysics can be viewed as a genealogy of 'filming' in which reason 'films' the ground of all beings."[33] Though Wurzer's important contribution merits far more attention than I can give it here, I take it up in part because it will help me show that the cinematicity of capital circulation is an "invention" in no way confined to Vertov and that capital confers the cinematic process itself. My use of Wurzer here also is designed to raise questions about the trajectory he posits for consciousness—one in which dialectics is ultimately transcended.

The principal claim of Wurzer's study is that it "inaugurates a reading of capital that opens an epoch, beyond the power of production, to a filming which judges freely" (Wurzer, 7). Despite the fact that I cannot remain with Wurzer in his Hegelian heights of Heideggerian rapture, in which filming becomes the absolute form of self-consciousness, exceeding the ground of subject and object precisely through a purported transcendence of the dialectic (the freedom from production), Wurzer's accomplishments are exceedingly illuminating. I do not disagree with him that filming restructures what might be called the architectonics of reality, and I do argue that this restructuring emerges at the end of one epoch of capital expansion; however, it inaugurates another. What Wurzer calls "filming" develops the relations for a shift in the mode of production and in no way achieves a release from the global violence that undergirds its phenomena.

For Wurzer,

> Filming, as it is named here, is not disclosed in Leonardo da Vinci's notion of camera obscura, nor in Thomas Edison's invention of the first workable motion picture camera. Indeed, filming does not belong in the archives of cinema and detailed studies of filmmaking. A historical and cultural theory concerning the very possibility of filming would certainly include such studies and many other cinematographic considerations. But our focus in this investigation is to expose filming as a non-photologocentric mode of judgment which accounts for the postmodern interplay of *Denken* [thinking] and *Einbildungskraft* [imagination]. (Wurzer, 31)

Wurzer's account is one that views filming as a historical tendency of consciousness. He continues:

> In modern metaphysics, we encounter the beginning of this mode of thinking in Kant's *Critique of Judgment*, in Nietzsche's *Birth of Tragedy*, and, more recently, in Heidegger's writings of the 1920s and 1930s. From a genealogical perspective, we may also discover filming in the epistemic, ontologic, and aesthetic issues of a metaphysics of subjectivity. The hidden history of filming, however, goes back much further and may initially have been presented, somewhat negatively, in the configurations of Plato's discourses on Eros in the *Symposium*. We can see that the question of filming is one that has not been raised explicitly with regard to a metaphysical text. In short, the history of philosophy, at least from Plato to Spinoza, has consistently repressed the notion of imaging and confined its importance to a logocentric view of reason. (Wurzer, 31–32)

Though I am in substantial agreement with this passage, I would like to suggest that logocentrism, which finds its concept only in the twentieth century, is itself built on the continuing exclusion of the rise of filming.[34] The reason that the question of filming has not been raised in the manner that it is raised here by Wurzer is not logocentrism, per se, but rather that political economy had not developed its impending cinematicity. The transhistorical elision of "filming," suddenly grasped and revealed by Wurzer, is utterly unconceptualizable without the materiality and technology, the camera obscuras and early film machines, that he elsewhere dismisses as inessential to filming. Wurzer's retroactive apprehension of thought freeing itself from reason and apprehended as cinema, or what he calls "filming," does not involve the transcendence of dialectics but is itself, as "filming," the phenomenological outcropping of a dialectical transformation. "Filming" is not a phenomenological shift, a new capacity of mind, brought into being by the striving of spirit for absolute self-consciousness under the sign of philosophy, nor can its significance be understood as the latest showpiece in some museum of the human intellect (however glorious) displaying a genealogy of concepts that finally transcends materiality, narrative, and reason itself; it is a historico-material displacement of the imagination, the extension of instrumental rationality into the visual. It is the increasing calculus of the image, bent on the rational organization of the imagination and necessary to the development of political economy through the intensification and elaboration of commodity fetishism. There are new affects, yes, but none is beyond the reach of History. The fact that, for Wurzer, the affectivity of cinema is not experienced as a dialectical shift in the structure of political economy does not discount that this shift is the condition of possibility for his insights.

Wurzer places filming in the metaphysical tradition and views it as the completion of the deconstructive project: "Filming thus deconstructs the dialectic empire in the genealogy of metaphysics. One can venture to say that it emerges in a philosophical discourse for which judgment is no longer under the spell of the identity of reason and ground, and in a time when judgment (Ur-teil) moves forward to a radically different terrain" (Wurzer, 2). This terrain is one of "radical disinterestedness" (Wurzer, 3). "Even in its withdrawal from dialectic, deconstruction cannot break out of the process of critique. So long as its mirror of reflection is unbreakable, it merely deflects from metaphysics. Filming, on the other hand, is the very shattering of the mirror. . . . Even the general text is erased as a new dynamics of power comes on the scene, a power which does not extend the hermeneutic desire of interpretation into a terrain of grafting one form of writing onto another" (Wurzer, 99). Wurzer is again correct in identifying the new order of abstraction he calls filming as the completion of the deconstructive project, but for the wrong reasons. Deconstruction's slow dissolve into the filmic is not the epic migration of higher consciousness seeking freedom. Deconstruction itself must be grasped historically as a crisis in the subject-function and its medium, that is, language—a crisis induced by a new politico-economic agent known as the image (and, it must be said, the antithesis of the image, which is, to use short-hand, the Third World). Like traditional society before it, the subject-form also must be fragmented and redeployed selectively and instrumentally in contemporary political economy. Deconstruction is the linguistic registration of a profound shift in the visual, that is, the rise of the visual economy. It is the death throes of the domination of language, an echo within language of its historically achieved inadequation to the new organization of the Real by capitalized visual technologies. Despite the fact that Wurzer must perform just the type of linguistic grafting he that criticizes in deconstruction to posit the terrain of filming, he makes his point: Filming exceeds dialectics and judges "capital as apparition" (Wurzer, 100).

> With filming there commences a radical questioning of the dialectic script imposed upon capital by infra/superstructural modes of interpretation. Breaking with this tradition, filming undertakes to expose capital differently. One may venture to say that capital is a prolepsis of filming. Prolepsis, derived from the Greek words pro ("before") and lambanein ("to take, to seize"), is an anticipatory movement which seizes representation before it (representation) imposes a metaphysical script upon time, a time that is to come (*Zukunft*). Capital, then, is a proleptic domain within filming, which disrupts the schematic power of images in order to release time from the imaginal. Breaking out of the genealogical space of continuity and discontinuity, capital sets the stage for a thinning out and fading of imaging, while simultaneously providing in advance the "promise" of a radically different time. In brief, capital "takes possession" of the gap subsequent to the filmic lapse and slippage of images. This postmodern seizure of a disjunctive space within imagination transposes imagination into filming, where filming's transformative modes of judging open up ways of seeing untainted by the prosaic relations of our epoch. (Wurzer, 83–84)

Though Wurzer claims that his "filming" can inaugurate a new critique of capital, the unqualified claim that there appear to be ways of seeing that are "untainted by the prosaic relations of our epoch" vitiates the relevance of any such critique. Film's dehiscence from that which is language-bound is not a sudden illumination but a process that has been developed and structured by language and economy for centuries. Wurzer's announcement of a new kind of consciousness, a consciousness as filming, indexes a historical shift in the character and possibilities of consciousness for the next century. In this he is quite correct. But as long as there are systematically excluded, suffering bodies on planet Earth, the idea of a radical disinterestedness is patently absurd. Disinterestedness, no matter how radical a departure it purports to make from the history and the philosophy of the subject, is nothing more, and can be nothing more, than bourgeois—art for art's sake. Wurzer correctly sees "filming" as an algorithm of capital and correctly grasps the emergence of a new order of visuality. His idealist twist—a ruling idea in the making—is a good example of the way in which the prosaic relations of our epoch work themselves back into filming.[35] Wurzer's move is to dissociate such visualization from the productive forces:

> Is Heidegger's "higher acting" of *Gelassenheit* operative in filming's prolepsis? In light of the sublime seizure of the imagination by capital, is the designation "higher acting" still appropriate? A glance at capital's genealogy illuminates filming as an "event of the head." It is therefore not unusual to speak of capital (caput, "head") in terms of the futural flux of reason. Capital is not regarded as a master concept dominating the relation of forces; it stands ahead of "events" only in the sense that it is a "coming-toward," a proleptic mode of thought. A moving texture which cannot be captured or reduced to an unequivocal concept, capital "consists" of diffuse scenes of filming without a theory gripped within practical reflections. If "higher acting" is complicitous with an overturning of the rigid interests of a theory/practice hermeneutic, it accords with the effacement of a normative dominance of images.
>
> Marx fails to highlight the possibilities of imaginal dehiscence, in that his reflections on capital are entirely governed by a "repressive hypothesis," that is, by the idea that capital is essentially deleterious so long as it cannot be unfastened from the production of commodities. (Wurzer, 85)

As Benjamin remarks about a passage detailing the futurist aestheticization of warfare, "This manifesto has the virtue of clarity."[36] The dialectical imperative of Marx entails understanding capital as simultaneously the best and the worst thing to happen in human history. As Benjamin put it, "Every document of civilization is simultaneously a document of barbarism." The overturning of a theory/practice hermeneutic that quickly (d)evolves into a postdialectical fantasy (common in France, though probably less common in the Murora atoll) is here followed by a disposition toward forgetting what insists on not being forgotten. Here, class hatred (for the bourgeoisie that informs everything of Marx's) is suppressed; even the discourse that speaks this essential kernel of hatred to the realm of thought is nearly forgotten, reduced, rather, to a repressive apparition. Capital is not something to be understood from some nowhere in which one might decide that it is not essentially deleterious. It is deleterious, if you live on the working edge of its production, if you experience its logic as the continual diminution of your existence. The release of productive forces is not in and of itself deleterious, but inasmuch as these forces exist for a privileged few and drive the majority of the world's population to a status outside of representation and into the unthought of the image, the release of the productive forces, even as "pure" thought, can be understood only if that understanding understands the violence presupposed in its very act of composure. Wurzer's eugenics of judgment rests on a forced elimination of all that threatens its purity. One would be hard-pressed to find a more brilliant endorsement of the poetics of the spectacle:

> Filming's contribution is only that of a question: What about spirit in an epoch that lets capital be? Its demand on judgment is complex not because capital is perceived to be a scene that films well but because capital leaps ahead of its time in search of a spirit whose time is yet to be. Does *Gelassenheit* become *Verlassenheit* [loneliness]? Does composure turn into destitution in the wake of the apparition of capital, the felling of ground and meaning? Is com-posure of spirit the complete erasure of history, of substance, of foundation? Is filmic excision poverty of life and being, a universal destitution? (Wurzer, 103)

Wurzer's answer is that "only a strict adherence to the principle of ground would make it possible to incriminate some relation of *Gelassenheit* to *Verlassenheit*" (Wurzer, 103), and film purportedly sweeps away all ground. Though it does so, it does so only as film, not as cinema. That is, only from an understanding of film as pure circulation can such an absence of ground be sanctioned or even imagined. "Filming," in Wurzer's usage, is revealed as the aesthetic counterpart to the circulation of capital, which, in appearance (consumerism), has broken away from the mode of production. This elevated aspect in the cycle of production "in search of a spirit whose time is yet to be" is embraced, while the rest (dissymmetrical exchange) is forgotten. But *cinema* recalls consciousness supposedly freed from materiality and historicity to its body. It shows filming to be the phenomenological pyrotechnics of the intensification of a capitalism that, no matter how treacherously difficult to apprehend from the standpoint of its apotheosis, still and always has its ground in the violation of bodies, the extraction of surplus-value. Thus, the postmodern mode of judgment that "denote[s] thinking without a metaphysical emphasis on the relation of the particular and the universal" (Wurzer, 102), and that is the triumphant realization of filming, depends on the universal violation of particular individuals. The particularization of the many oppressions, and the separation of bodies from each other and from the fruits of the historical amalgamation of human production and the universal process of "globalization," finds its most advance aesthetico-philosophical counterpart in Wurzer's "filming." Dialectics forces aesthetics to recall the conditions of its being, no matter how much we try to ignore them. And these conditions, conditions of systematic violation, rattle their chains even in the discourses that prefer, in an analogous systematic way, to exclude them. The moans are audible in the very language that strives to count them out.

"Filming," then (and here we begin our return to Vertov), is an inadequate account of production. Filming is a phenomenological formation with real effects. One such reality is that bodies, which are reduced to their pure particulars, mark their disappearance from materiality with their reappearance as images. Having conferred nearly all of their subjectivity, all of their living labor on a world that sweeps it away from them, they are, in their absolute impoverishment, not even present as subjects, therefore their objectivity fades into the state of relative non-being called the imaginary. They exist for others as images, and/or at the margins of images, as that which can be utterly appropriated and/or discarded. I discuss this relation further in chapter 6. Filming, as Wurzer uses the term, is the abstraction of this course of events, the de-subjectification, and hence de-objectification, of the spectral masses. It is an ideal(ized) expression of the dominant material relationships. "Cinema," as I am attempting to configure it here—perhaps against the high winds of history—would restore the historico-material development of filming.

6. Film as Capital. The Image of Production. The Attention Factory. Interiorization of the Technological Apparatus of Our Time.

I have said that film, as a new iteration of money, first posits objects as images and, second, circulates them as such. Thus, film takes on many of the functions germane to money—it develops the very properties of money. Money in Marx's third determination, that is, money as capital, in which money "is itself posited as an instrument of production" (*Grundrisse*, 152), has its corollary in the screen—that is, in film as cinema, where film is understood as an instrument of production. For here, finally, we reach the scene of the interface of images and bodies. And it is this scene that becomes the new, now de-territorialized factory of production. Vertov, who feared the unconscious and had an unsophisticated theory of the spectator, thought that his "factory of facts" would assemble the facts in the film, on the screen: "Shots enter into organic interaction; they enrich one another, combine their efforts, form a collective body, thereby releasing surplus energy" (Vertov, 272). Vertov did not fully grasp that to complete his facts, to give them the character of objectivity that is conferred only through belief and practice, the surplus energy would have to come from the spectator. As becomes clear with Eisenstein, film as an instrument of cinematic production does not refer merely to movie production: Cinema as "the organization of the audience through organized material" is utilized for social production in the largest sense of the word, for social production and reproduction, that is, for social organization and development.[37] It takes labor to build a world—the labor of the masses. For the first time, this labor will be systemically coming online through a visual pathway.[38]

Two convergent trends therefore must be grasped in Vertov's work. Cinema is well on its way to becoming a complex medium of value transfer, while money realizes an ever-increasing expressivity. Vertov's film of money—at once made of money and operating as an alternative medium of exchange—arises as film becomes money and money becomes film. Although one might want somewhat more nuance here, this dialectic is fundamental. Money's coverage of the human sphere interposes a unique distance between persons and things, and posits the image as the fundamental relation between subject and object. Put another way, the relation known as private property, which removes things from the grasp of the masses through abstract means, achieves a first-order dynamism in the money economy. In this economy, objects are already images—one may "look but not touch." Objects signify the will of another (an owner) and cannot be reached in their materiality except through the exchange of a discrete quantity of the general equivalent. Objects can be extracted from this relation and "belong to me" only through money. Furthermore, only in their complete amortization do they lose their abstract, imaginary dimension—they have no more exchange-value when they are used up. The flow of money itself is already filmic; that is, in tying the world together in a material array dependent upon abstraction, money places a film between the world of things and persons, a film that converts things into images and renders their materiality inaccessible (mediate). As one can surmise from Descartes, it is the relation known as the image (the hand before the face, the radical alienation of the visible) that constitutes the modern subject as well as the universe of mathematical objects. Film proper becomes the technological abstraction and intensification of this relation, a second-order dynamism of property relations that gives them simultaneously greater penetration and higher orders of expressivity—to the point where values in the human sense and values in the economic sense become indistinguishable not only in the last but also in the first instance. One cannot overestimate the necessity (for capital) of the amalgamation of the imagination and therefore of concrete bodies by media.

In Marx, the figure of circulation institutionalizes the commodity form because the exchange of two qualitatively noncomparable objects requires some abstract standard of equivalence (from which Marx derives the concepts of exchange-value and of abstract human labor time) in order that they be quantitatively compared and circulated. However, the perpetuation of the exchange of object for coin (commodity for money) cannot be explained from the standpoint of circulation alone:

> The repetition of the process from both points, money or commodity, is not implied in the conditions of exchange itself. The act can only be repeated until it is completed, i.e. until there has been exchange up to the amount of the exchange value [that is, until the resources in circulation are used up]. It cannot rekindle itself. Circulation therefore does not contain in itself the principle of self-renewal. Its moments are presupposed in it, not posited by itself. New commodities must continually be thrown into it from without, like fuel into fire. Otherwise, it goes out in indifference. It would be extinguished in money as the indifferent result. For in so far as it no longer related to commodities, prices, circulation, money would cease to be money and to express a relationship of production; it would now continue to exist only as a metal but not eco-

nomically. Circulation therefore, which appears as that which is imme-diately present on the surface of bourgeois society, exists only in so far as it is continually mediated. Considered in itself, it is the mediation of presumed extremes. But it does not posit these extremes. Hence it must itself be mediated not only in each of its moments but as the totality of mediation, as a total process. Its immediate being is therefore pure sem-blance. It is the image of a process occurring behind it. (*Grundrisse*, 186)

As Marx will reveal shortly, for circulation to continue, there must be some-thing behind the image of circulation—production, that is, labor. *Man with a Movie Camera*'s "image of a process occurring behind it" would seem to bring production into its sphere of visual circulation, and yet it does not. As Marx says, "Circulation therefore presupposes both the production of commodities by labor as well as their production as exchange-values" (*Grundrisse*, 186). Labor that produces exchange-values is the source that feeds the fire of circulation. Circulation, strictly understood, is the image of the process of production, but not production itself. In the case of Ver-tov, the representation of production is not enough to sustain his film work; "it goes out in indifference" (*Grundrisse*, 186). Or perhaps it was squashed out. In any case, the power that sustains the fire was missing. Circulation cannot sustain itself by itself but requires production, that is, productive labor. What Vertov did not figure out (and the question that Wurzer does not see) is how to get (enough) productive labor into the sys-tem of cinematic circulation to valorize the medium—a national currency works only if people work for it. Vertov's effort, though enormous, was in-complete. Like the bourgeois economists who wanted to circumvent crisis in capital—inflation, overproduction, and so forth—by issuing chits for objects (Marx points out that these would immediately behave like money and be traded on their own accord, like options), Vertov tried to alter the mode of production by intervening in circulation. He lacked an adequate theory of production—the factory of facts was not yet a fully functioning factory—and yet, one still hopes, as Michelson does, that history could have taken a different course. It is not that Vertov lacked a theory of film production, but rather that he lacked an adequate theory of social produc-tion with the cinema—of the cinema as a productive relation.

The greater instrumentality and greater success of Eisenstein, who trained as an engineer and saw himself as engineering consciousness, and the still greater success of Disney, of Hollywood, and of Microsoft (and now, fifteen years after I first wrote this essay, of Google) are instructive here. Each had, and, in the case of the latter three, has, a quasi-national or state endorsement and an "audience" interactive with their modes of production. They have inscribed themselves in the realm of necessity. Vertov struggled to achieve a circulation in *Man with a Movie Camera* alternative to capital circulation and therefore could not utilize circulation in accord with the phenomenology of its dominant appearance. The image (commodity) that is in circulation in daily life under capitalism is never experienced as Vertov represents it; rather, one experiences the phenomenal appearance of objects (and money) and their disappearance under the spell of reification, or, as Jean Baudrillard would have it, seduction. Vertov counters the phenomenological appearance of the commodity-image but cannot counter other emergent elements of the mode of production, specifically the emerging commodification of vision itself: the libidinal dimensions of the economization of perception and affect, and the subsequent deterritorialization of production.

If circulation "is the image of a process occurring behind it," and that process is production, then within the resolution of that image are the processes that sustain and amalgamate the world. As Marx writes, commodity production "presupposes circulation as a developed moment and appears as a constant process positing circulation and continually returning from circulation back into itself, in order to posit it anew" (*Grundrisse*, 186). The production *depicted* in Vertov's *Man with a Movie Camera* was not adequate to sustain the form of circulation it deployed. Therefore, we must posit a realm of production, of cinematic production, that was somehow unavailable to Vertov and his films. While it might be possible to imagine that cinema should remain in the realm of simple circulation as a product to be sold, like shoes, if capital is really becoming cinematic then the film itself must achieve a relation with spectators that can sustain its form. As with Marx's analysis of capital, production in this sense must take the form of labor-power released into the medium.

With Eisenstein, the labor that sustains cinematic circulation is provided by the spectator. This insight can be derived from the Pavlovian circuitry that Eisenstein built into his films in the form of the montage of attractions. For every image, so the theory ran, there is a programmed response. This response can be calculated, cut, organized, and re-organized: It is the spectator who returns living labor to the medium. As with workers in factory work, spectators must be formed in such a way, trained in such a way—through history and education, and through the movement of the world of objects (through production)—that they can work in the image-machines, the attention factories, present(ed) to them. For a variety of reasons, Vertov's images could not be valorized, at least to the degree required for their continued production and reproduction. Communism was not (yet) a viable virus. Its "failure" has to do with the lack of consideration of interiority and of psychosocial experience. Because everything in Vertov is geared toward the production of consciousness, we might say that Vertov did not anticipate adequately capital's total penetration of the sensorium. Despite the fact that Vertov thematizes production, he fails to grasp the unconscious visual component of production that develops hand in hand with the phenomenology of capitalist circulation. The non-rational, structurally unconscious, pyrotechnes of a new order of capitalism established deeper ties to viewers and the productivity of bodies and overpowered the Vertovian project.

When Vertov made *Man with a Movie Camera,* many other forms of production were extant from feudal times and bourgeois industrialism that also produced persons. It is arguable that though Vertov was able to make a conquest of space and time, he was unable to (dis)engage other circuits of perceptual and corporeal regulation that were protocapitalist, or becoming embroiled in the libidinal economy of capital. Indeed one could analyze the function of gender in *Man with a Movie Camera* (including the jokes with a bare female body and then the appearance of a long lens) to see some of the unreformed and/or underexplored dimensions of Vertov and his era. However, to imagine the kino-eye project realizing its proposed expansion and stated goals remains like an effort to solve a single equation with two unknowns. We know neither what the films should have looked like nor what the world should have become. What we do know, however, is that their production, and the production of the world they implied, could not be sustained. Vertov was correct to regard the visual as the next arena for the battle against the encroachment of capital on human becoming, but the relations of value transfer necessary to both an anticapitalist cinema and an anticapitalist universe—that is, relations that could at once do battle with capital and be self-valorizing—were not developed. To create a radical instrument and yet to avoid creating a radical instrument destined to become a subroutine of capital was a tall order and remains so today. *Man with a Movie Camera* was a momentary arresting of the becoming-media of capital and revealed what cinema already was becoming: a new moment in the consciousness of production necessary to production.

In a section of "The Work of Art in the Age of Mechanical Reproduction" excised from the English edition, Benjamin writes:

Primitive art, in the service of magic, set down certain notations that served praxis. It probably did so fully as much as for the sake of practice and rehearsal of magical procedures as for directions and indications, and also finally as the very objects of a contemplative meditation to which magical effects were ascribed. The objects of such notations showed human beings and their environment, and were represented according to the demands of a society in which technology as yet existed only in the form of ritual. Such a society stands at the antipodes of the present one, whose technology [technik] is the most emancipated. Yet such emancipated technology now stands over against contemporary society as a second nature and indeed, as economic crises and wars testify, a nature no less elemental than the one that confronted primitive society. Faced with this second nature, human beings, who invented it but have ceased to master it, are thrown back on a process of learning and pedagogical appropriation of much the same kind that earlier human beings had to summon in the face of original nature itself. Art once again places itself in the service of such a learning process. And film does so in particular. Film serves to train human beings in the practice of those apperceptions and reactions required by the frequentation of an apparatus whose role in their daily life ever increases. To make this whole enormous technological apparatus of our time into the object of human interiorization and appropriation [Innervation]—that is the historic task in whose service film has its true meaning.[39]

If, as Benjamin suggests, the historical task of cinema is to aid in the internalization of "second nature," that is, to produce the internalization of the logistics of the industrial revolution as the development and completing of the industrial revolution, then it is fair to say that cinema as an effect of the industrial revolution dialectically produces the consciousness of (and necessary for) the continued intensification of the industrial revolution, and moreover, it produces, dialectically again, those now reconfigured and fundamentally original sensate elements that marginalize, exceed, or transcend consciousness: affect, imagination, desire, proprioception, intensity, and so forth. These affective dimensions of industrial society—which challenge language's ability to process experience and throw us "back on a process of learning and pedagogical appropriation of much the same kind that earlier human beings had to summon in the face of original nature itself"—are the new modes of appropriation and the equipment for survival, and therefore are part of the reproduction of the worker. They take on an ever-increasing importance for late capitalist production. Cinema, ordained here as a total, social process that converts material circulation into sensual affect, becomes the condition of possibility for twentieth-century social production.

Vertov's work embodies and extends the logistics of the industrial revolution and produces them as a form of consciousness. His conversion of industrial process into dialectical vision, and thus into consciousness, is an effort to convert the totality of circulation into vision and consciousness. His visual production of the concept of totality, though a theoretical tour de force, was a practical failure inasmuch as it did not bring about the hoped-for end of prehistory or even its own continuation. Communism was the meaning of kino-eye, but not its significance. To laud Vertov's theoretical achievement in *Man with a Movie Camera,* while critically noting its failure, is not to lament the stupidity of the masses for not "getting it" but to critique a (historical) lack of imagination or preparedness and to investigate the historical limitations in the revolutionary production of the period. From a hermeneutic standpoint, Vertov succeeded spectacularly, but from an affective one, he did not. Indeed, the failure in Vertov to generate the necessary affective force was precisely the critique of Vertov offered by Eisenstein and the problem Eisenstein sought to remedy. The great question remains: Was there any (other) way for Vertov to appeal to the senses and remain Vertovian? What Benjamin refers to as "the violation of an apparatus which is pressed into the production of ritual values," took, for Vertov, the form of the acted cinema.[40] Was a total rejection of the acted cinema necessary?

Speculations on Vertov's failure to develop a more viable phenomenography would lead us far afield, demanding that Vertov invent a new psychology and a new sexuality in addition to the re-mediation of commodity reification. Again, as we shall explore more fully in chapter 2, Eisenstein's "solutions" to the problem of vision as a productive force in the building of socialism are plagued by their own failures. However, if, as Antonio Negri puts it, "antagonism is the motor of development of the system, the foundation of a continuous resurgence of antagonism each time that the project, the history of capital, progresses," then perhaps it is only in an inventory of the failed efforts and strategies of human liberation that the forces of oppression can be identified and fought effectively.[41] Is such not the legitimate task of the historian?

Vertov endeavors to span the totality of circulation, but circulation ordinarily is perceived through only a limited window into it—be it subjectivity, art, daily life, one's bank account, or television. The analytic perspective of capital (I should say, the *analytic* perspective of *Capital*) is clearly not what libidinally drives the majority of individual bodies; it is, in capitalist society, at any rate, the stirrings caused by partial phenomena, a momentary perception or a half-conceived idea, that drive the imagination: narratives, desires, attractions. Though Vertov clearly shows that orchestrated matter creates consciousness in ever fuller and more efficient ways, and that cinema, in its immanence and ostensible immateriality, organizes consciousness par excellence, his proof that cinema as such is "the ideal expression of the dominant material relationships" does not a revolution make.[42] Despite Vertov's aspirations, cinema as the new medium for the "ruling ideas" breaks a revolution. This is perhaps because the ruling ideas are no longer ideas. We are dealing with a calculus of the image.

The connection between the reproductions of the relations of production and cinematic reproduction brings both consciousness and material relations to a new stage of development. "In the act of reproduction itself are changed not only the objective conditions—e.g. village becomes city, the wilderness becomes cultivated clearings, etc.—but also the producers, who transform themselves in that they evolve new qualities from within themselves, develop through production new powers and new ideas, new modes of intercourse, new needs, and new speech" (*Grundrisse*, 418). In many ways, Vertov emphasizes the objective aspects of the development of cinema as "speech," hence his emphasis on both the external (objective) world and the cinematic apparatus proper. Movement becomes consciousness. It will take Eisenstein to consider formally the speech of film as a language and to self-consciously concern himself with (re)organizing the interiority of spectators through movement. By the time cinema becomes the lingua franca of capital, nearly all attempts to think visuality as language will be buried by electronic snow.

---

7. Revolution Not a Matter of Consciousness Alone.
Decolonization of the Sensorium. Use-Value of the Image
Is Its Exchange-Value. Dialectic of Cinema and the Psyche.
Image as a Notional Practice and a Material Abstraction.
Price as Proto-Image. Attention Theory of Value.
Cinema as De-territorialized Factory.

If, as Vertov's cinema can be understood to reveal, cinema is quite literally a form of capital, then it can, and indeed must, do other things than become self-conscious. In many respects, *Man with a Movie Camera* is for Vertov what *Reification and the Consciousness of the Proletariat* is for Lukács, because self-consciousness (for Lukács, the moment when the proletariat grasps itself as the subject-object of history) heralds the dissolution of the capitalist order. Although it is a necessary technique of capitalism to obscure the conditions of its own production and reproduction, and hence of its history, what Lukács and Vertov have in common (in addition to the tenet that in capitalism, social transparency equals revolution) is the principle that revolutions are matters of consciousness. In 1844, Marx could write, "Communism is the riddle of history solved, and it knows itself to be this solution."[43] The twentieth century teaches us that revolution (and counter-revolution) is not a matter of consciousness alone.

Although technology has extended the range of our perception, it has also—in intimately related ways—extended the range and extent of our subjugation. The conquest of space and time by cinema and by cinematic technologies that enables the utopian aspirations of Vertov also creates the conditions for a shift from an imperialism played out geographically and spatially (geographic domination as the pathway to the spatial containment of the body) to an imperialism played out physiologically and psychologically: Of course the reality of imperialism covered all these areas, but with cinema the administration of space and time becomes sensual. Individual bodies continue to suffer terribly, but the economy of means has developed. Territories are still dominated, but in addition to the traditional legal and military methods, they are also dominated by a deterritorialization that renders each of them affectively "global," a deterritorialization that occurs through the direct (local) entry of new logics into bodies through technological mediation. The conquest of geographical regions is not over—by no means—but the vanguard weapons of the postmodern conquistadors are computers, televisions, fax machines, cell phones, and films—technologies that work by inserting the spatial and temporal exigencies of the First World into Third World bodies and organizations, instantiating a juridical subject-function, altering their proprioception, infusing new aspirations and desires, proposing new groupings, and so forth, through what a century ago was called "the civilizing effect of foreign trade" (*Grundrisse*, 187). The same technologies also legitimate and/or obscure the actuality of violence and the sufferings of those who are the victims of imperialist war. Trade is not just the movement of money and objects; it is the movement of capital through sensoriums. Bodies give time for image in a new totalitarianism of the sensual. Like any other wage, the subsistence-level pleasure received in exchange for sensual labor is enough for survival, not justice. The capitalization of mass perception and consciousness is taking place on an unprecedented scale. Such an infusion of "culture" always accompanies the installation of export processing zones, the tolerance of World Bank and IMF lackeys as national leaders, and so forth. Capital ingrains new rationales and promotes new strategies of domination. Furthermore, it solicits our participation, our rejoicing, at every turn.

But I am getting ahead of myself, speaking drearily about products before having really undertaken the analysis of production. Vertov has helped us to begin such an analysis of the transformation of production by cinema by showing that the space, time, and movement of industrial production are all impacted in the image, that is, that industrial production circulates through the image and becomes a machine for the production of consciousness and, by implication, of social participation in all its myriad forms. The image becomes a form that results by passing through the totality of the spatial, temporal, and motional territories of the socius. These aspects of the social terrain are at once internal to the image and the condition of its circulation as an image. Thus, the cinematic image is precisely an abstraction of capitalized matter effected by the instrumental reassembly of its space-time movements and coupled to the sensorium and the viscera of spectators.

If we recall from Marx that "production is not only particular production, but it is invariably a definite social body, a social subject that is active in a wider or narrower totality of branches of production" (*Grundrisse*, 24), and, further, that the instruments of production are "also past, objectified, accumulated labor" (*Grundrisse*, 23), then the cinematic image not only as Vertov fabricates it but in general contains, as it were, the social totality. It is invariably a monad, a crystal of the socius, the totality of society registered in a crystalline form. Just as Edward W. Said can show how the micropolitics of a Victorian parlor novel depends on the British in India, one ought to be able to show how a still from, say, *Pretty Woman* is linked to concrete histories of patriarchy, the feminization of labor, and the formation of global commodity chains. Each image, like each commodity, potentially leads to the totality of the relations of production.

The crucial difference between the commodity-object and the image-object lies in the distinctive character of the image-object's circulation and consumption. The cinematic image is a sensualized abstraction with no physical content beyond its intellectual and sensual appeal, at least as far as the consumer of the image is concerned. It is a material formation emptied of its material, the label without the can—in some respects, the realization of what was once called the commodity's ersatz value. Thus, as cinema is a dematerialized form of circulation, the image is a dematerialized form of the commodity, the commodity without its material content. Indeed, this virtual, immaterial character might lead us to believe that the image is not a commodity at all, at least to the extent that it has no readily apparent use-value other than something that erupts in the zone of pleasure (use) and its psychic-ideological labyrinth, that is, until one considers its use-value for capital. In this usefulness for the valorization of capital, then, it is for the wage earner like money—the company scrip of U.S. Incorporated, a means to subsistence.

What is the use of the image? One cannot eat it or sleep in it; in the cinema, one cannot even take it home. If it is true that an image has no use-value in the practical, material sense, then it is pure exchange-value. Its use-value is its exchange-value. It circulates commodities through our sensoriums and exchanges itself for us. When we incorporate the image, we ourselves become exchangeable; we have/are social currency. In this respect, the commodity that the image most closely resembles is indeed money, the vanishing mediator, which, from the standpoint of the consumer, is the most general form of pleasure, the general form of social wealth, the means to life; and yet it is not money. One does not spend image; one performs it. As with money, the circulation of the image and its related phenomenological effects, along with the subroutines these imply, are essential for the valorization of capital.

To say that the spectator extracts subsistence use-values in a relation to exchange-value mediated by the image and valorizing capital is to reissue Theodor Adorno and Max Horkheimer's formulation, "Amusement under late capitalism is the prolongation of work." The next moment in the transformation of the interactivity of the image, cinema's legacy in email and the World Wide Web, makes this tendency patently obvious. The residual effects of money, so scrupulously noted by Simmel, are, in the moment of cinema, given a new turn: The residue of the circulation that is the moving image is the internalization of the consciousness of the industrial revolution and the subjugation of social performance to the logic of capital. This consciousness, and the array of affective states necessary to it, is itself necessary to the development of industry. Thus, Adorno and Horkheimer's assertion that the spectator's experiences "are inevitably after-images of the work process itself" describes not just the culture of industry but the political economic trajectory of industrial culture.[44] Circulation, then, is no longer simply "the image of a process occurring behind it," for in becoming image, the work of circulation such as that of truck drivers and stock boys is passed on to spectators and circulation becomes a for-profit service, ever more completely taking on the characteristics of production.

As the emergent interface between the body and the industrial revolution, the image is at once a consequence of and a prerequisite for the continuing development of capitalist exchange/domination. Like banking, it is at once an artifact of capital circulation, necessary to the process of circulation itself, and a point of capitalization. As an exchange-value, the image facilitates exchange, that is, the translation of forces that results in a metamorphosis of value. It scripts praxis through abstraction. As a capitalized fragment, that is, as a form of production for exchange, the image will introduce a new dimension to our old category "labor," shifting labor itself toward the province of mediation. As we shall see, the cyborg called the spectator comes online as the productive flesh in the emerging visual pathway of the capitalist machine.

If in the development of capital the object leans toward money, aspires to be money, then the next dialectical level of this iteration is a symmetrical leaning of the image toward the film frame. Each element of each pair has a proclivity toward the other element, and the two pairs resemble one another. Yet there is also a relation of intensification between the pairs: Objects strive to become photogenic, while images strive to become money, that is, the object tends toward the image, and money tends toward film.[45]

If money stirs the spectral heart of exchange-value within the object, the film frame brings forth from it the image. These two related extractions (abstractions) are notional practices more often than they are realized, which is to say that they are internalized as experience, incorporated into mental function as a form of apprehending the world. One does not need to have the price of a commodity in one's pocket to experience commodity fetishism, nor does one have to have a camera to frame an image, to experience the subjective affect, or the whatever, of the cinematic. Money frames objects as images, or, to put it another way, money frames the image of an object as its price. Money provides the aperture through which one grasps the (alienated) objective world. This statement brings us to a fundamental relation: Price is money's spectral representation of an object, and image is the film frame's spectral representation of an object. Price, therefore, is a proto-image, the image of the object's exchange-value. It is the meeting point of the object and money locked into capital circulation, the moment of exchange, the quantification of affect. Inasmuch as price implies a subject of exchange, the image implies the collapsing together (the tandem function) of these formerly discrete acts of production and subjective agency. The image delimits the fiduciary relation implicit in circulation by bypassing money, that is, by bypassing the need to realize the commodity's price in money, a process that was, in classical economics, the greatest moment of anxiety for the capitalist. The image, as a technology, extracts sensual labor (attention) directly in the moment of its apprehension. From an economic point of view, this cybernetic collapse is the more efficient administration of the potential crisis zone marked off by the classical gap between production and consumption—the valorization of capital in the exchange of the commodity for money.[46] In the regime of the cinematic the gap in the valorization process approaches zero, that is, it becomes almost instantaneous, because to recognize an image is to constitute a self and a world: To "see" is already to "buy," (I'll buy that), to look is to labor. The separation between buying and selling (one "buys" a commodity and "sells" one's labor in the same act of spectatorship, thereby bypassing the mediation of money) would be reconciled in the cinematic image. Vertov's film takes on a different cast when we can assess retrospectively that money in circulation is the film of the prices of objects, that is, the film of the movement of exchange. In *Man with a Movie Camera,* Vertov catapulted what was already the techno-historical tendency of material exchange toward the visible. Cinema is the evolution of this numismatic film of money into something like an operating system of the visual. The development of cinema appears as the historical trace of the dialectical development of capital, the material history of capital's binding of perception, of bodies, and of performative belief to its articulation of reality. These processes become the very processes of circulation and exchange. The pyrotechnics of the money form develop into the cinema, and the cinematic relation, in which all things attain to media, extends over the entirety of the *socius.* To fully grasp this is to glimpse the totalitarian character of contemporary life.

For the moment, let me say that the moving image represents an intermediate state, a synthesis, between money and other commodities. This synthetic space is the scene for the valorization of capital through the realization of surplus value. Money-Commodity-Money becomes Money-Image-Money as capital seeks a new armature to administer the extraction of surplus value.[47] As with the commodity's price in money, the image is the contact point between the general medium and its specific local content. The moving image (the shot), in its abstracting capture and circulation of particular objects, plays the same function as price, lubricating the flow of money against the gradient of commodities, because it itself is a representative of exchange-value. In ways still to be derived, the active consumer/viewer of the cinematic circulation of capital performs an element of this circulation with his or her own body. He or she transports the commodity to (through) the scene of its valorization and provides this transportation to capital at a discount. This performance, exchanging time for image, provides the counterflow to the moving image and as advertising revenues would indicate, is itself productive of value. This claim will lead to what I call the attention theory of value, along with a theory of cinema as a de-territorialized factory.[48] As all (commercial) shots become "money shots," Vertov's factory of facts gives way to the de-territorialized factories of affect/programming functioning in accord with the theory of the productive value of human attention.

I have put forth a description of the circulation of image-objects in a visual economy but have given only the briefest account of the means for the production of value in this economy. Kino-eye itself did not produce self-valorizing exchange-value or any other viable alternate productive organization that could allow it to develop as a historical practice along the vector of its own aspiration. Because *Man with a Movie Camera* does not achieve a self-valorizing perpetuation, the film as I have described it here constitutes only a form of circulation, a nonrenewable redistribution program.

Vertov saw capitalist cinema as having a hold over the unconscious. For him, it was at once a distillation and a refinement of state ideology. "Stupefaction and suggestion—the art-drama's basic means of influence—relate to that of a religion and enable it for a time to maintain a man in an excited unconscious state" (Vertov, 63). While the spectator remained in that "state of intoxication," cinema could "cram some idea, some thought or other, into his subconscious" (Vertov, 63). Though I have remarked that Vertov's distrust of the unconscious might well begin to explain his failure to theorize production adequately, the fault is not his alone. Kino-eye was finally to have established new conditions for the relations of production, to have become a new mediation of production itself. By making all relations conscious relations, seeing was intended to overcome money. The mediation of dialectics was to become practicable. Inasmuch as Vertov shows that "every form becomes immediately dissolved in the very moment when it emerges; it lives, as it were, only by being destroyed; every consolidation of form to lasting objects—no matter how short they last— is an incomplete interpretation that is unable to follow the motion of reality at its own pace," his cinema, albeit distantly, was approaching the logistic capacity of money.[49] However, despite his efforts to remediate the geographical dispersion and nonsynchronous temporalities of object production, his form of cinematic circulation did not insert itself as an indispensable force endemic to production and capable of reshaping both production and distribution.

Though Vertov's *Man with a Movie Camera* challenged capital, it did not overcome its organizational force. This perhaps constitutes both its failure and its spirituality. Though it strove to set up an alternative circulation of value, it was not a viable one. It did not, finally, effectually remediate the circulation of matter. Vertov's failure to do so, however, does not imply the general failure of cinema to do so. Indeed, it is the point here to show that cinema transforms all aspects of political economy, including production, distribution, circulation, labor, value, the senses, bodies, and consciousness. Cinema is their very transformation. Despite the many noteworthy acts of resistance and the myriad contestatory appropriations, the remediation of the circulation of capital by and as the cinematic has only increased the degree of uneven development in the world today.

With all the images of daily life in motion, the cinematic mode of production orchestrates the mise-en-scène for the production of consciousness and the consciousness of production. We cut, edit, produce, and direct; we watch, we process, we wait. You think all those movements, all that time, is your own consciousness, even though what plays on the screen in your theater comes somehow from beyond you. Vertov lives no longer, but the cinematic production of everyday life continues.

NOTES

1. See Dziga Vertov, "From Kino-Eye to Radio-Eye," in *Kino-Eye: The Writings of Dziga Vertov*, ed. Annette Michelson, trans. Kevin O'Brien (Berkeley and Los Angeles: University of California Press, 1984), 87–88. Subsequent references to *Kino-Eye* are cited parenthetically as Vertov. Michelson's descriptions of *Man with a Movie Camera* inform my own both here and elsewhere in this essay.

2. For Vertov, all aspects of cinematic decision fell under the sway of montage: "Every kino-eye production is subject to montage from the moment the theme is chosen until the film's release in its completed form. In other words, it is edited during the entire process of film production" (Vertov, 88).

3. The interval, a term derived from music that specifies the space/time between notes or passages, names the cinematic juxtaposition of two social moments between which the viewer must supply the intervening elements. Thus, it is a philosophical and conceptual term, specifying a construction through the shaping of hollows or empty spaces or absences. The interval specifies the mode by which the filmic presentation of

the social totality is possible. The viewer's activity is the mediation of the individual social moments presented and orchestrated in Vertovian cinema.

4. Georg Simmel, *The Philosophy of Money* 2d ed., ed. David Frisby, trans. Tom Bottomore and David Frisby, 2d ed. (New York: Routledge, 1990), 452.

5. "Of course, we do not want to underestimate film as a great and penetrating mass art, but it must also serve primarily as entertainment. . . . Therefore, entertainment cannot be merely on the fringe of public affairs, and cannot be neglected by the political leadership. . . . In this connection, film is one of the most valuable ingredients in utilizing the little time, aside from work, that is left to each German to renew his spiritual strengths. . . . Beyond these considerations, however, modern-day film is a foremost national instructional tool. In its influence, it can almost be compared with elementary school. . . . Film . . . continuously influences and educates adults and mature people on a national level. That is why the state cannot ignore the inherently tremendous possibilities." "Film as Teacher: Goebbels' Speech for the Opening of the Film Project of the Hitler Youth," trans. Richard S. and Gerda Geehr, *Film and History* 14, no. 2 (May 1984): 37–38. Goebbels's description of the pedagogical value of visual media for the infantalized masses, along with that of the occupation of excess or leisure time for the purposes of spiritual renewal coupled to state hegemony, points to the value-producing character of the image underpinning the existence of any of the media magnates mentioned above.

6. See Walter Benjamin, "The Work of Art in the Age of Mechanical Reproduction," in *Illuminations,* ed. Hannah Arendt, trans. Harry Zohn (New York: Schocken, 1969), 233.

7. Benjamin describes cinema in a way that, for me, always brings James Joyce's *Ulysses* to mind. See ibid., 236–37.

8. Ibid., 236.

9. Simmel, *Philosophy of Money,* 460.

10. "If the product of labor does not belong to the worker, if it confronts him as an alien power, this can only be because it belongs to some other man than the worker. If the worker's activity is a torment to him, to another it must be delight and his life's joy." Karl Marx and Friedrich Engels, *"Economic and Philosophic Manuscripts of 1844" The Marx-Engels Reader,* ed. Robert C. Tucker (New York: Norton, 1978), 78.

11. "What is to be avoided above all is the re-establishing of 'Society' as an abstraction vis-à-vis the individual. The individual is the social being." Marx and Engels, *Marx-Engels Reader,* 86; Simmel, *Philosophy of Money,* 460; Benjamin, "The Work of Art," 236.

12. I borrow this phrase from the title of Susan Buck-Morss's book on Walter Benjamin, *The Dialectics of Seeing: Walter Benjamin and the Arcades Project* (Cambridge: MIT Press, 1989).

13. "Kino-eye plunges into the seeming chaos of life to find in life itself the response to an assigned theme. To find the resultant force amongst the million phenomena related to the given theme. To edit; to wrest, through the camera, whatever is most typical, most useful, from life; to organize the film pieces wrested from life into a meaningful rhythmic visual order, a meaningful visual phrase, an essence of 'I see'" (Vertov, 88).

14. In *Man with a Movie Camera*, consciousness can no longer maintain capital's institutionalized division between mental and manual labor, nor, as Marx acerbically quipped in *The German Ideology*, "flatter itself that it is something other than consciousness of existing practice" (Marx and Engels, *Marx-Engels Reader*, 159). Consciousness is literally consciousness of existing practice and sees itself as such. Consciousness recognizes itself as at once produced by social conditions and in the process of producing them. Mental and manual labor fold into one another and are, in the last instance, indistinguishable—this dialectic is an ethic as well as an aesthetic. Thus, Vertov's phrase "man with a movie camera" expresses in the concrete reality portrayed by the film the abstract idea of the potentiality of humanity with a movie camera.

15. Unless, perhaps, they relentlessly endeavor to decode the conditions of their own formation, but even then they may still retain their fetish character. Do the images of Jean-Luc Godard, for example, which do indeed try incessantly to decode the conditions of their own formation in a historical moment quite different from Vertov's, avoid the fetish, the seduction of the commodity? Perhaps only in his latest: the unbelievably boring yet fantastic *Historie(s) du Cinema*.

16. See Wolfgang Schivelbusch, *The Railway Journey: The Industrialization of Time and Space in the 19th Century* (Berkeley and Los Angeles: University of California Press, 1986).

17. Karl Marx, *Grundrisse*, in *Karl Marx and Frederick Engels Collected Works*, vol. 28 (Marx: 1857–1861) (Moscow: Progress, 1986), 26. Hereafter, this work is cited parenthetically as *Grundrisse*.

18. Also cited in Annette Michelson, "The Wings of Hypothesis: On Montage and the Theory of the Interval," in *Montage and Modern Life, 1919–1942*, ed. Matthew Teitelbaum (Cambridge: MIT Press, 1992), 61, n. 2.

19. "The main and essential thing is: . . . The sensory exploration of the world through film. . . . We therefore take as the point of departure the use of the camera as a kino-eye, more perfect than the human eye, for the exploration of the chaos of visual phenomena that fills space . . . The kino-eye lives and moves in time and space; it gathers and records impressions in a manner wholly different from that of the human eye. The position of our bodies while observing or our perception of a certain number of features of a visual phenomenon in a given instant are by no means obligatory limitations for the camera which, since it is perfected, perceives more and better . . . We cannot improve the making of our eyes, but we can endlessly perfect the camera" (Vertov, 14–15).

20. Sergei M. Eisenstein, *Selected Works: Writings, 1922–1934*, ed. and trans. Richard Taylor, vol. 1 (London: BFI, 1988), 63. Hereafter, this work is cited parenthetically as *writings*. This is one of the primary differences between Vertov and Eisenstein: Vertov's assemblages are analyses that leave open the question of society for its members—the films were not to be once and for all but were to be renewed continually. Human activity might pass through other channels and affect the image. Though Eisenstein also made films for occasions, his were machines designed to impel the audience in a particular and precisely calculated direction. In short, Vertov utilized the materiality of machines to treat the viewer like a subject, while Eisenstein utilized the materiality of subjectivity to treat the viewer like a (Pavlovian) machine.

21. To portray Vertov and Eisenstein as diametrical opposites may be overstating the case somewhat. If one reads through the film theory of Eisenstein and Vertov, proceeding year by year, their constant influence and competition with each other becomes quite legible. Indeed, each takes several occasions to denigrate the other publicly while borrowing some of the other's best ideas. While there can be little doubt that Eisenstein, as a writer at least, was the more massive intellect, he borrowed often from Vertov, on occasion presenting a Vertovian idea as his own. The opposite may be seen in Vertov's rearticulation of the "theory of intervals" in the 1929 "From Kino-Eye to Radio-Eye" (Vertov, 85–92), which shares much with Eisenstein's far more highly articulated 1929 essay, "Beyond the Shot" (*Writings*, 138–50). Though Vertov takes pains to state that the theory of the interval was put forward first in 1919, he also refers to "the mutual attractions and repulsions of shots" (Vertov, 91), language that was absent in the earlier version. Similar though the theories of montage put forth by Vertov and Eisenstein at times may seem, fundamental differences necessarily exist, as can be gleaned directly from the most obvious implications of their theoretical musings: their films. Though Vertov believes that a montage fragment is a "film fact," while Eisenstein claims that a fragment "has in itself no reality at all" (Sergei M. Eisenstein, "The Dramaturgy of Film Form," in *Writings*, 178), their differences necessarily extend beyond their conceptualization of the building blocks to the manner in which they produce concepts. To be a bit simpleminded, Eisenstein believed that the concept must be induced by the collision and hence was limited only by the filmmaker's imagination for juxtaposition, hence his filmic practice was inductive. Vertov, on the other hand, believed that it was the job of the filmmaker to derive the resultant vector of a given theme, "to find amid all these mutual reactions, these mutual attractions and repulsions of shots, the most expedient 'itinerary' for the eye of the viewer, to reduce this multitude of 'intervals' (the movements between shots) to a simple visual equation, a visual formula expressing the basic theme of the film-object in the best way: such is the most important and difficult task of the author-editor" (Vertov, 91). Hence, Vertov's filmic projects were primarily deductive.

22. Vertov placed even higher hopes in the possibility of what we today call television: "The method of radio-broadcasting images, just recently invented, can bring us still closer in our cherished basic goal—to unite all the workers scattered over the earth through a single consciousness, a single bond, a single collective will in the battle for communism. This objective of ours we call kino-eye. The decoding of life as it is. Using facts to influence the workers' consciousness" (Vertov, 49).

23. "I would say Bentham was the complement to Rousseau. What in fact was the Rousseauist dream that motivated many of the revolutionaries? It was the dream of a transparent society, visible and legible in each of its parts, the dream of there no longer existing any zones of darkness, zones established by the privileges of royal power or the prerogatives of some corporation, zones of disorder. It was the dream that each individual, whatever position he occupied, might be able to see the whole of society, that men's hearts should communicate, their vision be unobstructed by obstacles, and that opinion of all reign over each. . . . Bentham is both that and the opposite. He poses the problem of visibility, but thinks of a visibility organised entirely around a dominating, overseeing gaze. He effects the project of a universal visibility which exists to serve a rigorous, meticulous power. Thus Bentham's obsession, the technical idea of the exercise of an 'all-seeing' power, is grafted on to the great Rousseauist theme which is in some sense the lyrical note of the Revolution. The two things combine into a working whole, Rousseau's lyricism and Bentham's obsession. . . . When the Revolution poses the question of a new justice, what does it envisage as its principle? Opinion. The new aspect of the problem of justice, for the Revolution, was not so much to punish wrong-doers as to prevent even the possibility of wrongdoing, by immersing people in a field of total visibility where the opinion, observation and discourse of others would restrain them from harmful acts." Michel Foucault, "The Eye of Power: A Conversation with Jean-Pierre Barou and Michelle Perrot," in *Power/Knowledge: Selected Interviews and Other Writings, 1972–1977*, ed. Colin Gordon, trans. Colin Gordon, Leo Marshall, John Mepham, and Kate Soper (New York: Pantheon, 1980), 152–53.

24. Though for Vertov social relations available for remediation meant primarily orthodox notions of relations of production and the consciousness thereof, there was, in theory, no limit to the kinds of relations that could have been represented. Decades later, Godard's own Dziga Vertov group would dismantle conceptions concerned with the unity of bodies, of bodies and voice, of narrative, of images, and of desire—all cinematic conventions that develop in the imaginary and function in art and life as relations of production. For polemical purposes, one might even say that it was Vertov's failure to develop a Marxist theory of sexuality (desire without fetishes?)—and hence of the unconscious—that predestined the general failure of his orthodoxy.

25. Georg Lukács, "Reification and the Consciousness of the Proletariat," in *History and Class Consciousness: Studies in Marxist Dialectics* (Cambridge: MIT Press, 1971), 22.

26. Michelson uses a passage from *The German Ideology* as the epigraph to her introduction to *Kino-Eye*: "The supersession of private property is, therefore, the complete emancipation of all the human qualities and senses. It is such an emancipation because these qualities and senses have become human, from the subjective as well as the objective point of view. The eye has become a human eye when its object has become a human, social object, created by man and destined for him. The senses therefore become directly theoretical in practice" (xv).

27. Karl Marx and Friedrich Engels, *The German Ideology*, in *Marx-Engels Reader*, 149.

28. See Andre Bazîn, *What Is Cinema*, trans. Hugh Gray (Berkeley and Los Angeles: University of California Press, 1967). See also Charles Musser, *Before the Nickelodeon: Edwin S. Porter and the Edison Manufacturing Company* (Berkeley and Los Angeles: University of California Press, 1991).

29. Ernst Bloch, *Heritage of Our Times*, trans. Neville and Stephen Plaice (Berkeley and Los Angeles: University of California Press, 1991), 97.

30. Andrey Tarkovsky, *Sculpting in Time: Reflections on the Cinema*, trans. Kitty Hunter-Blair (New York: Alfred A. Knopf, 1987).

31. Gilles Deleuze, *Cinema*, vol. 1, trans. Hugh Tomlinson and Barbara Habberjam, (Minneapolis: University of Minnesota Press, 1986), 40.

32. Guy Debord, *Society of the Spectacle* (Detroit: Black and Red, 1983), 66. That films can be bought for money, that is, made for money, should not deter us or cause us to think that film is somehow a lesser entity than money. Money can also buy factories, labor, and banks. One can buy money, debt, and other instruments of production with money. The question is: Can one buy money (and all that it implies) with cinema? The problem before us, then, is to find expression for the purchase that film has on the material world. "Being the external, common medium and faculty for turning an image into reality and reality into a mere image (a faculty not springing from man as man or from human society as society), money transforms the real essential powers of man and nature into what are merely abstract conceits and therefore imperfections—into tormenting chimeras—just as it transforms real imperfections and chimeras—essential powers which are really impotent, which exist only in the imagination of the individual—into real powers and faculties" (Marx and Engels, "Economic and Philosophic Manuscripts of 1844," *Marx-Engels Reader*, 105).

33. Wilhelm S. Wurzer, *Filming and Judgment: Between Heidegger and Adorno* (Atlantic Highlands, N.J.: Humanities Press, 1990), 2. Hereafter, this work is cited parenthetically as Wurzer.

34. See also Martin Jay, *Downcast Eyes: The Denigration of Vision in Twentieth-Century French Thought* (Berkeley and Los Angeles: University of California Press, 1993).

35. "The ruling ideas are nothing more than the ideal expression of the dominant material relationships, the dominant material relationships grasped as ideas; hence the

relationships which make the one class the ruling one, therefore, the ideas of its dominance" (Marx and Engels, "The German Ideology," *Marx-Engels Reader*, 172–73).

36. Benjamin, "The Work of Art," 242.

37. Sergei M. Eisenstein, "The Materialist Approach to Form," in *Writings*, 63. In the same essay, Eisenstein writes, "'The Strike' is the direct antithesis of 'Kino-eye'" (62).

38. In Eisenstein, one finds the development of the worker-spectator as the dialectical antithesis of the commodity-image. For more on this, see chapter 2.

39. This fragment (unpublished translation by Fredric Jameson) can be found in Walter Benjamin, *Gesammelte Schriften*, I, 2 (Frankfurt am Main: Suhrkamp, 1972–1989), 444–45. In the English translation of "The Work of Art," the fragment would follow what is section 5, p. 225.

40. Benjamin, "The Work of Art," 241. After a mocking description of the director's cinema ("According to your strict schedule, people fight and embrace. Marry and divorce. Are born and die"), Vertov writes, "We are at a film studio where a man with a megaphone and script directs the life of a fake land" (Vertov, 283).

41. Antonio Negri, *Marx beyond Marx: Lessons on the "Grundrisse,"* ed. Jim Fleming, trans. Harry Cleaver, Michael Ryan, and Maurizio Viano (Brooklyn: Autonomedia, 1991), 54.

42. Marx and Engels, "The German Ideology" *Marx-Engels Reader*, 172.

43. Ibid., 84.

44. Theodor W. Adorno and Max Horkheimer, *Dialectic of Enlightenment*, trans. John Cumming (New York: Continuum, 1991), 137. For Adorno and Horkheimer, the culture industry "bring[s] culture within the sphere of administration . . . [b]y subordinating in the same way and to the same end all areas of intellectual creation [and] by occupying men's senses from the time they leave the factory in the evening to the time they clock in again the next morning with matter that bears the impress of the labor process they themselves have to sustain throughout the day" (131).

45. If in the twin pairs of money/object and film frame/image it is money and image that seem to be the terms steeped in mystery, that is because the frame and the object appear inert, lifeless, reified. The object as an existential entity (existentialism as the experiential thrill [nausea] of the autonomous object wrenched from exchange in an act of perception consequent on social disenchantment) has all but disappeared (eroded by money), and the frame/screen has not yet achieved its full ascendancy as the cybernetic extension of all senses and sensibilities. These two, frame/object, fuse as surface and reappear as image/money. Yet as we have seen, objects, even before becoming images, are objectified humanity, and, as we know from experience, everything changes in the presence of a camera, just as previously everything changed in the presence of money. Like the commodity, the camera and film stock, that is, the early components of the frame, are also objectified subjectivity, but with a difference: They have

a higher technological coefficient for the production of subjectivity than does the simple commodity. In this the frame resembles money. Among its functions is precisely the creation of subjectivity, or, to employ the contemporary term, intensity, through circulation.

46. "The quality of money as mediator, the separation of exchange into two acts, already contains the germ of crises" (*Grundrisse,* 133).

47. A number of writers besides me have been working on a mediatic reformulation of the Marxian formulations C-M-C and M-C-M. See, for example, Richard Dienst, *Still Life in Real Time: Theory after Television* (Durham, N.C.: Duke University Press, 1994). See also Brian Massumi, *A User's Guide to Capitalism and Schizophrenia: Deviations from Deleuze and Guattari* (Cambridge: MIT Press, 1992).

48. Does cinema as the representative of exchange-value exceed the economic limits of money? Or, to put it another way, has money become such a complex form of mediation that it has become cinematic? The outline of the answer to this question can be discerned in the figure of sublation, the annihilation without destruction of dialectical categories. The commodity, like money, is not the highest form of capital; each is an iteration that derives its properties from a higher law that bursts forth from the shattering of the apparent unity of the lesser categories. Yet despite this shattering, the former categories nonetheless remain. So it is with the relation between money and cinema. In the largest business deals, managers work out the nitty-gritty while directors of nations traffic in images. Like virtual reality, an image provides a screen for a visceral imagining of the summation of a complex of relations. Such image making, however, is today at work at every level of economic endeavor. It is capital's imaginative projection.

49. Simmel, *Philosophy of Money,* 510.

Chapter 2

Production
The Spectatorship
of the Proletariat

*Revolutionary ideology, the coherence of the separate, of which Leninism
represents the greatest voluntaristic attempt, supervising a reality which
rejects it, with Stalinism returns to its truth in incoherence. At that point
ideology is no longer a weapon, but a goal. The lie which is no longer
challenged becomes lunacy. Reality as well as the goal dissolve in the
totalitarian ideological proclamation: all it says is all there is. This is a
local primitivism of the spectacle, whose role is nevertheless essential in
the development of the world spectacle. The ideology which is materialized
in this context has not economically transformed the world, as has capitalism
which reached the stage of abundance; it has merely transformed perception
by means of the police.* —Guy Debord, Society of the Spectacle

---

Prologue

Because today capital "thinks" several cycles in advance of itself, or,
to put it another way, because it has several historical stages of its own development simultaneously available to itself that can be utilized in varying
proportions, one could well argue that isolated labor strikes are made productive for capital and that phenomena such as the general strike or Samir
Amin's "de-linking" are impossible.[1] The argument for the productive value
of the strike for capital would not in itself necessarily be to ignore what
Jacques Derrida recently has called "Marx's injunction."[2] In discussing the
capitalization of the resistance to capital, given perhaps its most dramatic
form in and after 1989, one might still hear the ghostly admonitions of the
"specter of Marx," which, for Derrida "reaffirms the question of life and
death." Furthermore, one might hear the moans and intimations of such

an absent presence without oneself becoming as dead as Marxism is purported to be.

Though this essay is not directly concerned with the viability of the labor strike, it is most definitely concerned with the objective of the strike, that is, the reappropriation of historically sedimented human labor (the means of production) by disenfranchised individuals and groups. Such reappropriation of historically sedimented labor and of living labor is going on all the time; it is endemic to social change. As Antonio Negri argues, in endeavoring to establish the subjectivity of labor in history, not only does labor produce capital, but labor, in its resistance to capital exploitation, forces structural and technological innovations in capitalism. Though this is surely the case, we have lacked, since the advent of cinema in particular, a specific theory that accounts for the development of certain new regimes for the production of cultural and economic value via mental activity; we do not yet know how to account for the present-day dynamics of value production and appropriation that operate through the conversion of mental activity into social force. The capitalization of mental activity that calls into question the older distinction between mental and manual labor is an enabling factor in capital's ability to continue all previous forms of violation. By looking at the recycling of the resistance to capital by capital (the making productive of the strike against capital by capital) our *affective production* of hegemony may be foregrounded, while possibilities for the disruption of coercion and exploitation may be foregrounded as well. Toward those ends (and perhaps to the surprise of some), I would like to continue the discussion of the development of mass media during the time of early modern cinema, more specifically, those particular developments that can be found to crystallize in Sergei Mikhailovich Eisenstein's 1924–1925 film *The Strike*.[3] For it was here, precisely, in revolutionary cinema, that capital's encroachment into the visual sphere met with resistance. And yet, in spite of its intentions, *The Strike*, like capital itself, participates in producing a new regime of the sensorium by advancing an increasing integration of machines and culture, of labor and perception. We can use *The Strike* to mark an emergent socio-historical change in the character of what Marx called "sensuous labor" and, by direct implication, to mark as well a new strategy for the production and appropriation of value.

To talk here about the political economy of the reorganization of society in terms of the *simultaneously* economic and cultural value necessary for the reclaiming and restructuring of communicative pathways (media), and of sexual identities, of groups, of subjects, of time, and of institutional power, and the management of the world of objects, in short, social organization in general, suggests that the formation of identities, coteries, markets, subjects, groups, factions, are to be thought of as the formation of political blocs. Such formations require labor, which, in its product (and also in its production), may stand in some oppositional relationship to the dominant. Ideology is only one of the factors of amalgamation. As a prelude to new possibilities in a discussion of culture and economy, I have set myself the task of showing how what might be thought of as the political economy of organization comes into being.[4]

Manufacturing Logic.

The Strike remains an important film in cinema history for reasons inherent in its design and function as a mediator of social forces. It is a work of art conceived as a productive technology. For this reason, I am less interested in the "meaning" of *The Strike* as a text to be read and interpreted in the traditional way, and rather more interested in the specific significance of *The Strike* as an index of the potentialities of film technology during the 1920s and following.

For the Stalinist state to take its final form, the potential dictators had to be made over into spectators; their labor power had to be taken from them before, and through, their eyes. Bent by the exigencies of capital, the achievement of Eisenstein was, when understood on the largest historical canvas, the conversion of workers into spectators. To see this significance, it is necessary to "think" *The Strike* in a new way—not merely to interpret it but to understand it as a mediation, a form of agency. Hence, the kind of meanings in *The Strike* that, for example, allegorize the circumstances around the suicide of the worker-organizer whose stolen micrometer, according to the film's plot, might be imagined to have initiated the wave of strikes under the 1907 Czarist regime, are only of secondary importance here. That the micrometer was stolen secretly by the factory foreman in order to harass the workers and to create an excuse for increased surveillance in the factory, despite its practical and historical validity, seems to me as unimportant in the present context as Eisentein's ingenious idea of employing such an instrument—designed to measure tiny difference—to function as the cinematic sign for an infinitesimally small, yet crucial, moment in a larger process: The unjust removal of the micrometer serves as the flash point for a worldwide confrontation between labor and capital. These aspects of Eisenstein's film, though brilliant, must be stripped away if we are to approach the significance of *The Strike* in a new way, that is, at the level not of meaning, but rather of its consequences for political economy.

To begin the journey beyond meaning to significance, let us look at the worker's suicide note: "Comrades, the program accused me of thievery. I am not guilty but I cannot prove it. I cannot face being kicked out of the factory and branded a thief. I've decided to end it all and remember: I am not guilty." In the moments before the workers find their unfortunate comrade hanging from a beam, one shoe dangling off a foot that has now gone limp after convulsing, the camera shows him humiliated by the hypocritical foremen and managers in the management office. As this suspected labor organizer storms heatedly out of the office unable to find justice, the film, almost by way of contrast, provides spectators with the same tracking shot of the factory shown at the start of the film, when, as the intertitle told us, "all [wa]s quiet." The workers, lined up in rows from one end of the factory to the other, are stationed at their various spinning, stamping, pressing, and cutting machines, linked to an overhead power train by long, suspended leather belts. It is a long, beautiful shot that, in its synchronized complexity, reveals simultaneously the concrete organization of the factory and the relation of workers to power. Workers are on the receiving end of a power coming down from above, and they must manufacture according to the spatial and temporal (and by implication, economic) organization of the factory. The suspended belts function as parts or tools linking the workers' labor to a centralized source that increases their productivity (for the capitalist) and, simultaneously, as the film has been showing us, results in exploitation, sowing resentment and finally death for the worker. The belts, as machines, imply a whole system of interlocked operations, and they function emblematically, that is, at the most literal level, as a sign for the transformation of power into relations of production, and conversely, as a sign for the transformation of the relations of production into power relations.

The very next shot is a close-up of hands putting a slipknot in the belt, which, as we will realize a moment later, *The Strike's* suicide has removed from his own pants in order to use it to hang himself. This belt, also a machine, which, in this case, had held up the worker's pants, is turned into an instrument of the worker's destruction like the power belts in the factory. The abrupt cut argues that, like the factory structure itself, the belt that otherwise might have been a useful tool helps to rob the worker of his life, but in this instance not just little by little in the form of labor time stolen day after day but all at once. The worker, unable to find justice in the "proper" use of the belt, initiates an activity of destruction when he seeks it. In this case, the failure of justice results in the suicide/murder of the worker; the organizational structure of the factory has taken the worker's life. The belt, which ought to be a tool for the worker, confronts him as his enemy. This intensification and acceleration of the logic of the factory—the factory's taking of a worker's life in an instant—is the dynamite that sets off the strike. The instantaneous death of the poor factory worker, a death that robs him of all future sensuous activity and hence all future creativity and productivity, becomes the catalyst of the strike, because it reveals the slower truth for labor in the factory: *To hang from the end of a belt is to be dead.* The fact that an instrument that makes measurements as small as a micrometer does could be used to torment a man, and the fact that this small-scale torment sets off a strike, shows simultaneously the power of the capitalists, the scales on which their power operates, and the immanence of the workers' discontent. The instant consumption of all of the suicide's labor time, present and future, by the struggle between the worker and the management over the right to dispose of it, produces the value that solidifies the proto-union's organizational efforts up until that point and drives its members to strike.

These are the kinds of poetic resonances in the film-form that, though they at once show the extraordinary power of Eisenstein's dialectical mind and an aspect of his understanding of the relations between labor and power, I am interested in here only as they expand beyond meaning itself and point toward the growing agency of the organization of things. The strikers' affective appropriation of the labor power expended in the worker's death reveals that Eisenstein has a new theory of the relationship between value transfer and organizational form. Such revolutionary organization is, as we shall see, not so much a meaning but a historical watershed, at once a tremendous source of new semiotic possibility as well as the origin of a new dynamic of social production. It is true that in this discussion of *The Strike,* it will be necessary to traverse the course of a few more similarly signifying structures and even, if only by virtue of necessity, to give a reading of *The Strike.* However, the reading is not foremost. It is the more general and more significant phenomenon of the conversion of organized movement to a nearly immaterial signifying stratum (as also seen in Vertov) that concerns me here, and following that, it is the function of this nearly immaterial signifying stratum in social production. In this chapter, such an insight is more important than narratological dwelling. Even Eisenstein himself was interested in the force of his films far more than in their particular contents. "Nobody believes that the content of a newspaper consists of a report about the Kellog Pact, a scandal from the *Gazette de France* or an account of an everday event. The *content* [*soderzhanie*] of a newspaper is the principle by which the *contents* [*soderzhimoe*] of the paper are organized and processed, with the aim of processing the reader from a class-based standpoint."[5] "The principle of the organization of thinking is in actual fact the 'content' of the work" (*Writings*, 154). With this in mind, it is obvious that the kind of knowledge that a critical reading alone produces is available in any number of places; indeed, what I have said about the actual "meaning" of *The Strike* thus far only reproduces the hackneyed (if still goat-getting) claims of a hoary Marxism. It is not that readings are insignificant; they just produce a different kind and theory of work. Reading, especially as a bourgeois literary-critical practice, consists of the reassembling of textual events in a plodding and *reflective* way. It is after the fact, "a revolution behind," as Baudrillard says. I oppose this practice here, as does Eisenstein, to the *immediacy* of perception, affect, and activation: the modality of analysis versus the modality of event, the modality of theory versus the modality of practice. The register of concepts is connected only elliptically to the viscerality that is to be our province. In pursuit of this viscerality, we should note that as reading traditionally diverts our attention from the material operations of the text in order that we "understand," there remain those empty signs, those generally discarded shells of language that are perhaps best grasped in their totality as a *technology of affect*. Thought, as the philosophers use the term, is only one of the dimensions of affect, and perhaps not the most important one, especially today.

Though there is a great deal of difference between the technology of written language and of cinema, it is possible to think the continuity between consciousness and corporeality by partially shielding ourselves for a moment from the seductions of meaning and the pyrotechnics of images in order "to think" with the rationality of capital. It is by thinking like capital that we might think beyond thought. We are trying to understand what capital feels like, or, rather, to know what capital is "thinking" while we feel. Eisenstein, remember, regarded "cinema as a factor for exercising emotional influence over the masses" because it could deliver "a series of blows to the consciousness and emotions of the audience" (*Writings*, 39). I am interested here in the continuities between the development of Eisenstein's cinema and the development of capital. The cold rationality of capital helps us to understand the heat of social warfare.

Written language as a technology for the deterritorialization of consciousness was, as Hegel told us two hundred years ago, the condition of possibility for poetry, the highest art (followed in bulkiness by music, painting, sculpture, and architecture). For Hegel, the more completely art escaped from matter, mass, and spatialization, the more fully world spirit found its expression: "Poetry is, in short, the universal art of the mind, which has become essentially free, and which is not fettered in its realization to an externally sensuous material, but which is creatively active in the space and time belonging to the inner world of ideas and emotions."[6] This equipment-free aspect of poetry that (to speak a little bluntly) allowed consciousness unmediated access to world spirit will be challenged and indeed called into question by the advent of Marxism and then cinema. The Hegelian dialectic asserted that advancing societies would materialize ever more dematerialized issues of consciousness out of their own organizational processes. To tell the story in abridged and instrumental form, as world spirit came into being through the medium of history, the historical development of modes of expression allowed for the materialization of dematerialized Idea: the rarefied consciousness called poetry required the historico-material development of the world. By calling attention to the dematerialization of consciousness in written language and the read text with this thumbnail sketch of the Hegelian history of media, rather than just taking a generalized dematerialization of consciousness as a postmodern given, it becomes possible to think about lexical organization not merely as the index to a hermeneutic process called reading but as a historically embodied process of corporeal conversion. As Regis Debray has shown subsequently, the eloquence of various stages of expression (mediation) has wrought changes upon our techno-corporeal organization.[7] Dematerialized consciousness comes out of social development and feeds into it. Architecture, sculpture, painting, music, and poetry are, for Hegel, ascending developmental paradigms in the history of the expression of Idea, because, increasingly, Idea escapes from materiality. However, apparent independence from matter, as Marx taught us, is precisely *dependent* upon material organization. Cinema, arguably, combines the expressive abilities of all earlier art forms, while being even more immaterial: mere sound and light. If in the Hegelian paradigm cinema supersedes poetry, and even "the prose of thought," Walter Benjamin's famous words supply the necessary materialist qualification, "[I]n the studio the mechanical equipment has penetrated so deeply into reality that its pure aspect freed from the foreign substance of equipment is the result of special procedure[s]. The equipment-free aspect of reality here has become the height of artifice; the sight of immediate reality has become an orchid in the land of technology."[8]

The orchid in the land of technology as an expression of immediacy and of the production of affect helps us to understand the technology of expressivity as technology for corporeal reorganization—particularly if we see that the orchid in the land of technology is also the glimmering commodity shorn of its history of production. Bodies must be trained to interface with affect machines through the overcoming of certain physical encumbrances. Film's special role in the development of industrial capitalism lays the groundwork for the full commodification of the sensorium as it produces new affects. Beginning in Eisenstein's period, cinema dematerializes industrial processes, making them over into fodder for consciousness and sensuality, and projecting them into bodies through visual means. Film internalizes industrial movement and manifests it as forms of consciousness and sensuality. These forms are projected into bodies through the eye. Bodies then internalize industrial movement, making it inform their own consciousness. Film turns movement into thoughts and feelings, or, more generally, affect.

That the dematerialization of signifying strata historically emerges in a full-blown form (as consciousness, as cinema, as capital) simultaneously with forms of organization theory concerned with the material *embodiment* of organization is not a paradox. The more abstracted and ethereal the signifying stratum—that is, the greater the possibilities of expression without the appearance of apparatus—the more dependent the expression on the development of material and social organization. Anyone who has ever wanted to get information from a computer disk but who has not had access to a computer at a particular moment understands the socio-techno-historical embeddedness of signification on material organization. Without the complete history of the formation of the computer, that is, without the computer, its industrial base, and everything its existence implies (Silicon Valley, off-shore labor, imperialism, in short, the history of the world down to the present), the highly dematerialized information on the disk would be useless. Marx observed the same dependence of significance on social organization in the relation that he drew between the development of capital and the organization of bourgeois society. The more abstract capital became (as money, as debt), the more rigid and concrete, the more embodied bourgeois (capitalist) society became. With the increasing organization of bodies themselves (manners, culture) along with the increasing organization of the physical, intellectual, and visual pathways that they and their deterritorialized pieces traverse, comes the apparent dematerialization of expression.[9] The free-floating image is anchored in material social organization down to the quantum level.

The important thing to see in Eisenstein is his recognition of the principle that he saw behind regimes of organized movement. Eisenstein's conscious effort to put that principle into practice as more is expressed as follows: "An attraction," wrote Eisenstein, "is in our understanding any demonstrable fact (an action, an object, a phenomenon, a conscious combination and so on) that is known and proven to exercise a definite effect on the attention and emotions of the audience and that combined with others possesses the characteristics of concentrating the audience's emotions in any direction dictated by the production's purpose" (*Writings*, 41). Eisenstein was interested in control through the organization of attraction. "The method of agitation through spectacle consists in the creation of a new chain of conditioned reflexes by associating selected phenomenon with the unconditioned reflexes they produce" (*Writings*, 45). The script is "in our view a prescription or a list of montage sequences and combinations by means of which the author intends to subject the audience to a definite series of shocks, a prescription that summarizes the general projected emotional effect on the audience and the pressure that will inevitably be exerted on the audience's psyche" (*Writings*, 46). Because "the montage approach [i]s the essential, meaningful and sole possible language of cinema, completely analogous to the role of the word in spoken material" (*Writings*, 46). The juxtaposition of moving fragments became for Eisenstein a tool for the reorganization of the audience's psyche. The idea of montage, then, is the abstraction process itself, and cinema is its conscious utilization. In Eisenstein's famous phrase, direction is "the organization of the audience through organized material" (*Writings*, 65).

The fact that *The Strike* thematizes the general phenomena of movement as signification and that film theoreticians from Eisenstein to Pasolini were preoccupied with film *language* indicates their transitional places in a paradigm shift from signification to simulation (from meaning to stimulation) and provides a working periodization of this shift. This is the period of modern cinema, after which meaning recedes before pure affect (as in *Jaws*). What I want to emphasize about *The Strike* in particular, however, is that it is perhaps the first film that rigorously adopts the emerging paradigm of movement as signification to be the fundamental animating principle of its own organization. In so doing, *The Strike* attempts to incorporate the spectator into its very movement, its moving. As the worker in the Fordist factory becomes a component in the factory's orchestra (orchestration) of movement, a part in the machine, so also does the spectator become a component in the movement machines of Eisenstein. These films inflict their movement on and into the spectator who, though capable of reading their "meaning," realizes their significance only in and as bodily activity. The spectator embodies the resultant force of the motion transferred to him or her—a general situation of machine culture that envelops, and in certain ways exceeds, any particular meaning.

Eisenstein harnessed the dematerialization of material movement as not only meaning but as a direct *extension* of social force and developed its possibilities. Such an achievement makes *The Strike* an ideal case study for the contention pursued here that cinema, subjectivity, and corporeality come to operate on a continuum correlated via what Eisenstein calls a "manufacturing logic." If this is correct, it should turn out that the significance of *The Strike* is that not only interpretation but consciousness and viscerality itself are in our period cinematic, that is, endemic to a manufacturing logic that incorporates the body. This manufacturing logic, characterized simultaneously by the rational control of motion and the regulated production of consciousness, also turns out to be the logic of commodification. In the money economy, movement via capital circulation is the equivalent of commodification. I am suggesting that affect is increasingly the result of organized circulation; this circulation is a commodification effect. As disturbing a notion as the invasion of consciousness by the logistics of capital may be, it raises in the present a question that for some will be equally ghastly: "What is Marxism?"

Ploughing the Audience's Psyche.

Commenting on *The Strike* in "The Problem of the Materialist Approach to Form," Eisenstein confirms our argument thus far regarding the relationship between movement and expression:

> In *The Strike* we have the first instance of revolutionary art where the form has turned out to be more revolutionary than the content. . . . The historical revolutionary material—the *"manufactured"* past of contemporary revolutionary reality—was for the first time treated from a correct *point of view*: its characteristic movements were investigated as stages in a single process from the point of view of its "manufacturing" essence. The discovery of the manufacturing logic and the exposition of

the technique of the methods of a struggle that is the formal require-
ment I put to Proletkult in determining the content of the seven parts of
the cycle *Towards the Dictatorship*. (*Writings*, 59).[10]

Richard Taylor suggests that "the implication [of the phrase "'manufactured' past"] is that the past has prepared the present like a factory process
(*Writings*, 307 n. 2). What is at stake here for Eisenstein is the *self-conscious*
utilization of Marx's discovery of the human production of human
society—not merely as a *theory* of history and social production but rather
as a *method,* or, better, a *mode* of production. Eisenstein wants to use what
is nascent both in the method of industry and in its workers to make history. It is often suggested that revolutions fail to realize their utopian longings while succeeding in innovating a shift in the mode of production.
Eisenstein's revolution in form was no exception. That the past manufactures the present seems correct, but that the present manufactures the past
was equally important to Eisenstein. He saw the revolutionary filmmaker's
role as taking this relationship and turning it into a method capable of
manufacturing the future. To manufacture history, Eisenstein employed
the latest industrial methods.

In Eisenstein's words, "the revolutionary quality of *The Strike* was exemplified by the fact that it took its renewing principle not from the ranks
of 'artistic phenomena' but from those that are *directly utilitarian:*
specifically, the principle of the construction of the exposition of the manufacturing processes in the film" (*Writings*, 60). To show that the workers'
strike as a revolutionary activity is itself something manufactured is, for
Eisenstein, "a choice that is significant because it goes beyond the limits of
the aesthetic *sphere* . . . all the more so because what was in material terms
correctly ascertained was precisely that *sphere* whose principles alone *define
the ideology of the forms of revolutionary art just as they have defined revolutionary ideology in general: heavy industry,* factory production and the forms
of the manufacturing process" (*Writings*, 60). The strike must be manufactured out of the conditions that give rise to its necessity.

The sphere of production then, according to Eisenstein, is that which is
manifest in *The Strike* in the content, certainly, but also, even more dra-
matically, in the form. One misses the significance of *The Strike* if one sees
it merely as an exposition of the conditions of a strike. The film is itself conceived as a tool. It is, as it were, the third of three belts, this last one feeding off of the power train of the new (cinematic) mode of production to
transfer powers to the workers in a new way.

Revolutionary form is the product of correctly ascertained technical methods for *the concretisation of a new attitude and approach to objects and phenomena—of a new class of ideology*—of the true renewal not just of the social significance but also of the material-technical essence of cinema. It is not by revolutionising the forms of the stagecoach that the locomotive is created but through a proper technical calculation of the practical emergence of a new and previously non-existent kind of energy—steam. (*Writings*, 60–61)

The steam of Eisenstein's cinema, its "new kind of energy," is, he suggests, the organization of the masses through organized material—a new phenomenology of objects produced via industrial processes. This is the theory and practice of Eisenstein's historical materialism. For Eisenstein, cinema is not a mere representation of revolutionary practice but is directly engaged in the sphere of production. This theory of production is not empty rhetoric, because, as Eisenstein aptly puts it, this production produces "a new class of ideology," a suture with the social world that is of a new type. Eisenstein, who trained as an architect and an engineer, is designing machines to manufacture a new social order. With his characteristic knack for structural precision and his usual economy of means, Eisenstein sums up his views on the purposeful integration of machines, a proletariat rapidly emerging from agrarian life, and revolutionary art: "In our conception *a work of art* is first and foremost a *tractor ploughing over the audience's psyche in a particular class context*" (*Writings*, 62). For Eisenstein, the cinema is a machine that transforms mental life, and, as we shall see, subordinates it to a new logic.

Organization—Dematerialization of Material Movement.

Lenin's words stressing the importance of organization are quoted at the opening of *The Strike:* "The strength of the working class lies in organization. Without organization of the masses the proletariat is nothing. Organized it is everything. Organization means unity of action, unity of practical operations." Following this organizational directive, *The Strike* sets out to catalog various moments in the organization of the revolutionary proletariat at the same time that it strives itself to be a moment in the organization of the revolutionary proletariat. It constructs a continuity between the past and the present, and portrays the proletariat's revolutionary role in the reorganization of society. Indeed, the opening of the film is staged as the struggle between two communicative regimes that have at stake the resolution of a schism between two competing models for the practical organization of the workers and the state. The capitalist owners, for their part, have telephones, the power structure of the factory itself, and spies who report back to management. Ultimately, the owners can depend on the state in the form of police and military power for the enforcement of their hold over the workers. The capitalists, along with their managers, machines, spies, and police, form an entrenched organizational network. It is a living architecture of power. Meanwhile, the workers have for themselves only what they can create out of the conditions of their existence. In the fantastic shot sequence showing the interlocking components of the Czarist state and the regime of private property, a factory foreman, who early on believes trouble to be brewing, calls his superior, who then calls his superior on up to the capitalist owners and the military police. As the call goes up the ladder of command, talking heads listen to a phone in one ear while picking up a phone for the other ear in order to send the message on up the line. It is here that the film not only shows the technological immediacy of the connections between capitalist industrial management and other forms of state power but suggests that people's functions within that mediating network are determined by their position in the organizational array. In a certain way, the telephone has more agency than its user—at least when its users are capitalists or the lackeys of capitalists engaged in the oppression of forces (workers) that threaten to transform the organizational integrity of their systems. This telephone medium functions somewhat like cinema does in the hands of Eisenstein. The bureaucrats' heads mechanically transmit the message just as the capitalists and their state can do nothing but attempt to suppress the strike. The telephone cable, thin as it is, embodies tremendous organizational force. That the call reaches its final destination at the military commander, who has at his disposal the public records (maps of the city and images of spies whose photographs immediately begin to move), goes to show that the call for coercive counterrevolutionary force will animate already existing structures on its way back down the hierarchy toward its oppressive realization.[11]

Unaware of impending defeat, the workers use their life-energy to organize by word of mouth, by pamphleteering, and under the cover of art. During leisure time by the water, the handsome leaders argue and plot while reposed on an anchor. Their fraternal bond forged in working together for a common cause is perhaps, for Eisenstein, the libidinal core of a revolutionary society. We get several shots of men in repose taking advantage of leisure time to organize. Sitting among a tremendous mountain of piled iron train wheels, the workers, planning yet again, seem to draw inspiration from a material intimation regarding base and superstructure: rolling stock cannot roll without its wheels. In a factory bathroom, they are again conspiring until, upon the unwanted entry of the boss's foreman, they tear down their pants and face the urinals or sit on the pots in individual stalls—innocently going about their business. And under the superimposed cover of an accordion that opens and closes as if breathing a message in and out, we see bands of workers and their families walking, singing, and talking among themselves as a title states "spreading the word." On printed leaflets, too, the workers call for an immediate strike. This is the organization of the workers' countermovements. They are building revolutionary consciousness and a revolution.

In solidarity with the workers' use of their own spaces and creative force to assemble a strike, *The Strike* organizes the myriad movements and patterns of daily life to orchestrate a message. However, this message is not only meant to be understood, that is, it is not, as the above paragraph might seem to imply, merely a handbook of revolutionary activity. As the capitalists and the workers attempt to outmaneuver each other using their networks of organization and communication, it becomes clear that in the case of the workers, it is movement itself that is their medium of communication. They set up an alternative circulation and express themselves in the concrete reorganization of their surroundings. This reorganization is, as it were, the film-language of *The Strike*. The placing of things in motion is the form of this society's expression. Capitalists orchestrate movement according to their interests, while workers try to orchestrate their own form of movement. To move differently in a society of highly regimented motion is already to express something else. Alternative motions may defy, or even exceed, the dominant social order. Indeed, it is the workers' goal in *The Strike* to rip the factory partway out of the capitalists' network of organization and control, and to incorporate it into their own. They move to make its moving parts move for them.

In *The Strike*, the reorganization of movement (space and time) is made eloquent. Set apart from the capitalists, who are caricatures, and their spies, who are named for animals, the humans who appear as "The People" (who, in Eisenstein's films, Roland Barthes notes are "always lovable") are the only ones able to exercise autonomous agency.[12] In moving for themselves, the people claim their humanity. It is as if revolutionary movement itself begins to reverse Marx's description of the animalistic conditions imposed by capitalism, in which, "What is animal becomes human and what is human becomes animal."[13] For Marx, the animalistic conditions of the workers' lives under capitalism exist because all of the workers' creative energy (human labor) belongs to the capitalist. Though in their exploitation of workers the capitalists behave inhumanely, they appropriate the human attributes of the workers whom they have caged. The worker, in only being able to reproduce his or her own subsistence, is reduced to an animal, as "an animal only produces what it immediately needs for itself or its young. An animal produces only itself whilst man reproduces the whole of nature."[14] However, the workers' movements, organized for revolutionary change, produce something beyond immediate subsistence and reveal that it is the capitalists and their lackeys who, through their lack of agency, are capable of producing only themselves. The workers' movements in *The Strike* reveal the capitalists' animal nature. It is as if the spell that turned the workers into animals by freezing their humanity in the objects they made and that now cage them could be broken through the reorganization of movement. In Eisenstein, humanity remains a specter while the world is under capital's enchantment.

It is not for its own sake that I have raised the animal/human dichotomy present in Eisenstein, Marx, and, as will become important for us shortly, the imaginary of this period. Because capital was, in fact, *producing* animality, Eisenstein's concern with the relationship between animals, humans, and social organization was, at the turn of the century, part of a widely debated problematic. One need only think of H. G. Wells's *Island of Dr. Moreau*, the tropes used by late colonial and emerging imperialist powers to characterize racialized others, or Pavlovian behaviorism here. This constellation of capital, animality, and humanity suggests the deeper powers of metamorphosis latent in the communicative aspects of movement, since reorganization potentially breaks the spell of Circe, that is, of capital, of animality. For the moment, the important point here is to see the conjunction of capital and animality with the process of communication. For Eisenstein, communication arises as a result of the organization of production and functions as a form of production. Furthermore, it transpires directly in the movement of materials. That movement is itself communication is made most explicit in a scene in *The Strike* that occurs once the work stoppage is underway and some of the workers in the foundry refuse to join. An angry mob of striking workers picks up the raw materials of what will soon be a hail of cobblestones and, heaving them, breaks jagged holes in the windows of the foundry. There is no doubt about what they are doing in making the stones fly: They are sending a message that even an animal could understand: "Get out!"

That the movement of material is made expressive in Eisenstein is only slightly less extraordinary than the fact that it actually occurs via the dematerialization of the movement of material. But this dematerialization of material movement is the moment that goes beyond the mere meaning of the film in the sense that I indicated previously and marks its significance for the reorganization of the material and the materiality of signification. It is here, in the abstraction of material movement away from materiality, and in the ensuing phenomenological and visceral effects, that the cinematic mode of production comes into full presence. From now on, perception will be more or less consciously engineered according to the protocols of circulating materials. Because *The Strike* is itself a materialization of the movements that have begun to inhere in social organization as language, it is the materialization of a "language." *Language* is, however, as inadequate a term as *meaning*, inasmuch as what is accomplished in *The Strike* is less the speaking about something and more the transferring of its very motion, the transferring of revolutionary movement.

In "The Third Meaning," Roland Barthes used Eisenstein stills to arrive at a concept of the filmic, which surpasses the realm of the signified. For Barthes, "the third meaning," that which he calls "the obtuse meaning," is that which exceeds language—a "signifier without a signified."[15] In his words, "the third meaning—theoretically locatable but not describable—can now be seen as a passage from language to significance and the founding act of the filmic itself."[16] I am suggesting that "filmic" encounters take place in a translinguistic environment, which at once utilizes thought and is beyond it. Cinema is a technology for the organization of the scene of this encounter—let us provisionally call this space the space of the Real. Material reorganization of the world of capital and animality is, for Eisenstein, designed to produce psychic reorganization, physical reorganization, and, hence, social reorganization. That this organizational force materializes in, and as, the dematerialization of material movement only suggests that there is a new kind of energy for the transformation of the material organization of society—steam! Utilizing the technological organization of the Real, the gaseous film in all its airy immateriality extends the circulation of movement beyond its immediate place and time and into the arena of its employment—the social and the sensuous.

Cinema: A Technology of the Real. Consciousness Tends Toward Consciousness of Commodities. Productive Value of Human Attention. Cinema as Organizational Paradigm.

In *The Imaginary Signifier*, Christian Metz announces his psycho-analytic investigation of *capitalist* cinema as an effort "to disengage the cinema-object from the imaginary and to win it for the symbolic, in the hope of extending the latter by a new province, an enterprise of displacement, a territorial enterprise, a symbolic advance."[17] The symbolic advance that he intends entails extending the language of theory into the territory of cinema, since, for him, "cinema is a technique of the imaginary."[18] We should add here that cinema is a *technology* of the Real. In the winning of cinema for the symbolic, Metz wants to be able to articulate epistemologically that which occurs in the encounter between the cinema and the psyche. For Metz, the cinema performs tasks in the space of the imaginary that can be analyzed descriptively and logically. In short, Metz intends to figure symbolically the interface between the cinema and the body.

The parallel of Metz's work with my own effort can be found in my attempt to show that what is known about cinema in some empirical way (by watching and reflecting) and what is experienced can be expressed in another code. For Metz, this code is theory—the symbolic. By way of introducing what follows, what I would like to add here to Metz is that the experience of cinema not only can be, but indeed *is being* expressed in another code—though it is a type of code for which not all the units are meaningful *for us*. More and more thoroughly, these units have quantifiable, statistical significance *for capital*. The informatics of capital outpace meaning. If, as Georg Simmel writes, "money may be compared to language, which also lends itself to the most divergent directions of thought and feeling," the reverse is also true.[19] In taking the form of industry, that is, in being an extension of it, film-language takes the form of capital. Thus, I do not enter into the territory of cinema only to provide a theory of cinema; I want to show how capital has been developing a "theory" of cinema all along through the articulation of its form. Though the meanings of cinema are found in language, its significance is not language; its significance is in the symbolic known as capital. This symbolic, it should be noted, is not legible to all subjects and indeed signifies in a register far different from everyday perceptions in the cinema. In principle, all of the possibilities, affects, and experience available in the cinema are capable of being symbolized as capital—in other words, converted to exchange-value at some earlier or later stage of social production. Thus one sees the conversion of affect to money, of money to affect. Or such might be an abridged history of mediation since Eisenstein.

The aforementioned shift from language as the arbiter of value to what is ultimately cinematic capital as the arbiter of value—that is, the shift from linguistic code being conceptualized as the bedrock of reality to simulation as the affect of capitalized reality is *experienced* as a shift by the subject, that is, by the sensorium.[20] The most generic name for this new kind of experience resulting from the erosion of the stability of language is "the postmodern condition"—the phenomenology of which is best indexed by the term *simulation*. In the shift away from a linguistic code that is signaled by "simulation," another quite different code remains, the code of exchange-value, that is, the code of commodification. Indeed, to speak figuratively here (for to show the myriad ways in which exchange-value is becoming the obverse of not just cinema in the sense in which we ordinarily understand it but of perception and thought would be to establish a new political economy and a new aesthetics, not to mention a new psychology), capital's assembly line (as the montage of capital) not only provides the form for cinema, capital provides the formal model for the basic cinematic unit, the frame. The cinema is the concrete realization of what is already implicit in Marx: All things pass through the frame of capital. As Gilles Deleuze tells us, "The frame ensures a deterritorialization of the image" because it "gives a common standard of measurement to things which do not have one—long shots of countryside and close-ups of the face, an astronomical system and a single drop of water."[21] This principle of equivalence perfectly parallels and indeed extends the principle of equivalence implied by exchange-values (which can be compared directly), becoming the other side of use-values (which cannot be compared directly). In short, Deleuze suggests that the frame functions like money, as the general equivalent. The cutting up of reality according to the abstract logic of the frame suggests that the cinema is both a consequence and a source of fragmentation. Robert Bresson writes, "This [fragmentation] is indispensable if one does not want to fall into representation [which capital surely does not]. See beings and things in separate parts. Render them independent *in order to give them a new dependence*" (my emphasis).[22] Such disarticulation from traditional relationships and the reorganization into new relationships enacts the very process of capital.[23] Indeed, the form of cinema *is* the process of capital. With the cinematic organization of the world, the logic of capital moves us beyond representation and into simulation. In

Deleuze's words, "Money [becomes] the obverse of all the images that the cinema shows and sets in place."[24] The images have begun to move like money, and their affects demand the organizational work of capital. Eisenstein's exquisitely articulate resistance to this new regime of organized movement, and its attendant regime of the sensorium, also brought it into being.

Steven Shaviro, whose work is part of an attempt to explore the new aesthetics mentioned parenthetically above, forcefully states in *The Cinematic Body* that "when the real is fragmented as a result of being permeated with machines, the opposition between subjectivity and objectivity, between the observer and the observed, vanishes."[25] Such a phenomenological condition, thought to be endemic to postmodernism, is, in general, only *suggestively* allied with *postindustrial* society. A correspondence between economics and consciousness is taken for granted—shifts in consciousness are taken as *signs* of economic shifts. I am suggesting here that the dematerialization of industrial process *as* cinema can be taken to mark the inauguration of consciousness's conversion process—its generalized conversion to the commodity form. *Consciousness tends towards the consciousness of commodities*—that is the great lesson of Debord. We dream the dream of things. In cinema lies a key to the structure and relations, the physics and the metaphysics, the subjectivity and objectivity, in short the underlying *logic* of postindustrial society. The organization of consciousness is coextensive with the organization of postindustrial society, and the media are the belts that forge these organizing connections. Cinema inaugurates a shift in the economics of social production, and if it can be shown that such a shift achieves critical mass in cinema and its legacies of television, computer, internet, then it can be argued that cinema is not merely a *specific phenomenon* in which the sensorium becomes subject (subjugated) to a code existing beyond itself and indeed beyond "natural language," *but the general case*—the culmination and the paradigm of a historical epoch that supersedes the bourgeois mode of production by introjecting capitalized industrial process directly into the mindscape.

Shaviro comments that, in opposition to semantic and psychoanalytic film theory, which "remains so preoccupied with the theme of ideology and representation" and "regards editing primarily as a technique for producing . . . an illusion by suturing the spectator and perspectivizing the gaze, [a] wide variety of cinematic pleasures are predicated explicitly upon the decentered freeplay, the freedom from the constraints of subjectivity that editing and special effects make possible."[26] Although I agree with Shaviro up to a point, I also see such new forms of experience as essential modes of perception for existence in the nonsynchronic, schizophrenic milieu of postmodern society. They are the conditions of possibility for its perpetuation—a technology of management. In the cinema, we learn to cope with contradiction and discontinuity. By this, I mean to show that the affects produced by cinema are themselves engaged in manufacturing biosocial interfaces in late capitalism.

Benjamin writes of a Baudelaire, who

> speaks of a man who plunges into the crowd as into a reservoir of electric energy. Circumscribing the experience of the shock, he calls this man "a *kaleidoscope* equipped with consciousness." Whereas Poe's passersby cast glances in all directions which still appeared to be aimless, today's pedestrians are obliged to do so in order to keep abreast of traffic signals. Thus technology has subjected the human sensorium to a kind of training. There came a day when a new and urgent need for stimuli was met by the film. In a film, perception in the form of shocks was established as a formal principle. That which determines the rhythm of production on a conveyor belt is the basis of the rhythm of reception in the film.[27]

Though with today's television and email, the terms and conditions of movement through space have evolved beyond those met by the pedestrian, technology continues to train us to interface with the environment. The present analysis questions how "there came a day" when cinema, and later media in general, performed this entraining. It also explains the consequences of media's relation to "production on a conveyor belt." Today, in desperate measures to keep our world from flying apart at the contradictions, we are perhaps more apt to restrain the impact of shock with suture and continuity; however, discontinuity, illogic, and schizophrenia have their functions, also, as, to take but one example, the entirety of a book such as Noam Chomsky's *World Orders Old and New* implies.[28] As Paul Virilio writes, "videos and walkmans are reality and appearance in kit form: we use them not to watch films or listen to music, but to add vision and soundtracks, to make us directors of our own reality."[29] Such manufacturing of interfaces between bodies and machines requires labor from bodies and is productive of value—both cultural and economic. Social organization does not happen automatically, it requires work, labor power. Remarkably, it was Eisenstein who inaugurated the building of the first machines really suited to take advantage of this. Eisenstein's intention was to foster the 1917 Revolution by using *The Strike* to organize the labor necessary for its continuation and development. What he achieved, however, was the revolutionizing of a machine that would give capital a new hold on the living labor called perception.

In Deleuze's *Cinema* books, which, as I have suggested elsewhere, might have gone under the name *Cinema* in our century for reasons similar to those that prompted Marx to write under the name of *Capital* in the last, Deleuze writes that a cinema that has surpassed movement and has become a cinema of time "restores belief in the world," calling such belief "our only link."[30] Returning to our discussion of Metz, I would like to suggest that it is this "belief" that manifests itself in a variety of forms (none of which necessarily take the form of unified subjectivity or ideology), that is, even now, developing out of and into a new code, that is in the process of becoming symbolized. This symbolization is experienced subjectively as the production of new affects, desires, and identity formations. It also is experienced as the sublimity of the status quo. Objectively, the symbolic that is capital is digitalized, statisticized, militarized, and economized—it has the capacity in theory and practice to trump natural language. I am referring in the most literal way to the pricing of belief, and more generally of affect, by capital: to wit, the Orwellian language of contemporary nationalism and the aestheticization of fascist culture. What are corporations and politicians buying when they buy "airtime" if not, in the words of Antonio Negri, "productive social cooperation."[31] It is in response to the horror made possible by the increasing domination of the "natural" world and "natural language" by the affects of such economic calculus that Adorno wonders if there can be poetry after Auschwitz. No one, however, wondered if there could be movies. As global trends from statistical marketing to new social movements to the new fundamentalisms imply in as much as they represent the *formation* of nontraditional forms of social agency and action, belief is bought and sold, it organizes, it produces, it is, in short, labor. The labor of belief is one of the strong forms of what I call the *productive value of human attention.*

Through this general discussion, I am attempting to render an architectonics of the relationship between cinema—conceived as an advancement over the industrial mode of production—and human bodies. It is my hypothesis that cinema becomes, in its interaction with and incorporation of bodies, a mode of production in its own right. Cinema is a paradigm shift in the relation between organization and representation and is the characteristic effect of capitalized movement in general. As we shall see toward the end of this chapter, when Eisenstein's relationship to reflexology and Taylorization is discussed, film discovers new ways to do things to bodies. It is less *representation* than *presentation;* "signalization" in Pavlov's terms. Cinema as a process, a complex of movement, bodies, and consciousness, which I will refer to as cinematic process, becomes the dominant mode of production itself. Not all production passes through cinema in the institutional sense, but global production is *organized* as cinema is. Consciousness is dominated by the organization of movement—the organization of materials produces affect. In the cinematic organization of global production and reproduction, this logic will be interiorized in, and as, the postmodern to the extent that for the postmodern sensorium the world is a world of images. Cinema provides the architectonics of the logistics of perception for capital. Indeed, it represents their fusion. Hence, the cinematic has been machining the postmodern for nearly a century. In this sense, we can say that during the twentieth century, much of the world is literally in cinema, much in the way that the futurists intended to put the spectator inside the painting.[32] In other words, what Ken Surin calls "the consumption of society by capital," is made possible by the cinema and cinematic organization.[33] Reification, to take one example, is only a first-order approximation of the phenomenology of capital-driven movement. As capital envelops the environment, the entirety of affect (potentially) can be correlated with capital. Unlike Metz, then, I am not seeking to cause by theory what transpires in the imaginary to emerge in or as the symbolic. My project here is to isolate the organizational transformation of (in psychoanalytic language) the imaginary and the symbolic by the Lacanian Real, what in Jamesonian Marxism is known as History. Such a project takes the form of an indexical articulation of the industrialization of the sensorium; it is a necessarily schematic registration of a shift in the mode of production and the attendant transformation of the regime of value. Ideology, consciousness, cinema are not reflections of the material base—for *production passes through them.* Given the association of History with the Real, one can see that *The Strike,* as a product of the "manufactured past," is a historical formation, over and above its imaginary content that can be symbolized in and as a reading; it is, in a way that exceeds all its myriad gestures and interpretations, immersed in the space of the Real. At a level distinct from meaning, cinema is on a continuum with the Real. That Real (History as organization) is cut into the Spectator as a development of the unconscious with imaginary, symbolic, and *numismatic* effects.

Though other film theorists have argued that one encounters the Real in the cinema, none have shown that the *logic* of the Real manifests itself in cinema.[34] Of course, the notion that there is a logic to the Real runs counter to traditional notions of the Real itself; however, the Real (in Lacan's phrase, "that which eludes symbolization") is, for us, neither immutable nor ontologically given but historical. From the allegorical strategies of reading developed, for example, by Jameson and Terry Eagleton, which owe a tremendous debt to Althusser's idea of the Real as the mode of production, one can deduce that if the film is immersed in the space of the Real, then it is part of the mode of production. The Real is the manufacturing essence of the social—what hurts, in Jameson's phrase, but also what heals, and finally what moves. In the present mode of production, it is correct to say that, for Lacan, repetition is the encounter with the Real; but it is more useful, perhaps, to say that in Fordist and post-Fordist societies, repetition *is* the working of the Real. Meals, machine-guns, movie-film, DNA, and binary code all support such a claim.

Metz, I would suggest, only scratches the surface of a notion of the cinema as an agent of the Real when he touches on the structuring of the psyche by cinema, noting that "the cinematic institution is not just the cinema industry (which works to fill cinemas, not to empty them), it is also a mental machinery—another industry—which spectators 'accustomed to the cinema' have internalized historically and which has adapted them to the consumption of films."[35] Though Metz is right to state that cinema actively machines certain mentalities, the film industry does not, as Metz would have it, merely create its own consumers. Although cinema most assuredly has psychological repercussions for spectators, the "mental machinery" of the psyche has never been external to political economy. The cinema is a technology that develops in dialectical relation to the psyche's changing function in political economy. Gramsci already argued along similar lines when he asserted that Fordist manufacturing requires for the worker a new "psycho-social nexus."[36] Mental phenomena always have been a part of the production process, but cinema posits consciousness (perception?) as a general equivalent.[37] Consciousness becomes the medium and the frame that allows for the interface of bodies and society in the coming society. Cinema opens consciousness to the playful tyranny of exchange-value previously reserved (on a global scale) for bodies laboring only in a traditional sense. Cinema insists that consciousness (perception) work on exchange-value as exchange-value passes through it. Indeed, cinema is an elaboration of a process that was already taking place, albeit in primitive forms. It is a technology for mining consciousness (mental activity) of value.

Though there is still much to say regarding this point, I would like to put forth some of the claims and consequences that follow from the idea of the projection through the eye of the manufacturing logic of production for exchange-value by cinema (as well as other media, which are the developments of cinema):

1. Cinema is at once an organizational paradigm of social relations, a necessary technology for the conversion of the commodity form into an image, and a prototechnology for the capitalization of human attention. It is, in short, the paradigmatic technology for the commodification of human life up until the age of television. Just as private property, according to Marx, is not at first the cause of alienated labor but rather it is the effect, neither is cinema the cause of objects turning into images but the effect of their transformation. The conversion of objects into images is immanent in the commodity form. Cinema is an elaboration of the spectral aspects of the commodity in motion.

2. The cinematic mode of production relies upon a tandem structuring of perception and organization that results in the commodification of each—capital becomes the arbiter of the value of various organizational forms. It does this in the intensification of the circulation of the commodity-image. Tautologically, though accurately, stated, the more value the tandem structuring of perception, and organization produces, the more value it has. Cinema as cinema (as opposed to cinema as capital) is the perceptual excrescence of the material organization of an entire society. Cinema as cinema is the institutional matrix of bodies, perception, and industry, while cinema as capital is that institution functioning at once in its politico-economic dimension and as the paradigm for the totality of political economy. Capital-cinema posits, finally, the political economy of the society of the spectacle. Consciousness is the screen on which the regime of commodity movement carves its visceral speculations. Increasingly, all things are absorbed by cinema (capital) and appear on (or disappear from, depending on what is required) the screen of perception.

3. Therefore, the "symbolizing advance" that I intend concerning what Metz calls cinema's "second machine, that is, the social regulation of the spectators' metapsychology," extends far beyond the concept of

cinema's adaptation of spectators to the consumption of films, and indeed beyond psychology itself.[38] I am interested in the structural, psychological, libidinal, and corporeal adaptation of spectators to the protocols of global production. This conversion of spectating, generally conceived as a consumer activity, into a socially productive activity depends on the establishing of media as a *worksite* of global production. Today, mass media functions as a deterritorialized factory, where the maintenance and retooling of a transnational, transsubjective infrastructure composed of human beings, factories, cottage industries, service sectors, as well as programmed software and electronic hardware is *essential* to the valorization of capital. The cinematicity of objects is harnassed as an alternative force and used to intensify production. The cinema and its technological descendants extract the labor for the maintenance and calibration of the social totality. Without television, as well as fax-modems, telephones, computers, and digitized, computerized money, production would grind to a halt. Each of these media burrows its way into the flesh of the globe.[39] "The media" orchestrate production through the fleshy media of mind and body, while *appearing* as culture (or, for that matter, "democracy"). Cultural imperialism is not just culture in a one-dimensional sense, it is *imperialism*. As such, it puts into play all of traditional imperialism's dynamics of value exploitation (gated neighborhoods, police-states, unbearable working conditions, etc.), but it also puts up other barriers, as well (invisible walls that are visceral, ideological, perceptual), and extends the range of the body's malleability (through rhythm, desire, learning). The putting of non-Western and otherwise peripheral populations on line with the system's language of Western capitalism (the world-system) is an inexorable function of television. In short, the hypothesis here is that mass media, taken as a whole, is the deterritorialized factory, in which spectators do the work of making themselves over in order to meet the libidinal, political, temporal, corporeal, and, of course, ideological protocols of an ever-intensifying capitalism.

This hypothesis concerning population control does not rule out alternative practices; indeed, resistance takes place (as it traditionally has) in the very arena of domination. This aspect of political confrontation is precisely why Eisenstein was forced to use cinema to combat the encroachment of capital—capital was already invading visual perception. Television and other mass media are, more than anything else, technologies of social organization. What we do "there" today (moving our heart strings, internalizing rhythms, learning the codes of fashion and behavior, learning, above all, to fit in) is partially, in Marx's language "necessary labor." However, we also perform surplus labor, which becomes available as surplus value. More generally, this description of our activity characterizes productive participation in the cinematic machine of commodity circulation and distribution. The struggle over the appropriation and distribution of the value produced and channeled via spectatorial labor (most spectacularly and concretely manifested in the question of where the military hardware comes from and how is it used, but also visible as the vicissitudes of television news coverage, foreign policy, public opinion, institutional posts, and of all things created by the capturing of human attention [and human attending]) is arguably the most important struggle facing the coming century. Marx's *Capital* is, above all else, an analysis of how the general population's life is stolen from itself. The commodification of the public sphere and the attendant commodification of the sensorium brings the struggle with capitalism to the senses. Commodification, which derives its historical conditions of possibility from the induction of exchange-value in circulating use-values, a process that gave the use-value a spectral presence, finds its development in the production of image-value. The image marks the increasing eloquence of the specter of the commodity. Cinema is the possibility of the domestication of this very specter. Of course, such eloquence, such force, has its effect on the dynamics of human organization. *The Strike*, which contests the encroachment of capital on its own terms, marks an aggressive advance in the battle for the body according to the logistics of modern capitalism.

Because it falls outside of the orthodoxy of the labor theory of value and its rather nineteenth-century version of value-productive activity, spectatorial labor, which in the following chapters I will develop as a concept by following out the hypothesis of the productive value of human attention is only now beginning to be perceptible. The invisibility of the productive value of human attention for Marx is not a mere oversight; rather, it is an index of the historical development of the market economy. Bound by a particular historical conception of space, Marx could not think of the prosthetic extension of factory work outside of the space of the factory itself. The cinema had not yet been invented. Thus, for him, the circulation of capital is "the image of a process occurring behind it," not the production process itself.[40] For Marx, circulation is part of the process of production but not production itself; circulation is not the scene of labor. Today, the Nielsen ratings, for example, show that attention is becoming commodified formally as was labor under capital: What advertisers will invest in a certain media pathway depends on these ratings, because they index the quantity of attention available for production. Spectatorial labor gives up its attention to the specter of the object and merges with it, increasing its value. Such expropriation through commodification, already in place, demands a theory adequate to the sophistication of its practice. Given the long-standing "suspicion" regarding the perniciousness of the capitalist media, it is somewhat surprising that it has taken this long to suggest the possibility of a detailed political economy of its production of domination. However, the invisibility of domination has been one of the necessary aims and conditions of its production.

The concept of the economic alienation of sensual labor (and hence the senses) has been with us since the 1840s. In a formulation that might have inspired Benjamin's "orchid in the land of technology," Marx tells us in *The German Ideology* that German philosophy's "man" "does not see how the sensuous world is, not a thing given direct from all eternity, remaining ever the same, but the product of industry and of the state of society; and, indeed, in the sense that it is an historical product, the result of the activity of a whole succession of generations, each one standing on the shoulders of the preceding one, developing its industry and its intercourse, modifying its social system according to the changed needs. Even the objects of the simplest 'sensuous certainty' are only given through social development, industry and commercial intercourse."[41] That television and telecommunications are seen only as instruments of circulation suggests that Marx's concept of circulation—the mediation of value described above ("the image of a process occurring behind it")—needs to be rethought. Marx's rather cinematic trope signals that, in and of itself, circulation cannot produce value because the creation of surplus value takes place at a deeper level, in the production process itself, in other words, at the worksite. However, I am suggesting that the production process no longer occurs uniquely *behind* the image created by the commodity form in motion (what Marx here calls the movement of money); it occurs in the dynamics of the image itself—in its circulation, movement, incorporation.

In our experience with the fetish character of the image, we know one of the forms that this invisible labor of vision takes. This is more readily understandable when one realizes that, today, all things are images, in addition to whatever else they are. Put another way, all objects are signs—

how else could there have been semiotics? As we read them (Coke bottles, sneakers, automobiles, whatever), we produce their signification. The image is perceived not only in and of itself but as a consequence of the perception of others. The density of this perception of others is part of the quality of the image—its *caché*. In perceiving the fetish component of the image, we perceive the value accrued to it from the looks of others. Thus, we perceive that the media, as a deterritorialized factory, has become a worksite for global production. The value of our look *also* accrues to the image; it sustains the fetish. This new type of production is not a happy *accident* of the postmodern condition, a fortuitous cyber-buzz, but a cipher of the transformed dynamics of the global mode of production, a modality of the gaze that is infinitely repeatable and transferable. It is, at the same time, an innovation that works to stave off the falling rate of profit, since it increases the sites at and times during which value may be extracted. Cinema is an innovation in productive efficiency. Though I cannot develop this point here, let me say simply that if the circulation of capital is not grasped simultaneously as productive and exploitative, *then there is no more Marxism.*[42] Marxism is the active dialectical critique of the price of capitalist society. Despite Baudrillard's claim, in *For a Critique of the Political Economy of the Sign,* that it is the sober dialectic that collapses when all objects circulate and, as a result, become mediators, that is, ambiguous signs in polysemous movement, the jury is still out on the fate of the dialectic.[43] With all due respect to the Godard of Marxism, in cinematic spectatorship we are dealing with what the sociologists today call "disguised wage labor."

To Look Is to Labor. Struggle for the Body and Its Labor-Power.

This study of Eisenstein, then, concerns itself with the industrial and physiological conditions of possibility for the claim that to look is to labor. *How does industrial society fashion (posit and then presuppose) workers as spectators and then spectators as workers?* The psychological affects interrogated by Metz remain a highly relevant aspect of a general theory of cinema, even as, in the postmodern, psychology itself, as an autonomous arena of thought, begins to corrode. However, objects, the integrity of bodies as well as of traditions and of (certain aspects of) the nation-state also corrode during the twentieth century; all that is solid melts into film. To put this general theory of cinema in the context of Metz's discussion, it will be necessary to think the unthought of his textualized cinema described as an "institution [that] as a whole has filmic pleasure alone as its aim."[44]

As I have been trying to suggest, many other politico-economic elements besides the spectator's pleasure are mobilized in the exchange between spectators and films. Moreover, the circuit traversed by spectatorship is far more complex than the relation described by Metz—unless, perhaps, one takes his statement regarding "filmic pleasure" to be an incomplete expression of the consciousness-effect of present-day global organization. His metaphor of cinema as an internal machine could then be read as an intimation of the cinematic mode of production itself. This misreading, which depicts the "great Globe (of globalization) itself" as an institution that has as its sole aim the production of the pleasures of the global spectacle as the gateway to the profit system, is partially correct. "Filmic pleasure," then, is at once an effect and a necessary condition of the capitalist world-system. Such a misreading would make of Metz's efforts to win cinema for the symbolic a remarkably intuitive, yet finally unsuccessful, effort to chart the commodification dynamics of the image. The symbolic, in the psychoanalytic sense, is a rudimentary form of commodification, a realm of cutting and rendering that is in practice similar to commodification but in form analogical—not fully digitized. One might be tempted to read the symbolic itself as an allegory of the Real, in other words, as the mode of production. The language of phonemes and graphemes, however, is, from the present perspective of postmodern production, simply low tech; they belong to the modern. So much of what actually gets done in the world gets done without entering language (even though it places pressures on language and creates fissures in it). Although, from the standpoint of late capitalism, the symbolic is proto-commodification, it is, as intellectual work readily bears witness in the ages of cinema and television, commodifiable and commodifying. Words, too, have changed; they have become cinematic. We structure phenomenon and circulate their images in the marketplace of ideas. Cinema is, for Metz, an encounter in the imaginary, which can be won for the symbolic. In the view that I am elaborating here, cinema as cinema is an exemplary form of a generalized system of relations that is fully inscribed in the mode of production today, an affect machine inducing new forms of labor for the new state of capital.[45] In other words, it already has been won for the symbolic; that is, cinema is a victory of the symbolic of capital in that it is the archetypical medium in the battle for the body waged (via "seduction," but, more generally, enframing) for the symbolic of capital (money, or human attention, depending upon which moment in the dialectic production is being thought from).

The twentieth century marks the emergence of the struggle for the body in the realm of the visible. Today, consumption is productive not because it is part of the necessary circulation and destruction of objectified labor time (value) that takes place elsewhere and that is essential for the valorization of capital but because it is labor power itself that appropriates and valorizes commodities to particular ends, which are themselves productive of images. In giving his or her attention to an object, the spectator modifies both him or herself and it, thereby producing and reproducing the ever-developing infrastructure of the status quo.

Behaviorism, Scientific Management, Cinema.

The movement toward the twenty-first century brings with it the emergence of the visual as a realm of heightened political struggle because it becomes a realm of political economy. However, the commodification of the visible world is consonant with the fact that the most barefaced regimes of power have undergone a sort of transformation during the twentieth century: from military dictatorship to military spectatorship. The groundwork is laid early on for this shift to military spectatorship, in the development of the eye as a pathway for the regulation of the body. By the beginning of the twenty-first century, the eye becomes the preeminent link between body and world.[46] But in addition to the organization of the visual there are other significant developments in corporeal regulation that coalesce as cinema.

Eisenstein's cinematic practice, inasmuch as it is an endeavor to organize bodies, is not idiosyncratic but emerges out of a conceptual framework that was shared by other important innovators of his period. Especially important for us here are two other organization theorists, Ivan Petrovich Pavlov and Frederick Winslow Taylor. In the remainder of this chapter, I shall sketch the manner in which Eisenstein's work is a synthesis of the most important aspects of Pavlov and Taylor's findings. Taken together, the shared elements of their work represent the emergence of a new strategy for the controlled organization of bodies and society. Pavlov is concerned with the microprocesses of the biological organism; Taylor, with the macroprocesses of the social organism, and Eisenstein, with the synthesis of the two. Their work, predicated on techniques of selection, repetition, and conditioning, as well as on the logic of the location and isolation of discreet processes that then can be mechanically coordinated, develops technologies capable of putting bodies in line with the new protocols of intensifying industrialization.

In the failure of the dictatorship of the proletariat to come into being in the Soviet Union of the 1920s and in the grave disappointment known as state capitalism, we find the first fruits of an organizational practice that, in effect, renders the conversion of the proletariat from potential dictators (sayers) into spectators (watchers). In the absence of the libidinal (cinematic) incentives of the free market, cinema itself was called upon explicitly to "motivate" workers. "Of all the arts, film is for us the most important," Lenin is reported to have said (*Writings*, 155).[47] Stalin went so far to describe the artist as "an engineer of the soul."[48] It is, finally, in the form that this motivation/engineering took that we discover the production of the spectatorship of the proletariat. Such a phenomenon occurred simultaneously in the West, and indeed reigns today, but we can detail its emergence more readily in the Soviet Union.

In many ways that were partially unnecessary in the West, cinema had to compensate for the lack of a fully industrialized milieu. It had to extract some of the work on Soviet sensoriums that the cinematic organization of daily life extracted in the Western industrialized world. Because Soviet cinema had to bear a greater responsibility for achieving industrialization by adjusting workers to their tasks (and to their task of watching) than did cinema in the West, one finds in the Soviet cinema of the late twenties a more concentrated form of the tendencies of cinema generally to convert the worker into a spectator first and, later, to make him or her produce online, in the worksite of the sensorium and the public sphere, that is, during spectating, as spectator. In Eisenstein's work, early twentieth-century means of production (industrial and scientific) are re-engineered as means of representation—that is, industrial technologies and manufacturing logic codify as cinema and yield a method of representation. However, in the hands of Eisenstein, this new means of representation remained quite self-consciously a means of production. Representation was designed with social production foremost in mind. The dual (dialectical) function of Eisenstein's cinema achieves the maturation of the conditions immanent early on in the cinematic mode of production, because it regulates consciousness via industrial means for the sake of industrial development. This is not to say that the cinematic mode of production begins with Eisenstein, or that it even requires him; only that his work is paradigmatic of the structure and function of a mature cinema. The inauguration of a spectatorial economy in which spectators and spectatorial labor are involved directly in production is an important step forward in the realization of processes that are the preconditions of postmodern culture and economy. But let me here broaden the base of my argument.

In stating the overriding motivation for the entirety of his work, Pavlov writes in *Conditioned Reflexes* that, for the future, "it may be hoped that some of the more complex activities of the body, [such] as 'playfulness,' 'fear,' 'anger,' and so forth, will soon be demonstrated as reflex activities of the subcortical parts of the brain."[49] The rationalization of the function, the full predictability, and the final controllability of affect implied by Pavlov's statement are in many ways the ultimate goals of his work. For example, Pavlov dramatizes the struggle of the scientific quest for control on the occasion of finding in a dog that "simply could not remain quiet when it was constrained" for experiments, what he dubs "a special *freedom reflex*" that could only be "overcome by setting off another against it—the reflex for food."[50] Though couched in a rhetoric of objective inquiry, Pavlov's goals of mental and corporeal control may be compared here with Taylor's avid description of the fruits of scientific management in important ways. For Taylor, "scientific management consists in a complete revolution in the mental attitude and the habits of all of those engaged in the management, as well [as] the workmen."[51] Science and industry (whose technologies are, at the turn of the century, on a convergence course that only materializes fully in the political economy of the contemporary military industrial complex—that is, in the technology that Howard Rheingold refers to in a celebratory manner as "The Reality-Industrial Complex") have, each in their own way, the regulation of brain function on their agendas.[52] Both science and industry were attempting to find social methods of physiological regulation. While Pavlov wants to map and control the neuronal network, Taylor wants to redesign the industrial productive apparatus to similar ends. Each of their endeavors requires a similar ideology of manipulation and control, which puts the priorities of the thinking scientist before those of the "object" of study. Each develops scientific forms of consciousness (as science) and other, quite different forms of consciousness for the organisms subjected to, and affected by, their science. Though Pavlov and his battalion of scientists speculated on the long-range implications of their work for animals and humans, there is in their writings little or no registration of the experiences of the experimental subjects, animal or human. Indeed, the goal of reflexology was to understand the organism by bypassing subjectivity. It must have seemed to most of the scientists that their more immediate task was only to reconceive the structure of the lower animals, not to impose it. However, the violence of their methods speaks otherwise. A similar relation inheres in Taylor's system: While workers were often conceived of as animals (Taylor's "trained gorilla") and treated accordingly, there was never any question among scientific managers that scientists were human researchers furthering human goals and knowledge. Managers and scientists had only to reconceive their roles; workers and animals, on the other hand, had to be reconceived.

It is important to reiterate here that Eisenstein synthesizes the organizational aspects of Taylorization and Pavlovian logic as cinematic practice. One sees the general form of the synthesis of neuronal and industrial research, of Pavlovian logic (what Eisenstein refers to in his own writings as "reflexology") and Taylorization, in Eisenstein's famous phrase, "Reforging someone else's psyche is no less difficult and considerable a task than forging iron" (*Writings*, 49). The type of reforging that engages Eisenstein has physical, psychological, and industrial dimensions. Cinema is the conjunction of these social formations. Because the "manufacturing essence" of cinematic movement meets and then incorporates the body of the spectator by mediating between the microstructures (neuronal networks) and the macrostructures (the world-system) in which the human animal is immersed, it follows that Eisenstein's cinema is an extension of capital logic into the bodies it regulates. As will be seen, reflexology and Taylorization correspond to various crises in the development of the productive forces of society—crises of intensifying capitalism. Eisenstein's extension to the cinema of Pavlov's and Taylor's functionalist "solutions" to these crises of capital (the control of populations for the sake of profit) is at the same time an extension of capital logic into the cinema. The translation of the organizational logic of scientific method to the body via the cutting together of industry and the eye is an aggressive effort to organize a spectator proper.

Animals, Labor, History.

Consider for a moment the truth content found in the well-known photograph of Eisenstein giving one of his rare smiles as he shakes hands with Mickey Mouse.[53] Eisenstein's ostensible political project was oriented toward the obliteration of capitalist relations; however, his (necessary?) belief that there were laws of production existing somehow above or beyond their presentation (theory that translates into practice rather than theory *as* practice) would betray him. Ultimately, the early films are propaganda machines (of a very complex kind) designed to capture the imagination of the masses. For as rooted in the social fabric as *The Strike* is, and seems, the artist's point of view comes from a different place, and that, an alienated one. In his writings, Eisenstein always was engaging in the play of light and shadow, always boasting or insulting or prevaricating. He was relentlessly ironic. Of course, this pose is the vantage point of his genius, but it was also the lived testament of his failure. *The Strike* and *Potemkin,* at least, are finally utopian carrots. This pretense of possible utopia makes the machines that Eisenstein built Wizard-of-Oz-like, greater than the man who built them. In film history, such a relation makes for fantastic cinema; in national history, when the machine is greater than the people, it is Stalinism that is made. Like Moses, Eisenstein and his "beloved" workers would never enter the promised land. But then again, neither would anyone else.

Eisenstein stood outside his work, trying to manipulate the Real from the symbolic, trying to change History, in Jameson's sense of the word, via political theory. If one were to replace "History" with "animals" and "labor," such a conceptual architecture suddenly would appear to be common to the thought of Pavlov and Taylor respectively; it would reveal the scientistic aspect of their work. History is to political theory what environment is to science and what the market is for scientific management, the ground of theoretical inquiry and experimentation, and the site of practical application. Eisenstein, Pavlov, and Taylor each engage in the practical conceit that their innovations require—in Althusser's words, "the understanding of the overdetermining force of one structure on another."[54] We can descry this relation in Eisenstein's assertion of "the ideological character of form," for example, which implies that form is an instance or an iteration of a particular type of consciousness, practice, or worldview.[55] The necessary corollary here is that *his* revolutionary worldview should determine artistic form. His deep-felt sense of the truth of this statement, the equivalent of believing Marx's dictum that "Great men make history but only such history as they can make," while simultaneously believing oneself to be a great man, ought to be known as the Stalinist's bind. For Eisenstein, his perception of the *correct* practices for the development of socialism had direct *formal* consequences on his work.[56]

Similarly, for Pavlov, an overcoding machine exists that will determine, and has determined the structure of the nervous system. This machine, which for Pavlov presents itself as a baseline reality in the form of the natural environment and the process of natural selection, is immanent in the very idea of "conditioned reflexes." The nervous system develops in an environment that determines its structure through functional selection; some responses are hardwired, others have a degree of variability that can be altered by conditioning. The nervous system therefore can be mapped by noting the effects on behavior of controlled stimuli. Like Eisenstein, Pavlov believes in a hierarchy of structure. Natural selection and environment overdetermine the structure of the nervous system: Animals find their niches. For Pavlov, by controlling the elements of the selective environment, one eventually controls the brain.

For Taylor, the untheorized but still overarching structure that overdetermines the logistics of labor is capitalist relations and the falling rate of profit. Although the falling rate of profit is not theorized by Taylor, combating it is precisely what he means by "efficiency." (Gramsci recognizes the same exigencies in the innovations of Fordism, seeing it "as the ultimate stage in the process of progressive attempts to overcome the law of the tendency of the rate of profit to fall."[57]) Scientific management is a strategy for Taylor but also a destiny, an ethos, a "philosophy." Management, according to this philosophy, is the medium via which labor will be tailored to meet the objective and overarching exigencies of a capitalism intensified via science. For Taylor, management and the laborer are media that, for capitalism's expansion, it requires in order to reorganize the structure of the labor. For Pavlov, the nervous system and, finally, the science of reflexology, are media that natural selection requires in order to reorganize the structure of animal responses. For Eisenstein, film and the spectator were the media that socialism required in order to reorganize the structure of society. In a manner germane to the ethos of all three "scientists," Taylor calls for "the substitution of science for the individual judgement of the workman" and uses scientific management effectively to wrest control of the shop floor from labor (SM, 114). The same limiting effect on the individual organism's agency championed by scientific management is also found in Pavlov's management of the brain, or, for that matter, Eisenstein's management of the spectator. The key in all three cases was the manipulation of life force in accord with agency imposed from outside the individual organism. Although in the name of revolution the workers in The Strike were represented as men, they were being treated like dogs—more specifically, like Pavlov's dogs. From Taylor's "trained gorilla," Pavlov's dogs and chimpanzees, and Eisenstein's proletariat (who are always lovable, like dogs), we can see that all three of their techniques target the agency and cognitive experience of subaltern "animals."

Victory over the Brain. Forging the Audience's Psyche.

Pavlov's work on conditioned reflexes, along with the technical means that he used to establish experiments and controls, were well known and tremendously influential in postrevolutionary Russia. For Pavlov, "a stimulus appears to be connected of necessity with a definite response, as cause with effect" (*CR*, 7). His input/output concept of organisms, human and otherwise, did not so much bypass the psyche as conceive of it as a machine-like residue of cause and effect. He thought of the brain as a mediating artifact, however complex, of stimulation, and, hence, as a scientifically malleable formation. The nervous system was a developing medium for the translation of signaled stimuli into responses. "Reflexes, like the driving belts of machines of human design may be of two kinds—positive and negative, excitatory and inhibitory [P]hysiologists are succeeding more and more in unravelling the mechanism of these machine-like activities of the organism and may reasonably be expected to elucidate and control it in the end" (*CR*, 8). Into the psyche, Pavlov projects the organizational principles of mechanization. He diagrams a "manufacturing essence" internal to the body, a machinic communication system connected by belts and pulleys *within the body* that has a structure much like the image of Eisenstein's factory in *The Strike*. The image of the factory was also an image of the nervous system. The historical project was to alter its organization. Tragic as it may be, nervous system, factory, and cinema manufactured what is now a past, which, in 1989, was brought online with official capitalism.

The introjection of the formal organization of manufacturing into the nervous system was in some respects the paramount achievement of Pavlov's work. At the close of a series of public lectures delivered, appropriately, at the Military Medical Academy in Petrograd during the spring of 1924, Pavlov wrote, "In concluding this series of lectures which have set as their object a purely physiological interpretation of the activity of the higher nervous system [w]e have indisputably the right to claim that our investigation of this extraordinarily complex field has followed the right direction, and that, although not a near, nevertheless a complete, success awaits it" (*CR*, 410). This "complete success" is twofold: the total mapping of the manufacturing essence of the higher nervous system, and a corresponding victory over the brain—its total control. If the human being could be conceived as a group of machines, it could be modified as one.

Even more eagerly received than the work of Pavlov was Taylor's theory of Scientific Management. This doctrine, whose oxymoronically stated objective was "to secure the maximum prosperity for the employer, coupled with the maximum prosperity for the employee" (*SM*, 9), quickly became a national and then an international theory of organization known in Europe as Americanism. Like Pavlov's concept of the human body, in which "the whole activity of the organism should conform to definite laws" (*CR*, 7), Taylor posits the same ideals for industrial management: "When men, whose education has given them the habit of generalizing and everywhere looking for laws, find themselves confronted with a multitude of problems, such as exist in every trade and which have a general similarity one to another, it is inevitable that they should try to gather these problems into certain logical groups, and then search for some general laws or rules to guide them in their solution. The philosophy of scientific management places their solution in the hands of management" (*SM*, 103). This excavation of laws, with an eye toward a trinity of efficiency, predictability, and social control, informs a conceptualization of industrial production that is at one with Pavlov's conceptualization of the laws governing the function of the human organism. In both cases, the laws can be discovered and manipulated for "productive" ends. Eisenstein synthesized the "philosophy" of laws governing industrial production and the "science" of laws governing the nervous system in order to create machines that for the sake of helping the young Soviet state to compete with capitalism, would "forge the audience's psyche."

Audience as Material and Medium.

The combination of the fleshy microstructures posited by Pavlov and of the industrial macrostructures posited by Taylor finds expression in the following words of Eisenstein: "I am a civil engineer and mathematician by training. I approach the making of a motion picture in much the same way as I would approach the equipment of a poultry farm or the installation of a water system. My point of view is thoroughly utilitarian, rational, materialistic."[58] Eisenstein invokes engineering not as mere expressive rhetoric, that is, as analogy, but as a method. *The Strike* functions as an excellent example of this method. Throughout his career, and even beyond what some see as a shift in his preoccupations with the mechanistic reflexology of Pavlov and Bekhterev to ideas of organicity and unity, Eisenstein pursues this vision of cinema and reiterates it as late as 1937: "I am regarded as one of the most 'inhuman' of artists. The description of the human being has never been either the central or the most fundamental concern of my works. In my basic cast of mind I have always been more pre-occupied with *movement*—mass movements, social movements, dramatic movement—and my creative interest has always been more keenly directed towards *movement itself.*"[59]

In many respects, the words of one of Eisenstein's cold war critics remains correct: Soviet Cinema represented "a triumph over humanity."[60] The triumph of movement over humanity, equally well indexed by Taylor's slogan, "In the past the man has been first; in the future the system must be first" (*SM*, 7), indexes two distinct phases of social development. The shift from the first (humanity) to the second (movement) is clear; it is the crisis called modernism, the transformation of traditional societies into machine societies, of organic life into life plagued by shock and constrained by Max Weber's iron cage of reason. However, in Taylor's second phase, the "future," two separate moments of systemic dominance must be differentiated. In Stage 1 of this future, Taylor posits the worker as a part of the productive machine and represents him as such. In cinema history, one of the most extraordinary early *representations* of his imperative "the system must be first" can be found in the representation of the worker on the assembly line in Charlie Chaplin's *Modern Times*. As a worker, Chaplin's movements are represented as being dictated and then conditioned by machine technology. But Eisenstein—who initiates a transition from Stage 1 (the *positing* that human function can be controlled by rationally designed machines) to Stage 2 (the *presupposition* that human function can be controlled by rationally designed machines) did not *represent* the human being as a part in the machine; rather, *he presupposed it as such*, taking a primarily behavioristic approach toward his audience. The conception of a mechanical fit of human being in a social and cinematic system was incorporated into Eisenstein's cinematic strategy, not as a matter of representation, but as a matter of practice. Eisenstein thought it possible to "envision in both theory and in practice a construction, with no linking plot logic, which provokes a chain of the necessary unconditioned reflexes which are, at the editor's will, associated with—predetermined phenomena and by this means to create the chain of new conditioned reflexes that these phenomena constitute" (*Writings*, 49). For him, "this [accomplishment] signifies a realization of the orientation [of the spectator] towards the thematic effect, i.e., a fulfillment of the agitational purpose" (*Writings*, 49). *The audience is already built into the system, part of the raw material on which the social machine may work.*

Audience of Dogs.

"A work of art is first and foremost a tractor ploughing over the audience's psyche in a particular class context" (*Writings*, 62). This phrase shows that for Eisenstein, human subjects not only are homogenized as raw material by cinema but are made interchangeable, exchangeable. As with the carefully conditioned dogs of Pavlov, and the workers who made it through the brutal weeding-out processes of Taylor, Eisenstein's "audience is known and selected in advance for its homogeneity" (*Writings*, 41).[61] "The script," for Eisenstein, like the carefully controlled experiments of Pavlov, and like Taylor's daily directions written to the workers, "expresses the purpose of the experience that the audience must undergo" (*Writings*, 34). It is "a 'prescription' that summarizes the general projected emotional effect on the audience and the pressure that will inevitably be exerted on the audience's psyche" (*Writings*, 46). Such prescribed techniques of mechanical manipulation also begin to show that, in effect, Taylor's workers and Pavlov's dogs may be thought of as earlier types of audiences, experimental spectators. Eisenstein, Pavlov, and Taylor create machines that produced subjective effects, as they met objective necessities. These effects were necessary to their machines' function. By conceiving the masses as interchangeable components of the cinematic machine, Eisenstein endeavored to engineer a cinema that would engineer a population. The echo of Pavlov can be heard in Eisenstein's words: "We want to restore the *qualitatively* differentiated and the alienated and individualized into something that is *quantitatively* correlated" (*Writings*, 156). This "restoration" is much like the effect of the money economy on the object world: objects, though qualitatively different as use-values, may be "quantitatively correlated" as exchange-values. Eisenstein's films are intent upon converting workers into subjects—subjects of history, perhaps, but subjects whose behavior he could control.[62]

As director, Eisenstein saw his responsibility as "the organization of the audience through organized material" (*Writings*, 63). Structurally, the director here has the same role as Taylor's manager and Pavlov's scientist. Like Taylor's efforts to "organize" his workers, and Pavlov's efforts to organize his dogs, Eisenstein's cinema can be seen as a first effort to lock onto the spectator's sensorium in a scientifically calculated way. That workers, spectators, and animals were imagined as a single amalgamation is not simply an idiosyncrasy of Eisenstein or of this analysis.[63] Wherever instrumental rationality pressed, animality appeared. We may discern this general case here, in 1924, when Maxim Gorky wrote: "The fundamental obstacle in the path of Russia's progress towards Europeanisation and culture is the zoological individualism of the peasantry."[64]

As I have noted, the calculated orchestration of the audience's emotions and activities, so much a part of Eisenstein's filmwork, was in many ways, in direct contradiction to the explicit thematics of Eisenstein's films. Thematically, his films emphasized workers' autonomy and their revolutionary role. Given the historical path of the Soviet "experiment," however, Eisenstein's cybernetic incorporation of the spectator into the cinematic machine runs counter to the films' explicit ideologies. His mobilization of the masses conceived of spectators as fuel for his engines of change—to be blunt, a new form of labor to be harnessed, "steam!"—and he harnessed them through a vision of their own humanity. Even if the workers had a revolutionary role, in the end, it had little to do with their autonomy. Eisenstein, I believe, knew this in spite of his hope to the contrary, hence his irony.

This assertion is not to claim that Eisenstein was not part of a revolution, only that in the historical long view, the revolution of which he was a part largely differs from the one thematized in his early films. The production of film as a factory for laboring sensoriums is widespread today. Presciently, Eisenstein felt that the spectator inevitably was conditioned by the cinematic apparatus, even warning that "th[e] pure method of training the reflexes through performance effect deserves the careful attention of people organizing educational films and theater that quite unconsciously cram children with an entirely unjustified repertoire of reflexes trained through performance" (*Writings*, 49). Hence, it is not only ideology in the sense of false consciousness that the spectator is subject to, but a physical attuning. For Eisenstein, the solution to this danger was that the spectator should be made over properly by placing the cinematic apparatus in the capable hands of a politically correct director. Filmed material was to be found "(as in *The Strike*) [by] snatching fragments from our surroundings *according to a conscious and pre-determined plan calculated to launch them at the audience in the appropriate combination, to subjugate it to the appropriate association with* the obvious *final ideological motivation*" (*Writings*, 63). Such an experience was to re-energize the workers, giving them the ideological motivation, as well as the physical ability, to meet the demands of the production process. That they were being exploited as they made "their" revolution was, and remains, a problem for history to solve.

"The organization of the audience through organized material" also accurately describes the strategy of Pavlov's work on his audience of dogs. The phrase also describes the strategy of the method regarding Pavlov's audience of students, military men, doctors, and scientists, who are, according to the theory of reflexology, on a continuum with the dogs that served as examples. Here, I have two senses of the word *organization* in mind: 1) the production of organs themselves, through their identification and through the determination and delimitation of their function; and 2) the extension of such an "organizing" principle to the institutional and bureaucratic process of the research itself. *Organization* implies the organization of both the nervous system and of knowledge itself in accord with scientific rationality. The principles of organization projected onto the dogs' nervous systems contain in miniature—holographically, as it were—the architecture of the bureaucratic and institutional organization of Pavlov's scientific research in general. In the research, and in the object of research, there is an uncanny mirroring effect that amounts to an epistemological tautology.

Pavlov partitioned out his research to many different students and doctors, each with his own reflex to explore, each with his own dog or monkey to corporally cut and—I might as well say it—edit. The same mechanical principles of division and functionalism thought to organize the brain of the dog also organized the research itself. Like individual nerve synapses, the scientists would convene, reporting the state of their stimuli in order to make (scientific) consciousness.[65] The research, organized as described, took place on an object organized by the same logic and provided a rational picture of a rational system that then could be generalized to the human brain. In other words, the spread of organizational partitions begins to make the observer look like the observed until, finally, they are one and the same. The knowledge of the brain is organized like the brain itself. In this circuit of relations, the structure of scientific knowledge itself becomes manifest proof of its claims regarding the structure of the brain. The structure of legitimacy (science) ratifies legitimate structures (reflexes). This relation extends the logic of rationality into the dual provinces of knowledge and the body. The direct relation between the organization of the object (the nervous system) and the organization of the medium for the perception of the object (science) takes the form of the idea that knowledge is structured like the brain. Object (the nervous system) and media (science), science proudly announces, each have a rationalized manufacturing essence, a like organization. This like organization, however violently imposed, creates the effect of a harmonious relation between observer and observed.

Antithesis of Vertov's Object-Image Is Eisenstein's Spectator-Worker. The Dominant Mode of Production Becomes the Dominant Mode of Representation.

To emphasize the full significance of the organization of a spectator, it will be necessary for me to return to Dziga Vertov's *Man with a Movie Camera*. In chapter 1, I showed how *Man with a Movie Camera* posits cinema as a specific mode of production's highest form of self-articulation. This extraordinary film inaugurates, for Vertov, a revolutionary epoch that goes beyond mere man: humanity with a *movie camera*. Technologically mediated, perception opens for Vertov possibilities of social transparency regarding the mode of production, collectivity, and critique. In chapter 1, I suggest that it is, in effect, the convergence of the industrial processes that produce commodities and of the industrial processes that produce images that makes Vertov possible. Not only does cinema depend on industrial technologies, it takes the form of the assembly line; moreover, the assembly line takes the form of cinema. The dynamics of the object (ordinarily reified under the regime of commodification) and the dynamics of the image coalesce and are unified in one process: cinema. Vertov reveals this relation. Each object/image is in circulation, each is produced in industrial processes, each signifies, and each has value. In Vertov, each image is a socially produced object, and each object is an image. It is in the circulation of these object-images that consciousness is produced. Using the technology of capital, Vertov endeavors to institute cinematically a form of circulation alternative to the reificatory circulation of capital(ism).

The significance of Vertov's object-images for my discussion of Eisenstein is as follows: The production of the spectator from the worker (the spectator-worker) in Eisenstein will be the other side of the convergence of commodity (industrial object) and image (the object-image) in Vertov, its dialectical antithesis. Thus, the spectator and the image replicate at a dematerialized (higher) level the relationship between labor and commodities. The being-integrated processes of vision and work coalesce in the spectator, as do the being-integrated processes of representation and commodity production in the image. The generalized form of the commodity-image that one finds posited in Vertov requires, antithetically, the generalized form of the worker-spectator posited in Eisenstein.

Keeping in mind the convergence of image and commodity, on the one hand, and of labor and vision, on the other, we may better grasp how the relations of capital become steadily dematerialized. As I am attempting to show, the organizational movement of capital has a tendency toward cinema. Even before the invention of cinema proper, the movement of capital was cinematic. It should be possible, therefore, to read a text such as Marx's *Grundrisse* as a form of early cinema. There especially, capital is the frame through which the metamorphosis of the world appears. That the organization of capitalist production is becoming the organization of the cinematic production of society is true not only in cinema proper but also in science and industry. Because of the overall tendency of capital to pass between the poles of image (commodity) and spectator (worker) through the media (circulation), science and industry begin to resemble cinema. In Eisenstein's period, the dominant mode of production becomes the dominant mode of representation, and, in doing so, the dominant mode of production achieves a qualitative shift. A half-century or so down the road this dominant mode of representation will itself become the dominant mode of production. When the industrial means of production become a means of representation, they inaugurate a new mode of production. What Eisenstein makes from Pavlov and Taylor serves as a demonstration in miniature of what cinema makes from the money economy and what the money economy makes out of cinema. In placing the commodity-image in dialectical relation to the worker-spectator, cinema becomes the organizational paradigm of capital. In the process, the society of the spectacle supersedes bourgeois society; the industrial mode of production is superseded by the cinematic mode of production.

True to the critique of Eisenstein made by Vertov, Eisenstein endeavors to make the spectator over in the form of the image.[66] The dominant vector of expression in Eisenstein is not an effort to articulate the totality of social relations, in which the spectator is a producer of the conditions of possibility of the image itself, as in Vertov. Rather, Eisenstein's films work wholly within the said totality occluding its dynamics by positing it as concept, or as somewhat less than a concept, as an ideal, a goal to be achieved. Hence, Eisenstein renders invisible the subtle dependence of the social totality, upon an infinity of interactions, leaving it to the province of theoreticians such as himself.

The Strike, unlike *Man with a Movie Camera,* is not an effort to articulate the viewers' places in the social totality so that viewers might understand themselves as a creative part of a variegated social fabric and base their actions on that understanding. Eisenstein dismissed this contemptuously as contemplation; *The Strike* is an effort to *put the viewers in their place* utilizing an image that assumes a prior and superior knowledge of totality.

Thus, his films are, in many ways, antithetical to Vertov's. The violence of Eisenstein's cinema comes from the effort to force an unspecified, but supposedly shared, past and present into an equally unspecified, but *projected*, future. His films are machines for particular situations, and they are designed to get the job done. Eisenstein, the planner, wants to affect a change within totality by harnassing a force. He puts himself in the position of the avant-garde, however, since he assumes the position of the one who knows the nature of that totality and the direction necessary for it to move in order for it to achieve its goals. As Eisenstein said, commenting on Vertov's films, "It is not film-eye we need but film-fist!" Because Eisenstein conceives of his films not merely as a representation of revolutionary practice but as revolutionary practice orchestrated according to methods that he might have described, by using Taylor's phrase, as "the one best way," he runs the risk run by all avant-gardes: the making of the wrong revolution. Eisenstein wrote, "There is only one way for making *any* film: the montage of attractions," and in his work, he found it unnecessary, or impossible, to incorporate a dynamic self-representation of totality open to critique, as did Vertov; in its stead, he supplied a monolithic image (*Writings*, 65). He treated his viewers like subjects in his image, subjects with the same formation as himself, but lesser inasmuch as they required no theory, no consciousness of the image's formation. That was for the filmmaker. Viewers were to realize the goals of the film. Directed, as it were, from above, *The Strike* submits the psyche to a new phase of industrialization that assumed a lesser degree of individual agency, for workers and spectators alike. This reduction of individual agency, for the sake of mass agency (what Eisenstein called "correlation," and elsewhere "subjugation"), was the goal.

Universality of Montage. Cut, Paste.

What is perhaps most extraordinary about Pavlov's work is that the rationalized stimuli perpetrated on the dogs—aural tones, violent lacerations, shades of light and dark, acid enemas, electric shocks, amputations—and the development of methods for the accounting of responses, were only a prelude of things to come in science, cinema, and in society generally. The gulags, the concentration camps, and U.S. imperialist wars during the twentieth century are only the most pronounced realizations of the emerging technologies of population control. Not only do Pavlov's experiments with electricity, lamps, and knives give a new meaning to the surgical cinema mentioned by Walter Benjamin, but the process of cutting culture into bodies as endemic to mediation is becoming clearer.[67] Such a concept of culture is now generally understood since Michel Foucault's work on discourse, or, even more appropriately here, the work of Elaine Scarry, especially her book *The Body in Pain: The Making and Unmaking of the World,* but the role of media, which does much of the work done by discourse and war, remains to be explored.[68] Opinion polls, market research, credit profiles, viewer surveys, and television programming in general are today's statisticized equivalents of methods of accounting for pain. Though on the surface such forms of accounting may not seem as painful, they are at present endemic to a society that thrives on generalized pain inasmuch as pain is productive, just as is labor, starvation, or killing in war. All such orchestrations of corporeality are, at present, endemic to social production and reproduction; they are myriad responses to the stimulus of capital. The modification of bodies through pain (as well as exemption from pain, even pleasure) is synonymous with the logistical development of the mechanics of capital. Today, stimulus-response logic, the rationalized orchestration of stimulation, is known in the vernacular as programming. Whether in computers or televisions, programming converts movements into data and data into images, which then feed back into and influence movements. Consciousness is influenced by material organization in the circulation of value. Though this is an old story, it has reached new proportions, cinematic proportions. Because the value produced in mediation accrues back to the proprietors of the media, cinema and television today function to reconcile the irreconcilable: capitalism and democracy. As we see in the work of Taylor, who insisted upon the necessity of regulating the habits of workers both within and *outside* the workplace (he wanted to regulate their morality, their drinking habits, even their dreams), the rationalized and instrumental orchestration of stimulation arises simultaneously with the rationalized and instrumental orchestration of movement. In full-blown cinema, these two registers are combined. This combination is the condition of possibility for democracy under capitalism—people are perfectly free to move in the ways that they are programmed to move.

The table that follows summarizes the comparison of Pavlov and Taylor with Eisenstein thus far.

That Eisenstein, Pavlov, and Taylor all utilized montage requires some elaboration. For Pavlov, "external stimuli [that] have been from the very birth of the animal transmitted to a definite center, can, notwithstanding, be diverted and made to follow another route, becoming linked up by the

Comparison of Pavlov, Taylor, and Eisenstein

	Pavlov	Taylor	Eisenstein
Organizational principle	Scientific method	Scientific management	Manufacturing
Overdetermining force	Environmental selection	Falling rate of profit	Mode of production
Achievement	Reflexology	Taylorization	Cinema
"Object" of knowledge	Biological organism	Industrial production	Socialism
"Subject" of knowledge	Dog/Audience	Worker/Audience	Spectator/ Audience
Media	Reflexology/Brain	Management/ Worker	Film/Spectator
Method	Montage	Montage	Montage

nervous connection to another center, provided always that this second center is physiologically more powerful than the first" (*CR*, 36). Strong, repeated stimuli, what Pavlov called "signalization," can resequence behavior. It should not come as a surprise that such cutting and editing processes are also endemic to industrial production (assembly-line production, global distribution), penetrating, finally, the totality of social practices. Indeed, montage can be isolated as the principle conceit and the principle practice of modernization. Through generalized fragmentation and assemblage, the "montage of attractions" produces the unity (as well as the tyranny) of capital.

Montage, as the cutting and coupling of fragments, was the Ur-form of assemblage during the period when cinema was dominant. Taylor's own original form of editing and montage goes well beyond the literal use he made in his research of the movie camera and the stopwatch. It can be seen from the manner in which he began to edit his production: "*First*. Find say 10 or 15 different men (preferably in as many separate establishments and different parts of the country) who are especially skillful in doing the particular work to be analyzed. *Second*. Study the exact series of elementary operations or motions which each of these men uses in doing the work which is being investigated, as well as the implements each man uses. *Third*. Study with a stop-watch the time required to make each of these elementary movements and then select the quickest way of doing each element of the work. *Fourth.* Eliminate all false movements, slow movements, and useless movements. *Fifth.* After doing away with all unnecessary movements, *collect into one series* the quickest and best movements as well as the best implements" (*SM,* 117–18; last emphasis mine). Taylor edits the labor process like a film. As in Pavlov's experimental elimination of unknown variables and Eisenstein's elimination of material, which programs "an unjustified repertoire of reflexes," Taylor edited his material for an economy of action.[69]

Like the achievements of Taylor and Eisenstein, which are easily understood as responses to crises within capitalism, Pavlov's *Conditioned Reflexes* pertains to a particular crisis of capitalism, as well. The theater of cruelty, played first to Pavlov's audience of dogs and later to his audience of scientists, utilized a variety of cinematic techniques, not the least of which was cutting. Such cutting of movements and of workers was also characteristic of the assembly line, the *chaîne de montage.*[70] In industrial process, capital is cut into pieces to buy raw materials that are then cut up and combined to produce commodities. Each cut and splice sends value down a different production pathway in order to modify and streamline the product. The products are reassembled as the unity of capital. Workers, as Marx shows, are also products. In the case of Pavlov, the product whose mode of production needed to be altered was quite simply the "zoological peasantry."

The surgical alteration of brains and spinal columns, the extirpation of cortices, vivisection in the manner depicted in H. G. Wells's *The Island of Doctor Moreau* all lead up to a reinvention of animals that, since Darwin, have been placed on a developmental continuum with humans. In Pavlov, the continuum can be discerned immediately from the way in which he phylogenetically extends the findings of his experiments to humans—the "complete success" he mentions. To substantiate his claims concerning the relevance of his work to human life, Pavlov also experimented on children and mentally "deficient" persons as intermediate links in the chain of being that extends from humans to the lowest organisms. One could argue here that Pavlovian experiments on animals understood as evolutionary precursors of humans coincide with the social experiments being done on peasants "freed up" from their lands in Russia and more generally with the emergence of all sorts of new natives during the Age of Empire. *These peoples, as "raw materials," had to be retooled for the purposes of "civilization."*[71] Eisenstein desired to produce the "quantitative correlation" of those who were to pass as the revolutionary proletariat as energetically as others called for "the civilizing influence" of capital. These impetuses toward exchange-ability (the machinic interchangeability of individual bodies) should be compared with the globalizing program of television to convert populations into juridical subjects, "consumers" with "rational" needs. Because of the historical moment of Pavlov's experiments and the emergence of huge populations being first "separated" from the land by the money economy and then, once free, needed for wage labor (or state capitalism) by industrial production, Pavlov's experiments resonate with these other efforts to determine how one might manipulate liminally human, "zoological" populations with technology.[72] To assert this intention simply reverses the assumed polarity of scientific purpose. Rather than conduct research in a set of controlled experiments to discover the workings of the outer world, the point becomes to conduct research on the workings of the outer world in order to discover a set of controls.

Vivisection.

As with the technologies that media moguls develop for their particular publics, Pavlov continually returns to the contest between the ingenuity of the instrument makers in developing precision instruments and the extraordinary discernment of dogs' senses. The instruments must match the range and complexity of the dogs' nervous system. The goal of machining more and more finely honed instruments, which are able to further isolate particular nervous functions, becomes the production of more and more precise controls. In Pavlov's work, "the investigation of the cerebral hemispheres is brought into line with the investigations conducted in other branches of natural science[;] their activities are studied as purely physiological facts, without any need to resort to fantastic speculations as to the existence of any possible subjective state in the animal which may be conjectured on analogy with ourselves" (CR, 16). Because, for Pavlov, the nervous system is objectively rational, he allows himself in his writings many occasions to lament the inconclusiveness of a set of shocks, lacerations, and stimuli that result in the dog's "micturation and defecation in the stand," as well as "violent neurotic-like outbursts" and death. Often Pavlov recommends that another year-long series of experiments using redesigned instruments be conducted on a new dog. Pavlov's inability to feel anything for the dogs he traumatized translates into Taylor's failure to identify with the workers he cut or pasted, even though he himself emerged from the working class. He treated workers as labor without consciousness. Such treatment had certain objective goals in mind, namely, increasing the efficiency of value production. But he also had certain subjective goals in mind: "As there is practically no stimulus of whatever strength that cannot, under certain conditions, become subjected to internal inhibition, so also there is none which cannot produce sleep. Very powerful electric shocks applied to the skin led, after many months of use in the experiments of Dr. Erofeeva, to a progressively increasing internal inhibition in spite of continuous reinforcement, and in the experiments of Dr. Petrova they became the most effectual agents in inducing sleep" (CR, 252). Regular electronic shocks produce sleep; Clockwork Orange–like, the systematic application of pain inhibits the "freedom reflex" and annihilates the power to resist or even to feel.[73]

If the scientific rationalization of body processes can be read as a response to psycho-economic anxiety about emergent populations and manifests the need to manipulate populations with machine-like precision, Eisenstein expresses the same anxiety in his representation of spies and the lumpen as animals in The Strike. In the film, only the capitalists and the revolutionary masses have human consciousness, and, as we have noted, the capitalists only marginally, since they respond almost automatically to stimulus. Even more like animals, The Strike's lumpen live in holes in the ground and can be conditioned easily (with sex and liquor) to follow the capitalists. Recall also that the spies of the capitalists are animals as well, trained dupes of the ruling class. Endemic to such animality is the aggressive and violent aspect of Eisenstein's cinema; however, the contradiction here is that the proletariat, figured as humans, are treated as animals. As in capitalism, organization is won through the perfecting of animality. For H. G. Wells and Pavlov, animals have to be cut up in order to attain human form; similarly, for Eisenstein, awakening spectators to their human state requires that they be shocked and stimulated as animals are. Animals, the raw material of humanity, have a proximity to labor, the raw material of industrialized society. Labor, like animals, is without real consciousness; hence, a predictable behavior must be forged. In Eisenstein's work, the iron cage of reason captures the animals by sending them calculated signals. The violent transformation (via cutting and editing) of organisms conceived as animals into humanoids constitutes these animals as spectators. In one gesture, scientifically managed signalization constitutes spectators and asks them to find an image for their world in a human face.

Working within the framework of capital's manufacture of the relationship between animality and humanity, Eisenstein sees his films as a form of vivisection, a hewing of fragments from world historical reality with "the axe of the lens" and arranging them in such a way as to forge the audience's psyche. "In *cinema*, by *selective treatment* [the director] recarves *reality*" (*Writings*, 64).[74]

Material Industrialization of Consciousness.
The Circuit of Production.

We have seen how industrial production and scientific rationality were aspiring toward cinema, and how cinema was, in many respects, the fulfillment of the logic nascent in the practices of industry and science. Cinema marks the moment when the dominant mode of production becomes the dominant mode of representation. This representation itself surpasses representation as such, passing into a technology for the rational production of affect and becoming part of the general cycle of production.

The meshing of the microprocesses of the biological organism outlined by Pavlov with the macroprocesses of the socio-industrial organism outlined by Taylor in the cinema of Eisenstein is predicated upon the logic of isolated organs, rationalized functions, repetition, selection, and conditioning. The extension of this logic to the body through the eye shows that a cybernetic integration of social mechanisms is occurring; radically different mechanisms are being shot through with systemic compatibility. In computer talk: Industry, the nervous system, and representation are all beginning to speak a compatible language, a compatible machine—or systems—language. After Eisenstein, the cinema as a logistics of production and sensation rapidly develops and extends to a point in which all of its subtle affects and increasing complexity are able to extract a growing portion of the labor of social production. In the rational throws of profit, a consciousness is born. This consciousness is at once linguistic and visceral, discursive and "filmic"—it is our very seeing. The assertions of Metz that the cinema and the spectator are both locked into the circulation of capital remains correct. But the dynamics and consequences of this circulation extend beyond the imaginary and the symbolic and into the Real.

The New World Order.

For Capital, the worker does not represent a condition of production, but only labor. If capital can get it performed by machinery, or even by water or air, tant mieux. *And what capital appropriates is not the worker, but his labor—and not directly but by means of exchange.*
—Marx, Grundrisse

The true definition of a productive worker consists in this: a man who requires and demands absolutely no more than is necessary to enable him to bring his capitalist the greatest possible advantage.
—Marx, Grundrisse

The surplus value of capital rises, but in an ever diminishing ratio to the development of productivity. Thus the more developed capital is, the more surplus labor it has already created, the more tremendously must it develop productivity if it is to valorize itself, i.e., to add surplus value even in small proportion.
—Marx, Grundrisse

I have tried to suggest here that dialectical development of productivity drives relations of capital into the media—the meaning of dialectics as mediation is today actualized as media if not understood as such. Though all previous stages of development still obtain (there remain today pockets of feudal societies and slavery, as well as tremendous populations working in industry), capital seeks new ways of valorizing itself by increasing its efficiency, its ability to withhold itself from producers while capturing labor time. In cinema, and now in TV, spectatorial producers no longer receive money in exchange for their labor (attention) but are paid in another type of image—company scrip. By helping us to perform the necessary production and reproduction of the workers—of ourselves—the affects received in exchange for our attention endeavor to help us meet certain needs as they strive to ensure our domination. Willing to see almost anything, willing to believe almost anything (even the triumph of capitalism [a belief that helps to produce that triumph]), and needing to be a little different every day, we modify ourselves as we watch. Remade daily, we go about our diurnal course in a more or less docile manner, even though we are outraged. The latest "vanishing form of subsistence," as Marx called the money paid to workers in exchange for their labor, is "entertainment," the consciousness of choice.[75] We valorize the organization of society in our very bodies as we add value to the media by watching it and make ourselves over in socially acceptable forms. In the twentieth century, the vanishing mediator takes on the form of media itself.

In 1924, Eisenstein wrote in "The Montage of Film Attractions," "We see that the methods of processing the audience are no different in the mechanics of their realization from other forms of work movement and they produce the same *real, primarily physical* work on their material—the audience" (*Writings*, 56). By 1928, at the age of thirty, he had released *The Strike, Battleship Potemkin,* and *October,* and had written some of the most important works of film theory to date. Also in 1927 and 1928, while finishing *October* and working on *The General Line,* Eisenstein wrote "Notes for a Film of *Capital*," a film he would never make.[76] If it is correct to say that historical truth exists only as irony, then perhaps Eisenstein never made *Capital* because he had already made it in *The Strike.*

The spectatorship of the proletariat raises once again the specter of humanity, but this time on the screen of consciousness. Today, the cinematic specter—humans becoming images becoming cyborgs—raises along with the questions regarding the production of value the question of the legacy of the human body. Given all the pathways of its interface with the *socius,* to whom or to what will it belong? Robert Reich's "immaterial labor" and Deleuze's "society of control" are indicators that we are in the presence of "the real subsumption of labor under capital instead of the formal subsumption of labor under capital."[77] If this is the case, then surely the fate of bodies—who occupies them, who thinks or feels in them, what they want—is again in question. If we are occupied by cinematic consciousness, what is the value of our seeing, our thought? The specter haunting the (movie) house of capital will never disappear, because it is the persistence of unfulfilled promises made to the suffering, the laboring, and the dead. Though Eisenstein's revolution was finally a revolution in and over the imagination, consciousness still perceives a realm of freedom, even if only in its absence. What struggles are yet to be waged at the edge of thought and feeling?

In this analysis and indictment of the media-system, I have tried to open a way through political economy to investigate how many of the small-scale pleasures and freedoms that we enjoy are simultaneously used against us and against others. I also hope that this chapter will raise questions against the egocentric and imperialistic works that currently celebrate the liberatory power of mass media. Capital's micrometry of our sensual satisfaction functions systemically to ensure that the energy of our "freedom reflex" is ever more precisely controlled, absorbed, and set against us. According to its logic, our satisfactions are to take place enframed by the network of capital, or not at all. Such satisfactions should be partial, at best, since not the least part of them is enabled by the continued invisibility (alienation) of most of humanity's pain. In the presence of new technologies for the strict regulation of suffering and death, and for the global calibration and synchronization of violent exploitation in all its historical forms, one realizes that the "New World Order," as a military-industrial spectacle nearly a century in the making, is no mere phrase; it is the massively mediated crowning of a new order of capital. It is necessarily, then, the harbinger of new forms of revolution.

NOTES

1. Samir Amin, *Delinking: Towards a Polycentric World,* trans. Michael Wolfers (New York: Zed Books, 1990). For a discussion of the productivity of the individual strike, see my essay, "Desiring the Involuntary: Late Capitalist Circulation and the Machinic Assemblage in Deleuze and *Robocop 2,*" in *Global/Local: Cultural Production and the Transnational Imaginary,* ed. Rob Wilson and Wimal Dissanayake (Durham, N.C.: Duke University Press, 1996).

2. Derrida read from his then forthcoming book *The Specter of Marx* on 4–5 October 1993, at Duke University. Drawing heavily on Hamlet and Marx, Derrida suggests that when the time is out of joint, that is, when *différance* reigns, the specter of the past appears in order to raise the question of inheritance. What are the dead calling for? In our disjointed time, the specter that appears is the specter of Marx. For Derrida, who seems to be attempting to think an alternative way to impel the course for historical movement without resorting to metaphysics or utopia, the specter of Marx demands a reaffirmation of the question of life and death by raising questions of inheritance and justice. The world is the trace of postgenerations; for whom is it?

3. *The Strike* was produced in April to November of 1924 and released in April of 1925. See the excellent chronology of Eisenstein's life in David Bordwell, *The Cinema of Eisenstein* (Cambridge and London: Harvard, University Press, 1993).

4. The reader's forbearance is requested in the discussion that follows.

5. Sergei Eisenstein, *Selected Works: Writings 1922–1934,* vol. 1, ed. and trans. Richard Taylor (London: BFI Publishing, 1988), 154. This work hereafter is cited parenthetically as *Writings.* Unless otherwise noted, all italics are Eisenstein's.

6. The citation finishes, "Yet it is precisely in this its highest phase, that art terminates, by transcending itself; it is just here that it deserts the medium of a harmonious presentation of mind in sensuous shape and passes from the poetry of imaginative idea

into the prose of thought." From Georg Wilhelm Friedrich Hegel, *The Philosophy of Fine Art*, in *Critical Theory Since Plato*, ed. Hazard Adams (New York: Harcourt Brace Jovanovich, 1971), 530. Though for Hegel the prose of thought is philosophy, for us the transcendental prose of the sensuality of cinema is the numismatics of capital.

7. Regis Debray, *Media Manifestos*, London: Verso, 1996.

8. Walter Benjamin, "The Work of Art in the Age of Mechanical Reproduction," in *Illuminations*, ed. Hannah Arendt (New York: Schocken Books, 1969), 233.

9. Such a radical dematerialization produces the perspective that is the condition of possibility for Pier Paolo Pasolini's statement that "All life, in the entirety of its creations, is a natural living film." Pier Paolo Pasolini, *Heretical Empiricism*, trans. Ben Lawton and Louise K. Barnett (Bloomington and Indianapolis: Indiana University Press, 1988), 204. Life can be a natural film for Pasolini only because film has come into being historically both as a technology and as an abstraction. Cinema as "the written language of reality" is only possible in a world in which movement itself has taken on new meanings for vision. For Pasolini, film is to "the language of action" as writing is to oral language. The eye achieves new functions in the processing of a dematerialized reality (images), because material reality is organized in such a way as to make these new functions possible. A cinematic order comes to underlie all movement and its meaning. The structure of reality converts objects into images and signs. In a world of highly organized systems, organized movement itself becomes significant (hence the first volume of Deleuze's *Cinema* is subtitled *The Movement-Image*); in this context, disorganized movement also becomes significant. With the origin of cybernetics, the relations between movement, patterns of movements, and meanings not only become explicit, but enter into the conceptualization of life itself. "Life is an island here and now in a dying world. The process by which living beings resist the general stream of corruption and decay is known as *homeostasis*. We can continue to live in the very special environment which we carry forward with us only until we begin to decay more quickly than we can reconstitute ourselves. Then we die. . . . We are not the stuff that abides, but patterns that perpetuate themselves." And then, presciently, "A pattern is a message, and may be transmitted as a message." Norbert Weiner, *The Human Use of Human Beings: Cybernetics and Society* (Garden City, N.Y.: Anchor Books, 1954), 95–96. Pasolini's filmic introduction of disorganized movement into a society of increasingly organized capitalist and heterosexist libidinal relations (disorganization that he saw as something akin to non-reified life-force) in a film such as *Arabian Nights* (1974), is the heretical aspect of his empiricism. In a highly regulated society, to intensify existing disorganization through an alternative ordering was, simply speaking, to inaugurate revolution. But that was the sixties. Today, it is more difficult to believe that jouissance and revolution are one, or for that matter, that they can even inhabit the same constellation of ideas.

10. As Richard Taylor tells us, "*The Strike* was originally intended as one of the epi-

sodes in th[at] larger cycle," *Towards the Dictatorship,* which was never completed (*Writings,* 307 n. 3).

11. Near the bottom of the capitalist hierarchy are the spies. These men are given animal names such as Fox, Owl, and Bulldog, and are, like the capitalists and the military themselves, only minimally presented as subjects. Rather, the spies are unthinking creatures who report everything to their masters. After the strike is well underway, one of the spies uses a camera hidden in a pocket watch to capture the image of one of the leaders of the strike. This image is then used to identify and capture the leader himself. As with the other communications media utilized by the capitalists, the developed film in the capitalist chain of organization becomes, like the phone cable, an instrument of power against the working classes. Just as the capitalists' control of certain media allows them to exercise power over the workers, the pocket watch-camera suggests the dynamic consequences of such a practice for the twentieth century: Whoever controls the image controls the time and indeed, the times; conversely, whoever controls the time controls the image. Using the watch-camera, the owners put the striker in the service of their time. The regulation of images and time, which is precisely the achievement of industry as cinema, becomes the new key to the control of social organization. Though *The Strike* as a whole is ostensibly an attempt to wrest images and time (history) away from capitalism, the watch-camera sequence shows, à la Paul Virilio's *War and Cinema,* that cinema and industrial capital develop in tandem: capturing the image of the organizer is tantamount to capturing him. ("'If I had to sum up current thinking on precision missles and saturation weaponry in a single sentence,' said W. J. Perry, a former U.S. Under-Secretary of State Defense, 'I'd put it like this: once you can see the target, you can expect to destroy it.'" Paul Virilio, *War and Cinema: The Logistics of Perception,* trans. Patrick Camiller [London: Verso, 1989], 4). Indeed, his capture follows almost immediately upon the developing of his photograph. Like the cable and the belt, the image is here another leash on the worker.

12. Roland Barthes, "The Third Meaning," in *A Barthes Reader,* ed. Susan Sontag (New York: Hill and Wang, 1982), 317–33.

13. Karl Marx, "Economic and Philosophic Manuscripts of 1844," *The Marx-Engels Reader,* 2nd ed., ed. Robert C. Tucker, (New York: Norton, 1978), 74.

14. Ibid., 76.

15. Barthes, "The Third Meaning," 326. It is worth noting that this definition is the antithesis of the prevalent definition of the sublime, "a signified without a signifier." See, for example Jean-Francois Lyotard, *The Postmodern Condition* (Minneapolis: University of Minnesota Press, 1989), 81.

16. Barthes, "The Third Meaning," 330.

17. Christian Metz, *The Imaginary Signifier: Psychoanalysis and the Cinema,* trans.

Celia Britton, Annwyl Williams, Ben Brewster, and Alfred Guzzetti (Bloomington: Indiana University Press, 1982), 3.

18. Ibid.

19. Georg Simmel, *The Philosophy of Money*, 2nd ed., ed. David Frisby, trans. Tom Bottomore and David Frisby. (London and New York: Routledge, 1990), 470.

20. See my essay, "Cinema, Capital of the Twentieth Century," *Postmodern Culture* 4, no. 3 (May 1994). Available at pmc@unit.nsu.edu.

21. Gilles Deleuze, *Cinema 1*, cited in Steven Shaviro, *The Cinematic Body* (Minneapolis and London: University of Minnesota Press, 1993), 38.

22. Robert Bresson, in Shaviro, *The Cinematic Body*, 40. Quoted from Bresson's *Notes on the Cinematographer*, trans. Jonathan Griffin (London: Quartet, 1986), 84.

23. "The bourgeoisie cannot exist without constantly revolutionizing the instruments of production, and thereby the relations of production, and with them the whole relations of society. Conservation of the old modes of production in unaltered forms, was, on the contrary, the first condition of existence for all earlier industrial classes. Constant revolutionizing of production, uninterrupted disturbance of all social conditions, everlasting uncertainty and agitation distinguish the bourgeois epoch from all earlier ones. All fixed, fast-frozen relations, with their train of ancient and venerable prejudices and opinions are swept away, all new-formed ones become antiquated before they can ossify. All that is solid melts into air, all that is holy is profaned, and man is at last compelled to face with sober senses his real conditions of life, and his relations with his kind." See Marx, *Marx-Engels Reader*, 476.

24. Gilles Deleuze, *Cinema 2: The Time—Image*, trans. Hugh Tomlinson and Robert Galeta (Minneapolis: University of Minnesota Press, 1989), 77.

25. Shaviro, *The Cinematic Body*, 39.

26. Ibid., 40–41.

27. Walter Benjamin, "On Some Motifs in Baudlaire," in *Illuminations*, 175.

28. Noam Chomsky, *World Orders Old and New* (New York: Columbia University Press, 1994).

29. Paul Virilio, *War and Cinema*.

30. Deleuze, *Cinema 2*, 172.

31. From Antonio Negri's brilliant "Twenty Theses on Marx: Interpretation of the Class Situation Today," trans. Michael Hardt, *Polygraph #5: Contesting the New World Order* (1992): 154.

32. The spectator "must in the future be placed in the center of the picture. He shall not be present at, but participate in, the action." See, "The Exhibitors to the Public, 1912" in H. B. Chipps, *Theories of Modern Art* (Berkeley: University of California Press, 1968), 296.

33. Kenneth Surin, "'The Continued Relevance of Marxism' as a Question: Some Propositions," *Polygraph 6/7: Marxism Beyond Marxism?* (1993): 52.

34. Slavoj Zizek, *Looking Awry: An Introduction to Jacques Lacan through Popular Culture* (Cambridge: MIT Press, 1991).

35. Metz, *The Imaginary Signifier*, 7.

36. Antonio Gramsci, "Americanism and Fordism," in *Selection from the Prison Notebooks*, ed. and trans. Quintin Hoare and Geoffrey Nowell Smith (New York: International Publishers, 1971), 279–318.

37. I equivocate between consciousness and perception here because I have not yet worked out the basis upon which to mark the distinction, and this is not the place to do it. For now, let me say that consciousness is beginning to resemble money, "the vanishing mediator," while thought and perception express particular relations of capital. Marx's tripartite definition of money as measure of value, means of circulation, and as representation of wealth (i.e., as capital) culminates in money's achieving a consciousness of its own. "Money in its final perfected determination now appears in all respects as a contradiction which resolves itself, which drives itself to its own resolution. As the general form of wealth, it is confronted by the whole world of riches. It is their pure abstraction—hence comprehended as such, it is mere imagination. Where wealth appears to exist as such in a quite material, tangible form, it has its existence merely in my mind, is a sheer figment of the imagination. Midas" *Grundrisse*, 166. I am suggesting that not only do workers in capitalism have the Midas touch, but spectators in late capitalism have the Midas gaze. Whatever we look at turns to gold, for someone.

38. Metz, *The Imaginary Signifier*, 7. The first and second machines elaborated by Metz are both part of what I refer to as "cinema as cinema." Only when understood in their politico-economic dimensions are they to be understood as "cinema as capital."

39. "Computer programming is really a branch of moviemaking," Theodor Nelson said, quoted in Howard Rheingold's *Virtual Reality* (New York: Simon and Schuster, 1991), 176; see also 286. "Computers are theater. Interactive technology, like drama, provides a platform for representing coherent realities in which agents perform with cognitive, emotional and productive qualities. Two thousand years of dramatic theory and practice have been devoted to an end which is remarkably similar to that of the fledgling discipline of human-computer interaction design; namely, creating artificial realities in which the potential for action is cognitively, emotionally, and aesthetically enhanced" (quoted in Brenda Laurel, *Computers as Theater* [Reading, Mass.: Addison-Wesley Publishers, 1991]). Rheingold groups together these and other such citations under the provocative heading "The Reality-Industrial Complex."

40. Marx, *Grundrisse*, 186.

41. Marx, *The German Ideology*, in *Marx-Engels Reader*, 170. In *Economic and Philo-*

sophic Manuscripts of 1844, Marx notes, "The forming of the five senses is a labor of the entire history of the world down to the present" (*Marx-Engels Reader*, 89).

42. If one still believed in Marx's notion of species-being, one might be tempted to paraphrase the Marx of the 1840s: Our senses no longer belong to us. Like sensuous labor, our senses are alienated from us and us from them. Our sensual activity is taken from us, and then used against us. The more we sense, the poorer we become, and the richer the capitalists (celebrities of all stripes) become. One can only hope to succeed by sensing nothing. Of course, such rhetorical forms posit a humanity that no longer exists, that is only a spectral trace (or so our senses tell us).

43. Jean Baudrillard, *For a Critique of the Political Economy of the Sign*, trans. and intro. Charles Levin (St. Louis: Telos Press, 1981).

44. Metz, *The Imaginary Signifier*, 7.

45. Hence the connections being made between cinema, the gaze, and consumption in historical studies. See, for example, Anne Friedberg, *Window Shopping: Cinema and Postmodernism* (Berkeley: University of California Press, 1993).

46. There is much work on transformations of the eye and its function during the modern period. See, for example, Jonathan Crary, *Techniques of the Observer: On Vision and Modernity in the Nineteenth Century* (Cambridge: MIT Press, 1990); Martin Jay, "Scopic Regimes of Modernity," in *Vision and Visuality*, ed. Hal Foster (Seattle: Bay Press, 1988); and Paul Virilio *War and Cinema*.

47. As is well known, both Lenin and Stalin emphasized the preeminent place of cinema in Soviet culture.

48. Eric Rhode, *A History of the Cinema from its Origins to 1970* (New York: Hill and Wang, 1976), 88.

49. Ivan Petrovich Pavlov, *Conditioned Reflexes*, trans. and ed. G. V. Anrep (New York: Dover Publications, 1960), 4. This work is hereafter cited parenthetically as *CR*.

50. "We began to give the dog the whole of its food in the stand. At first the animal ate but little, and lost considerably in weight, but gradually it got to eat more until at last the whole ration was consumed. At the same time the animal grew quieter during the course of the experiments: the freedom reflex was being inhibited" (*CR*, 11–12).

51. Frederick Winslow Taylor, *The Principles of Scientific Management* (New York: Norton Library, 1967), 131. This work is hereafter cited parenthetically as *SM*.

52. Rheingold, *Vitual Reality*, 129ff.

53. See *Eisenstein on Disney*, ed. Jay Leyda, trans. Alan Upchurch (Calcutta: Seagull, 1986). On the propagandistic aspect of Disney, there are many works; see especially Ariel Dorfman and Armand Mattelart, *How to Read Donald Duck: Imperialist Ideology in the Disney Comic*, trans. David Kunzle (New York: International General, 1975); and Eric Smoodin, ed., *Disney Discourse: Producing the Magic Kingdom* (New York: Routledge, 1994).

54. Louis Althusser, in Louis Althusser and Etienne Balibar, *Reading Capital* (London and New York: Verso, 1990). That "science" is also the method of dialectical materialism is a troubling issue, indeed.

55. "Form is *always ideology*. And form always turns out to be *real ideology*. That is, ideology that *really* applies and not what passes for ideology in the idle prattle of the talkers" (*Writings*, 24).

56. Barbara Herrnstein Smith may help us to unpack Eisenstein's self-privileging. She writes, "The decisive moves in the generation and maintenance of [a] double discourse of value are commonly made under the quasi-logical cover of *We must distinguish between:* for example, we must distinguish between mere price and intrinsic value, between mere consumers and discriminating critics, between true artistic creativity and technological skill, and so forth. The question posed here and throughout this study is *must* we and indeed *can* we? (The attendant question 'Who are "we"?' is of course as relevant here as everywhere else.)" See *Contingencies of Value* (Cambridge, Mass.: Harvard University Press, 1988), 127. Eisenstein pushes the matter of taste, selection, and discrimination to its limits; *he* is someone who knows, and "we" are someone who needs to be shown.

57. Gramsci, *Prison Notebooks*, 280.

58. Quoted in Standish Lawder, "Eisenstein and Constructivism," in *The Essential Cinema*, vol. 1, ed. P. Adams Sitney (New York: Anthology Film Archives and New York Univesity Press, 1975), 60.

59. Sergei Eisenstein, *Selected Works: Towards a Theory of Montage*, vol. 2, ed. Michael Glenny and Richard Taylor, trans. Michael Glenny (London: BFI Publishing, 1991), 1. For an excellent discussion of the evolution and consistencies of Eisenstein's theoretical writings see Jacques Aumont, "Montage Eisenstein I: Eisensteinian Concepts," *Discourse* 5 (Spring 1983): 41–99.

60. Robert Warshow, *The Immediate Experience* (New York: n.p., 1962), 204, cited in Rhode, *A History of the Cinema*, 87.

61. A typical example of Taylor's selection process can be found in his description of his work at the ball bearing factory. "For the ultimate good of the girls as well as the company it became necessary to exclude all girls who lacked a low 'personal coefficient.' And unfortunately this involved laying off many of the most intelligent, hardest working, and most trustworthy girls merely because they did not possess the quality of quick perception followed by quick action" (*SM*, 89–90).

62. The modern subject is a spectator, the postmodern subject is a schizophrenic; some ornery paranoiacs remain.

63. One only has to assemble a short list of canonical modern authors to remark the all-pervasiveness of animals as figures for marginalized subjects at the turn of the century: Mann, Wells, Kafka, Ibsen, Bulgakov, among others.

64. Cited in Rhode, *A History of the Cinema*, 108.

65. Jim Beniger writes in his stunning book, *The Control Revolution: Technological and Economic Origins of the Information Society* (Cambridge and London: Harvard University Press, 1986), "Foremost among all the technological solutions to the crisis of control—in that it served to control most other technologies—was the rapid growth of formal bureaucracy" (279). "With the rapid development of rationalization and bureaucracy came the succession of dramatic new information processing and communication technologies that contained the continuing control crisis of industrial society in production, distribution, and consumption of goods and services" (285). In this section, I am endeavoring to show how bureaucratic organization invades both knowledge and the body and emerges as media. Media itself becomes the conduit of organization; it is organization *in principle*. The ultimate consequences of this fact can be gleaned from Edward S. Herman and Noam Chomsky, *Manufacturing Consent: The Political Economy of the Mass Media* (New York: Pantheon, 1988). *Manufacturing Consent* brilliantly documents how the technology for the organization of knowledge and bodies (and therefore money and arms), once in place, functions in particular case scenarios.

66. Insisting, in "The Factory of Facts," that "The growing adoption of kino-eye's external manner by the 'acted' film (*The Strike* and *Potemkin*) is only an isolated incident, a random reflection of the ever-growing kino-eye movement" (Vertov, 58), Vertov gives his assessment of acted cinema: "You find yourself in a small but extraordinary land where all human experiences, behavior, and even natural phenomena are strictly controlled and occur at precisely determined times. At your command and whenever you wish, rain may fall, a thunderstorm or tempest arise. If you like, the downpour will stop. The puddles will immediately dry up. The sun will shine forth. Perhaps even two or three suns. If you wish, day will turn to night. The sun into the moon. Stars will appear. Winter will replace summer. Frost patterns will cover the windows. You can, if you choose, sink or save ships at sea. Cause fires and earthquakes. Make wars and revolutions. Human tears and laughter obey your command. Passion and jealousy. Love and hatred. According to your strict schedule, people fight and embrace. Marry and divorce. Are born and die. Die and come to life. Die again and again come to life. Or kiss endlessly in front of the camera until the director is satisfied. We are at a film studio where a man with a megaphone and script directs the life of a fake land" (Vertov, 283). I read this passage not only against Eisenstein but against Stalin as well.

67. Benjamin, "The Work of Art," 232–34.

68. Elaine Scarry, *The Body In Pain: The Making and Unmaking of the World* (New York: Oxford University Press), 1985.

69. The exigencies of such a generalized economy of action are emphasized by Gramsci in his essay "Americanism and Fordism." When, speaking of the future of the industrial proletariat, he predicts, "A forced selection will ineluctably take place; a part

of the old working class will be pitilessly eliminated from the world of labour, and perhaps from the world *tout court.*" See Gramsci, *Prison Notebooks,* 303. Global reorganization, it seems, requires some radical cutting and pasting. As science approached cinema by imposing the economy of its representation on its object, and as industry approached cinema by imposing the economy of its representation on its object, and as industry approached cinema by imposing the economy of its movement on its object, dogs and workers encountered the rationalized shocks, which Benjamin has described elsewhere as the shock characteristic of modern life.

70. Geoffrey Nowel-Smith points this out in Eisenstein, *Selected Works: Towards a Theory of Montage,* 2, vol. xiii.

71. I am indebted here to Neferti X. M. Tadiar for this insight into H. G. Wells's *The Island of Doctor Moreau,* which I have here transposed to Pavlov.

72. Annette Michelson has argued that Pavlov's work has its origins in the Enlightenment and traces it back to La Mettrie's *L'homme Machine.* La Mettrie "abolishes the dualism of Descartes (whom Pavlov claims invented the idea of the reflex) and works in the tradition of Locke." Michelson also traces his work forward, as it were, to Vsevolod Meyerhold, Eisenstein's mentor and friend, and argues persuasively that Eisenstein inherits the Enlightenment. Annette Michelson spoke at Duke University in March 1993 on Pudovkin's chilling *Mechanics of the Brain,* a film shot in Pavlov's laboratories. She also showed the film. Although I had been thinking about the constellation of Eisenstein, Pavlov, and Taylor in relation to rationalization for some time, her lecture and the film persuaded me of the viability of the project. I owe a great debt to her work, which I would like to acknowledge here. See especially her work on Dziga Vertov, *Kino-Eye: The Writings of Dziga Vertov.*

73. Gramsci proposes certain limits to such intensive repetition. In industrial work, "The only thing completely mechanized is the physical gesture; the memory of the trade, reduced to simple gestures repeated at an intense rhythm, 'nestles' in the muscular and nervous centres and leaves the brain free and unencumbered for other occupations. One can walk without having to think about all the movements needed in order to move, in perfect synchronization, all the parts of the body, in the specific way that is necessary for walking. The same thing happens and will go on happening in industry with the basic gestures of the trade. One walks automatically, and at the same time thinks about whatever one chooses. American industrialists have understood too well this dialectic inherent in the new industrial methods. They have understood that 'trained gorilla' is just a phrase, that 'unfortunately' the worker remains a man and even that during his work he thinks more or at least has greater opportunities for thinking, once he has overcome the crisis of adaptation without being eliminated: and not only does the worker think, but the fact that he gets no immediate satisfaction from his work and realises that they are trying to reduce him to a trained

gorilla, can lead him into a train of thought that is far from conformist." See Gramsci, *Prison Notebooks,* 309–10.

74. Eisenstein also spoke of the classic "mists" in *Potemkin* as functioning as the "cows" in *The Strike,* that is, as "a sharply honed razor that will cut the viewer 100 per cent in the place that needs it at a particular moment" (*Writings,* 68). In a reply to Vertov, he writes, "We must cut with our cine-fist through to the skulls, cut through to final victory and now, under the threat of an influx of 'real life' and philistinism into the Revolution, we must cut as never before! Make way for cine-fist!" (*Writings,* 64).

75. Marx, *Grundrisse,* 219.

76. See Sergei Eisenstein, "Notes for a Film of *Capital,*" *October* 2 (1976): 3–26.

77. I owe this formulation to Michael Hardt. Ken Surin extends the argument: "The current phase of capitalist expansion has created a social order in which all the conditions of production and reproduction have been directly absorbed by capital—by consuming society capital itself has become entirely social in nature. Capital has to extend the logic of command over productive cooperation to envelop the whole of society in order to enable further the extraction of new forms of surplus value, new forms it has to invent as a way of dealing with the crisis of the Fordist or Keynesian paradigm of accumulation." See Kenneth Surin, "The Continued Relevance of Marxism," 52.

Chapter 3
The Unconscious
The Unconscious of the Unconscious, or, The Work of Consciousness in the Age of Technological Imagination

The alienation of the spectator to the profit of the contemplated object (which is the result of his own unconscious activity) [emphasis mine] is expressed in the following way: the more he contemplates the less he lives; the more he accepts recognizing himself in the dominant images of need, the less he understands his own existence and his own desires. The externality of the spectacle in relation to the active man appears in the fact that his own gestures are no longer his but those of another who represents them to him. This is why the spectator feels at home nowhere, because the spectacle is everywhere. —Guy Debord, Society of the Spectacle

---

For the Moment I am Not Fucking

Let us recall Wlad Godzich's words referenced in the introduction to this volume.

> The problem is that a dissonance is now manifesting itself: images are scrambling the functioning of language which must operate out of the imaginary in order to function optimally. Images are parasitical noises on language at first—and then they supplant it: it must be recalled that the technology of images operates at the speed of light, as does the world. Language could slow down the world, thanks to its tremendous negative capability, but it cannot slow down images, for they operate out of the very imaginary that language would have to be able to organize in the first place."[1]

Given what we have said so far regarding capital's organization of the imaginary, Godzich's account of the effect of images on language-function under the auspices of the cinematic mode of production would imply that the scene of production is unconscious, or, alternately, there are strict limits with respect to a consciousness of production. This unconsciousness occurs because cinema is "a technique of the imaginary," and the imaginary is being organized and harnessed as a productive force, even as language cannot organize this imaginary. What this reasoning suggests is that the theory of the unconscious, up until very recently itself devoid of consciousness of production, has its own unconscious in mass media, or image-culture, or to speak at once historically and in a vocabulary consistent with my work here, in cinema. I want to begin my discussion of what I call the unconscious of the unconscious with something like a demonstration of how this double unconscious functions, using some of the prime exemplars of the contemporary autism that Godzich describes as the postmodern predicament: Beavis and Butt-head.

Dying of thirst in the desert in *Beavis and Butt-head Do America,* somewhere in the middle of the film (which just happens to be the middle of nowhere), Butt-head has one of those hallucinations that a close brush with death inevitably brings on. Dehydrated unto death, his life, spent in front of a television set, flashes before him—first he is on the couch with Beavis in swaddling clothes, then they are toddlers on the couch, then they are elementary school kids, and then they are the teenagers they are and whom we have all seen. Reflecting on this series of dissolves that are his memory Butt-head turns to a dying Beavis and relates, "My life just flashed in front of me," followed by a thoughtful pause and then, "It was cool." Then it is Beavis's turn to hallucinate. Confronted with death and at the limits of what his body can endure, he reports that he is beginning to "feel weird." A look of despair comes over him, and then of ecstasy as his physical degeneration brings on a vision which he announces is "like a music video."

The ensuing hallucination, which is a kind of movement through concentric worlds toward some fundamental center, is full of Heronomyous Bosch–type creatures, grooving monsters, dancing girls, funky skulls with eyes, a slug with an eye-ball at one end that moves like an inch-worm through a landscape of rotting corpses (it is the phallic seeing tentacle of Japanese anime in a devolved form), all throbbing and jiggling to a rock-and-roll beat. In one of the circles of this ecstatic hell, a giant green devil plays guitar, and in another the skulls watch part of the performance on a primordial TV that is somehow climactically revealed as being the bedrock of the entire sequence. The dance of death raves on, and in the innermost circle of hell, rotting corpses watch it on a TV out of the Flinstones. In the depths of the mind, at the core of the psyche, at the center of the human experience, is television.

In thinking further about the significance of Beavis and Butt-head's autism in the face of visual culture, one is tempted to recall here Jacques Lacan's memorable phrase regarding linguistic function spoken during the thirteenth seminar of *The Four Fundamental Concepts*, "For the moment I am not fucking, I am talking to you."[2] The statement is meant to be a summary of one of the aspects of Freud's concept of sublimation in which the sexual finds expression in the symbolic. Speaking about sublimation as the "satisfaction of the drive without repression," Lacan adds, "Well! I can have exactly the same satisfaction [talking to us] as if I were fucking. That's what it [sublimation] means. Indeed it raises the question of whether in fact I am not fucking at this moment."[3]

Taking Lacan's phrase in conjunction with Godzich's account cited above of the interruption of language brought about by image culture raises certain troubling questions about Beavis and Butt-head (B&B). If for the moment B&B are not fucking—for this, indeed, is their inaugural problematic—what on earth are they doing? For it is certainly clear that they are not adept talkers. Lacan's point is that utilization of the symbolic order, which for the moment we can call language, can provide access to satisfaction, so far as satisfaction goes, and without going into the details of the argument, this satisfaction is sexual. The libido, what Deleuze and Guattari will identify in its combinatory activities with the outside world as "desiring-production," invests language as a scene of production and . . . reproduction. Desire is productive of language, which following Kristeva is "eminently productive of culture," which in the postmodern is productive of value, as argued in the present work. Thus to speak, write, and engage in discourse is also posited as creating value, but Beavis and Butt-head do little of this work.

Beavis and Butt-head's condition of not fucking, it must be noted, is essential to the movement of the film's plot; it is the basis of the narrative. Theirs is an enabling silence. In their MTV homeland, the dynamic duo is most often positioned as our surrogates, quasi-idiotically watching the same music videos we're watching and saying the one or two things that we presumably might say, if we were truly in touch with our inner dweeb. As the images speed by, B&B throw out the name of a fetishized body part ("he said, 'dick'"), and laugh (heh, heh), or pronounce on it ("cool"). This stammering inactivity is a tried and true formula for TV, at least judging by their popularity and by the condition of many television viewers, but you could never make a Hollywood film like that. In the commercial cinema, you must narrativize whatever postmodern intensities are there to be experienced, at least to a certain extent.

So Beavis and Butt-head's silence must be put to work. Another key point about the plot, and viewers will remember this if they have seen the film, is that it doesn't get going until Beavis and Butt-head's TV set gets stolen, which, necessarily, is at the beginning of the film. The absence of TV provides the characters so-called "motivation;" only in television's absence is it possible to tell a story. The fact that the story turns on their struggle to get their TV back so that they may free themselves from the exigencies of cinematic narrative back into the stupefied plenitude of televisual turpitude, poetically holds forth the possibility of elegant closure. Poetically, because such closure is an allegory of the weakening of narrative and the associated, catastrophic implosion of consciousness in the postmodern.

Beavis and Butt-head are thus the perfect incarnations of Godzich's postmodern predicament, broken-down, sputtering language machines, barely up to speed. As is apparent from the Grateful Death sequence alluded to above, the marginalization and decay of language wrought by televisual images is absolutely central to the being, if you will, of these animated characters. This hallucination scene is to *Beavis and Butt-head Do America,* as Hans Castorp's hallucination scene in the blizzard is to Thomas Mann's *Magic Mountain,* or as Mark and Daria's hallucinogenic lovemaking in the desert is to Michelangelo Antonioni's *Zabriskie Point.* It is a confrontation with truth, a revelation, in short, a figure for their spiritual immersion in a truth that transcends everyday time. When Beavis's life flashes up before him, he discovers (or we do) that at the core of his psyche is Television. What are the consequences and implications of this apparent metaphysical inversion, so brazenly thematized for our analysis? Correlatively, if TV knows that it is inside our heads, why don't we?

First, as far as Beavis and Butt-head are concerned, they are naught but empty shells nibbling on the margins of the symbolic-order. Their investments are elsewhere, even though they hardly know where. Not only do Beavis and Butt-head's identities and appeal depend upon their particular use/misuse of language, what I am calling their autism, but the entire plot of *Beavis and Butt-head Do America* relies upon a series of radical misreadings related to their linguistic handicap and driven by the fact that they are not fucking. As soon as their TV is stolen, Beavis and Butt-head embark on a search for their lost bliss and mistakenly enter a hotel with a "TV" logo on the marquis. While in this place where they don't belong (we surmise that they got there because the only word they can read is TV, which is, after all what they're after) they get an offer from an arms dealer to "do" his troublesome wife. This proposition takes them all over the country. They think "do" means "fuck," but it really means "kill"; the Bruce Willis arms dealer character thinks that Beavis and Butt-head have contracted to kill the Demi Moore troublesome wife character while they think that they have agreed to have sex with her. These usages of the word "do," I would suggest, should be read back into the film's title in order to glean the consequences of B&B's constitution. *Beavis and Butt-head Do America* becomes *Beavis and Butt-head Fuck America* and *Beavis and Butt-head Kill America*. These are two immediate results of having a TV in your brain. However, since TV is quintessentially American and, as we have just seen, B&B have it in their brains, the terms are reversible: "America does Beavis and Butt-head," thereby fucking and killing them as well.

Here's the evidence that America is fucking and killing these animated detritum of the world system (our stand-ins): As the plot "thickens," B&B become entangled in an international arms cartel and the stratagems of FBI men, each of whom have their own complex agendas regarding the military-industrial complex and each of whom uses the stunted facilities of Beavis and Butt-head with the symbolic order for his or her own purposes. By the time we meet B&B in the desert, they are leaving Vegas and walking toward Washington, D.C., with a deadly chemical weapon in their underwear. Despite being told that Washington, D.C., was "three thousand miles thataway," they turn without a thought and walk into the desert, not even bothering to bring water, TV having provided them with absolutely no sense of geography. All this time and through to the end of the film, when they finally get their TV back, B&B are willing if unconscious participants in the schemes of others, led around as they are by their penises, or more accurately, by their addiction to whatever it is they substitute for not fucking—the narcissism of the imaginary.

Although the situation of B&B may appear absurd to some, a mere ruse to attract puerile viewers, it is arguable that their situation of being unconsciously used by various multinational interests who represent the war and money business, and of being led around by an autistic yet absolute identification with their visually modulated, genitally programmed desires, is the situation of most Americans. The evidence supports this in as much as we observe that the relatively successful programming of even this film depends upon a deep structural knowledge of the conditions by and through which the film constitutes its successful characters and affects. Beavis and

Butt-head are the linchpins of a society undergirded by the exigencies of the world-system. Geographical incapacitation, intellectual autism, total identification with one's genitalia, homophobia, and a general imperviousness to learning and logic are some of the central conditions of possibility for the production and reproduction of the American superstate. Such pleasures are among the fallout of the cinematic mode of production.

To conclude this section, spectacle master Guy Debord:

> "In clinical pictures of schizophrenia," according to Gabel, "a degradation of the dialectic of the totality (of which dissociation is the extreme form) and a degradation in the dialectic of becoming (of which catatonia is the extreme form) seem to be intimately interwoven." Imprisoned in a flat universe bounded on all sides by the spectacle's screen, the consciousness of the specator has only figmentary interlocutors which subject it to a one-way discourse on their commodities and the politics of those commodities. The sole mirror of this consciousness is the spectacle in all its breadth, where what is staged is a false way out of a generalized autism.[4]

Media to the Core

Let us now take more seriously the dramatization of the centrality of image technologies for the production of buttheads of all stripes, keeping in mind that such humanoids are not, from a structural point of view, end-products, but rather moments necessary to general production. All that pent-up libido and pent-up language, first organized in the early days of modernity and presently all but stymied by visual technologies, accomplish what is known colloquially as economic growth. But let's use a finer-meshed analysis to see the details and the historicity of this dynamic as it affects the function and architecture of the psyche.

In order to resolve cinema as the unconscious of the unconscious, two distinct motions must be attempted simultaneously. First, the understanding of the unconscious must be transformed; one must historicize the conditions for the emergence of psychoanalysis—its struggle with the visual and the optical. Second, but simultaneously, the understanding of cinema must undergo a similar shifting in order to appear in its proper relation to industrial development and capitalism.

In many respects, the cinematic apparatus is a technology for increasing the eloquence (efficiency) of capital through the optical and the visual. In the conceptualized space known as "the mode of production," the cinematic apparatus and the unconscious as two separate entities may be apprehended as part of the same machine. They are two tandem technologies/effects for/of the re-organizing and expansive development of consciousness, of production, and of the at times seemingly inexorable growth of that dynamic immensity called capital. Furthermore, when one apprehends that the cinematic apparatus and the psychoanalytic unconscious are in effect parallel technologies for the processing of new environmental conditions forever transformed by capitalist expansion, one grasps the extent to which subjective experience is coordinated with alienated production by cinematic capital.

Lacan tells us that "discontinuity is the essential form in which the unconscious first appears to us as a phenomenon" (*FFCP*, 25). I will proceed then by asserting a link through discontinuity as such and discontinuity 1) as it inheres in industrial production (the assembly line along with the rationalization, fragmentation, and alienation of production); 2) as manifest in the forms of experience industrialization produces (the modern experience of shock, at work, at war, and in society at large—the shattering of traditional societies); and 3) as the essential form in which cinema first appears. In cinema, discontinuity manifests itself not only as persistence of vision, in which twenty-four still images per second give the "illusion" of movement (it is no more of an illusion than anything else), but also and more strikingly as montage. It is essential here—in each of the above cases—to grasp discontinuity, that is, the cut, as *simultaneously* the form through which continuity—the continuity of character, narrative, and the mise-en-scène of daily life—is generated.

Though the idea of character and narrative being spliced together from discontinuous fragments is clearly a presupposition of filmmaking shortly after its origins in 1895, it is also a discovery and indeed a "truth" of psychoanalysis. Take, for example, the role of the organization of the drives in identity formation. As Lacan says, "If there is anything resembling a drive, it is a *montage*" (*FFCP*, 169). And again, "the drive is precisely that *montage* by which sexuality participates in psychical life in a way that must conform to the gap-like structure that is the structure of the unconscious" (*FFCP*, 176). I will have more to say regarding "the gap-like structure that is the structure of the unconscious," and "discontinuity" momentarily, but first let me comment on this term "montage," a term whose cinematic dimension does not appear in Lacan's text. Rather, it is associated immediately with painting, meant, as Lacan hastens to add, "in the sense that one speaks of *montage* in a surrealist collage" (*FFCP*, 169). This statement is characteristic of the general de-emphasis of the cinematic in Lacan and the corresponding importance of the painted. Freud tells us that "in the dream-work a psychical force is operating which on the one hand strips the elements which have a high psychical value of their intensity, and on the other hand, *by means of over-determination,* creates from elements of low psychical value new values, which afterwards find their way into the dream content. If that is so, *a transference and displacement of psychical intensities* occurs in the process of dream-formation, and it is a result of these that the difference between the text of the dream content and that of the dream-thoughts comes about."[5] What I am suggesting is that the "dream-content" of Lacan's Seminar XI comprises part of what we are accustomed to regarding as psychoanalytic theory, but the "dream-thoughts" are, as it were, displaced. As the remainder of my discussion labors to show, what is displaced is a struggle with the emerging power of the visual and the cinematic. As we shall see, the dreamwork performed by the seminar finds its traumatic analogue in the half-awake visual work of consciousness in the life-world.[6] Though Lacan does not seem interested in the visual per se, drawing on it by way of example in order to elaborate the structure of the subject of the signifier, "the dream is, as it were, differently centered from the dream-thoughts—its content has different elements as its central points."[7]

Slavoj Zizek reminds us that for Freud, "we must get rid of the fascination in th[e] kernel of signification, in the 'hidden meaning' of the dream—that is to say, in the content concealed behind the form of the dream—and center our attention on the form itself, on the 'dream-work' to which the 'latent dream-thoughts' were submitted."[8] It is for this reason that it is not enough to exclaim here that, yes, the cinematic mode of production is the latent content of *The Four Fundamental Concepts of Psychoanalysis!,* in spite of the fact that this is indeed the case. To perform the analysis, it is necessary to account for the form of the dream—at least up to a point. Thus it will be necessary to highlight certain instances of condensation and displacement (as with Lacan's usage of "montage"), as well as to sketch the forces of overdetermination that at once construct the dream elements (Lacan's examples, arguments, asides) and displace a complex trauma stemming from a new order of images, and lying at the core of psycho-analysis—as well as at the frazzled core of the contemporary psyche.

Dr. Green, one of Lacan's seminar auditors, sums up Lacan's position on the montage of the drive ("the drive is ultimately destined to the combinatory of the fact of discontinuity") in order to pose a question from "the economic point of view" (*FFCP*, 170).[9] I read Dr. Green's question as a remark on the affinities between the form of the drive and the form of industrial manufacturing, finishing with a pointed question regarding Lacan's elision of labor: The "energy of the system," or again, "the element of thrust," where does it come from? Although Lacan sometimes invokes economics, he answers Green's question in terms of energetics—the economic question remains, as does cinema, at the extreme margins of his discourse. If one listens closely, however, one hears in Dr. Green's question a request for Lacan to address the homologous character of the montage of the drive and the montage of materiality, that is, assembly-line production and monetary exchange. Lacan's lack of a response here provides a gap for the initiation of interpretation, in a manner consistent with his theory of the unconscious.

The perception that there is an overlap in the structure of the psyche and in the structure of political economy is taken up by Zizek, among others.[10] Zizek, who claims that "according to Lacan it was none other than Karl Marx who invented the notion of the symptom," reminds us that Marx set out to "penetrate the 'secret' of the value of commodities," that is, to examine the ostensible continuity of the commodity as rupture.[11] Though in both psychoanalysis and Marxism it is a long way from originary rupture to a theory of alienation, the presence of symptom as false continuity leads us to a simple principle: With the increasing forms of discontinuity and rupture emerging through the simultaneous historical development of mechanization, perception, and capital itself, new forms for the imposing of continuity are created that modulate and indeed extend the shattering of reality into fragments by capitalized machinery—among them (and in addition to the commodity and psychopathology) Marxism, psychoanalysis, and cinema. In the cases of commercial cinema and of psychoanalysis, at least, it is probably fair to say that these orchestrations of discontinuity as continuity are predominantly forms of mediation for putting the Humpty-Dumpties of capital back together again.[12] Of course, in a list of media for the shattering of reality and its subsequent reorganization one also would have to include war-machines, factories, print advertisements, planes, trains, automobiles, and computers.[13] However, cinema, with its intellectual, visceral, and *optical* mediation of machinery, economy, desire, and vision turns out to be the decisive technology of our age, the archetype of a new organizational fusion of disparate systems.

Posing the metaphysical question of the identity of fragments, Lacan asks:

Is the *one* anterior to discontinuity? I do not think so, and everything that I have taught in recent years has tended to exclude this need for a closed *one*—a mirage to which is attached the reference to the enveloping psyche, a sort of double of the organism in which this false unity is thought to reside. You will grant me that the *one* that is introduced by the experience of the unconscious is the *one* of the split, of the stroke of the rupture. (*FFCP*, 26)

Let us imagine that this proto-post-structuralist assertion of Lacan is speaking simultaneously about the split subject, the film character, and narrative unity, "I spoke with you about the concept of the unconscious, whose true function is precisely that of being in profound, initial, inaugural relation with the function of the concept of *Unbegrif*—or *Begriff* of the original *Un*, namely, the cut" (*FFCP*, 43).[14] Lacan asserts "a profound link between this cut and the function as such of the subject, of the subject in its constituent relation to the signifier itself" (*FFCP*, 43). As with a dream, the manifest content of Lacan's statement about the unconscious appears to the analyst as a cipher of a latent content. How does one account for the form of the dream—in this case the unconscious itself? It could be said that Lacan's claim that the "one" who appears as the artifact that unifies the gaps that are the experience of the unconscious *masquerades* as being a statement about false closure as the structure of the subject. In the mode of psychoanalysis we may state, "Clearly these dream elements are drawn from Lacan's diurnal immersion in the discourse of psychoanalysis and displace a deeper trauma!" The latent content here lies in an intuition about the mode of production itself, the crisis that is the generalized emergence of discontinuity in all aspects of life (so well documented by modern literature and Modernism in general). In accord with classical psychoanalytic theory, we may say that the unconscious takes this particular form because the dreamwork that here is psychoanalytic theory itself, functions to present controversial material (the technological and the economic) in a way that maintains the equilibrium machine called "the ego" of the analyst. This machine is a socio-political entity at once brought into being to unify discontinuity (the history of the modern subject) and evermore under siege (and hence driven) by intensifying modernization. What is censored from the Lacanian dream is the mode of production in its cinematic aspect—because, to acknowledge industrial technology and the intensification of the visual at the core of the psyche would be to denature the psychoanalytic project, which for Lacan is the very fantasy that enables psychoanalytic subjectivity. As Freud taught, the dream censor does not eliminate but only distorts elements from the unconscious; therefore, the cinematic mode of production appears in disguised form in the words such as "montage" and "cut," as well as in the very figurations of psychic architecture. Indeed, taking "montage" as an index of a repressed element, the above passage and the entire institution of psychoanalysis can be seen to comply with the subject's need for a generalized repression of technologically mediated production of an unprecedented scale. Such is the precondition of all twentieth-century humanism. Consider New Criticism.

Psychoanalysis reads generalized discontinuity as a gateway to the understanding of personality and strives to place the personal and the individual—or at their extreme limits the specie-al and the biological—in the foreground of complex structural effects that daily threaten to annihilate these. It manifests a commitment to language function that global organization is rapidly rendering problematic. Lacan's summation of Freud's contribution to knowledge, "here, in the field of the dream, you are at home" (*FFCP*, 44), belies the psychoanalytic wish to find reason in an ostensibly irrational presentation that for us equally could be the dream, as Freud intended the term, or the dream-world (virtual reality a la Baudrillard) of technologized life (*Vanilla Sky, The Matrix*). In either case, what besieges the subject is an erumpent vision—a moving picture troubling the word. It is no secret that psychoanalysis is the epic of the subject under siege, the story of Ulysses institutionalized, but the causes of that siege, the Oedipus Complex, castration, and ontological lack secret another element in their mytho-poetic aspect. In short, the cut.

For Freud, the dream is a rebus, "a picture puzzle" that must be solved. "Our predecessors in the field of dream interpretation have made the mistake of treating the rebus as a pictorial composition."[15] Though Freud is certainly not as ocularly invested as is Lacan, he often describes the dream as a contest between the image and the word and deploys strategies to stabilize the otherwise moving image. "But obviously we can only form a proper judgment of the rebus if we put aside criticism such as these [dream images are non-sensical pictures] of the whole composition and its parts and if, instead, we try to replace each separated element by a syllable or a word that can be represented by the element in some way or another. The words which are put together this way are no longer nonsensical but may form a poetical phrase of the greatest beauty and significance."[16] This act of taking the image as a signifier in disguise is a primordial operation of psychoanalysis (and a little later, of semiotics). The unconscious is the unsaid or the to-be-said of images.[17] This claim is implicit in Martin Jay's historical narrative regarding Lacan's formulation of the mirror stage.[18]

Godzich, in the essay cited above, argues that,

> The structure of objective images achieved by our technological innovations brings about a new relation: photographs coincide with the world to the point of denying themselves as images, but the world they make present to us is imaginary. . . . We are living in the midst of a prelogical affirmation of the world, in the sense that it takes place before the fact of the *logos,* and it threatens us with an alienation that modern thinkers could barely conceive. For what happens is that immediate (non-mediated) reality becomes the very expression of the imaginary and substitutes itself for it. The imaginary becomes free of the *logos* since the world speaks itself in its own terms. Such a world is defined without us."[19]

Thus, and in a way that begins to vitiate Sartre's existentialist yet redemptive concept of creative participation, the unconscious as "the discourse of the Other," as the gap in the language of the "I," undergoes something like a quantitative increase with the emergence of photography that renders a qualitative transformation in language's ability to preside through and in a certain way over the discourse of the Other by creating the illusory "one." This shattering of the subject's continuity is what Godzich means here by "an alienation that modern thinkers could barely conceive." Images that supplant language as the discourse of the Other ("the world speaks itself in its own terms") reveal two related tendencies—the crisis of language as the arbiter of expressivity and the simultaneous fading of "the Other" ("such a world is defined without us"), since images are not really a discourse at all. The poles of the subject-Other relation begins to dissolve—not via psychoanalysis or within the structures of subjectification, but in spite of psychoanalysis and beyond its parameters. Images begin to seem like indifferent nature—undifferentiated, non-intentional, non-signifying landscape—nothing for no one. The transformation of the world into images asserts two contradictory trajectories: Everything begins to exceed signification (legibility for the subject) and yet (in fact, objectively) remains shot through with intentionality. This intentionality no longer can be subsumed by any particular "one" or "Other," or be figured in any existing "language." Intentionality therefore becomes at once deterritorialized and systemic while being neither attributable to God nor conceptualizeable. Such a perceptual situation subverts the identity and indeed the very structure of the subject who, with the help of analysis, might once have presided over "his" unconscious. If the unconscious meant the standing reserve of the *to-be-said* or the *to-be-represented* that informed the internal world of the subject, then cinema means the *to-be-filmed* aspect of the world *within* which (postmodern) consciousness is "found."

If filming is a form of realization that exceeds the capacity of consciousness to language it, then the ethic known as "film-language" was and to a certain extent remains an effort to subjugate the world of images, the imaginary, to the law of the *logos*. One thinks here of Pasolini's cinematic ideal of "representing reality with reality," and the subsequent endeavor to derive a grammar for this new language. Cinema, as "the written language of reality," was, for Pasolini, an earth-shattering world-historical technology, to visual language the equivalent of what writing was to spoken language.[20] Pasolini's is a quasi-ontological claim (the world is cinematic in its basis and film is the long-awaited technology capable of representing its true communicativity), but again, the relevant question is the historicity of his insight—he's right, but not transhistorically. What is noteworthy here is that cinema as the phenomenological appearance of organized fragments in the visual field defines, over and above verbal language and in terms of sheer proportion, a new relation of representation to the linguistically unrealizable. When the linguistically unrealized rises up and overwhelms the capacity of the *logos* for realization, the world that once was fully present in and as language begins to feel like an island. This sensation explains the rise of the term "intensity" as a substitute for "experience"—the latter being narrative in character and requiring duration in order to ripen. Intensity on the other hand is utterly deterritorialized, denoting some perception of some consciousness somewhere. Consciousness, as Deleuze and Guattari have characterized it, becomes a "recording surface"—the concept of intensity is a figuration for a consciousness in crisis; it shows consciousness's apprehension of its own marginalization and its failure to constitute itself as a subject.[21] Of course, this is supposed to be a good thing, but I do not wish to debate its merits here. Again:

> The problem is that a dissonance is now manifesting itself: images are scrambling the functioning of language, which must operate out of the imaginary in order to function optimally. Images are parasitical noises upon language at first—and then they supplant it: it must be recalled that the technology of images operates at the speed of light, as does the world. Language could slow down the world, thanks to its tremendous negative capability, but it cannot slow down images, for they operate out

of the very imaginary that language would have to be able to organize in the first place. Indeed, the question is one of dissonance: can language bring the speed of images under control, that is, turn images into a kind of language (but the failure of visual semiotics is not reassuring on this score) or are we to *see* a world, images of this world, and an imaginary all traveling at the speed of light in a universe without *logos,* an alogical universe?[22]

Though Godzich poses above a fundamental question of the new relation of consciousness to politics, I will have to bracket it here. However, cinematics must be understood as an effort to redeploy the negative capability of language in order to grasp the logic of a universe operating at the speed of light. It must show the *modality* of the instantaneous, global operation of mega-structures in the shaping and indeed the control/annihilation of experience. I only want to add here that consciousness's own perception of itself as a structural effect of a world operating at the speed of light, creates, beyond, yet as part of its self-constitution, new difficulties for the subject to purposefully map itself into a world whose intelligence exceeds its own. The organizing mind must work from its own conditions and take itself, along with its *necessarily* perverse conceits, as a part of the "objective" situation.[23]

The eruption of the unconscious through the structure of the gap emerges as a crisis in signification, and psychoanalysis appears as a linguistic endeavor to remedy a breakdown of language. It follows then, albeit parenthetically, that, from an historical standpoint, with the blossoming of psychoanalytic theory there is more and more unconscious around. Psychoanalysis, the investigation of parapraxis, sleep, and other breakdowns, is the discovery of the build up of the unconscious at the moment it reaches critical mass, and it may be taken as one technology to stay the rising tide of the unconscious in and by its very endeavor to language it. It establishes a continuity to discontinuity. As such, the unconscious is at once generative and controlled, generated and controlling. The unconscious is a breakdown of language; its activity increases with the presence of images. "The Unconscious" expresses an inability (at once destructive and productive) on the part of language to give an adequate accounting of experience. One might go so far as to define the unconscious as the effect of the inadequacy of language to render experience. Hence the famous "decline of experience" noted by Walter Benjamin.[24]

It would not be wrong here to deduce that the *quantity* of ambient unconscious (both as concept and activity), if I may be so bold, at the end of the nineteenth century is, like the quantity of environmental destruction that might be taken as its analogue, minuscule compared with that which is in our midst at the beginning of the twenty-first. Linguistic interruption and dysfunction have achieved new heights. The massive breakdown of language that brings about and indeed is a tremendous spilling forth of unconscious, is not just some piddly-diddly development in the history of ideas. Rather, it is part of the very same techno-economy responsible for global warming and the destruction of the ozone layer. In the present over-heating of consciousness that results from language on overdrive, the unconscious floods forth like water from the poles of reason, engulfing all. *Solaris*-like, it leaves only islands of thought whose limits, when pursued, threaten to reveal their free-floating character, the utterly cut-loose character of a new kind of being that has lost all ontological guarantees—even those of its immediate presence. Rather than appearing in the verbal slip, the unconscious is the generalized slipperiness of the contemporary world as mise-en-scène, that is, the world as resistant to language—dreamy and unconceptualizable, in the philosophical sense. Consciousness today is mere flotsam in the swirling convection streams of the massive tide of unconsciousness that, as—and here is the point—the excrescence of capitalized mediation (media here in the most general sense, the translation of forces, that is, social organization as we know it) threatens to swallow up all knowing as such.

Postmodernism itself attests to the increased thermal activity of the unconscious, which, in a serialized and ubiquitous way renders consciousness itself unconscious.[25] Of course, the unconsciousness of consciousness was the fundamental polemic that founded the inauguration of psychoanalysis, but the sheer quantity of that which is not conscious and yet informs the character and nuance of all aspects of life from the most objective and external to the extremely subjective and innermost zones of experience, has increased exponentially. The zones of social production are at once more numerous and more intense. Less "blindness and insight" and more "blindness and incite!" This increase in the quantity of unconscious is not only from the vertiginous circulation of images—the rise of image culture is a dialectical symptom here. The global warming of the psyche, caused by a consciousness, which as an artifact of the symbolic is driven beyond its linguistic capacities, places consciousness in a virtual sea of unconsciousness and in many ways reverses the polarity of the terms. Rather than a firmly solidified consciousness capable of soberly presiding over the pyrotechnics of the fissures of the unconscious, consciousness appears only as a function of the unconscious morass—*its* dream. Without here giving further commentary on Borges' short story "The Circular Ruins," in which the ostensibly autonomous creative subject is revealed as merely the dream of a larger homologous system, a cog in the dream of a mystical and potentially infinite machine, it is sufficient here to say that it is this imaginary characteristic of consciousness itself as doing the dreamwork of society that characterizes the postmodern. We are society's dreams. Postmodernism and its ethos of surface, its denial of depth, represents the triumph of the unconscious. The *Unconscious* expands beyond the limits of the individual subject and individual experience—you no longer have, what in retrospect was "your unconscious." The proliferation of images prevents conscious rationality from exerting mastery and providing meaning—even, perhaps, the meaningful explanation of traumatic non-meaning that psychoanalysis claims as its field of engagement. Therapy is a lost cause—our ironic detachment from belief in reality is already the "cure." To a large extent the postmodern "subject" recognizes the loss of objectivity and therefore intuits that he or she is a particular nodal instantiation of an unconceptualizable machine—a serialized screen across which a variant of the world passes.

Psychoanalysis, then, only hails (and to a certain extent produces) the birth of the modern subject (necessarily simultaneous with the beginnings of its demise). Because it is axiomatic that innovations in cultural form express corresponding transformations in the mode of production, the appearance of psychoanalysis simultaneously hails a shift in the mode of production. To reify my terms for a moment: The appearance of psychoanalysis in the superstructure indicates a transformation in the economic base. But this transformation is expressed and realized more completely by cinema, which, with its visual capacity, its higher speed, its tremendous conveyance of data, and its tremendous production of suture in the image, emerges as the greater technology of this crisis in production by bringing the industrial revolution to the (*its*) senses. To a great extent, psychoanalysis is merely cinema's shadow.

The Scopic, or, the Agency of the Visual Object

We have begun to observe the crises that the technological development of the image represents for language, for the order of representation. The "noise" of the image on language links the emergence of the unconscious with the visual, and, as I shall further elaborate, it is the visual that provides the basis of Lacan's ocularcentric theory of the subject. In the work of Lacan, the struggle of the symbolic with the unconscious is founded on the struggle of the symbolic with the visual. It should be noted that Lacan studies *Freud's* unconscious, which emerges, coincidentally, with cinema. This unconscious, which in Freud first appears as ruptures in language, in Lacan's analysis is *derived scopically*.

In the latter half of *The Four Fundamental Concepts of Psychoanalysis*, one may grasp that the subject as an effect of the signifier is transposed from a visual relation. Citing Merleau-Ponty, Lacan specifies that in terms of our being (as distinct from our function as subject), "we are beings who are looked at in the spectacle of the world. That which makes us consciousness institutes us by the same token as *speculum mundi*" (*FFCP*, 75). Having specified the mise-en-scène of human being, Lacan immediately introduces an important qualification: "The world is all-seeing, but it is not exhibitionistic—it does not provoke our gaze. When it begins to provoke it, the feeling of strangeness begins too. What does this mean, if not that in the so-called waking state there is an elision of the gaze, and an elision of the fact that not only does it look, *it* also *shows*. In the field of the dream, on the other hand, what characterizes the image is that *it shows*" (*FFCP*, 75). The emphasis here is on a certain bivalence of the gaze that Lacan will develop at some length. We are seen in the world, but it is only with the inauguration of our seeing that the dialectics of subjectivity emerge. For Lacan, the bivalence of seeing is embodied in a split between being and meaning, the eye and the gaze. "In so far as I am under the gaze, Sartre writes, I no longer see the eye that looks at me and if, I see the eye, the gaze disappears" (*FFCP*, 84).

The point is that this involution of the eye and the gaze introduces into perception an imaginary dimension. In Sartre's example, there is a demonstrable oscillation, "when I am under the gaze, I no longer see the eye," that is, I imagine being looked at by the Other and in doing so perceive myself as seen. "If I see the eye, the gaze disappears," that is, when I look, when I see the eye as an object or image, I do not see (that I am seen). In each direction, as it were, of this fundamental dynamic between self and Other, something is missed. The imaginary element (the point from which I am seen) is in the field of the Other. The *objet a*, as that upon which the desiring gaze cathects, is caught up in/as this oscillation—it is simultaneous with the gaze, and as Lacan will say, indeed is the gaze in the visual field.

In the Lacanian theory of the gaze, Sartre's example is a specific instance of the general case—the oscillation of the gaze is impacted (into objects: the *objet a*) and generalized to all objects of desire in the visual field. "[T]he interest that the subject takes in his own split is bound up with that which determines it—namely a privileged object, which has emerged from some primal separation, from some self-mutilation induced by the very approach of the real, whose name, in our algebra, is the *objet a*" (*FFCP*, 83). From this relation in which "the subject is suspended in an essential vacillation of the gaze" (*FFCP*, 83), two things become clear. First, "*the* objet a *in the field of the visible is the gaze*" (*FFCP*, 105), meaning that each of these two terms (gaze, *objet a*) is a standpoint in a single dynamic of subjectification, and second, the *objet a*, as always already in the field of the Other, becomes the model for the unconscious as "the discourse of the Other." Vision provides the ontology for signification.

The lesson from Seminar XI entitled "What is a Picture?" forms a prelude to Lacan's discussion of the unconscious as the discourse of the Other and of alienation in the symbolic: "In the scopic field, everything is articulated between two terms that act in an antinomic way—on the side of things there is the gaze, that is to say, things look at me, and yet I see them. That is how one should understand those words so strongly stressed, in the Gospel, *They have eyes that they might not see.* That they might not see what? Precisely, that things are looking at them" (*FFCP*, 109). This relationship described by a bivalent vision constituting the subject in relation to an object (an object that has a certain subjective dimension: remember, the gaze is "on the side of things" (*FFCP*, 109)) will later be objectified in the algorithm of the signifier. "The subject is born in so far as the signifier emerges in the field of the Other. But, by this very fact, this subject—which was previously nothing if not a subject coming into being—solidifies as a signifier" (*FFCP*, 199). The subject that solidifies as a signifier, an "I," is always already in the field of the other (*Je est un autre*); the architecture of the specular relation lays the groundwork for the symbolic relation, before passing into it. In languaging the gaze and the *objet a*, Lacan develops in the symbolic the abstract form that ultimately will be the very architecture of the symbolic.[26]

As with signification, which is always already in the field of the Other, "[i]n the scopic, the gaze is outside, I am looked at, that is to say, I am a picture" (*FFCP*, 106). Lacan will recuperate the picture as Freud does the rebus, but at a more generalized level of abstraction. The visual field, and the fact of being "a picture," assures the ontological character of the symbolic. However, this ontologicalization of "some primal separation, from some self-mutilation induced by the very approach of the real" (*FFCP*, 83), works by a sleight of hand.

> This is the function that is found at the heart of the institution of the subject in the visible. What determines me, at the most profound level, in the visible, is the gaze that is outside. It is through the gaze that I enter light and it is from the gaze that I receive its effects. Hence it comes about that the gaze is the instrument through which light is embodied and through which—if you will allow me to use a word, as I often do, in a fragmented form—I am *photo-graphed*. (*FFCP*, 106)

Through the use of an uncanny anachronism, the camera is employed to invoke the ontological character of sight. Lacan produces a model to show how we are inscribed in the visual field by the gaze, but the model that is to show the visceral, ontological, and quasi-biological character of "the institution of the subject in the visible" grounds its function on photographic technology. Because "the *objet a* in the field of the visible is the gaze" (*FFCP*, 105), it is the *objet a* that inscribes the subject in the visual field. Things are looking at me! What is implied of course is that the camera only plies this relation. However, the recursive possibility that the camera—along with the advent of visual technologies and modern visuality—induces and intensifies the inscription is cut off.

In dreams, "the things I see, see me just as much as I see them."[27] If observant objects populate the dreams of both Valery and Lacan, it should not surprise us too much that the camera is at the basis of a world in which things look at us. These dreams are dreamt in history—that is, in a world in which objects, in Marx's phrase, "confront us as something hostile and alien." Objects have taken on a new agency via the massive economic alienation and reification of subjective activity within the terms of capitalist production. The camera is an image for the agency of objects; moreover, it exemplifies their practice in visual terms—it is the object par excellence and marks the impact of alienation on the visible. The camera is, to a certain extent, the paradigmatic object of late capitalism.

For Lacan, the *objet a* is a *function,* an object of desire as easily supplied by/as a person or a commodity. This interchangeability of the object of desire and its being defined as such in terms of function is in accord with the logic of the photo-graph because objects—in a world where virtually all elements, from the atomic to the "natural" to the national pass through the economic—are nothing but raw materials fused with reified, alienated human activity, or better, matter combined with frozen human subjectivity. These willful, alien objects photograph us, that is, they inscribe us in the visual field. Such is the other side of our looking at them.

Marx's notion that the history of capital is also the history of the development of the senses is useful here. Given the conditions of production in which human agency is impacted in objects to such an extent that nearly everything is historically mediated, that is, man-made, it is not surprising that there is a convergence in the perceiving of objects and the perceiving of human beings: Humans are taken as objects, and what is more, objects are taken as humans. The Lacanian visual economy depends upon such a sentience of objects, their artificial intelligence. Furthermore, perception itself activates this economy, inducing as it does a radical *maiconnaissance*. Such an activation may be grasped simultaneously as being productive of subjectivity as well as productive of the relations implied by capital: our non-knowledge that what we have made is ours, or, to put it another way, our non-comprehension of the spectacle as a social relation. These products (subject, alienation, spectacularity) are the expression of the same logic in different registers of experience.

Lacan's fundamental operator, the *objet á*, hails from the visual field and is the touchstone through which he figures the visual economy of the subject. As such, the *objet a* is the hallmark of the effort of psychoanalysis to "bring the speed of images under control" and "turn them into a kind of language."[28] All such constructions endeavor to territorialize the *objet a* in fields of signification. The *objet a*, in other words, is precisely Lacan's term for the image. Cinema that engages the animation of the object-world in earnest by giving visual objects at least the full impact of another's subjectivity is nothing less than the technological elaboration of the productive yet internecine convergence of alienated human subjectivity and the object world. This convergence itself was signaled in industrialization (with the machine-mediated combining of human labor and raw material—where workers' products confront them as "something alien"), only to be realized in its cinematic aftermath.

The collation of subjectivity and objectivity by industrial and cinematic capital is exemplified in Lacan's description of the eye. "[T]he true function of the organ of the eye [is] the eye filled with voracity, the evil eye" (*FFCP*, 115). It is "the eye that must be fed" (*FFCP*, 115), "the eye [which] carries with it the fatal function of being in itself endowed—if you will allow me to play on several registers at once—with a power to separate" (*FFCP*, 115). Both the rationalization of work and the alienation of the worker from the fruit of his/her labor allies this separation with its essential function for capital—the cut of exchange-value that culminates in the radical separation of the spectacle. Furthermore, this separation of workers from their products feeds the maintenance of two distinct yet intertwined hungers, that of capital for profit, and that of the worker for food. The voracious eye is the eye of capital, as well as of labor in capital.

As I develop my reading of Lacan, I intend to indicate the extent to which the Lacanian theory of the subject is the theory of managerial consciousness *in* global capital.[29] For it is not enough merely to assert that the Lacanian subject is the subject in capital or even that it is the subject *of capital*. One must trace the migration of various properties of material relations into the visual field and back, for it is through capital's colonization of the visual that capital tracks and finally, to a very great extent, appropriates (subsumes) the symbolic. In *capital's* articulation of the imaginary, it wins the symbolic. With one tine in for-profit industry and the other in the desire of subjects in capital, cinema embodies the fusion of economic and psychological exigencies. Its coordination of both through the construction of the image is, from a social-science standpoint, paradigmatic, that is, cinema both signals and realizes the terms of the twentieth-century subject's being in the world. It is the proof of the thesis that there is an eye of capital (the voracious eye) that dialectically produces consciousness in capital.

Subjectivity as Screen

The Lacanian account of the gaze is the manifest content of a dream in history whose latent content is cinema. Being "photo-graphed" in the operation of the gaze induces a split in/as the subject, a separation between what one is for oneself, and what one is for/in the eyes of the other, so to speak. Lacan's term for the region in which the play of the image occurs is consistent with the visuo-optical discourse he employs: It is "the screen" (*FFCP*, 106). Again within the biological he unearths the technological:

> Only the subject—the human subject, the subject of desire that is the essence of man—is not, unlike the animal, entirely caught up in this imaginary capture. He maps himself in it. How? In so far as he isolates the function of the screen and plays with it. Man, in effect, knows how to play with the mask as that beyond which there is the gaze. *The screen is here the locus of mediation.* (*FFCP*, 107; italics mine)

Thus the screen is that surface on which the subject negotiates his appearance, the illusory space of the masquerade. The Lacanian formula that "man's desire is the desire of the Other" (*FFCP*, 115) can be grasped here, because it is on the screen of appearance that man manipulates his masks in order to lure the desire of the other. The mapping, of course, is the assignation of meaning to the image through the signifier. Lacan continues:

> Last time, I alluded to the reference given by Maurice Merleau-Ponty in *La Phénoménologie de la perception* in which, from well chosen examples based on the experiments of Gelb and Goldstein, one can already see, simply at the perceptual level, how the screen re-establishes things in their status as real. If, by being isolated, an effect of lighting dominates us, if, for example, a beam of light directing our gaze so captivates us that it appears as a milky cone and prevents us from seeing what it illuminates, the mere fact of introducing a small screen, which cuts into that which is illuminated without being seen, makes the milky light retreat, as it were, into the shadow, and allows the object concealed to emerge. (*FFCP*, 107–108)

In this interlude with the cinematic apparatus, a semblance of it, and not just its properties, is utilized to figure the psyche. The introduction of a screen into a beam of light serves to model the gaze, at once bringing into focus an object of desire and marginalizing the real. "At the perceptual level, this is the phenomenon of a relation that is to be taken in a more essential function, namely, that in relation to desire, reality appears only as marginal" (*FFCP*, 108). The focusing of the gaze with the illuminated screen images the operation of the gaze in vivo. The marginalization of the Real appears as a natural function of desire.

The censor of the dream called psychoanalysis blocks the appearance of cinema and performs its duty in the above passages in order to sustain the psychoanalytical wish for an ontological/biological basis for its researches, and for the establishment of, in accord with what is, ostensibly at least, the central concern of *The Four Fundamental Concepts:* psychoanalysis as a quasi-science.[30] Disguised forms of cinema only serve as elliptical examples, never as basis.

Such displacement takes yet another form toward the end of "What is a Picture?" In a kind of quadruple remove, Lacan, in an effort to elaborate the gaze via comments about the paintings of Cezanne, refers to "the delightful example that Maurice Merleau-Ponty gives *in passing* in his *Signes,* namely, that *strange slow-motion film* in which one sees Matisse painting" (*FFCP*, 114; italics mine). In the dreamwork of Lacan, the rebus that is Seminar XI signals a profound anxiety regarding the unpalatable, anti-humanist, non-biological, and indeed non-psychological notion that at the heart of the psyche smolders technology and economics, that is, "the inhuman." We must pass through Cezanne, Merleau-Ponty (whose formulation of the situatedness of the perceiver seems somewhat more open to the historicity of consciousness than is Lacan), and Matisse, to arrive at this "strange slow-motion film" (*FFCP*, 114), that is actually at the core of the seminar.[31] The number of mediations here is striking. Says Merleau-Ponty for Lacan (Lacan paraphrases him here): this film, which overwhelmed Matisse because the "gesture, enlarged by the distension of time, enables us to imagine the most perfect deliberation in each of [his] brush strokes" (*FFCP*, 114), "is an illusion. . . . What occurs as these strokes, which go to make up the miracle of the picture, fall like rain from the painter's brush is not choice, but something else" (*FFCP*, 114). Even though this strange slow-motion film engages viewers and painter in precisely the structure of subjectification that is the topic of this seminar, that is, the imaginary positing of intention behind the image, the film is deemed unreliable (a trick), and neatly contained by an elaboration of painting: "Should the question [what is a picture?] be brought closer to what I called the rain of the brush?" Lacan will use the picture in place of the film to dramatize the relationship between an image and its significance, that is, its signification. Despite the fact that the film's effect precisely figures the positing of subjectivity through the image, the mechanical mediation renders it unworthy—it is used only as a false version of a true illusion. Though Lacan is himself working out what is nothing less than the parameters of a *technology* of the subject, in which its very existence and possibilities are overdetermined by the structure of signification and the gaze, he remains with what he takes as the organic activity of bodies and natural language. And despite the fact that Lacan's modeling of the subject goes a long way toward the dismantling of what Derrida will call the "myth of presence" (Lacan's deconstruction of "the one"), Lacan's dream cannot recognize consciousness as a technological, that is, cybernetic, effect, but naturalizes its processes by gesturing toward animal behavior. Despite Lacan's mechanistic ("scientific") presentation, presence as an illusion of language, the illusion of "the one" as a sealing off of the unconscious, remains securely within the realm of humanism. The illusion produced by the film, the clear imposturing of a machine, must be degraded because the consequences threaten the very ontology of the signifier.

If the filmic effect of the apparent deliberation in Matisse's brush is allowed to stand, then the locus of the masquerade is no longer in the human realm—it is the machine that means. Photography introduces this lecture, and its very title "What is a Picture" could be read as a distorted reference to cinema (as in "the pictures"). Because of an intense unconscious techno-phobia, Lacan uses paintings to elaborate the visual economy of the scopic field. However, I would suggest that Lacan's statement "I am a picture" really means to say "I am a film." This displacement occurs, and must occur, finally, because paintings contain human-scale examples of the gaze and its dynamics, about which Lacan can develop a humanist psychoanalytic discourse, while cinema would end up containing psychoanalysis as an example.[32]

The Gaze of Capital

Psychoanalysis as spilt revolution (an endeavor to heal the subject without social transformation) takes the lack that informs Marxism (as the dialectic of impoverishment against capital's self-valorization) and registers its transference to the visual field. Desire is one with lack. Consistent with Zizek's arguments for the correlation between enjoyment and surplus-value, that is, profit, my argument is nothing short of the admittedly somewhat grandiose claim that economic investment (for the sake of profit) reappears as a visuo-libidinal economy: "the *objet a* in the field of the visible is the gaze" (*FFCP*, 105), meaning that the gaze mediates production. According to Zizek, and almost as if in answer to Dr. Green's earlier question, "Lacan modeled his notion of surplus-enjoyment on the Marxian notion of surplus-value. The proof that Marxian surplus-value announces effectively the logic of the Lacanian *objet petit a* as the embodiment of surplus-enjoyment is already provided by the decisive formula used by Marx, in the third volume of *Capital*, to designate the logical-historical limit of capitalism: 'the limit of capital is capital itself, i.e. the capitalist mode of production'"[33] After going through a "dumb" reading of this axiom, in which one would conceive that it means that capital grows to a certain size, works for a while, and then sheds its skin to expand, and a "smart[er]" reading of it in which *"this very immanent limit, this 'internal contradiction', . . . drives capital into permanent development,"* Zizek writes,

It is this paradox [the immanent limit] which drives surplus-enjoyment: it is not a surplus which simply attaches itself to some 'normal,' fundamental enjoyment, because *enjoyment as such emerges only in this surplus,* because it is constitutively excess. If we subtract the surplus we lose enjoyment itself, just as capitalism, which can survive only by incessantly revolutionizing its own material conditions, ceases to exist if it 'stays the same,' if it achieves an internal balance. This then is the homology between surplus-value—the 'cause' which sets in motion the capitalist process of production—and surplus-enjoyment, the object-cause of desire. Is not the paradoxical topology of the movement of capital, the fundamental blockage which resolves and reproduces itself through frenetic activity, *excessive* power as the very form of appearance of a fundamental *impotence*—this immediate passage, this coincidence of limit and excess, of lack and surplus—precisely that of the Lacanian *objet petit a,* of the leftover which embodies the fundamental constitutive lack?[34]

What I am suggesting is that the *objet petit a,* a.k.a. "the gaze," is to a great extent like money in its function as capital—in a way analogous to Althusserian interpellation but less discursively based, it grasps the subject and forces him to produce himself according to certain protocols. These protocols are at once inherent, as it were, in the structure of a visual economy overdetermined by capital, and specific to the particularities of both subject and object under industrial and then cinematic capitalism. It is the general point, that in the cinematic mode of production the gaze is manifest as a medium that invests with an eye toward profit (surplus value/surplus enjoyment)—whether one is regarded by a commodity or a more immediately human object of desire—and marginalizes other concerns, that is at issue here.[35] This activation of the gaze as capital is not a mere analogy, but a *materialization* of capital logic occurring as capital invades visual perception with technology. It is a movement of the logistics of capital into the visual arena—the mutual articulation of capital by vision and vision by capital.

Like the passages in the *Grundrisse* in which Marx shows 1) the capitalist as the subjectification of capital (desirous of a profit) and 2) the construction of modern subjects through the process of exchange (each brings his exchange-value to the market and, through the money relation confronts the other as an equal, a relation of equivalents), Lacan shows the process of subjectification in and as the gaze. However, the gaze—which marks the meeting of objects as subjects as well as the simultaneity of desire and lack—is a relation of capital having achieved an idealist, that is, psychological (one might say psycho-pathological) dimension.[36] This is not to say that the psyche is "mere" superstructure, or that its dynamics are false. The modern psyche is a production-effect that will itself be productive for capital—the Althusserian subject that "works" via an imaginary relation to the Real.[37] Such is ultimately the highest order of cinema: auto-matonic consciousness as a function of a visually dominated, technologi-cally animated universe (Beavis and Butt-head as spectators par excellence). The present psychoanalysis of this idealist iteration of capital under the category of the subject is an ideological analysis of the psyche of modern capital—a psyche that could be characterized as a functional architecture that is "ideological" in the sense specified below.

As Zizek shows in his analysis of ideology as practice (he cites Pascal: one doesn't pray because one believes in God, one believes in God because one prays), the very *forms* of thought exist in what Zizek calls "practical con-sciousness" before they exist in "theoretical consciousness," and, even more importantly, in excess of their existence in theoretical consciousness. "If we want to grasp this dimension of fantasy, we must return to the Marx-ian formula 'they do not know it, but they are doing it.'"[38] In accordance with the Lacanian schema in which the ego is defined as "that nucleus given to consciousness, but opaque to reflection," one is blind to the prac-tice as soon as one thinks the theory.[39] "Philosophical reflection is thus subjected to an uncanny experience similar to the one summarized by the old oriental formula 'thou art that': there [for example], in the external effectivity of the exchange process, is your proper place; there is the theater in which your truth was performed before you took cognizance of it. The confrontation with this place is unbearable because philosophy as such *is defined by* its blindness to this place: it cannot take it into consideration without dissolving itself, without losing its consistency."[40] Similar to Al-thusser, Zizek's point here is that "'*Ideological*' is not the 'false consciousness' of a (social) being but this being itself in so far as it is supported by 'false con-sciousness.'"[41] My calling psychoanalysis ideological here means that the being of psychoanalysis is supported by the non-knowledge of the techno-economic.

The Investing Gaze, The Value of Envy

The fact that in the discourse of psychoanalysis the psyche appears as the artifact of a primary structure, rather than as a dialectical iteration of the economic suggests that the psyche is an abstraction of social relations of an ideal variety, ideal in the sense of "the ruling ideas" that Marx elabo-rates in *The German Ideology*, with an added proviso that we might call the Zizekian twist. The point for Zizek is that even as one thinks one knows about, for example, commodity fetishism, one proceeds as a "practical solipsist"—that is, the knowledge does not in fact vitiate the activity—Marxist or not, one is a fetishist in practice.[42] "Thus we have finally reached the dimension of the symptom, because one of its possible definitions would also be 'a formation whose very consistency implies a certain non-knowledge on the part of the subject': the subject can 'enjoy his symptom' only in so far as its logic escapes him—the measure of the success of it's interpretation is precisely its dissolution."[43] In other words, if Lacan *really* understood the economic and visual examples that color and indeed ground his discourse, that understanding would destroy the possibility of developing psychoanalytic theory as such.

It is true that psychoanalysis investigates the image as the cut-out of the gaze. Sensing that consciousness itself is structured cinematically, psychoanalysis sets out to investigate the gap and finds "the discourse of the Other." However, this outside that is inside, is in the *weltanschauung* of psychoanalysis, structurally neutral, existential, existing only in individual variations of the same inexorable condition. But an organized visual realm as the exterior of the subjective fantasy is a different kind of animal. This realm, which is also inside (of psychoanalysis as well as the subject) is the culture industry, B&B's TV—a fully integrated arm of capital, and a full-fledged member of the oligopoly that includes nation states and the military industrial complex. It is, in short, part of the global machinery of immiseration for the sake of "economic growth," the capitalization of the visual dynamic instituted by capital. The New World Order is an Order of Images.

An investigation into precisely the same structure of repression through the cut as is staged in psychoanalysis was the aim of Marx's research. By taking economic crisis as a kind of parapraxis, Marx develops the terms of his political economy. In other words, the labor theory of value and its consequences is Marx's theory of the unconscious of bourgeois capitalist production. In the Marxist theory of the unconscious of capitalist production, profit is the *objet a*. Labor-power as that which adds surplus value to capital is, in terms of the process of production, the discourse of the Other, precisely that invisible surplus necessary for the valorization of the capital. In the visual arena, labor will be drawn out of the subject in the imaginary, that is, as the subject constructs himself in the field of the Other. As such, labor's role in the production of surplus value remains the unconscious from the standpoint of capitalist representation, for the commodity and for consumers (through reification and naturalization). Though labor attains a certain self-consciousness, for example, in Lukacsian Marxism, vision as a form of socially productive labor has been entirely unselfconscious of its social function up until now. The labor theory of value is the theoretical expression of the actual robbery of worker's life energy through an unequal exchange with capital. The theory of the productive value of human attention, which I advance throughout *The Cinematic Mode of Production,* is the theoretical expression of the robbery of the spectator's vision in particular, and of his or her sensuality, perceptivity, activity, and consciousness in general. Historically speaking, capital no longer posits merely "labor-time" as alienated and productive for capital, but all *human* time. To put it another way, the logics of capitalist production and of the psyche are proto-cinematic in their systemic organization of the discontinuous. Materiality, labor, and profit are conjoined in an insatiable and thus infernal infinity, just as are vision, the gaze, and pleasure. Cinema proper announces the tandem organization of these two continuums as "visuality."

In "What is a Picture," Lacan's analysis of the painted picture's function accounts for historical variations in the form of patronage and in the content of works of art while instituting the same fundamental relation between painter and work: "It is the painter as creator who sets up a dialogue" (*FFCP*, 112). Thus, the law of the same in which images are always already converted into language (dialogue) is taken as the quasi-ontological socio-psychic relation with an economic dimension:

> The painter, it is said, no longer depends on aristocratic patrons. But the situation is not fundamentally changed with the advent of the picture dealer. He, too, is a patron, and a patron of the same stamp. Before the aristocratic patron, it was the religious institution, with the holy image, that gave artists a living. The artist always has some financial body behind him and it is always a question of the *objet a,* or rather a question of reducing it—which may, at certain level, strike you as being rather mythical—to an *a* with which—this is true in the last resort—it is the painter as creator who sets up a dialogue. (*FFCP*, 112)

By making the painting vanish into dialogue, the painter utilizes the economy of the gaze to insert himself into the intersubjective and therefore fiscal economy. With the Christ painting, for example, "What makes the *value* of the icon is that the god it represents is also looking at it. It is intended to please God . . . [it] may arouse the desire of God" (*FFCP*, 113; italics mine). In the dream text of Seminar XI, the importance of this example is to illustrate subject formation in the dynamic of the picture and to foreshadow the role of the symbolic. Thus in Lacan's account, "a certain pact may be signed beyond every image" (*FFCP*, 113). But in tracing back the forces that overdetermine the dreamwork, the process by which the gaze as investment returns a profit becomes legible. By capturing the visual attention of others, the artist generates his income—what will, after the advent of the modern period, be his capital (or, at the very least, the gallery's capital).

While seeing clearly the material components (institutions) that sustain the production of the work of visual art, Lacan is quite specific about the particular, non-materialist, that is, ideal realm in which the image, as the screen on which the economy of subjectivity plays itself out, is negotiated:

> What is it that attracts and satisfies us in *trompe-l'oeil*? When is it that it captures our *attention* [italics mine] and delights us? At the moment that the representation does not move with the gaze and that it is merely *trompe-l'oeil*. For it appears at that moment as something other than it seemed, or rather it now seems to be that something else. The picture does not compete with appearance, it competes with what Plato designates for us beyond appearance as being the Idea. It is because the picture is the appearance that says it is that which gives the appearance that Plato attacks painting, as if it were an activity competing with his own. (*FFCP*, 112)

The picture, then, is a token of the Idea as well as the coin by which subjects are constituted—*that* is the pact signed beyond the image. The picture appears both as what "is" and simultaneously reaches beyond its appearance and posits an exchange between subjects. It is at once a use-value and an exchange-value. Like a monetary transaction, the picture posits a relation of social equivalence on each side of the exchange, a ground in the realm of ideas for what Lacan calls "dialogue." The visual material is a means to an ideational exchange. In the case of the *trompe-l'oeil*, its apprehension implies that the visible world is an illusion that testifies to the presence of a subject, be it the painter, the proprietor, the Platonic forms, or God. This idea that the medium is a means for the creation of subjective effects and that it is these effects that are noteworthy is, by the way, the traditional approach of film theory to its medium (with Hitchcock to thank?)—the director as the spectator's alter-ego is almost always posited.

Since the gaze is that which "photo-graphs," the visual economy that has the picture as its coin has its circulation via an economy of gazes. Cinema is the industrial organization of this visual economy, the slow form of which is the picture. But as I am endeavoring to show, the gaze is already cinematic, which is to say that cinema, as a technology of the gaze, both in-forms and builds upon its properties. These properties stem from capital's organization of the psyche and its encroachment on the visual field as a field of production—an encroachment that will exceed subjective effects. This delimitation of the visual field already has occurred historically when Lacan performs his retroactive reading of the function of a picture—he reads the picture in terms of the subject in spite of the fact that it functions in excess of the subject. The picture itself does not necessarily fall under the regime of signification, only its e-valuation does—and this, only to a certain extent. The development of capital during the period of its visual encroaching is industrial, and cinema is the decisive achievement of in-dustrialization, the bridge to "post-industrial" society. Thus one can trace the dialectic from industry through the psyche to cinema. The subject is at once produced by and producing the mechanized industrial process that is moving toward image culture. When Lacan theorizes the gaze, he theo-rizes a gaze whose practices are long extant, having at once given rise to cinematic industry and been shaped by it.

In developing the relation of the gaze and the *objet a,* derived from the picture, into a model for signification, Lacan's metaphor for the effect of the image—the *signing* of a pact—and the inauguration of *dialogue* func-tions with an excess that indicates particularly significant affinities of the visual economy with the money economy. The voracious eye, for which the picture is a "showing," is somehow satisfied by the painting: "The appetite of the eye that must be fed produces the hypnotic value of the painting" (*FFCP,* 115). I will return to the viewer's eye in a moment. The painting from the standpoint of the creator is, for Lacan, described by Freud's analy-sis of artistic creation as sublimation and further, by "the *value* it assumes in the social field" (*FFCP,* 111; italics mine).

Freud declares that if a creation of desire, which is pure at the level of the painter, takes on commercial value—a gratification that may, all the same, be termed secondary—it is because its effect has something prof-itable for society, for that part of society that comes under its influence. Broadly speaking, one can say that the work calms people, comforts them, by showing them that at least some of them can live from the ex-ploitation of their desire. But for this to satisfy them so much, there must also be that other effect, namely, that their desire to contemplate finds some satisfaction in it. It elevates the mind, as one says, that is to say, it encourages renunciation. (*FFCP,* 111)

In other words, the painter quite literally capitalizes on the imaginary satisfaction of viewer's desires. Since I already have established that in the dreamwork of this seminar the picture stands in for the film, I will not dwell on the fact that the above reformulation of Lacan's hypothesis about the method of the painter better describes the role of the commercial filmmaker. For it is film that elevates the mind, though in a slightly different sense, and, generally speaking, encourages renunciation. In the practice of his craft, the commercial filmmaker creates a commodity that in many ways is the realization of the commodity form: A visual representation of "pure desire" that provides imaginary or virtual satisfaction and encourages renunciation. As Debord puts it, "The spectacle is the money that one only looks at, because in the spectacle the totality of use is already exchanged for the totality of abstract representation."[44]

Concerning the visuo-economic trauma that is the latent content of Lacanian psychoanalysis, the so-called "secondary gratification" of commercial success that haunts the above passage as the specter of the gaze is an instance of the return of the repressed. It is disguised to the extent that the repressed visuo-economic scar appears in a way that elides the single most important element in the determination of a painting's economic value— its fetish character. With the unique work of art, its fetish character is the ultimate measure of the success of the painter's "pure desire." The fetish, which is nothing in our culture if not an economic determination, is capital's measure of just how "profitable" the painter's "exploitation of desire" has been.

The economic content of the fetish is further visible in Lacan's description of envy, a structure that better explains the commercial value of the painting (if Lacan would but let it) as it sheds light on the primary forces for the determination of value in the visual arena.

Invidia comes from *videre* [to see]. The most exemplary *invidia*, for us analysts, is the one I found long ago in Augustine, in which he sums up his entire fate, namely, that of the little child seeing his brother at his mother's breast, looking at him *amare conspectu*, with a bitter look, which seems to tear him to pieces and has on himself the effect of a poison.

In order to understand what *invidia* is in its function as gaze it must not be confused with jealousy. What the small child, or whoever, *envies* is not at all necessarily what he might want—*avior envie*, as one improperly puts it. Who can say that the child who looks at his younger brother still needs to be at the breast? Everyone knows that envy is usually aroused by the possession of goods which would be of no use to the person who is envious of them, and about the true nature of which he does not have the least idea.

Such is true envy—the envy that makes the subject pale before the image of a completeness closed upon himself, before the idea that the *petit a*, the separated *a* from which he is hanging, may be for another the possession that gives satisfaction. (*FFCP*, 115–16)

Despite the fact that the example from St. Augustine is from another era, Lacan's statement that envy is "aroused by the possession of goods which would be of no use to the person who is envious of them" intimates the approximation of the gaze to the logic of private property and commodity fetishism. "To see is to have at a distance," in the words of Merleau-Ponty.[45] The account of envy provides an excellent elaboration of the relation of the commodity in the visual field to the Lacanian formula that man's desire is the desire of the Other—the value of the picture is dependent upon the satisfaction that it is perceived to be able to provide to others. Its objective value, that is dollar value, produces a split in the subject whose lack inevitably is plied in his viewing.[46] Such is even more true in the case of the spectacle, the perfection of the subject's encounter with "an image of completeness closed upon himself" (*FFCP*, 116). Although the phenomenon described by this observation gives rise to marginal utility theory in contemporary bourgeois (fascist) economics (someone will pay just a little more than what somebody else will pay for a particular commodity because it is more valuable to him than to others, and this individual choice, not exploited labor, is the source of profit), what this accretion of gazes on the surface of the image-commodity shows, precisely, is that the gaze is an economic medium, its lingering is productive of value. The more others who are deprived of completeness through one's possession of the unique work of art, the greater its value. The gazes of others create this value: *to look is to labor*. The fetish character of the unique work of art is produced precisely through the accretion of gazes upon a privately owned image. The visual layering of the subjectivity of others becomes inseperable from the work. Like capital, the gaze is a structure of organization (the *objet a* draws the gaze, is, in fact, the gaze) that demands a certain kind of work from the body, from some bodies. Increasingly, part of the value of the commodity, be it a painting or a Hollywood star, comes from the amount of (unpaid-for) visual attention it has absorbed. This severing of the laborer from the industrially produced object that first generated the fetish is complemented by the severing of the attender (spectator) from the mediatically produced object (the image). In this analysis lies the solution to the mystery of the fetish-character of the commodity.

Of Vanishing Mediators, Unconscious Conversions, and the Mechanization of the Abstract

At the beginning of *The Four Fundamental Concepts,* Lacan describes what he calls "the *pulsative* function . . . of the unconscious, the need to disappear that seems to be in some sense inherent in it—everything that, for a moment, appears in its slit seems to be destined, by a sort of pre-emption, to close up again upon itself, as Freud himself used this metaphor, to vanish, to disappear" (*FFCP*, 43). The gap/unconscious bridges a disjunction—it is a vanishing mediator between two things that are not the same in spite of the fact that for everyday consciousness they are held together by the principle of identity. Understood at a formal level, this suture is identical to that which is performed by that other vanishing mediator, money. In exchange, money posits the identity of two qualitatively distinct commodities.

Contemporary geo-political life requires the increasing co-function and coordination of the psychic, the political economic, and the visual.

The following chart is designed to facilitate thinking the dynamics of that complex immensity synchronically inscribed as "The World System." The slippages in the listed categories relevant to the analysis of what is perhaps better described as the World-Media System are at once questions and invitations to think about the multitude of gaps that necessarily riddle my account.

The cinematicity of the mode of production and of the psychoanalytic unconscious can only appear and disappear in partial glimpses, stolen partial images of its immensity. However, one might posit a dialectic in which money appears as the first order of the vanishing mediation (as thesis), while the unconscious appears as a second order mediator (antithesis). Cinema itself appears as a third order (synthesis) vanishing mediator, indeed it is a "higher" *form,* a development of the forms of money and the unconscious—in spite of the fact that it cannot be separated from either. The production of the global spectacle, the multifaceted capitalized spectacle of globalization, is the sublation of these earlier forms—"earlier" because logically and materially primary—the massive *méconnaissance* that bends bodies in all their multifaceted, subjectified, capitalized modes to their acquiescence to power. Cinema, understood as the moving images of pro-

Comparison of Psychoanalysis, Marxism, and Cinematics in the World-Media System

Psychoanalysis	Marxism	Cinematics
Unconscious	Mode of production	Cinematic mode of production
Theory of the unconscious	Labor theory of value	Productive value of human attention
Subject	Subject of exchange	Spectator
objet a	Commodity	Image
Desire	Money (as measure)	Image-object (subject matter)
Identity	Money (as medium of exchange)	Suture
Gaze	Wage-labor	Duration/attention/ performance
Transference	Circulation	Narrative/continuity
Symbolic	Capital	Mediation/cinema
Alienation	Alienation	Spectacle (separation)
Enjoyment	Profit/surplus value	Enjoyment
Reproduction	Reproduction of conditions of production	Watching television

duction, is the next advancement in the history of abstraction, one which already has occurred in material practice but is only now finding its language. For it is, finally, in and with images that everything from massive financial flows to the unconscious are negotiated and renegotiated—from budgetary allotments for the Pentagon to the kinds of bodies that are desirable. Vision and visuality, which for Lacan, as well as Sartre, Merleau-Ponty, and more generally the surrealists and situationists, were taken as quasi-primordial relations, received the attention they did not because of their ontological character, but because of their eschatological tendencies.

NOTES

1. Noteworthy again here is Godzich's discussion of the temporal fallout of the image. "We have a withdrawal of meaning. Ideas are leaving the suprasensible forever to go over to the sensible, where they get lost, where they abolish themselves as ideas.

Something of this nature is happening to time. The traditional way to think of a decisive action was articulated around the three tenses, past, present, and future, but today we are moving toward a two-tense system: real time and differed, or replay time. The future has disappeared into the calculations of supercomputers as well as into this strange entity called 'real time,' which contains both a part of the present and a part of the immediate future, as, for instance, when one sees on a radar screen the approach of a threatening missile in real time" Wlad Godzich "Language, Images and the Postmodern Predicament," in *Materialities of Communication*, ed. Hans Ulrich Gumbrecht and K. Ludwig Pfeiffer (Stanford: Stanford University Press, 1994) 368. The point here, as in that related phenomenon known as "Live TV" is the inexorability of flow without the possibility of human scale intervention. This is the time of Certificates of Deposit, road projects and the budget of the Pentagon.

2. Jacques Lacan, in "The Deconstruction of the Drive," trans. Alan Sheridan (New York and London: W.W. Norton and Company, 1981), 165.

3. Ibid., 165–66.

4. Guy Debord, *Society of the Spectacle* (Detroit: Black and Red, 1977), statement 218.

5. Sigmund Freud, *The Interpretation of Dreams,* trans. James Strachey (New York: Avon Books, 1965), 342–43.

6. I might add here that the term "dreamwork" is in many respects tailor-made for this analysis, since it is precisely my purpose to show in *The Cinematic Mode of Production* that consciousness as society's dreams of itself performs much of the work, now in the Marxist sense of the word, of amalgamating hegemony. Anne Friedberg suggests as much in *Window Shopping* when in discussing the effects of the advertising of commodities she asserts that recognition in any form affirms the status quo. See Anne Friedberg, *Window Shopping: Cinema and Postmodernity* (Berkeley: University of California Press, 1993).

7. Freud, *The Interpretation of Dreams*, 340.

8. Slovoj Zizek *The Sublime Object of Ideology* (London: Verso, 1989) 14.

9. Dr. Green's question reads as follows, "One point you have raised obviously seems quite crucial. This is the fact that the other qualities that specify the drive must be conceived as discontinuous elements. My question concerns the element of thrust that you have rather pushed to one side, in the course of your talk today, because, I think, it seemed to you one of the easiest ways of getting misled. But if, as you show, the drive is ultimately destined to the combinatory of the fact of discontinuity, it posits for itself the problem of the contradiction inherent in the energy of the system, which is conceived as a force that is both constant and subject to variation. It is this question that I would like you to develop in more detail if you can, in so far as it introduces the point of view that remains for me very important, and which I do not see very clearly in your teaching, namely, the economic point of view" (*FFCP*, 170).

10. See also Jean-Joseph Goux, *Symbolic Economies: After Marx and Freud*, trans. Jennifer Curtiss Gage (Ithaca: Cornell University Press, 1990).

11. Zizek, *The Sublime Object of Ideology*, 14. As Zizek points out, the important question for Marx, as for Freud, is not assumed by the content of the secret: "Classical bourgeois political economy has already discovered the secret of the commodity-form; its limit is that it is not able to disengage itself from the fascination in the secret hidden behind the commodity-form—that its attention is captivated by labor as the true source of wealth. In other words, classical political economy is interested only in contents concealed behind the commodity-form, which is why it cannot explain the true secret, not the secret *behind* the form but *the secret of the form itself*" (15).

12. Lacan would demur here, I believe, and argue that it is American ego-psychology that endeavors to reconstruct the subject. However, he would not and could not claim to have a theory of revolution.

13. The war-machine, for example, destroys the spaces and narrative unities of a population, and strives to impose a new order on both. This is the fundamental role of capitalized media in general. The computer as a tool for the visually mediated reorganization of the world is an extension of cinema.

14. Zizek insists that Lacan is not a post-structuralist—because, I think, "being" is still an operative category for Lacan. In the words of Kevin Dalton, "Lacan transforms a metaphysics of presence into a metaphysics of absence, but metaphysics remain" (email correspondence, 1996).

15. "Anyone who has ever tried to recount a dream to someone else is in a position to measure the immense gap, the qualitative incommensurability, between the vivid memory of the dream and the dull, impoverished words which are all we can find to convey it: yet this incommensurability, between the particular and the universal, between the *vécu* and language itself, is one in which we dwell all our lives, and it is from it that all works of literature and culture necessarily emerge." Fredric Jameson, "Imaginary and Symbolic in Lacan: Marxism, Psychoanalytic Criticism, and the Problem of the Subject," in *Literature and Psychoanalysis*, ed. Shoshana Felman (Baltimore: Johns Hopkins University Press, 1980), 338–39.

15. Freud, *The Interpretation of Dreams*, 312.

16. Ibid., 312.

17. It might be objected here that many of Freud's examples of dream condensations are not images but words. I would suggest that these verbal condensations are also images, and that indeed they allow us to penetrate the very character of the image as rebus. Freud's word-images are radical condensations, troubling perturbations that, when taken as a signifier, inaugurate the interpretations that posit the unconscious as such.

18. Martin Jay, *Downcast Eyes, The Denigration of Vision in Twentiety-Century French Thought* (Berkeley: University of California Press, 1994). See especially chapter 6, 329–

80. The Marxist theory of overdetermination implied by Marx's familiar statement that the laws of capitalism are the laws of chance can be elucidated by a comment of Lacan's that shows the psychoanalytic relation to the image and elucidates the character of cinema's capacity for abstraction. Lacan writes:

> Freud considers, with a view to the interpretation of dreams, the consequences of the chance transcription, and the arbitrary nature of the links made—why link this with that, rather than with something else? Freud certainly brings us here to the heart of the question posed by the modern development of the sciences, in so far as they demonstrate what we can ground on chance.
>
> Nothing, in effect, can be grounded on chance—the calculation of chances, strategies—that does not involve at the outset a limited structuring of the situation, in terms of signifiers. When modern games theory elaborates the strategy of two partners, each meets the other with the maximum chances of winning on the condition that each reasons in the same way as the other. What is the value of an operation of this kind, if not that one's bearings are already laid down, the signifying reference points are already marked in it and the solution will never go beyond them.
>
> Well! As far as the unconscious is concerned, Freud reduces everything that comes within reach of his hearing to the function of pure signifiers. It is on the basis of this reduction that it operates, and that a moment to conclude may appear, says Freud—a moment when he feels he has the courage to judge and conclude. (*FFCP*, 39–40)

The unconscious as a theoretical category is a conceptual machine for the conversion of datum into signifiers. Just as in Marx's formulation in which chance is already circumscribed within the realm of capital—in which one is born rich, another, more likely, is born poor, one invents a new widget, another invents nothing at all, but all function within the statistical and structural architecture of capital's field of organization—in capital, as in the unconscious, there are no meaningless accidents. Capital's orchestration of exchange-value inflects the structuring of all formations—all production falls under the laws of exchange. In the field of unconscious as theoretical matrix, everything is converted into a signifier and hence falls under the rules of signification. Cinema, which does to the entire world what the unconscious does to its datum, and what capital does to its commodities, signals the tandem operating of the rules of signification as understood in all their complexity in the linguistic sphere and of exchange-value as understood in all their complexity in the sphere of political economy. Cinema puts all of its objects in a form of circulation that confers upon them a like ontological status. Everything appears in its sign-function and simultaneously, this sign-function is given a dimension that extends beyond the province that we usually recognize as thought—call it viscerality, experience, what have you. Cinema, both as the films we watch in the theater and as the visuo-sensual mediation of capital, extends capital logic into the body both through the signifier and beyond the signifier, as experience. Cinema therefore engages the body in a conversion process analogical to what has been theorized as the process(ing) of the unconscious and the process(ing) of capital, but is not itself an analogical form since it is the synthesis of these processes. Put another way, political economy and psychoanalysis taken in their entirety are two partial (proto-) images of cinema. Cinema not only engages in the manipulations of the basic units of each of these two fields (signifier, exchange-value), but it engages all of the metaphysical and phenomenological consequences of each.

19. Godzich, "Language, Images and the Postmodern Predicament," 368.

20. See Pier Paolo Pasolini, "The Written Language of Reality," in *Heretical Empiricism,* ed. Louis K. Barnett (Bloomington: Indiana University Press, 1988), 187–222.

21. See Gilles Deleuze and Félix Guattari, *Anti-Oedipus: Capitalism and Schizophrenia* (Minneapolis: University of Minnesota Press, 1983) particularly chapter 1, pp. 1–50.

22. Godzich, "Language, Images and the Postmodern Predicament," 370.

23. The writer must realize that that which cuts up his or her drive for realization and which must therefore be languaged over is indeed the expression of the historical conditions in which he or she is immersed. The writer's subjectivity is part of the objective situation. Writers organize what the world cuts into them.

24. See Walter Benjamin, "The Storyteller," in *Illuminations,* ed. Hannah Arendt (New York, Schocken Books, 1969).

25. The non-knowledge of so much of what is—and I am not talking about "the classics"—is the pre-condition for what some writers like to call "the American Mind."

26. This move is essential because it reestablishes the relationship with Freud by languaging psychic phenomenon and makes space for the account of the subject's alienation in the signifier and of the transference ("the enactment of the reality of the unconscious" (*FFCP,* 146). This places meaning entirely in the realm of the signifier: "What is a signifier? A signifier is that which represents a subject. For whom?—not for another subject, but for another signifier" (*FFCP,* 198).

27. Pal Valery cited by Walter Benjamin in "On Some Motifs in Baudlaire," in *Illuminations,* 189.

28. Godzich, "Language, Images and Postmodern Predicament," 370.

29. Freud writes, "A daytime thought may very well play the part of *entrepreneur* for a dream; but the *entrepreneur,* who, as people say, has the idea and the initiative to carry it out, can do nothing without capital; he needs a capitalist who can afford the outlay, and the capitalist who provides the psychic outlay for the dream is invariably and indisputably, whatever may be the thoughts of the previous day, a wish from the unconscious." Freud, *The Interpretation of Dreams,* 599–600; cited in Neferti Xina M. Tadiar, "The Fantasy-Secret of Killing Time In a Warm Place," *Diliman Review* (June 1996).

Best, for the understanding of the historicity of psychoanalysis, to allow Freud's comparison to move in two directions at once: a wish from the unconscious is capital, and capital is a wish from the unconscious.

30. Lacan raises the following questions in the first lecture of Seminar XI and returns to them throughout: "Was Freud really the first, and did he really remain the only theoretician of this supposed science to have introduced fundamental concepts? Can we even say that what we are dealing with are concepts in the strict sense? Are they concepts in the process of formation? Are they concepts in the process of development, in movement, to be revised at a later date? . . . I think this is a question in which we can maintain that some progress has already been made, in a direction that can only be one of work, of conquest, with a view to resolving the question as to *whether psycho-analysis is a science*" (*FFCP*, 10–11). Here, as everywhere, Lacan's tropes, in this case of work and conquest, are noteworthy.

31. For a brief précis of this position, see "An Unpublished Text by Maurice Merleau-Ponty: A Prospectus of His Work" and "The Primacy of Perception and its Philosophical Consequences," in Maurice Merleau Ponty, *The Primacy of Perception*, ed. James M. Edie (Evanston, Ill.: Northwestern University Press, 1964), 3–42.

32. Breaking with this technology taboo (in concepts such as "the machinic assemblage") is a foundationally enabling gesture of Deleuze and Guattari's *Anti-Oedipus*, as well of their *Thousand Plateaus*.

33. Zizek, *The Sublime Object of Ideology*, 50–51.

34. Ibid., 52–53.

35. The particular affects that are mass produced through the mass mediation of the gaze, and the economics thereof, is a separate branch of inquiry beyond the scope of the present chapter.

36. Regarding Marx, one cannot help but add that it is a testament to his extraordinary intuitive powers that he describes ideological accounts of reality that place the realm of ideas above social conditions to function by making the world appear upside down—as if in a camera obscura. For the next evolutionary level of what Marx means by "ideology" will occur precisely in the optical and the visual—indeed, the rise of the visual is already implicit in Marxism's empiricism. Lacan's discourse, which is incapable of registering structural inequality, though not incapable of perpetuating it—everyone is equal under the law of the signifier, and difference is often labeled "asymmetry"—derives its form from the dynamics of the visible. In other words, his seminar marks the progress of the transition from capital's ideology to capital's optical illusion; as a discourse, psychoanalysis is ideology, but as a dream to be read, it provides the schematic diagram for the human perceptual machine as the camera obscura necessary for the development of capital.

37. However, the critique that discovers capital to be the meaning of technology (for

what else could Heidegger really mean by the technological "enframing" of human being and the technological positioning of human beings and nature as technology's "standing reserve"?), threatens to disturb the homeostasis of the universal psyche, because, unlike the symbolic, it *engenders* two different subjective instantiations: capital and labor. The discourse of psychoanalysis, however, at least as it is handled by Lacan, is unable to register inequality—difference is an after-image registered in the play of an ontological structure, for example, "In the psyche there is nothing by which the subject may situate himself as a male or female being" (*FFCP*, 204). Although these two terms, capital and labor, could be (and in fact are unconsciously) mapped as the phallus and castration, or male and female, Lacan conflates such differences in and through the function of the psychic economy as terminus, while Marxism stages this antagonism of what is, generally, empowerment and disempowerment, as class struggle. In the symbolic, everyone is screwed, while in capitalism, everyone is screwed, but some pigs are screwed less than others.

38. Zizek, *The Sublime Object of Ideology,* 30.

39. Jacques Lacan, *Ecrits,* trans. Alan Sheridan (New York: W.W. Norton, 1977), 15.

40. Zizek, *The Sublime Object of Ideology,* 19–20.

41. Ibid., 21.

42. Ibid., 20.

43. Ibid., 21.

44. Debord, *Society of the Spectacle,* #49.

45. Merleau-Ponty, "Eye and Mind," in *The Primacy of Perception,* 166; cited in Vivan Sobchack, "The Scene of the Screen: Envisioning Cinematic and Electronic Presence," in *Materialities of Communication,* ed. Hans Ulrich Gumbrecht and K. Ludwig Pfeiffer (Stanford: Stanford University Press, 1994), 91. Lacan himself was already aware of the proprietary qualities of vision referring to the "*belong to me* aspect of representations, so reminiscent of private property" (*FFCP*, 81).

46. Of the voracious eye of the viewer of the image, Lacan says "its power to separate goes much further than distinct vision. The powers that are attributed to it, of drying up the milk of an animal on which it falls . . . of bringing with it disease or misfortune—where can we better picture this power than *invidia* [envy]?" (*FFCP*, 115).

Chapter 4
Inspiration of Objects, Expiration of Words
Cinema, Capital of the Twentieth Century

The history which is present in all the depths of society tends to be lost at the surface. The triumph of irreversible time is also its metamorphosis into the time of things, *because the weapon of its victory was precisely the mass production of objects according to the laws of the commodity. The main product which economic development has transferred from luxurious scarcity to daily consumption is therefore history, but only in the form of the history of the abstract movement of things which dominates all qualitative use of life. While the earlier cyclical time had supported a growing part of historical time lived by individuals and groups, the domination of the irreversible time of production tends, socially, to eliminate this lived time.*
—*Guy Debord*, Society of the Spectacle

The time of production, commodity-time, is an infinite accumulation of equivalent intervals. It is the abstraction of irreversible time, all of whose segments must prove on the chronometer their merely quantitative equality. This time is in reality what it is in its exchangeable character. In this social domination by commodity time, "time is everything, man is nothing; he is at most the carcass of time" (Poverty of Philosophy). *This is time devalued, the complete inversion of time as "the field of human development."*   —*Guy Debord*, Society of the Spectacle

---

Capital Cinema

So what is cinema? Let me here begin again this kind of thinking about cinema with a brief discussion of the "Capital Cinema" shown and shown up by the Coen brothers in their 1992 film, *Barton Fink*. In their film, Capital Cinema is the name of the late 1930s pre-war Hollywood production-studio that, according to the story, provides the conditions of possibility for cinematic expression. This company, as a representative of the studio system, is used by the Coen brothers to demonstrate that cinema is at once a factory for the production of representation *and* an economic form, that is, a site of *economic* production. As factory and as economic system, cinema is inscribed in and by the dominant mode of production: specifically, industrial capitalism and, here, its war economy. As a factory of representation, Capital Cinema dictates limits to the forms of consciousness that can be represented, but as an economic form inscribed by the larger cultural logic, Capital Cinema dictates limits to forms of consciousness per se.

The film *Barton Fink*, in which the Jewish writer Barton (played by John Turturo) falls from celebrated playwright to abject existentialist hack as he tries to make the shift from New York playwrighting to Los Angeles screenwriting, is about the spaces and sensibilities that fall out of (are absent from) a cinema that is a fully functioning component of the capitalist economy. The movement from New York to Los Angeles marks the movement for Barton, but also for representation in general, into a new era.[1] The climax of the film occurs when the film confronts the limits of its own conditions of representation.

Indeed, the thesis of *Barton Fink* is that there remains an unrepresentable for cinema: experience that refuses commodification. Numerous incidents marking the unrepresentability of experience occur in the film via specific instantiations of race (Jewishness), gender (the oppressed wife who has written all of her alcoholic husband's books), sex (the homoerotic tensions in the hotel room scenes), and class (the inner life of the encyclopedia salesman)—all of which to varying degrees are rendered invisible by the screened world and therefore are legible only elliptically, as effects. More interesting still, is the film's construction of invisibility as such as a general case in capital cinema, a predicament of disenfranchised (non-capitalized and non-capitalizable) elements in others and in ourselves. The writer Barton is trying to create a script about the real man, about "everyman," but when the film finally encounters the existence of everyman's never-told biography in the form of the biography of the failed encyclopedia salesman (played by John Goodman), that is, precisely the biography that Barton, being preoccupied with his capitalized script, has not had the time to listen to, the encounter is and can be only indirect—off-screen as it were, and that, as a crisis. At the moment of the encounter between cinema and the experience of "everyman," that is, at the moment when the essence of the encyclopedia salesman's character would emerge, a conflagration erupts. Inside the frame, the film set is burnt, while outside the frame in the space beyond the film, the very edges of the frame curl and burst into flame. The medium literally self-destructs as the reality principle of the film is destroyed in the confrontation of its limits.

By "reality principle," I mean the set of logics, conventions, and strategies by which the film creates the reality effect of the narrative and the mise-en-scène. The term is particularly apt since it is the immanent eruption of various repressions—intimated in an otherwise realist narrative by sinister sounds and the walls dripping ooze—which in the film threatens the integrity of the reality principle before its final catastrophe. Sigmund Freud's elaboration in *Beyond the Pleasure Principle* of the reality principle as that principle which replaces the pleasure principle and works "from the point of view of the self-preservation of the organism among the difficulties of the external world" coincides precisely with my thesis here that consciousness in its dominant forms is the cinematic excrescence of social organization.[2] To put it very crudely, organized more and more like movie production, capitalist production creates difficulties and contradictions that must be resolved in the space-time of cinematic representation/consciousness. The excess is driven off the screen into the unrepresentable/social unconscious. For the sake of the economies of the gaze, spectacularity, narrative, and profit, cinema represses other forms of interference. In other words, for the sake of the perpetuation of capital cinema, certain contradictions and possibilities do not cross the threshold of cinematic consciousness.[3] In Debord's terms, "[I]ndividual experience of separate daily life remains without language, without concept, without critical access to its own past which has been recorded nowhere. It is not communicated. It is not understood and is forgotten to the profit of the false spectacular memory of the unmemorable."[4]

Freud tells us that "under the influence of the ego's instincts of self-preservation, the pleasure principle is replaced by the *reality principle*. This latter principle does not abandon the intention of ultimately obtaining pleasure, but it nevertheless demands and carries into effect the postponement of satisfaction, the abandonment of a number of possibilities of gaining satisfaction and the temporary toleration of unpleasure as a step on the long indirect road to pleasure."[5] In his development of this formulation Freud could well be describing the representational strategy of Capital Cinema: "In the course of things it happens again and again that individual instincts or parts of instincts turn out to be incompatible in their aims or de-

mands with the remaining ones, which are able to combine into the inclu-
sive unity of the ego [or in this case, the film]. The incompatible "instincts"
[here embodied as the encyclopedia salesman's entire life—his class, his
failures, his repressed homosexuality, and his vengeance] are then split off
from this unity by a process of repression, held back at lower levels of psychical development and cut off, to begin with, from the possibility of satisfaction."[6] That Freud uses the trope of cutting is perhaps no accident. If the
"incompatible" instincts succeed "in struggling through, by roundabout
paths, to a direct or to a substitutive satisfaction, that event, which would
in other cases have been an opportunity for pleasure, is felt by the ego as
unpleasure. . . . Much of the unpleasure that we experience is *perceptual*
unpleasure. It may be perception of pressure by unsatisfied instincts; or it
may be external perception which is distressing in itself or which excites
unpleasurable expectations in the mental apparatus—that is, which is recognized by it as 'danger.'"[7] The ego here can be seen at once as the psychic
consequence of a repressive social order pitted against a polymorphously
perverse, or at least untameable body, and as a theater of perception. As a
matrix of mediation, it occupies the bio-social space that during this century has been overtaken by cinema in the special sense of the word that I
attempt to develop here. The language/function of the ego has been interface and it becomes a subroutine of the spectacle. In a film steeped in the
protocols of profit, the particular experiences of Goodman's mad encyclopedia salesman, that is, the myriad experiences of failure in capitalism
(and experiences of the failure of capitalism), fall below the threshold of
knowing possible—or at least legitimated—in capital cinema and are precipitated only as effects. These effects, much like a labor strike or terrorism
seen from the standpoint of bourgeois reason, confront the mode of production as a sort of inexplicable and phenomenal irrationality, and hence
as a crisis that halts its smooth functioning. The *real experience* of Everyman—vanishing since World War I according to Walter Benjamin—is in
this representation by the Coen brothers nearly uncommodifiable by definition and therefore cannot be represented in Capital Cinema.[8] Its emergence or, better still, its eruption, threatens to destroy the medium itself.

If we consider the hypothesis that consciousness in late capitalism, generally speaking, functions like film-language—relatively unable to think
beyond the exigencies of capital—then it is important to note at the outset
that film-language as consciousness is overdetermined by capital *regulation*. Cinema, as money that thinks, fuses the protocols of representation
and capitalist production. This claim remains relatively unproblematic

until one takes cinema not only as a form of representation but as endemic to the workings of consciousness itself. Simply put, something like the Coen brother's Capital Cinema manufactures not just films, but consciousness in general, complete with its possibilities and lacunae.[9] This process is dramatized by Barton Fink having to adopt himself and his perceptions to the exigencies of the film industry as he struggles to write a viable script. Cinematic consciousness is shown as the hegemonic form of consciousness in late capitalism. If what I call the cinematic mode of production can be shown to have infiltrated human minds and converted their function into a kind of money that thinks, then this script writer's dilemma can be shown to pertain generally. Such thinking money, what Marx called the "truly creative power," is money of a special form, not money as a mere medium of exchange but, simultaneously, money functioning as capital. It is money that has transcended the money form, becoming part of what Marx called the General Intellect.[10] The screenwriter for the studio, like the professor for the university and the citizen for the state, must from some position of accountabiltiy be a source of profit. Capital consciousness has a variety of perceptual possibilities, thresholds, and limits that at once provide standards of productivity and spur certain kinds of innovation. Here, as well as elsewhere, it is essential to see these innovations as being labor-driven, that is, forced upon capital by the efforts of workers to free themselves. Capital's innovations are thus strategies of containment and strategies to combat the falling rate of profit, no matter what else they might be.

In explaining this idea more fully, I first will show the manner in which the mediated colonization of the sensorium combats the falling rate of profit. In previous chapters, we have seen the cinematic circulation of capital followed by the cinematic production of capital, followed by cinema's spectral presence in the discourse of the unconscious. Here we will begin to explore the necessity of capital's transgression of limits—its deterritorialization of the material, the visual, and the body. The perceptual and biophysical transformations wrought by cinema impact upon the object world. Put another way, the character of objects, already a relation among people, that is, a mediation and hence a medium, shifts as the technical structure of perception and the internal composition of the psyche shift. In reality, these shifts are subtle and are orchestrated simultaneously, but in the temporality of critique they must be observed as moments. Thus, in an analysis of the auratic phenomenon noted by Benjamin, I will show the palpability of the form of value innovated in and as a visual economy.

An important dimension of an undertaking that aspires to a political economy of consciousness via a political economy of cinema involves an analysis of cultural imperialism. Imperialism is an economic undertaking as well as an ideological and libidinal one. The phrase "cultural imperialism" indicates a mode of production for which certain dimensions remain more or less unconscious. I mean to suggest here that whatever the project of imperialism was, it does not cease in the presence of the fantasy called the postcolonial. Rather, as world poverty indexes readily show (infant mortality, life expectancy, access to health care, literacy), the pauperization process is intensifying. The "expiration" of national boundaries and the purported "obsolescence" of the nation-state only imply that these national forms are being superseded (sublated) even as they continue to do their work.[11] The thesis here is that cinema and cinematic technologies (television, telecommunications, computing, automation) provide some of the discipline and control once imposed by earlier forms of imperialism (torture, violent intimidation, humiliation, covert war, though there is still plenty of that), but the media work to organize these previous forms of discipline and control that remain extant plus innovate entirely new forms. The two wars in Iraq, and the coordination of the exigencies of the military industrial complex with the programming of corporate media and the function of the consciousness of Americans provide ample testament to the continuation of the old imperialism via the new technological means. Our objects and images are all embroiled in this bloody melange.

Transnational capitalism, which today finds its very conditions of possibility in computing, telecommunications, and mass media, shows that these media are playing a fundamental role in new modes of value production and value transfer. The cinema is a first instance of these other "higher forms" of mediation. By unlocking the dynamics of cinema, a new critique of its later iterations becomes possible. With the globalization of capital, economic expansion is presently less explicitly a geographical project and more a matter of *capturing* the interstitial activities and times between the already being-commodified endeavors of bodies. Contemporary cultural theory works in the interstitial spaces of the West and of Western domination, in the uncharted subjective and historical vicissitudes of ethnicity, gender, sexuality, and epistemology. That theory, as well as the practical relations that it aims to describe, finds its locus there in the gaps, because it is there precisely that the newest struggles over the production of value(s) have shifted. This emergence of such interstitial sites is apparent not only for theory and for politics, but for the psyche and for intellectual-corporeal activity. Every movement and every gesture is potentially productive of value. I am speaking here of media as cybernetics, of capital expansion positing the yet-unalienated zones of the body as the new frontier, a new frontier for production.

We are thus dealing with two distinct yet interactive sets of relations here. In the first set, capital cinema regulates perception and therefore certain socio-libidinal pathways to the body. It is in this sense that it functions as a kind of discipline and control akin to previous methods of socialization by either civil society or the labor process (e.g., Taylorization). The second moment, related yet distinct from the first, is the positing by capital cinema of a value-productive relationship that can be exploited—that is, a tapping of the productive energies of consciousness and the body in order to facilitate the production of surplus value. The worker, once enveloped in the machine a la Charlie Chaplan's *Modern Times* or Fritz Lang's *Metropolis,* is now the "social-worker" in Antonio Negri's special sense of the term— an actor whose body and consciousness are enveloped entirely by the deterritorialized factory of capitalist social organization, exactly as in the Wachowski brothers' contemporary social realist film, *The Matrix.*

Reconfiguration of Existence Itself
by the Falling Rate of Profit

Before I move on, let me recall and briefly summarize the first two dialectical hypotheses of *The Cinematic Mode of Production,* that of the image-commodity and the spectator-worker:

1. As I showed in chapter 1, cinema simultaneously images and enacts the circulation of economic value. It images *the patterns of circulation* (the tracing of space, time, movement, production) and intensifies the imagistic aspect of the commodity. What was implicit in the fetish character of the commodity as the phantom limb of its severed relations of production (at once the cipher of alienated labor and of its repression), increases quantitatively to the point where the commodity becomes an image, an image-commodity. The alienated living labor become-dead labor that constitutes the commodity finds new expressiveness in and as the cinematic image. In *Man with a Movie Camera,* we saw that cinema enacts *the circulation of economic value itself* (capital), and I suggested that though the fact of this process, visible in Vertov, is suppressed from cinematic diegesis after Vertov, it nonetheless continues to pertain. The moving image is the

circulation of capital, indeed the circulation of images is a higher form of the circulation of capital. Cinema is the very *form* of capital circulation, its materialized abstraction, that is its functional ability to abstract an object via its practical dematerialization. Through a visuo-sensual cybernetic interface, it changes the relationship between the body and the commodity, which immediately implies a shift in the mode of production.

2. As I showed in chapter 2, the image-commodity finds its dialectical antithesis in the spectator-worker. The circulation of value (in the cinema-spectator link, that is) through the spectator-worker, is itself productive of value because looking is posited as a form of labor. I should emphasize here that all previous forms of capitalized labor remain intact. However, looking as labor represents a tendency toward increasingly abstract instances of the relationship between labor and capital, a new regime of the technological positioning of bodies for the purpose of value extraction. Though this tendency is becoming dominant, which is to say that the relationship between consciousness and mechanization is more important than ever before, all previous forms of exploitation continue—they are managed, justified, intoned, and made invisible through the cinematic production of consciousness. When a visual medium operates under the strictures of private property, the work done by its "consumer" can be capitalized and made to accrue to the proprietor of the medium. The celebrity, to give just one example here, is the epitome of the contradiction of individual identity posited by private property (s/he owns his or her image) and massive communal dissemination. In other words, some people make a profit from other people's looking. The ways in which this profit is produced and channeled fundamentally defines the politics of cultural production and of the state. This dynamic abets not only the perpetuation of a hierarchical economic pyramid in what is nominally "democracy" via, for example, the mass-sanctioned, frenzied, and continual building of bombs, it ensures that their "collectively" chosen targets are chosen by a self-interested super-elite. Furthermore, it continues to disguise class, race, and imperialist wars as struggles for freedom, peace, security, and justice. As an industry on a continuum with other industries, the spectacle is productive of value for itself (for its proprietors) and also in what might be considered a short circuit of the money relation because viewers are paid in social "know how" and "enjoyment," for capital in gen-

eral. In a longer circuit of production, the spectacle also demands that spectator-workers labor to produce their own modifications of themselves and therefore their ability to cope (or cooperate) in the social matrix. I will have more to say on the consequences of the instantiation of both the image-commodity and the spectator-worker in what follows.

3. Such revolutionary methods for the extraction, appropriation, and channeling of value from the human body have as profound an effect on all aspects of social organization as did the assembly line—they change the dynamic of sight forever, initiating a visual economy, and finally an economy of the senses and cognition. These methods deterritorialize the body and multiply the sites of socio-technological interface. As I shall chart briefly in a discussion of Benjamin, this economy has been developing for some time.

4. Understood as a technology capable of submitting the eye to a new disciplinary regime, cinema may be taken as a model for the many technologies that in effect take the machine off of the assembly line and bring it to the body in order to mine it of labor-power (value).[12] Cinema, and the media that extend its practices, constitute deterritorialized factories, paradigms of flexible accumulation. The implication is that value is extracted across the image and the spectator-worker is "paid" through enjoyment or other forms of social utility ("knowledge," affects, other types of social software that can be "downloaded" through viewing). This represents a the shift in the wage that corresponds to the shifts in circulation and capital described above.

The hypothesis that vision and more generally human attention is today productive of economic value can be supported by showing that the labor theory of value is a specific instance of a more general hypothesis that is possible concerning the production of value. This I call the hypothesis of the productive value of human attention, or the attention theory of value. It is derived from the way in which capital process occupies human time in the cinema and in other media. Assuming for the moment that human attention is a value-adding commodity sought by capitalized media, it can be shown that if to look is to labor, then at least a partial solution to the dilemma posed to the political economist by the very persistence of capitalism presents itself. Capitalism thrives in apparent violation of the labor theory of value and the law of the falling rate of profit. These two limitations on the expansion of capital cause Marx, Lenin, Luxemburg, and others to predict a critical mass for capital—a catastrophic point beyond which it cannot expand. Unable to expand and hence unable to turn a profit, fully globalized capital was expected to self-destruct. With the end of an outside for capital, the law of value was to have been necessarily overcome and a world in which any of us, should we so desire, could hunt in the morning, fish in the afternoon, and criticize at night, as Marx expressed it in a euphoric moment, was to have come into being. Clearly, and despite the globalization of capital, this auto-annihilation of capital has not happened. I am suggesting that, from the standpoint of capital, as geographical limitations are in the process of being fully overcome by capital, capital posits the human body as the next frontier. By colonizing the interstitial activities of bodies, each muscular contraction or each firing neuron is converted into a site of potential productivity.

Instead of occasioning an attack on the fundamental premise of Marxism, that value production under capital requires the extraction of surplus value (i.e., that value production is fundamentally exploitative—implicit in the abandonment of the labor theory of value and expressed in false hypotheses regarding conditions of choice and equality that underlie economic conditions of production/consumption, for example, the marginal utility theory), we can show the manner in which media and allied technologies have developed to combat the falling rate of profit via what is in effect, informal labor (disguised wage labor), and further how this penetration of the fabric of existence by capital forever transforms the objective qualities of things. Let me develop this argument by elaborating from a few tenets of Marx.[13]

1. "Capital is not merely, as A[dam] Smith thinks, command over alien labor, in the sense in which every exchange value is that, because it provides its owner with *buying power,* but that it is the power of appropriating alien labor *without exchange, without equivalent,* but under the guise of exchange" (*Grundrisse,* 474; emphasis Marx). Marx refers here to the extraction of surplus value in wage labor. Since, according to Marx, value is and can only be added to capital through labor, for workers to make money for their capitalist, they must be paid for less than what they actually produce.

    Marx shows that once society has passed subsistence production, workers, because of increased productivity, have to labor less than an entire working day in order to subsist—socially necessary labor time decreases. Capital, however, pays subsistence wages, that is, it pays for socially *necessary* labor (the labor necessary to reproduce the worker), and appropriates the unpaid, that is, *surplus* labor from the remainder of the working day for itself. One can see in a more detailed examination of Marx's work than I can engage in here that in early capitalism this surplus labor was a small percentage of the day up to, say, one-half of a day, while with the increasing efficiency of workers (the sheer amount one worker can produce via machinery, etc.) the surplus labor amounts to proportions along the line of 99 percent of the day and greater for itself. The point is that although the worker is forced to work an entire day, he or she is paid only for an increasingly small fraction of the value that his or her labor produces. The remainder is taken "under the guise of exchange," in a relationship that through force of convention, law, violence, and necessity is made to appear inevitable, natural, and right. The question here is, under what other guises ratified by "custom" has capital evolved strategies for the extraction of surplus value?

2. "Circulation can *create value* only in so far as it requires additional employment—*of alien labor*—additional to that directly consumed in the production process. This is then the same as if more *necessary labor* were directly required in the production process. Only the real *costs of circulation* increase the *value* of the product, but they reduce surplus value" (*Grundrisse*, 471; emphasis Marx). Though Marx clearly grasps circulation as a *moment* of production, circulation *as such* is for him never production. A transport company, for example, can make a profit by employing alienated labor, but the cost of transport is added directly to the product. If it costs 8 hours worth of labor (abstract universal labor time) to move product X from point A to point B, then the value of X at point B is X + 8 hours, that is, the transportation was necessary labor, the necessary labor of circulation, and its value is added to the value of the product. However, this does not keep the transport company from paying for only 2 hours of the necessary labor provided and realizing a profit, that is, in effect appropriating 6 hours of labor-time under the guise of exchange. (The worker who has worked 8 hours and received 2 hours wages takes his "day's" wages and can exchange it for only 2 hours of objectified labor time in the open market.) Thus circulation as necessary labor in the exchange of commodities does not add value to capital (it is like the cost of raw materials and therefore does not *create* value), but circulation as a capitalized business can produce value for capital in

general in the alienated production process of *its* product, that is, transport, mediation, circulation.

3. "*The production of capitalists and wage workers is . . . a major product of the valorisation process of capital.* Ordinary political economy, which considers only the objects produced, entirely forgets this. Inasmuch as this process posits objectified labor as simultaneously the *non-objectification* of the worker, as the objectification of a subjectivity confronting the worker, as the *property* of someone else's will, capital is also necessarily a *capitalist*" (*Grundrisse*, 436; emphasis Marx). *The articulation of social form in and through the medium of history is a necessary product of capital.* Capital produces the conditions in which labor must confront capital and the forms in and through which capital confronts labor. Though Marx personifies capital in the *Grundrisse* (since capital personifies itself in and as the activity of the capitalist), to an unprecedented degree capital today is also necessarily the momentum of capitalist society in all of its aggressively proclitic infiltrations confronting workers as the property (properties) of someone (thing) else's *will*. I am speaking here of society as a force of alien will bearing down upon isolated individual bodies. Many times this no longer will take form as belonging to a subject, but as part of "nature," "culture," "the facts of life."

4. "Capital's creation of *absolute surplus value*—more objectified labor— is conditional upon the expansion, indeed the constant expansion, of the periphery of circulation. The *surplus value* produced at one point requires the production of surplus value at *another* point, for which it may be exchanged. . . . A condition of production based on capital is therefore *the production of a constantly expanding periphery of circulation*, whether the sphere is directly expanded, or *whether* more points within it *become points of production* (*Grundrisse*, 334–35; emphasis Marx). Though Marx here is thinking of geographical extension and urban intensification (what will be called imperialism and urban industrialization), I am suggesting here that capital presently throws its network of control over bodies and masses of bodies in similar though technologically and dialectically advanced ways. Many of the forces for the regulation of material production have been dematerialized. Urban architecture poses certain constraints on the worker, but today, so also does computer architecture. The expansion of the periphery of circulation expands not only geographically but extends rhizomatically into and around bodies as zones of flow.

It should by now be clear that the four conditions of capital expansion specified above, that is, (1) the appropriation of labor without exchange, (2) the value added to commodities by the necessary labor of circulation, (3) the developing subjectification of capital as alien will and the corollary (en)forced structuring of social practice, and (4) the expansion of the periphery of circulation, are all met in my account of mass mediation. Capital strives to infiltrate the entire terrain of sociality, structuring the dynamics of all appearing, and binding existence to appearance. What needs to be shown, and what can be quickly demonstrated, is the structural manner and the degree of efficiency with which mass media counters the falling rate of profit.

The countering of the falling rate of profit, which historically was accomplished in a variety of ways, including longer work hours and increasing efficiency through the utilization of Taylorization and machinery, is today still accomplished, in effect, by extending the working day. But the means are different. After what is officially known as work, spectator-workers "lounge" about in front of TV or at the cinema, producing more of the world, for capital. Circulating capital's products, ratifying the shifts and nuances in its subjectivity, opening unknown regions of our bodies for its penetration, developing whole new sets of capacities and affects, spectator-workers release living-labor to capital without equal exchange. Though I will have more to say about the forms that such near-mandatory activity takes, what I want to do here is to show the surprising significance such an extension of labor time has for capital.[14]

Marx shows that "surplus value always depends on the ratio between the whole working day and that part of it which is necessary for the worker to keep himself alive" (*Grundrisse*, 261–62). Therefore, "the increase in the productivity of living labor increases the *value* of capital (or diminishes the value of the worker) . . . because it reduces *necessary* labor and thus in the same proportion creates *surplus labor*, or, what amounts to the same thing, surplus value" (*Grundrisse*, 264). If, therefore, necessary labor is one-half of a day and capital (through technological innovation or scientific management) doubles productivity so that necessary labor becomes one-quarter of a day, capital increases its rate of profit from one-half of a day to three-quarters of a day, that is, the ratio of surplus labor (profit) to necessary labor increases by 50 percent. But a little simple math shows the following: "The surplus value of capital rises but in ever diminishing ratio to the development of productivity. Thus the more developed capital already is, the more surplus labor it has already created, the more tremendously must it develop productivity if it is to valorize itself, i.e., to add surplus value even in a small proportion—because its barrier always remains the ratio between that fractional part of the working day which expressed *necessary labor* and the whole working day" (*Grundrisse,* 265).

Without here going into all of the reasons for capital expansion, massification, competition among the many capitals, I can represent numerically the basis of this relation. Recall that in the above example, doubling productivity gave capital a 50 percent increase on the rate of profit. If, however, productivity already has increased to such an extent that necessary labor is 1/1,000th of the working day, than a renewed *doubling* of productivity (necessary labor = 1/2,000th of a day), means only an increase for capital from 1,998/2,000th of a day to 1,999/2,000th of a day, that is, 1/2,000th of a day or 0.05 percent. A doubling of productivity that earlier on yielded a 50 percent increase in the rate of profit now only increases this rate by a slight fraction (0.05 percent). As productivity grows, the increase in the rate of profit falls off asymptotically, that is, *as long as the length of the work day remains the same.*

However, if an absolute increase in the working day can be engineered, the growth rate can increase profits at the higher rates occurring during the historically earlier doublings of general productivity. For example, if one were to consider the whole of the average per capita television time as labor, that is, 6 hours per person per day in the United States, which capital could then add to the better part of the 8 hours that it already has appropriated, capital increases its rate of profit from nearly 8 hours per day [(999/1,000)*(8)] to nearly 14 hours per day [(999/1,000) *(8) + 6], or approximately 75 percent. One can easily see that not all of the productive value of television time (labor time or what I am calling attention time) need accrue to capital for the proportional increases here to exceed increases in productivity engineered by capital during the working day. Television, as sort of a second job, creates surplus value for capital that allows it to combat the falling rate of profit. No wonder people sleep less today than at any other time in history. No wonder children watch so much TV. No wonder we spend so much time in front of the development of that interface doing things like email, web-research, and the like. The increasing efficiency and development of new attention-siphoning technologies becomes the central province of endeavor for later twentieth-century capital. Cinema and television quite literally represent an evolution in the form of capital.

In order to follow this developmental trajectory of ever-expanding capital (of which cinema, as the first fully realized form of media-capital is so crucial a part), one must consider the cyberneticization of the flesh—what Virilio calls "the habitation of metabolic vehicles."[15] For it is the extension of machines into the body, the incorporation or enframing of body components by capitalized forces of mediation, that best characterizes the development of late capital. Like the road itself (the productive value of which Marx intuited but never showed), such machine/body interfaces clearly shift the distribution of the body over its techno-mechanical linkages, opening up many more sites and times for the production of value, multiplying, as it were, the number of possible work sites. Capital expands not only outwards, geographically, but burrows into the flesh. This corkscrewing inward has profound consequences on life-forms. The argument I am making about the historical modification of the body in and by social (cinematic) process should have important consequences for studies of sexuality, identity, the history of art forms, and communication research, not to mention political economy. Seeing how modern visual technology tools the body for new labor processes during the twentieth century suggests parallel studies of other arts, technologies, and periods, past, present, and future. Art as cultural artifact has been a diverting pursuit, but art and culture as a social interface, as a panoply of technologies shot through with historical, libidinal, and visual necessity promises a more compelling account of human (cybernetic) transformations. Cultural forms must be grasped as technologies—machines for the engagement of human flesh. And equally, machines, objects, and images must be grasped as cultural forms, that is, social relations. The technologically articulated body does not undergo transformation merely in order to reflect new social relations or express new desires; the retooling it undergoes is central to the transformed economics of social production and reproduction—a necessary *development* of social relations.

Cinema is the development of a new medium for the production and circulation of value, as important in the reorganization of production and consciousness as the railroad track and the highway. Human endeavors generally grouped together under the category "humanities," and (perhaps) once experienced as realms of relative freedom, can be and *are being* figured as economically productive. The entire history of cinema remains as a testament to this practice; advertising, television, and culture generally today *testify* to it.

Certain relationships between looking and value, that is, images, already are and will continue to become sites of extensive legislation and political struggle. The photographs of Robert Mapplethorpe, the pink triangle, English words in French advertising, images of genitals in American films shown in the Philippines, are examples of the politically charged link between looking and value. The legitimacy or lack thereof of these images is not "merely" about ethics, identities, or politics; they activate the battles over the terms of the capitalist enfranchisement for the embattled groups advocating or suppressing them. Other forms of contention over the image include corporate competition for industry standards in High Definition Television, satellite communications, and computing. It is a mistake to think that the first group and the second are different realms—culture in the case of the former and industrial technology in the case of the latter. All are struggles over interfaces that will empower certain communities and *disempower* others in a society in which empowerment has come to mean capitalization more than anything else. Here, at the most general level, I am speaking about the commodification of culture and mediation, about *culture as an interface between bodies and the world system*. Much work already has been done on this problem of the commodification of culture, but little has been done that is fully conscious of the problem of the quantitative as opposed to merely the qualitative or metaphorical capitalization of culture. A sense of the quantification of cultural value as capital proper begins to shed light on how radical indeed the qualitative shifts in culture have become. Furthermore, this sense of transformation of the value form poses a strategy of inquiry that adds another dimension to the significance of cultural shifts. The corollary here is that academic, philosophical, historical, and aesthetic concerns are essential aspects of socio-economic transformation, designs for haptic processes that integrate the body with social production in general. The amalgamation of the labor involved in such processes as the production of cultures, identities, and desires, is already and will continue to be the way in which political blocs, however ephemeral, are formed and persist in postmodern society. The cinematic organization of fragments is at once the mode of tyranny and tyranny's possible overcoming.

The Thinking Person's Fetish

As one of my leitmotifs might suggest, we might imagine for a moment that at a certain point in history (Taylorism and Fordism) the world began to be organized more and more like a film. Geoffrey Nowell Smith points out that the form of assembly-line production easily invokes montage—hence, the French phrase *chaîne de montage*—thus the movement of capital itself may as well be thought of as a kind of cutting. As film stock is edited as it travels along a particular pathway to produce a film-image, capital is edited as it moves through its various determinations in assembly-line production. Like the screen on which one grasps the movement of cinematic production, capital is the standpoint or frame through which to see the movement of value, the scene in which emerges a moment in the production process. *Capital provides the frame through which one observes economic movement.* The finished commodity or image (commodity-image) results from a "completed" set of movements. When the circulation of capital is grasped as a kind of cutting, one grasps the generalized cinematicity of social organization, the spectacular arrangement of production, in short that the world is organized like a film. Cinema then, already is implied by capital circulation; dialectical sublation, as the metamorphosis of capital, is a slow form of film. Janet Staiger has noted that "Hollywood's mode of production has been characterized as a factory system akin to that used by a Ford plant, and Hollywood often praised its own work structure for its efficient mass production of entertaining films."[16] Although I do not disagree with this I am arguing the opposite as well: Rather than cinematic production copying Fordism, I would argue that it is an advance over Fordism. Cinematic production uses the practices of Fordism but begins the dematerialization of the commodity form, a tendency which, more than anything else, characterizes the course of economic production during this century. Rather than requiring a state to build the roads that enable the circulation of its commodities as did Ford, the cinema builds its pathways of circulation directly into the eyes and sensoriums of its viewers. It is the viewers who perform the labor that opens the pathways for the flow of new commodities.[17]

We can trace proto-cinematic technologies even further back in historical time than Fordism or, for that matter, Marxist dialectics. The standardized production of terra-cotta pots, the Roman minting of coins, the Gutenberg press, and the lithograph mentioned by Walter Benjamin in his essay "The Work of Art in the Age of Mechanical Reproduction" are early forms of cinema.[18] Like shutter, frame, and filmstock, each reproductive technology mentioned above repeats a standardized and standardizing act while striking an image that subjugates the eye to a particular and consequential activity. From the recognition of money to the reading of print, these activities place the eye within the discipline of a visual economy that corresponds to the type and speed of the mode of production. For each mode of production there necessarily exists a particular scopic regime. With the advent of cinema and the speeding up of individual images to achieve what is called "the persistence of vision" (that is, the purported "illusion" of a smooth continuity of movement among individuated images), an equally dramatic and corresponding shift occurred in the relation of the eye to economic production. From the historical moment of the viewer circulating before the paintings in a museum to the historical moment of images circulating before the viewer in the movie house, there is an utter transformation of the visual economy, marked by the movement from what Benjamin called "aura" to what today postmodern theory calls "simulacra." This movement was accompanied by a changeover from yesterday's ideology to today's spectacle. With the increased speed of its visual circulation, the visible object undergoes a change of state. In apprehending it, the textures of the object, its tactility, and indeed, the very properties of consciousness are transformed.

The Greek casts for terra-cottas and coinage, the woodcut, the printing press, the lithograph, the museum, all of which Benjamin elaborates as precinematic forms of mechanical reproduction, are also all technologies designed, from the point of view of the historical development of the senses, to capture vision and to subjugate it to the mechanics of various and successive interrelated economies. These forms of mechanical reproduction, with their standardized mechanisms and methods of imprinting are, in effect, early movies. That upon its emergence the "aura," which Benjamin theorizes, is found not on the visual object but in the relationship between the perceiver and the perceived (it accompanies the gaze, the gazing) is consistent with Benjamin's dialectical thesis that the sensorium is modified by the experience of the modern city. The development of film, like the development of the metropolis, is part of an economy that has profound effects on perception. As Benjamin writes, "The film is the art form that is in keeping with the increased threat to his life which modern man has to face. Man's need to expose himself to shock effects is his adjustment to the dangers threatening him. The film corresponds to profound changes in the apperceptive apparatus—changes that are experienced by the man in the street in big-city traffic, on a historical scale by every present day citizen."[19] That modernization modifies perception coincides with the dialectical notion that in the production and reproduction of their own conditions human beings modify themselves. Perception's aura, I suggest, is the subjective experience of the encroaching commodification of vision, the becoming-media, that is becoming-capitalized media, of the object.

The becoming conscious of aura in the historical moment that is Benjamin's writing is the last cry, the quantum emission of the existential object, as it is subsumed through a change of state induced by capitalized perception.

Today, because of the exponentially increased intensity of the image's circulation, the simulacrum produced by mass media is utterly emptied out and "means" only its own currency in circulation, far more than John Berger's painted masterpiece.[21] Indeed, meaning is but a subroutine, a fine-tuning of the ballistic trajectories of social force delivered via the impact of the image. What is important is flow and effect. Meaning is but one modality of grasping the image and one of decreasing importance as far as the project of the capitalist organization of society is concerned. This emptying out of images and objects, what is called simulation, is the latest consequence of the long-term strategies of appropriation of alienated sensuous labor (that is, alienated attention) by the object in circulation. Previously, this transformation was registered in the changed character of the particular work of art and of art in general. First, in modernization, mechanical reproduction liquidated the "original," and now, as Baudrillard informs us, any possibility of the "copy" is liquidated in the frenzy of the circulation of the postmodern image.[21] We should pause here to remark that with the pure simulacrum, we are looking at the pure fact of other people's looking at a particular nodal point in media flow—a fact of a new seriality that wreaks havoc on the organization of space and time. The simulacrum is primarily an economic image, the first object-image that is in terms of its qualities, principally an economic *function*. Seen as the production of the gazes of others, the simulacrum is a touchstone for the frenetic circulation of the gaze.

The spectacle, as Guy Debord puts it, "is not a collection of images, but a social relation among people mediated by images."[22] Aura as "a unique distance" never was anything other than the slow boiling away of the visual *object* (the painting, for example) under the friction of its own visual circulation. The painting in the museum becomes overlaid with the accretions of the gazes of others on its surface. This statement, like Debord's, is merely a reformulation in visual terms of Lukács' analysis of commodity reification, "underneath the cloak of a thing lay a relation between men [*sic*]."[23] With the painted masterpiece, which, as a unique object, has been seen in serial fashion by so many others, the viewer's image of it is necessarily measured against all other *imagined* viewers' images. The media-system that has the painting in its grip has a perceptual effect. The edifice built by the gazes of others on the work of art has a perceptible effect on the imagination, which is to say that when we view a cult image in the form of a painting, we view a generalized and imaginary image imposed upon the material surface of the canvas.

Though Benjamin's use of the term "aura" is varied, it subtends an object's relation to its past and to its production—the trace of the potter's hand in the pot, as Benjamin put it in the Baudelaire essay. The trace of production past, to which Benjamin ascribes the aura, at a later moment becomes the fetish character of the commodity. The aura as the phantom limb linking an object to production and history is transformed into the spectral quality of the fetish character for the unique work of art as the circulation of such a visual object in the visual field begins to affect the quality of its prior visual harmonics. Put another way, the aura is the thinking person's fetish. The thing that Benjamin calls "aura" is worked on by visual circulation; it is altered by all that looking. By the time the museum patron confronts the masterpiece on the wall, s/he must compare her/his experiences of the object with her/his perception of all the perception that has accreted to it—in short, everything that accounts for its canonical status as art, that valorizes the object socially, and that valorizes the viewer who establishes a relation to the art object. It is in such a moment that we might grasp the tremendous scale in terms of space, time, visual objects, numbers of persons, and social institutions mediating our relations to one another. These relations necessarily become imaginary and it is here that the image begins its decisive ascension over the signifier. The viewer's perception of the painted image includes his or her perception of the perceptual status of the object—the sense of the number and of the kind of looks that it has commanded. This abstracted existence, which exists only in the socially mediated (via lithographs, museum's reproductions, etc.) and imagined summation of the work of art's meaning (value) for everyone else (society), becomes the fetish character of the unique work. Its uniqueness stands in contradiction to its mode of appropriation. The stature of the unique work of art is the other, supplemental, fate available to objects in a situation of mass-production. Thus relations of production in the production of the value of art are abstract—they depend upon the mode of appropriation generalizeable to the entire society in which the unique work is seen and understood. Because they are abstract, that is, not visible in the object itself, and because they heretofore have lacked a theory, these relations of production that inhere in "high" art have been hidden, despite their practical realization as the price of art masterpieces.[24]

The visual fetish emerges when one cannot see the visual object in its totality (the totality of looks in which it has circulated)—part of the art object's value comes from its very circulation. The fetish character intimates a new value system; the aura intimates visual circulation in a visual economy. As the $60 million price tag of a Van Gogh investment practically demonstrates, this circulation is productive of value in the classical terms of the labor theory of value.[25] All that alienated attention, in the form of those dutiful, or worshipful, or revelational, even disdainful fetishizing gazes, in the form of Christy's promotions, monographs, postcards, what have you, accretes to the image and its proprietor. Both particular works of art *and* the entire art-system are infused with value of this sort. Art-objects and the institutions that sustain them become capitalist machines extracting and expropriating value through alienated attention.

Use-Value and Exchange-Value in Every Byte!

"It is half the art of storytelling to keep a story free from explanation as one reproduces it."[26] What Benjamin understood as "information"— that is, events, "shot through with explanation"—the rise of which coincides with the fall of the story, the decline of experience, and the dawning of full modernity, is now recognizable as a predominant feature of new forms of mediation in the capitalist economy.[27] In the intensification of the logic of capitalist information society, the pure and immediate visible object becomes ever more recondite, the oceanic bond with it ever more distant. As the distance from the eye to some originary visual object approaches infinity, as the visual becomes the ob-scene, the "essentially pornographic," "visuality" or the medium in which every iteration is inscribed in its seam with "use only as directed," aura either "withers away" or passes into simulacrum.[28] In either case, what this means, effectively, is that "the thinking person" is gone.

As with information, which must appear "understandable in itself," and the coin, so with binary code and the media byte.[29] The media byte is media functioning in two determinations: 1) as its particular content, mediation in its synchronic form; and 2) as part of a system of circulation. As with all objective forms that must be reified (taken out of capital circulation, at least conceptually) in order to be constituted as an object, the media byte traveling at a certain speed (in the form of a nineteenth-century painting in the nineteenth century, for example) has a fetish character or aura. Language can try to catch up with it. As the image accelerates, the aura undergoes its quantum shift (quantity [of gazes], to quality [of image]) and becomes simulacrum. Simulacra travel so fast, circulate among so many gazes, that the content (as context, as socio-historical embeddedness) is sheared from the form, making the history of their production ungraspable. Simulacrum is the sublime in the ridiculous, truth as the removal of the ground for truth. Indeed, to a certain extent, that is, within simulacra's own realm, the category "history" no longer applies to them (except, of course as simulation, as "history"). The simulacrum has value and nobody knows why. That is because its metaphysics of value are in another dimension, on a different string, if you will. What replaces historic imbeddedness of the image-object is mediatic regulation. This result should be taken as a gloss on Marshall McLuhan's famous phrase "the medium is the message." The aura, in its conversion to simulacra, signifies the regime of mediation, not necessarily denotatively but practically. Experientially we encounter simulation, practically, they realize profit. The specter of the visible (aura) has become the substance of the visual (simulation). In the visual arena, as in the object universe before it, exchange-value overtakes use-value, forcing vision itself to partake directly in the dynamics of exchange. The local confounding of metaphysics releases a whole new battery of affects that become the software algorithms for postmodernity. Hence today there is an almost palpable integument overlaying society. This integument can no longer properly be described as "ideology" (since ideology is a concept welded to a narrative and therefore a quasi-historical core) but is more adequately denoted by the term "spectacle."[30]

Aura, then, is to ideology as simulacrum is to spectacle. Aura is of the subject. In the simulacrum, the particular content of a message, its use-value, is converted into nothing but pure exchange-value. The amplitude of the message itself is liquidated under the form that it takes. Media bytes realize their value as they pass through the fleshy medium (the body) via a mechanism less like consciousness and more like the organism undergoing a labor process—call it an haptic pathway. Media bytes are thinking money, or better, affective money (that becomes thoughts in the subroutines of language). In the course of their flow, new synapses uniting brain and viscera are cut and bound. Internal organs quiver and stir. We arise from our seats in the cinema and before our television sets remade, freshly ennervated from a direct encounter with the dynamics of social production and reproduction. "We see that the methods of processing the audience are no different in the mechanics of their realization from other forms of work movement, and they produce the same real, primarily physical work on their material—the audience" (*Writings*, 1:66).

Properly speaking, contemporary media bytes do not have an aura, but have become simulacrum. The term "aura" is better reserved for the painting hanging on the gallery wall—its circulation among gazes transpires at a slower speed. As I noted, the painting's aura derives from the gap between what one sees and its status as a work of art in circulation. It also derives from the fact that one constructs oneself as a "one." One covets the authentic knowledge of an object which is slowly boiling away under the gazes of passersby only to be reassembled as an abstraction of what the many eyes that have gazed upon it *might* have seen. The painting becomes a sign for its own significance, a significance that is an artifact of its invisble mediations, its circulation through myriad sensoriums. Simulation occurs when visual objects are liquidated of their traditional contents and mean precisely their circulation: *It is at this object-image that myriad people have looked.* Liquidated of its traditional contents and intimating the immensity of the world system, the affect of the visual object as simulacrum is sublime.

The aura of authenticity experienced by Benjamin in the presence of the museum painting marks historically the emergence and intensification of the fetish character of vision.[31] It is the watermark of the commodification of sight. Aura indexes the falling of vision under the sway of the capitalization of vision which itself is falling under the sway of the cinematic mode of production. The frustratingly mystical properties of the aura are due to the fact that it is the index of the suppression of the perception of visual circulation. The aura is the perception of an affect and indicates the moment where the visual object is framed by the eye with the desire to take it out of circulation. Like the fetish character of the commodity, it marks the desire to convert exchange-value into use-value, to free the object from the tyranny of circulation, and to possess it, to have a unique knowledge of it. It marks the desire to overcome that unique distance, or what could be understood as the disappearance of humanity from the world of things. The fetish character of the commodity is the result of capital's necessary suppression of the knowledge of the underbelly of production, that is, exploitation at once desired and disavowed; it is the mystification of one's relationship to the products for consumption—the consequences of the very alienation of the produce of production from producers. Here, this mystified relation, expressed most generally, is our inability to think the production of value through visual means, that is, our inability to thoroughly and immediately perceive the properties and dynamics of the attention theory of value in the production of aesthetic, cultural, and economic value. All those looks at a painting, though invisible, leave a residue that makes the painting what it is. The aura is the living tissue of now absent attention and social practices that congeal around the work and continue to exercise a palpable effect despite the fact that they are invisible. The fetish also marks the independent will of objects, their monstrous indifference to our puny desire, their sentience, that is the registration of their animation in circulation—their cult value. But the fetish marks the invisible relations capital that haunt the object while the aura marks the now absent uses and properties that make the object what it is.

The personal quality of certain strains of modernism and the very cult of genius or personality as a signifying structure in modern art supporting individual works that otherwise would be lost in the world of intending objects, is a consequence of the amplification of such characteristics (personality and individual will over and against the sentience and indifference of objects). Thus personality and genius are not only hermeneutic mechanisms for the interpretation of modern artworks, but compensatory mechanisms imputing human characteristics to a world where these characteristics are disappearing among the general population in the face of the market. Like the experience of Everyman in the Coen Brothers' Capital Cinema, the personal touch, unaccommodated by massive, visual mediation (massively intending, widely circulating, institutionally enabled, capitalized objects) is doomed by capital to extinction.

Though no longer personal, because so highly mediated, such modernist masterworks confront us with a socially magnified image of our own lack. The utopia they represent, in which their creator's personality is valued for what it is, passes through the market of alienated labor and attention. The value produced by our personal relationship to them, accrues to them, their media, and their masters. Such is the logic of celebrity. Commodity fetishism, which is a variation on precisely the same structure of alienation, is the necessary ruse and consequence of free enterprise—its sublimity is the antithesis of social transparency. We want what has been taken away from us. This sublimity is further intensified (as is social opacity) with simulation in the postmodern—simulation is the intensification of social opacity.[32] The viscerality of simulation attests to the depth of the penetration of alienation into the core of the collective (Western? Global?) soul.

The aura, as either a visual component or analogue of the fetish, specifies the character of representation, visual and otherwise, under capitalism during the modern period. Simulation, which occurs at a higher speed and greater intensity of visual circulation, specifies the character of representation in the postmodern period. In Debord's words, "The spectacle within society corresponds to a concrete manufacture of alienation. Economic expansion is mainly the expansion of this specific industrial production. What grows with the economy in motion for itself can only be the very alienation which was at its origin."[33] Thus the visual fetish implies that the production of alienation has entered the visual field. In the case of the painted masterpiece, it is the mark of so many eyeprints, each having left its unaccounted-for trace in the production of value.

The Money-Image

In his explicitly multinational and self-consciously contemporary work *Until the End of the World*, new German filmmaker Wim Wenders films the cinema as an explicitly politico-economic complex. There, optical machines interfaced with computers and the human sensorium allow the blind to see through the eyes of another person. This other person, the filmmaker, so to speak, must be in a state of empathy with the blind. He or she must go out to see things and then during the playback of the images remember them with the feelings that accompanied them in order that the recorded images may pass first through his or her consciousness and into the consciousness of the blind. According to the logic of *Until the End of the World* then, the filmmaker's role, in a manner a la Vertov and Kino-Eye, is to aid those who, in post-industrial society, cannot see because of their bio-historical restrictions; cinema is a prosthetic device for the enabling of those who, because of where they are and who they are in a world such as ours, live with limitations. The filmmaker does not have to create an image of totality in order to achieve some form of social remediation, as in *Man with a Movie Camera*,—what is required is simply an image rooted to the world by passing through a human and humanizing mind. The film lasts until the end of the world, that is, until the cinema is overtaken by video.

In the late capitalism of *Until the End of the World*, a converging course for visual representation and the unconscious is portrayed. This convergence, thematized as video, threatens Wenders' cinema-on-a-human-scale. The human-friendly technology that is described above as drawing upon memory and the unconscious in positive ways is shown to contain within itself dire possibilities. These adverse tendencies, which for Wenders threaten the very being of analytic thought, are activated when vision and the unconscious are impacted in a third term, the commodity. In a new innovation, the same technology that during the early part of *Until the End of the World* is being developed to allow the blind to see, is utilized to record and replay an isolated individual's dreams by cutting out the filmmaker-other, in effect, undermining the structuring-field of the signifier as the constitutive condition for self/other or subject/object. As signaled by the quasi-anachronistic presence of a Sony camcorder in this futuristic film, this technology turns out to be an elaborate form of video. The film's female love interest, who is involved in the research on this new technology, develops an addiction to the ghostly, colored electronic shadows of her own pixilated dreams that flicker on her eye-screen and then vanish only to coalesce once again as, for example, liquid blue and yellow silhouettes walking hand in hand on a blood red beach. Rather than surrealism without the unconscious, what appears on the video (and by implication what video is) is the spectacle of her own unconscious, exempt from the triangulation performed by the self-other-signifier relation. Endlessly she watches the movement of the abstracted forms of her desire mediated and motivated only by technology *and her own narcissism,* rather than seeking an encounter with the outer world through another visual subject. Her addiction feeds off of her dreams and her dreams feed off of her addiction. That this "indulgence" makes her inaccessible to the men who desire her, and that this self-separation from heterosexist patriarchy might be a good thing or have some elements of a good thing, is not explored adequately by the film. Indeed, here, it only stimulates the men's fascination and their need to save her from her own (attractive) narcissism. Within Wenders' logic, she is caught in a dead-end loop. This video within a film is portrayed as capital's shortest circuit—an environment where the individual immediately and addictively consumes her own objectification.

Staring endlessly at video, only breaking off in order to sleep, the *female* antagonist is immersed in the time of the unconscious—in time that is unconscious—and therefore cannot be reached from outside. The time of the unconscious articulated in the videographic hallucinations secreted on the screen is taken also as a sort of ur-time of late capitalism—a temporality resulting from the infinite fluidity and plasticity of a money that responds to desire before desire can even speak. This desire, which is pre-symbolic and in certain respects a result of capital's penetration of the infantile, is a desire that, no matter what else it is, is necessarily (if unconsciously) a desire for money, the very medium of the addiction. Hence her desire, in passing through the technological, is mediated by capital in the sense developed in chapter 2, that is, capital structures the conditions of the emergence of her desire, even if that desire is not structured by the symbolic of language. As emphasized by the setting, a James–Bond style cave full of high-tech imaging equipment staffed by aboriginal people in the middle of the Australian outback, the strangest outcroppings of capital circulation are under scrutiny here. Because, as the multiplying characters and the multinational plot would imply, capital is shown to traverse all circuits as global flow, technological society and the money economy appear as the real in *cinematic* representation, even if not accessible as such in the *videographic* hallucinations. What the film *Until the End of the World* shows that the video cannot is that when the batteries run out, another world appears. It is therefore a critique of virtual reality, an attempt to map the reality behind virtuality. The film stages the new terms of a crisis in which a kind of involution occurs—most of what was formerly reality becomes unrepresentable within the videographic/unconscious, and that which was unconscious stands in the place of the reality principle, that is, in place of wakefulness. Unconsciousness tends to subsume consciousness. In late capitalism, three strands—representation, the unconscious, and the commodity—tend to converge in the image.

This flattening out of the space between the unconscious and representation (i.e., the end of representation as such) is precisely the argument, albeit with shifting emphasis, implicit in a variety of socio-linguistic analysis from George Orwell to Jean Baudrillard: With a certain amount of pressure on the signifier (pain), depth (as history, as the unconscious) vanishes and things *are* as they appear. Freudian representation becomes Pavlovian signalization. All of the would-be contradictions, yesterday's contradictions, are on the surface, and since there is nothing but surface they are no longer contradictions. This surfacing of signification appears in two dimensions: the elimination of depth, and the annihilation of laws and boundaries that have, in the past, delimited the movement of the signifier. In Orwell's famous example, *with enough electricity,* 2 + 2 can equal 5. Though I will not elaborate the idea here, these two altered dimensions in the transformation of the signifying stratum are just two effects of the same process of the technologically mediated overloading of signification. Absolute depthlessness and incessant ecstatic exchange come into being simultaneously as new fields of power and organization (capitalized mediation) overtake the field of signification.[34] As signification is overwhelmed and overdetermined by capitalized visual technologies, as it is subsumed by the economics of the imaginary, it is converted in its interface with bodies into a productive activity compatible with industrial labor and then visual attention. All of signification's spatial and metaphysical properties undergo a shift—its internal, organic logic is sublated by capital logic. This transformation of the laws presumed to striate signification conventionally, such as referentiality, logic, or narrativity, has been called poststructuralism and postmodernism, but very few of the discourses emitted in and as these formations have been able to figure adequately the economic as an overdetermination effect on the new (im)possibilities of signification. Because of the dissolution of the referent, language's inability to posit its own beyond, the economic, along with the unconscious and the Other, has an annoying quality of evaporating just where one might hope to find it. However, this shift in the character of language away from being a representation of reality to being under erasure, that is, at its extreme, unconsciousness itself, can be historicized.[35]

We already have seen that for an image of the inadequation of language and contemporary visuality, one need look no farther than that fabulously undynamic duo of Beavis and Butt-head. Situated *within* MTV, endlessly watching music videos, they only interrupt their viewing to describe the intensities of their visceral urges (with an economy of language that would make Hemingway envious). Then they immediately fall back into their visual stupefaction (which is sutured to the home-viewer's) in front of undulating, eroticized musickified bodies. In their movie premier, *Beavis and Butt-head Do America,* much as in *Until the End of the World,* it is noteworthy that the plot cannot get going until Beavis and Butt-head's television is stolen, that is, only in the absence of this prosthesis can narrative begin. Overall, language offers only the most rudimentary punctuation of corporeal intensities. Meanwhile, virtually disempowered, Beavis and Butt-head serve the purposes of others.

Let me suggest here that because the sign is swamped by images, it takes on the commodity form. Its structure is less signifier/signified (signifier over signified) and more exchange-value/use-value (exchange-value over use-value). To an ever-greater degree (and with apologies to poets, struggling or otherwise), the social signification of the sign can only (also) be capital. Like other bits of exchange-value moving in a global commodity chain, the exchange-value that is the signifier must follow its capitalized vector, while its use-value becomes, as is the case with money, primarily its capacity to valorize capital. In other words, the sign is integrated vertically with the spectacle, but in such a way that the spectacle is above it (rather than the unconscious being below it). Thus the sign is the unconscious of the spectacle—"the non-represented." The traditional properties of language do less to inflect the trajectory of the signifier than do the laws of capitalized informatics.[36] The space of the fold between signifier and signified that registers alienation, what Lacan conceptualized first as the cut and later as the rim, has all but disappeared—because we have fallen into it. We become the unrepresentable because representation itself becomes a marginal riptide in the intensive flux of capitalized signifying matter. God is a shout in the street. As far as capital is concerned, at least, the meaning of everything is capital. The laws by which subjects are constituted are superseded by the laws of capitalized signification (the discourse of cinema's third machine). When the subject no longer can constitute itself as the subject of oppression because of the inadequation of language to visuality, when dystopia is no longer recognizable as such, there is the postmodern. As in some of the work of Tarkovsky or David Lynch, or, for that matter, in the novellas of Can Xue, we *are* the unconscious. To the Orwellian Trinity "War is Peace, Freedom is Slavery, Ignorance is Strength," one can add a maxim for the theorist: *Consciousness is Unconsciousness*—indeed, such is approximately the dictum ("Orthodoxy is unconconsiousness") employed by the high priests of Newspeak. The corollary: If the subaltern cannot speak, neither can you, or what's left of you. And the rest, well what's that?

Lacan, in fact, says pretty much the same thing in the discussion of *aphanisis*, the disappearance or fading of the subject, in the lecture on alienation in the *Four Fundamental Concepts of Psychoanalysis*. However, the differentiating element between a Lacanian modernism and the postmodern, one might suppose, is the temporality of the subject's fading. The constitution of the subject constantly functioning as the process of its disappearance in the signifier can be glimpsed from the following account of the drive: "in the profound relation of the drive, what is essential is the movement by which the arrow that sets out towards the target fulfills its function only by really re-emerging from it, and returning on to the subject" (*FFCP*, 206). The Lacanian diagnosis of the acceleration of this process of the drive immediately follows: "In this sense, the pervert is he who, in short circuit, more directly than any other, succeeds in his aim, by integrating in the most profound way his function as subject with his existence as desire" (*FFCP*, 206). By Lacan's definition, Beavis and Butt-head as well as the video-addict in *Until the End of the World* are perverse. So too would be the speaking subaltern, who, excluded from speech, "exists" as desire.

The perverse in Lacan's universe is something like "bad oedipalization," if I may be so bold. Though in many respects Wenders' locating such a "flaw" in a woman shows the conventionally sexist character of his notions of gender (woman as perverse, narcissistic, addicted to money), nonetheless, his equation of video with the feminine is not entirely off base—at least inasmuch as it endeavors to modulate the view that in the culture of capitalist patriarchy the phallic subject is the oedipalized subject and the pre-(non?)-oedipal subject is the unknowable/as-yet-unknown zone of the non-subjective feminine. In other words, the film embraces a kind of sexist naturalism in which that which is to be brought under the dominion of the phallic subject is feminized. It recapitulates the absence of Woman in the phallogocentrism of the symbolic. Though phallic and patriarchal, this naturalizing of the zone of the non-subject is not superficial, indeed it reveals the ground on which much first- and second-wave feminism stages its struggle. The feminine as glyph of another universe and as object of male desire corresponds to the postmodern mode of *écriture* that Alice Jardine calls *Gynesis*: "a new kind of writing on the woman's body, a map of new spaces to be explored, with "woman" supplying the only directions, the only images, upon which postmodern man feels he can rely."[37] Wenders' registration of a feminizing techno-narcissism as a threat both to the subject and to the subject of history, and his effort to recontextualize it in the oedipal domain, present a lucid crystal of the simultaneously profound and hegemonic perceptions of gender, technology, and power. I should say up front that I am deeply ambivalent about this presentation. What are the possibilites in the intersections of the technological violation of the subject and feminism and/or antiracist feminism? In Wenders' presentation, much like the lose-lose situation of the O.J. Simpson trial, in which spectators are invited to be either racists or misogynists, we are given the choice of techno-feminist narcissism blind to issues of political economy, or sexist Marxism constitutionally opposed to experience beyond the purview of the phallic subject. Because Wenders seems to be saying that one might escape from patriarchy and yet not escape from capital, the "solution" that he offers in the final scenes of the film is that of a partially emasculated subject (the woman in command but in outerspace), ironically engaged in some form of environmental politics.

Before trying to untangle this ball of string, let me return to certain elements from chapter 3. Lacan, for whom the subject emerges in the field of the Other, tells us two things: "Everything emerges from the structure of the signifier" (*FFCP*, 206), and "the facts of human psychology cannot be conceived in the absence of the function of the subject defined as an effect of the signifier" (*FFCP*, 207). The subject is a signification effect. In Lacan's model of signification, "the processes are to be articulated . . . as circular between the subject and the Other—from the subject called to the Other, to the subject of that which he has himself seen appear in the field of the Other, from the Other coming back. This process is circular, but of its nature, without reciprocity. Because it is circular, it is dysymmetrical" (*FFCP*, 207). Such then is the subject in the field of cinema in *Until the End of the World*. As the love story shows, before video, the male subject emerges in the field of the other in a circular process without reciprocity—the generative situation of unrequited love—the dysemmetrical aspects of the relation implying or giving rise to time—narrative time. Man pursues woman in time. But the temporal twist in *Until the End of the World* that results in the videographic subversion of time itself, also shows that the film's theme-song refrain, "I'll love you 'till the end of the world," means nothing more than until video sucks in "subject, Other, and time."

The End of the World and the Beginning of Globalization

The significance of the paragraph below will not be lost on anyone who has endeavored to teach media studies to students with no formal training in critical theory, because televised images often as not are *not* perceived as "something for someone," but rather as something more like "nothing for no one."

> The whole ambiguity of the sign derives from the fact that it represents something for someone. This someone may be many things, it may be the entire universe, inasmuch as we have known for some time that information circulates in it, as a negative entropy. Any node in which signs are concentrated, in so far as they represent something, may be taken for a someone. What must be stressed at the outset is that a signifier is that which represents a subject for another signifier. (*FFCP*, 207)

Not only does this non-recognition of media feed as a signifier suggest that critical theory is itself an institutional response to the crises of the subject (a huge machine staving off its impending disappearance), it also suggests that only when images are taken as signifiers, and brought into the analytical and metaphysical mode of analysis, that their political dimension as ideological state apparatus emerges. The fundamental act of most media theory is to take mediated emissions as signifiers. In so doing, media theory posits its own subjectivity, that is, its position as analyst.

The subject-form is linked inexorably to politics and political thought;

Wenders fears the end of conscious politics. Such a fear is the old fear of rampant visuality, overwhelming, indeed emasculating, analytic thought. The spectacle is practical feminization, understanding that reasserts male power. Wenders, and he is not alone, believes that cinema can ponder the visual world in a philisophico-political mode. Such is the contest between cinema and video/television. However, the form of the subjective constitution—here the taking of non-subjectifying video feed as signifier—shows precisely through its fear of the visual that other mechanics accompany so-called signifying practice that precede and exceed those that can be apprehended in the realm of signification *qua* signification. Whether an audience is conscious or not, media make demands on it. The political exceeds the subjective. This is something that feminism has argued convincingly for some time. In many ways, Pavlov's term "signalization" is again more apt than "signification" to describe the consequences of media feed. Televisual images that do not emerge as signification (but are experienced rather, as "nature" or as "intensities") will not be taken as a someone and no subjects will be constituted. An observer, constituted as are all scientists, in the realm of signification, finds, in such a signalized miasma, nodes of intensities in a media-scape. Such an observer is probably in cinema as Wenders understands it, caught in the oedipal triangle, while the observed are videographic.

Lacan provides another name for such a non-inter*subjective* relationship to signification in his correction of what he calls the "Piagetic error," that is, Piaget's notion of "what is called the *egocentric* discourse of the child" (*FFCP*, 208).

> The notion of egocentric discourse is a misunderstanding. The child, in this discourse, which may be tape-recorded, does not speak for himself, as one says. No doubt, he does not address the other, if one uses here the theoretical distinction derived from the function of the *I* and the *you*. But there must be others there—it is while all these little fellows are there, indulging all together, for example, in little games of operations, as they are provided with in certain methods of so-called active education, it is there that they speak—they don't speak to a particular person, they just speak, if you'll pardon the expression, *à la canto*nade." (*FFCP*, 208)

Alan Sheridan, the translator of *The Four Fundamental Concepts*, quickly adds a note explaining that "*à la canto*nade" is at once a pun on Lacan's name and "to speak to nobody in particular." It is as an analyst of the signifier (that is, as one who takes their words as signifiers) that Piaget constructs these children as subjects. So one sees here the connection between the non-subjectivizing character of discourse in the mass media, feminization, and infantalization as well as the desire for the Other (subject) on the part of the analyst.[38]

We now have here three models of signification within mass media: 1) the self-other of linguistics and psychoanalysis that corresponds to the older cinema; 2) the active education or signalization model in which media speaks *à la cantonade* and, we must assume, provokes audiences to a great extent to respond in kind, adopting a similar utilization of the signifier, a kind of parallel play—this corresponds to television; and 3) the perverse, which would correspond to the purely videographic/virtual reality. Valorizing any one of these alone as harboring some inherent revolutionary character is over-hasty—the prospects for consciousness, dominant media, or even the promising category of perversity as a guiding light for the amelioration of historical problems seem irredeemably limited. However, taken all together these three forms yield the schematics of the psycho-perceptual regime of cinematic production in late capitalism. It is possible and indeed probable for any consciousness encountering this assertion to pass through all of these states. Thus Wenders' film, for all of its flaws, is a map of the dominant relations of production at the level of media, a realist representation of the postmodern: a quasi-Balzacian ideologeme.

The necessary refusal of a univalent plan for a solution to the global unfreedom of the majority of Earth's inhabitants gives rise to the relativistic strategies adopted by social theorists; however, it is precisely in the alternation among these modes that social cooperation is produced and maintained—to the detriment of so many. But neither, among the most radical strains of political engagement, has a unified model for social struggle come into being. If we choose consciousness and subjectivity as our mode of accounting and our paradigm for action, we risk enacting for the nth time all the violence of Western metaphysics and its discontents (logocentrism, patriarchy, imperialism). "Choosing" televisual "consciousness" corresponds, in the Deleuzian vocabulary, to a becoming woman, becoming child, that is to an effort to enter a pre- or anti-oedipal state. But to choose this may really be a choice for door number three, since one cannot in fact choose the pre-oedipal and therefore one only embraces the anti-oedipal. This shows that the child and the woman of Deleuze are *virtual* enterprises, garments to wear, mantles to be picked up. Alice Jardine, in her chapter "Becoming a Body without Organs," encourages such doubts about "D+G's" (Deleuze and Guattari's) project. Her citation of Irigaray illuminates a troubling question about the discourse of D+G vis-à-vis the subject and feminism: "In order to make the 'body without organs' a 'cause' of jouis-sance, isn't it necessary to have had, with respect to language and sex—to organs?—a relationship which women have never had?"[39] Jardine also points toward the contradiction in Deleuze and Guattari's work that I have been plying here. She finds "D+G's 'woman' . . . endemic to an era of post-signification—an era, it would seem, that human subjects, their texts, and the world itself are rapidly approaching," while at the same time noting that "while taking the United States as their ideal, D+G's work remains over-whelmingly Francocentric in its philosophical teleology. The voyages to the outer continents of reason are firmly directed from their homefront."[40] Thus critical reactions to the encroaching era of post-signification threaten to repeat the logics of patriarchy and imperialism. "We" do not yet know how to make time flow backwards to bring us to a point before oedipalized subjectivity, before gender (unless television and virtual reality are pre-cisely technologies for such an undertaking), so the phallic subject is to work his way into the beyond of childhood or femininity, using these fig-ures as modalities or methods for negotiating the assemblage and finding the line of flight. But like Deleuze and Guattari's idea of the Oriental or of Faulkner's becoming negro, one can't help feeling that this form of gyne-sis or, now, "other-esis," these minoritarian simulations, are at once sus-pect and highly circumscribed, especially given that some empowerment of "minorities" has taken place precisely in marginalized groups' institu-tional self-constitution *as subjects*. Perhaps the historical conditions have not emerged for Deleuze and Guattari's thought manuals to realize them-selves beyond a virtuality all too comfortable with forgetting, I honestly don't know, but even if these lessons for dismantling the phallic subject from within are valid (as Jardine seems to suggest), I can't help, with re-spect to such poststructuralist escape hatches, but lean toward the spirit of Langston Hughes's remark that the average black person in America "hasn't even heard of the Harlem Renaissance, and if he has, it hasn't raised his wages any."

A different filmmaker might have ended his history of the world and of the disappearance of what Lacan calls "the lethal factor" from perception with a time-image marking the end of the world, that is, with the overtak-ing of *Until the End of the World*'s narrative with the videographic display, but Wenders, who has always painfully yet sometimes beautifully believed in the world, ends the film with a knowing farce: Returning not exactly to Earth, but to the logical time of official world history, the video junky kicks the habit and gets a little perspective on the planet by working in an orbiting shuttle for Green Space. Despite Wender's partial yet inadequate ironizing of such "political" alternatives that utilize the money-consciousness system with a little perspective, I think that we can take *Until the End of the World* and its closing aporia as exemplary of Deleuze's argument that *"the cinema confronts its most internal presupposition, money, and the movement-image makes way for the time-image in one and the same operation.* What the film within the film expresses is this infernal circuit between the image and money. . . . The film is movement, but the film within the film is money, is time."[41] In the strange temporality of *Until the End of the World,* the plot breaks down where the video starts.[42] The mechanism of what Deleuze finds beyond the movement-image and calls "a little time in the pure state" is revealed in the video-junky's techno-capitalist narrative dysfunction: Time cut out from movement and narrative is the expression of the transcendence of signification brought about by capital intensification. *Until the End of the World* is a film that wants two things: to be the world, and to restore a redeeming subject to the world. Whatever one wants to make of that as a political project, we can learn something from the film's portrayal of the video interludes dripping with the temporality of pure mediation. Locked into the circuits of economic flow, the time-image is a money-image as well. As Debord would have it, "The spectacle, as the present social organization of the paralysis of history and memory . . . is the *false consciousness of time.*"[43]

The time/money-image that reveals the end of thoughtful action, or inaugurates the paralytic contemplation of the unconscious/sublime, or even impels us toward what might be termed the narcissism of philosophy, is not the sole province of the latter half of the twentieth century. In *The Time Machine* of H. G. Wells, which is contemporary with the beginning of cinema, we have another harrowing time-image of the end of the world: The lonely time traveler sits in his now-ancient time machine on the last beach at the end of the world, a cold, thin wind arising as the giant red sun, gone nova, droops into the final sky. To avoid the tremendous crabs that slowly close in on him near the end of eternity, the time traveler first moves on a hundred years only to find the crabs still on the beach, so he moves forward a few million years more. The giant crabs are gone and the only living creature to be seen is a black sea-dwelling football-like animal that takes a single leap out of the dark ocean. The thin wind blows colder and in the twilight snow falls. This scene suggests that the forces of reason capable of producing the time traveler's time machine are also capable of hailing the foreclosure of the human species. Wells's time-image at the end of the nineteenth century as well as Wenders' at the end of the twentieth put forth two images of time and its ruins, or better, its ruining, at the end of the world. This "a little time in its pure state" is at once a meditation on the consequences of rationality, and equipment for living. If we reconstitute ourselves in the presence of the sublimity of an indifferent time that eats away at our very constitution, a temporality that is a result of the cultural logic of our era, perhaps we become inured to it as well. For time really has become this way and yet we must go on. In our responses, conscious, unconscious, visceral, what have you, we incorporate the terms and protocols of the new world—in this case perhaps, the impossibility of a future—and its new temporalities as it incorporates us.

What do the time machines of H. G. Wells and of the cinema have in common, then? Is not Wells's late-nineteenth-century time machine already a form (in Deleuze's terms) of "post-war" cinema, a device for the utter severing of the sensory-motor link? I am suggesting that the cinema machines this severing, that it is not a mere response to an objective historical moment that can be reified under the sign of the war. Rather, such a severing ought be thought of as a tendency of convergent logics and practices. True, the scale of military operations and those of corporations renders individual agency ever-more marginal, but are these thinkable without the war of images?

Antonio Gramsci, in his essay "Americanism and Fordism," predicted the necessary emergence of a psycho-physical nexus of a new type in which sensation and movement are severed from each other.[44] One must consume such severing to produce it in oneself. After all, like the spectator, the time-craft just sits there utterly motionless as night and day alternate faster and faster, as the solid buildings rise and melt away, and then, still accelerating, as everything goes gray and the sun becomes a pale yellow and finally a red arc racing around the sky. *The Time Machine's* bleak registration of the infinite extensionality of a time that yields only emptiness and extinction emerges directly out of the theory and practice of a scientific rationality that we know that Wells associated with specialization, capitalism, and imperialism. The time machine is the consciousness of these formations. It is also a figure for the cinema. In many ways, the story of *The Time Machine* prefigures Max Horkheimer's assertion in "The End of Reason" that the concentration camps are the logical result of instrumental rationality.[45] Rationality to the point of irrationality; temporality to the point of extinction—these are the trajectories emerging out of a cultural logic based upon the acceleration of production and the consumption of the future.

In processing the time-image, we produce our own extinction, a necessary condition for many of today's employees.[46] In capitalism, our labor confronts us as something alien, as Marx said. Today we work (consciously and unconsciously, if such a distinction can still be applied) to annihilate our own constitution as subjects and make ourselves over as different types of information portals able to meet the schizophrenic protocols of late capitalism. Just as in one era at the behest of social organization we built ourselves as consolidated subjects, in another mode of production we dismantle and retool.[47] Today we are schizophrenics—juridical subjects one moment, polymorphous pseudopodia of affect the next (for example, *Terminator 2*).[48]

If cinema is a time machine, then perhaps its sublime is precisely the image of our own destruction (as subjects, and therefore, in the "free world" as the components of "democracy"). The pleasure we get as we consume our own annihilation marks a contradiction as absolute as that which emerges, for example, from the awe inspired by the early 1990's I-Max film (an excellent name for a late-capitalist medium), *Blue Planet*. As our eyes, like those of Wenders' video junkie, experience the exhilaration of digging deeper and deeper into the infinite resolution, in this case, of six-story-tall images of entire continents shot with hundred-thousand-dollar optics on large-format movie film in outer space, the film proposes, with far less irony than Wenders' Green Space, that space observation might aid in saving the visibly eroded planet still swirling majestically below us. This proposition conveniently elides the notion that the present condition of an earth that requires saving is a direct result of the very technology (optical, military, communicational—and the economics thereof) that offers us such breathtaking and "salvational" views. The message of the universal project of Science (which here can be understood to be one with the universal project of "good" [American] Capitalism) is reinforced by the moving image of the awesome and eternal Earth. If, in the time images of Deleuze's "masterpieces," we confront the many forms of our own annihilation, "the impower of thought," and elsewhere, "the destruction of the instinctive forces in order to replace them with the transmitted forces", and if, in the time-images of our popular culture we confront the apotheosis of production/ destruction dynamic of capitalism, then we must confront the question of the significance of the aestheticization and philosophization of sublimity in lieu of a political economy of the time-image.[49] In *Blue Planet*, as in the logo of Universal Studios, the earth itself, in its now precarious (now that it can in fact be seen) but once-immutable majesty, becomes an image of the awesome destining of capital cinema.

Given the image of the globe of globalization as the sublime figure for our universal disempowerment, it should come as no surprise that the labor necessary to produce the manifold forms of our systemic compatibility is our (humanity's) own. On an immediate level, this claim implies that we work for big corporations when we watch their advertising, or submit to their p(r)ograms, but more generally, our myriad participations in the omni-present technology fest are engaged in ensuring the compatibility of our sensoriums with prevailing methods of interpellation, signalization, and unconsciousification, in addition to whatever else they're doing. These communiques reach us not only by calling us into identification in the Althusserian sense but by calling us to rhythms, to desires, to affects. Daily we interface with machines in order to "speak" the systems-language of the dominant and dominating socio-economic system. The retooling of ocular and hence corporeal functions is not a one-time event; retreading vision, sensoria, and psyches requires constant effort. It is important to note that we are thinking of organic transformation channeled not only through discourse, but through visual practice. (One must, of course, at this point acknowledge the ear and the nose as well—as music and now the perfume industry attest, other senses are being opened for capitalization.) Though certain hardware remains standard for a time, even the screen, for example, has undergone many modifications in its movement from movie to TV to computer. Today the screen again is being superseded by virtual reality—in the so-called "fifth generation" of computer technology we will be inside of information. As a citation in Howard Rheingold's *Virtual Reality* puts it, "Computer programming is just another form of filmmaking." Rheingold describes the generational development of computers as a slow meshing of human intelligence with artificial intelligence, a gradual decreasing of the distance between the mind and the machine. At first one delivered punched cards to an operator. Then one could input information oneself. Then there was a switch from base two to primitive code words, and after that more common language and the screen. In the fifth generation (VR), we will be *inside* information, able to fly through information spaces making simple physical gestures such as pointing, which will then perform complex computerized functions.[50] But this transformation will only put us literally where we already have been for some-time. Micro-adjustments and calibrations of the practices of concrete bodies have been and are being made all the time: as fashion, as sexuality, as temporality, as desire.

I have enumerated above several of the shifts in consciousness and perception characteristic of the cinematic mode of production without passing final judgment on these. To conclude this section, I would like to recapitulate two propositions concerning the question of value.

1. As the visual fetish testifies, the perception that images pass through the perception of others increases their currency and hence their value. Vision adds value to visual objects, value that is often capitalized. Inevitably, this value changes the form or the character of the image because this value is the bio-technological placing of the image in circulation, its very mediation. If circulation through sensoria creates value (recall the painted masterpiece), then this value is the accruing of human attention on the image. Because the images circulate in regulated media pathways (channels), the media itself becomes more valuable as its images do. As significance is displaced and messages are depleted, we move from "the medium is the message" to "the medium is the medium."

2. The accretion of "fixed" visual capital, the visual technologies that arise for its management (mediation), and the intensification of its productive strategies along with the increased rate of profit made possible through the colonization and domestication of life bring about a change in the very quality of human productive activity. In what sociologists would call an informal economy, value is produced by viewers as they work on their own sensoriums.[51] In other words, some of the effort in the near-daily remaking of the psyche, as well as the production of rhythms, desires, intensities, proprioception, zones of visibility, and zones of invisibility is provided by the labor time of the viewer. This tooling of the body to make it amenable to commodity flow—to make it know how to shift times and to operate at the different speeds that the non-synchronicity of late capitalism demands, to make it address certain ideologies and desires, to elicit certain identifications, to engender and transgender, to seek freedom in the well-lubricated groves of capitalist ambition, requires human labor time and is productive of value for capital.[52]

Thus, at a formal level, the value of media and of images is increased, while at an informal level we work on ourselves so that we may work in the world. This said, it is important never to forget that in the present regime of sensorial production, all earlier forms of exploitation (wage labor, slavery, feudalism, imperialism) coexist with the visual and the sensual production of value that I have described.

Twenty-First Century Addendum: Media-Capital of the Twenty-First Century

As the price of assets such as housing rise and as the medium wage in the United States decreases (adjusted for inflation), one might expect to find a growing discontent among a fragmented working class that could be countered only by the erosion of civil rights and imperialist war. While the global war on terror, with its patriot(ic) acts, clearly fills this gap, destroying social wealth in what appears to be for many a more or less psychologically satisfying way while preserving hierarchical society intact, it is important to see that this war, which has as its basic goal the destruction and/or expropriation of the individual's wealth in exchange for a fantasy of empowerment and/or security, is also characteristic of the new fundamentalisms and of consumerism. How does this phenomenon work? Is this the psychology of most, approaching all socio-economic exchange, including showing up for work, film-going, sporting events, attending meetings, and perhaps even your reading here? What actually happens as you give your life to this book? Are you giving away your labor time only because you believe (perhaps not incorrectly) that it will help you do battle in the capitalist competition of each against all? Is reading a way of capitalizing your investment of attention? And is it possible or does it matter that in doing so you are increasing the author's capital (little as it is . . .)? Assuming we are not direct antagonists, are we in solidarity or is this a business relationship?

This line of questioning is less about thinking the bling (only one) of academic glamour and more about pointing out the isomorphism of various forms of socially programmed investment—whether of one's social due(s) (the commons, including public education, welfare, the highways), one's labor or attention (work), or one's accumulated wealth (consumption) in a larger dynamic of symbolic empowerment. This would show that the other side of consumerism is to turn all social activity into investment—an investment in an/one's image. The pleasure derived from such investments is one of the payoffs (you feel important, secure, American)—a kind of surplus value. Being "American," in the religious sense of the word, is one place, a kind of conspicuous consumption/production, in which, for example, poor working-class people wager their fair share of the social wealth (past, present, and future) on an outcome that returns a profit in a way not too dissimilar to working to buy Prada, or doing what it takes (saying what needs to be said) to show everyone you're a good Christian.

In the end, it is the conspicuousness that is most significant here because it brings us back to the dynamics of the image and of film-language. In the investment in and production of a capitalized symbolic on the subjective side, in the calculus of the image on the objective side, a shattering or rather a sublation of all the categories of value is achieved—the categories are at once annihilated and preserved. Just as from a certain distance, Gauss's law allows physicists to treat an uneven distribution of charge as a point charge, the distinctions between use-value and exchange-value, production and consumption also may be ignored and utilized for certain calculations, such as the current price of Google's stock. However, what is going on at the surface, as it were, of that point of charge, is a whole new set of dynamics far different than the contradiction between labor and capital as played out on the shop floor in the industrial context.

This transformation of the form of value, finally, is the reason that cinema is the privileged figure of analysis in this text. As one can observe about my insistence on the relationship between the aesthetic and production—of the image as a productive interface between social capital and the body—the dynamics of capital accumulation will have to have been transformed for the productive aspect of the aesthetic dimension to be valid. A film, like a car, is neither a single commodity nor is it used up at one go. At certain junctures, each is treated as a discreet commodity, as when, for example, a car or a ticket is bought. However, each is not only an assemblage of commodities and processes that range across the entire planet, each is also "consumed" partially, in different instances of space and time. I put "consumed" in quotation marks because neither can be consumed fully or rather exclusively in as much as consumption also involves movement and hence circulation. Furthermore, this circulation, which is also a kind of consumption, requires the "throwing into the fire" of continual infusions of value (productive labor) in order to complete itself—either in the form of gassing up, (and working to do so) or sales of media and the utilization of media to/by different concrete individuals separated in space and time. While it would seem that neither GM nor Pixar makes any money from the gassing up or the actual watching (even driving), it is also obvious that cars and films stimulate other vast networks of production and consumption and that furthermore, these vehicles get people to work.

What this description says about the value form is that the complex amortization, production and re-production of media, introduces complexities that make commodities neither particle nor wave; they can and must be treated differently from different standpoints of analysis and of practice. For the capitalist, production implies consumption: This is an old thesis of Marx, but these two follow upon and overlay one another in new ways. Furthermore, the unit of analysis is not confined to the day, the hour, the Thaler, or the widget, rather, it has been shattered to the point where it is infinitely differentiable. The Armani suit, the tax write-off, the tear, and the genital tremor might all be moments of consumption that are now or years later turned to the purposes of production. It is as if, if one wanted to think in terms of abstract universal labor time, huge swaths of it were no longer available and capital had to depend continuously upon machines for fishing around for momentary fragments of such time. In "post-industrial: society, capital no longer can get the hose-line of abstract universal labor time as it could on the assembly line, or more accurately, even though it can and does get these hose-feeds, in many contexts it also must seek little pieces of abstract time."[53]

Indeed, Google's advertising strategy in 2005 (yes, it's 2005 already, which just goes to show that production also is parceled out over space and time), which has helped push its stock price above $400 per share, is to create a massive algorithm that takes into consideration all known variables about a particular user—address, online purchasing history, web pages viewed, gender, age, and very likely class and frequency of orgasm—to link auctioned advertising to searches run by Google users. This method of gathering, weighting, and bundling little pieces of attention more and more thoroughly distills units of abstract time to a universe of time/attention buyers. This computerized advance over the niche marketing practiced by television buyers and the product placement practiced by film and TV is linked to the practice of what Google calls the monetization of content— where every instance of content on the web can, in principle, be treated simultaneously as a commodity and a medium.

This means that every page view, every image if you will, is slated to be sold as a medium of labor power. Google has found its true function in the sifting and parsing of not just data but of human subjective activity. Under the guise of making information available to users, Google has made these users available to capital and thus have made them productive of capital.

Significant here is the Google Print program, which has secured the rights to major library holdings in order to source materials that have fallen out of copyright protection and to make them available online. Also, and like Amazon, Google is taking advantage of fair use laws to show a page at a time of other print works. Deals with libraries and publishers currently are being inked to allow these individual page views to be sold a page at a time. This cannibalization of prior media should be understood in conjunction with online music, image and digital video sales/distribution, as well as blogging. Time-Warner's acquistion of Myspace.com reveals that content producers, mostly kids, bands, and burgeoning (auto)pornographers are not just working for themselves as they craft their identities. In short, these devices are the means by which the real subsumption of society by capital is continued and intensified. They also mark a further moment of primitive accumulation—an expropriation of the commons (be it the old books or people's private lives collectively conceived) in order to privatize and capitalize it. And then there is the modestly christened Google Earth, which turns the entire planet into an image with the intention of eventually monetizing it. As one commentator aptly put it, "Soon you'll be driving your Google to the Google to get some Google for your Google."

NOTES

1. Not coincidentally, this shift from one representational paradigm to another coincides, historically speaking, with the break marked by Gilles Deleuze between the movement-image and the time-image. Gilles Deleuze, *Cinema 1: The Movement-Image,* trans. Hugh Tomlinson and Barbara Habberjam (Minneapolis: University of Minnesota Press, 1986), 209 and 215. See chapter 3 of the present volume.

2. Sigmund Freud, *Beyond the Pleasure Principle,* trans. James Strachey (New York and London: W.W. Norton, 1961), 4–5.

3. Very generally here, I mean a lack of solidarity with others, a dearth of historical self-understanding, and an absence of strategies for imagining the terms of the world as other than they appear.

4. Guy Debord, *Society of the Spectacle* (Detroit: Red and Black, 1983), #157.

5. Freud, *Beyond the Pleasure Principle,* 4–5.

6. Ibid.

7. Ibid.

8. This point can be made more forcefully still if we see with Walter Benjamin the category of experience fundamentally at odds with the commodification of culture during a certain historical juncture. Experience and narrative are in decline because of the emergence of rationality as shock and information. See Benjamin, "The Storyteller," in *Illuminations,* ed. Hannah Arendt (New York: Schocken Books, 1969), 83–109.

9. As I have noted previously, during the twentieth century the world is organized

more and more like a film; commodity production becomes a form of montage. Commodities, the results of the cutting and editing of materials, transport systems, and labor time, take on the status of filmic objects that are then activated in the gaze on the screen of consciousness. The transformation of consciousness, wrought by the cinematic organization of production and the transformed status of objects, is tantamount to consciousness's full-blown commodification.

10. See Paolo Virno, "Notes on the General Intellect," trans. Cesare Casarino, *Polygraph 6/7: Marxism Beyond Marxism?* (1993): 32–38.

11. One need only think of the crucial role that borders and passports continue to play in regulating immigration. Precisely because people can't move, capital, with its ability to cross borders, can pit one national population against another as they compete to sell themselves ever more cheaply than their neighbors. For an excellent discussion of the new form of the nation state, see Arif Dirlik's essay, "Post-Socialist Space Time: Some Critical Considerations," in *Global/Local: Cultural Production and the Transnational Imaginary*, ed. Rob Wilson and Wimal Dissanayake (Durham, N.C.: Duke University Press, 1994).

12. See my essay on *Robocop 2* entitled "Desiring the Involuntary," which discusses the cyberneticization of the flesh as a further realization of what cinema has been doing to its audiences all along, in *Global/Local: Cultural Production and the Transnational Imaginary*, cited above.

13. In order to avoid bogging the discussion down with sets of qualifications that ultimately would make it necessary to lay out in schematic form the whole of Marx's analysis of capital, I restrict myself to the skeletal components of a discussion and leave it to readers to raise questions and fill in gaps.

14. My example here is with absolute values for labor time utilizing what Marx calls "abstract universal labor time" as my measure. But it also should be possible to develop a kind of saturation coefficient to describe the number of sites and the intensities of capital's occupation of the human faculties.

15. See Paul Virilio, *Speed and Politics* (New York: Semiotext(e), 1986).

16. Janet Staiger, "The Hollywood Mode of Production to 1930" in David Bordwell, Janet Staiger, and Kristin Thompson, *The Classical Hollywood Cinema: Film Style and Mode of Production to 1960* (New York: Columbia University Press, 1985), 90.

17. In the cinema, the technologies for the organization of production and of the sensorium converge. Film/capital is cut to produce an image. Today, the convergence of the once-separate industries for image production and for other forms of commodity production (in advertising, for example, the image is revealed as the commodity par excellence) realizes the new and hybridized form of the image-commodity.

18. Benjamin, "The Work of Art in the Age of Mechanical Reproduction," in *Illuminations*, 217–51.

19. Ibid., 250, n.19.

20. John Berger, *Ways of Seeing* (London: British Broadcasting Corporation and Penguin Books, 1972).

21. Deleuze, in a characteristic and brilliant reading of Plato, provides an analysis of simulation and suggests that it always has haunted the house of philosophy. What I find characteristic about this essay is that in locating the need for idealism to banish simulation in Greek philosophy, Deleuze elides the historical problem of simulation: Why is it possible to his analysis *now*? See "The Simulacrum and Ancient Philosophy" in *The Logic of Sense,* ed. Constantin V. Boundas (New York: Columbia University Press, 1990).

22. Guy Debord, *The Society of the Spectacle* (Detroit: Red and Black, 1977).

23. Georg Lukács, "Reification and the Consciousness of the Proletariat," in *History and Class Consciousness* (Cambridge: MIT Press, 1971).

24. Here it is important to note that I am speaking about the production of value generally. Whether or not this value will be capitalized depends upon a variety of factors including how pervasively capital has pervaded the arena of the work of art's "consumption."

25. That Benjamin at one point extracts the aura from the solitary seer's gaze upon a tree branch serves only to prove that the supplemental excess of vision that is the aura is not particular to any one moment in an economy of vision, but is distributed along all nodal points in the economy of sight. That which Benjamin called "distance" is actually the irreducibility of the visual object into a static object free from the visual circulation that eventually annihilates the visual object as an object of sight. This finally is as simple as the fact that we cannot look at the same thing forever and that things impel us to look at other things. The way in which our gaze moves is directly related to the way in which our bodies and our eyes are plugged into the economy itself. "Distance," then, is a form of vibration between the two determinations of mediation. Like the commodity, the object of vision occupies two states simultaneously, it is at once a thing, a use-value; and a place holder in the syntax of an economy of vision, an exchange-value. The experience of unbridgeable distance registers the impending disappearance or submergence of any visual object back into the regulated circulation of vision itself. Distance, that is, aura, is the poignant registration of the visual object's oscillation between its two determinations: an object of vision, and a moment in the circulation of vision.

26. Benjamin, "The Storyteller," *Illuminations,* 89.

27. Ibid. Storytelling in the essay is pitted against the production of events designed for easy consumption, that is, what Benjamin presciently calls "information." The clash of storytelling and information in this wonderful essay stages the confrontation of two modes of production that also clash in "The Work of Art," the pre-industrial and the modern.

28. Information, as it turns out, has less use-value outside of the circuits of the market than did storytelling. It is not knowledge really; to function it must remain in channels.

It is important here to distinguish between mediation per se, as in the mediation of events by a medieval manuscript or the transportation of sugar cane on a barge, and mediation in its self-conscious form; that is, media as media that, like the commodity in circulation, has both a particular component (use-value) and an abstract component (exchange-value) in every "byte." To understand media thus is to argue that each infinitesimally small slice of media has value in its content, its information, and in its form as media itself. Media as media always posits and refers back to the circulatory system in which it has and is currency.

29. Benjamin, "The Storyteller," *Illuminations*, 89.

30. What Benjamin only peripherally perceives about the phenomenon that he dubs aura is that it is an artifact of a visual economy. His perception of it marks a shift in the speed of the circulation of visual economy. The aura, as observed and constructed by Benjamin, is a primordial form of the exchange-value of the visual object produced by the systematic circulation of looks, and hence of "images," in an emerging economy of sight. The labor power accreting on the visual object gives it a certain palpable agency; that is why compelling objects look back. In the moment of their looking at us, we encounter the indifference of the value-system to our own being. In the postmodern, objects look back at us with such intensity that they see through us. In their indifference to our individuality is their sublimity. Benjamin records earlier experiences of this kind of event. Quoting Proust he transcribes, "Some people who are fond of secrets flatter themselves that objects retain something of the gaze that has rested on them," adding, "The ability it would seem, of returning the gaze." As Benjamin notes, "To perceive the aura of an object we look at means to invest it with the ability to look at us in return." In his effort to define the auratic, he quotes Valery as well, writing, "To say, 'Here I see such and such an object' does not establish an equation between me and the object. . . . In dreams, however, there is an equation. The things I see, see me just as much as I see them" ("On Some Motifs in Baudelaire," in *Illuminations*, 188 and 189). The concept of the aura is the semi-conscious acknowledgment of the work or image as simultaneously commodity and currency—as being at once itself (an object) and a moment in the circulation of vision. As with storytelling itself, which for Benjamin becomes a topic on the eve of its extinction, the aura becomes observable as soon as there is a transformation in the status of objects. Visual objects, like the events that are no longer held in an organic relation by storytelling but instead appear as information, appear via a new mode of production in the modern. This mode of production functions at a new speed.

31. Though the aura does not apply to vision alone but rather denotes the specter of

tradition in the context of fragmentation (the specter of humanity in the context of objectivity), I emphasize the visual here because through the eye one may grasp most easily the dynamics of circulation in general.

Because such disappearance of authenticity is at once more clearly marked in the realm of the visual (Benjamin, Berger, Baudrillard) and, simultaneously, at present more characteristic of late capitalism, I will restrict my comments here to the visual component of aura.

32. If one takes the fetish as an intimation to the abject individual of the power of the world system, then it could be said that simulation as spectacle is a dim version of the sublime; it occurs when the shutter on the lamp of the unrepresentable is just barely open. If simulation is an excess of reference without a clear referent, then the sublime is an excess of referent without adequate reference. All the simulation in the world cannot represent the world system, even though the sublimity of such a spectacle evokes its ominous presence. This dual inadequation between a symbolic that cannot represent its object and an object that cannot find its symbolic representation defines the semantic field of the postmodern condition.

33. Debord, *Society of the Spectacle*, #32.

34. Adorno and Horkheimer show the practical causes and effects of the transformation of the signifier in *Dialectic of Enlightenment:* "The more completely language is lost in the announcement, the more words are debased as substantial vehicles of meaning and become signs devoid of quality; the more purely and transparently words communicate what is intended, the more impenetrable they become. The demythologization of language, taken as an element of the whole process of enlightenment, is a relapse into magic" (Max Horkheimer and Theodor Adorno, "The Culture Industry: Enlightenment as Mass Deception," *Dialectic of Enlightenment*, trans. Joda Cumming [New York: Continuum, 1976], 164). "Terms themselves become impenetrable; they obtain a striking force, a power of adhesion and repulsion which makes them like their extreme opposite, incantations. They come to be a kind of trick, because the name of the prima donna is cooked up in the studio on a statistical basis, or because a welfare state is anathematized by using taboo terms such as 'bureaucrats' or 'intellectuals,' or because base practice uses the name of the country as a charm. In general, the name—to which magic most easily attaches—is undergoing a chemical change: a metamorphosis into capricious, manipulable designations, whose effect is admittedly now calculable, but which for that very reason is just as despotic as that of the archaic name. First names, those archaic remnants, have been brought up to date either by stylization as advertising trademarks (film stars' surnames have become first names), or by collective standardization. In comparison, the bourgeois family name which, instead of being a trade-mark, once individualized its bearer by relating him to his own past history, seems antiquated. It arouses a strange embarrassment in Americans. In order to

hide the awkward distance between individuals, they call one another 'Bob' and 'Harry,' as interchangeable team members. This practice reduces relations between human beings to the good fellowship of the sporting community and is a defense against the true kind of relationship" (164–65).

35. Using symbolic logic, Lacan shows the fallacy of the static principle of identity (X = X), saying "the signifier with which one designated the same signifier is evidently not the same signifier as the one with which one designates the other—this is obvious enough. The word *obsolete*, in so far as it may signify that the word *obsolete* is itself an *obsolete* word, is not the same word *obsolete* in each case" (*FFCP*, 210). This logical operation of the signifier indexes and indeed constitutes the subject alienated from himself. Alienation in the signifier, which Lacan calls the vel of alienation, "condemns the subject to appearing only in that division [in which] if it appears on one side as meaning, produced by the signifier, it appears on the other as *aphanisis*" (*FFCP*, 210). In the choice between being and meaning, "If we choose being, the subject disappears, it eludes us, it falls into non-meaning. If we choose meaning, the meaning survives only deprived of that part of non-meaning that is, strictly speaking, that which constitutes in the realization of the subject, the unconscious. In other words, it is in the nature of this meaning, as it emerges in the field of the Other, to be in a large part of its field, eclipsed by the disappearance of being, induced by the very function of the signifier" (*FFCP*, 211). The meaning is no longer meaning for the subject posited by the signifier whose being now fades. This phenomenon, what Derrida identifies as "the trace," can be expressed by the phrase, "I am no longer in my words."

The vel of alienation "whose properties depend on this, that there is, in the joining [the intersection of the sets "meaning" and "being"], one element that whatever the choice operating may be, has as its consequence a *neither one, nor the other*" (*FFCP*, 211), is further elaborated by Lacan in an example that proves particularly relevant here: "*Your money or your life!* If I choose the money, I lose both. If I choose life, I have life without money, namely, a life deprived of something" (*FFCP*, 212). It is, of course, not an accident that Lacan places the imperative imposed by capital as the cynosure for the function of the sign, however, Lacan does not dwell upon this relation. Instead he finds the source of the alienating *vel*, in Hegel's master slave dialectic: "*Your freedom or your life!*" (*FFCP*, 212) and characterizes the unique element of this *vel* as the "lethal factor" (*FFCP*, 213). One chooses alienation in the signifier or death. For Lacan, the entry into the symbolic is not a matter of disposition, as he says, "this alienating *or* is not an arbitrary invention, nor is it a matter of *how one sees things*. It is a part of language itself. This *or* exists" (*FFCP*, 212). The persistence of this "or," coupled precisely to the historical transformation of how one sees things, accounts for the radical dislocation of political consciousness from political event.

36. Except perhaps at the level of individual experience. I mean "individual experi-

ence" in an almost technical sense, that is, as marking off a zone of conscious life at the threshold of capitalization in which one establishes a unique relationship to a particular event, signifier, or constellation of materials. Though one side of the product may emerge as capital (a life spent in the factory, a work of art), the other side is a residue of the greatest importance. See, for example, Georges Bataille's ideas for a "science of the heterogeneous" in *Visions of Excess,* trans. Allan Stoekl with Carl R. Lovitt and Donald M. Leslie, Jr. (Minneapolis: University of Minnesota Press, 1985).

37. Alice Jardine, *Gynesis: Configurations of Woman and Modernity* (Ithaca: Cornell University Press, 1985), 52. I want to emphaszie that Wenders does not bring us any closer to answering Jardine's question, "if . . . gynesis at work in the male text is rooted in male paranoia, what happens when women take over this discourse in the name of women?" (263).

38. Infantilization, in a way different from but not entirely unlike feminization as a model for televisual unconsciousness, raises certain questions about the celebratory character many postmodern writers have taken with respect to film and television's deterritorialization/re-organization/superseding/etc. of the subject. The question of the subject in the postmodern is an iteration of the effect of the image on language, and therefore equally on meaning and existence.

39. Jardine, *Gynesis,* 213 (fr., Irigary, *Ce sexe,* pp. 138–139).

40. Jardine, *Gynesis,* 210 and 209.

41. Gilles Deleuze, *Cinema 2: The Time-Image,* trans. Hugh Tomlinson and Robert Galeta (Minneapolis: University of Minnesota Press, 1989), 78.

42. One might recall here that this is precisely the function of images of women according to Laura Mulvey. See "Visual Pleasure and Narrative Cinema," in *Issues in Feminist Film Criticism,* ed. Patricia Evans (Bloomington and Indianapolis: Indiana University Press, 1990).

43. Debord, *Society of the Spectacle,* #158.

44. For Gramsci, Americanism implied not only a routinization of work experience, but the concomitant necessity of "breaking up the old psycho-physical nexus of qualified professional work, which demands a certain active participation of intelligence, fantasy and initiative on the part of the worker, and reducing of productive operations exclusively to the mechanical physical aspects." Antonio Gramsci, "Americanism and Fordism," in *Selections from the Prison Notebooks,* ed. and trans. by Quintin Hoare and Goeffrey Nowell Smith (New York: International Publishers, 1971), 277–318 at 302. I discuss Gramsci's idea of Americanism in chapter 6.

45. Max Horkheimer, "The End of Reason," in *The Essential Frankfurt School Reader,* ed. Andrew Arato and Eike Gebhardt (New York: Continuum, 1987), 26–48.

46. See Noam Chomsky, "Notes on Nafta: The Monsters of Mankind," in *The Nation,* March 29, 1993, 412–16. He argues that the necessary condition of transnational

corporations is the destruction of democratic consciousness. In any case, they are acting as if it didn't exist and putting policy into place to ensure that it doesn't exist at least at the level of representation. How much more effective when the mass media engages the microcosms of our own sensibilities to work in tandem with the macrocosmic interests of transnational capital.

47. This is the basic mise-en-scène of cyberpunk.

48. *Terminator 2* provides a perfect example of such malleability in the advanced terminator, the T1000. Without going into the Lacanian dynamics here, let me simply say that this humanoid machine provides a figure for and of the members of the audience. The T1000 can consolidate itself in order to produce a striking force, but it also can morph in order to become inconspicuous (famously, it became the very floor walked upon), trick others, and conceal its purposes. It can take on any face, any texture, any identity without giving up its final ends: to kill strategically with the purposes of infinitely perpetuating humanity's subjugation to its own machines, that is, the mechanics of capital. Once again, the stakes are nothing short of the foreclosure of the future.

49. In the program of the masochist from Gilles Deleuze and Felix Guattari, *A Thousand Plateaus,* trans. Brian Massumi (Minneapolis: University of Minnesota Press, 1987), 155.

50. Howard Rheingold, *Virtual Reality* (New York: Simon and Schuster, 1991).

51. The analogy here between self-employed trash-pickers and small-time vendors who find their niches within the interstices of the *socius* is not accidental here.

52. I would venture as well that it is this unrecognized value-producing activity, along with other kinds of informal economy (attention) described as disguised wage labor both in third-world economies by political scientists and in patriarchal economies by feminist socio-linguists, that make up the bulk of the unacknowledged maintenance of the world.

53. I want to thank Gopal Balikrishnan for this formulation and for a conversation on the form of value that inspired some of my remarks here.

Chapter 5
The Pyrotechnics of Control
Numismatics of the Sensual,
Calculus of the Image

The Vanishing Mediator

In "mention[ing] a final trait in the style of contemporary life whose rationalistic character clearly betrays the influence of money," writes Simmel, "by and large, one may characterize the intellectual functions that are used at present in coping with the world and in regulating both individual and social relations as *calculative* functions."[1] He adds that "Their cognitive ideal is to conceive of the world as a huge arithmetical problem, to conceive events and the qualitative distinction of things as a system of numbers. Kant believed that natural philosophy was scientific only to the extent that mathematics could be applied to it."[2] Because "the money economy enforces the necessity of continuous mathematical operations in our daily transactions . . . the exact interpretation of nature [is] the theoretical counterpart to the institution of money."[3] These tendencies toward abstraction and mathematical precision are characteristics of what Simmel calls "the objective mind" and mark the internalization of the logic of the movement of money. From Karl Marx's analysis of commodification, to Georg Lukács's analysis of categoricality and reification, to Jean Baudrillard's analysis of semiotic codification in *For a Critique of the Political Economy of the Sign*, much has been written (including the bulk of my own work) on the tendency toward increasing abstraction under capitalism. Commodification, itself a process of practical abstraction by which qualities are grasped as exchange-values penetrate ever more deeply into nature and perception itself, results first in the generalization of abstraction and second in what might be ordained as historical periods of abstraction. As shifts in the quantity of abstraction precipitate shifts in its qualities—for example, in the sequences Colonialism, Imperialism, Globalization, or Impressionism, Cubism, Neo-Realism, Virtuality, or Cinema, Video, Computer—shifts in the intensity of practices of abstraction coincide with different modes of perception. For the present purposes, I would like to describe that process thus: The practices of abstraction that become a general cognitive and indeed psychological tendency under the industrial reign of the commodity form, as noted in Simmel, are fully realized and then surpassingly transformed under the reign of the cinematic image; cinema becomes a new type of calculative function for regulating both individual and social relations.

While Christian Metz's model of "financial feedback" between the cinema industry and the spectator's metapsychology should come to mind here because it implies a model for the mutual modification of corporeal practices and aesthetic form, let us stay with Simmel for a moment. Simmel says of law, intellectuality, and money "that all three lay down forms and directions for contents to which they are indifferent."⁴ So too with film. Cinema, by which I really mean the moving image, requires celluloid moving through sprockets (and now tape across heads or CD-ROMs in drives), as well as a series of evolving conventions and program formats badly described as "film language." In both cases (of hardware and "language"), the medium is indifferent to the contents. In the previous chapters, I have argued that cinema is a new order of capitalization that brings the industrial revolution to the eye. Building on this thesis regarding *the industrialization of the senses,* we may deduce that while remaining embroiled in "material relations" *cinema is a techno-phenomenological institution, itself a registration of a shift in the affective intensity of the formal logic of the movement of capital.* As the predominant assemblage (machine-body interface) responsible for the general phenomenon of what might be called image-capitalism, cinema marks a movement from the rational to the sensual, from the calculative to the affective. This shift, which also has been observed in the history of advertising, accompanies what must be grasped as a dialectical transformation of the status of objects, first circulating as exchange-value in the pathways prescribed by capital, and then, in a later moment (in what amounts to a dematerialization of the object), as the image circulating in the new pathways of capital. The movement of the image is the new process of capital, and the zones across which it moves are capital's new pathways.

"Even if our cognition were an exact reflection of the objects as they are in themselves, the unity, correctness and completeness that knowledge approaches by mastering one thing after another would not derive from the objects themselves. Rather, our epistemological ideal would always be *their content in the form of ideas, since even the most extreme realism wishes to gain not the objects themselves but rather knowledge of them.*"[5] The epistemological ideal attendant to money, then, is precisely the image—the dematerialized object, the object, grasped in its essence by the mind. Though Simmel's consideration of the abstraction of material content places its emphasis on knowledge and cognition (the *philosophy* of money), film's unique poly-technic extension of the process of abstraction (a process that emerges with the institutionalization of exchange-value as the money economy and in-tensifies with the [dialectically] subsequent spread of production for ex-change under capital) restores to cognition its sensual aspect (the *practice* of money). In the arc that might be drawn from Rene Descartes' skepti-cism in "Meditations on First Philosophy" to today's "Reality TV," the alien-ation of the senses today returns as the sensuality of alienation.

Here's the difficult part. Money *as medium* is without quality or quan-tity; it is movement and organization. So also is that new order of money first recognized as the film. Provided that one grasps that film and its de-scendants (TV, video, computers) put objects into circulation in a new way, and also that one understands in exchange-value the abstraction of the ob-ject, that is, a kind of proto-image, one also will grasp that each medium (film, money) deploys a logic for the circulation of image-commodities. The classical commodity was, after all, a proto-image, a materiality and a fetishistic excess—it is only the ratio of these components that shifts due to the intensification of circulation called mass mediation. However, the shift in the ratio "materiality to affect" in the commodity, leads/testifies to dramatic shifts in expression.

The interpenetration of the psychic and the numismatic, analyzed at incredible length by Simmel, finds a genuine fusion in the cinematic. Money's philosophy, its thought, as it were, is recorded by Simmel, yet its mode of conceptualization achieves a higher expression in film—the "phi-losophy of money" as praxis. As we saw in the previous chapter, Deleuze all too succinctly puts it thus, "Money is the obverse of all images that the cinema shows and sets in place."[6] The twin tines of economistic calcu-lability and material sensuality, emerging in the dialectical schema from an originary alienation first expressed as the commodity-form (exchange-value/use-value) are reunited and merge in the consciousness induced by the image. It is by looking more deeply into the numismatics of the sensual that the possibility of a political economy of vision will emerge more fully.

Postmodernism: The Redistribution of Sense

If the conceits of modernism include rationalization, quantification, standardization, and consciousness (even if vis-à-vis the unconscious, for scientificity and the unconscious are two sides of the same coin), then the conceits of the postmodern include sensuality, qualification, flexibility, and simulation. As we remember the young Marx in a euphoric moment predicting that, "[a]ll history is the preparation for man to become the object of *sensuous* consciousness," we might reflect that in certain respects, the postmodern is the ironic fulfillment of this modern. As students of advertising and fascism well know, the image has eroded a rational-actor paradigm and set in place a model of society driven by rationally contrived irrational urges—Adorno's psychoanalysis in reverse. But we shall find that the image—the rational production of the non-rational, the truly generalized "end of reason"—provides not the restoration of the senses but the sensual illusion of the restoration of the senses. The commodity is repletion of a certain type; when there is no vessel left to fill, repletion becomes saturation.

The senses, evolving in dialectical relation to the medium that the medium of money inaugurates, have passed through a transformation much like land's conversion to private property through ground rent, and belong now to another logic, to something other than their apparent organic proprietors. In the Deleuzean vocabulary, the senses have been "deterritorialized." For the image economy demands the estrangement not of sensuous labor alone (although that, in its industrial and agrarian forms, remains woefully estranged) but of the senses themselves. Senses—vision, hearing, proprioception—are made to produce against us. They indeed have become "theoreticians," but theoreticians for capital.[7] In the language of a dated shorthand, we could say that false consciousness has become false sensuality, seeking gratification in modalities that presuppose and corroborate structures of hierarchical society.[8] Of course, the term "false" only makes sense in a pre-postmodern universe, within a (hypothetical) universe in which the subject-form has not been at least partially liquidated by the developments that I am trying to register, but the important thing here is the figure produced—that of expropriation (a relation that raises the question of a relationship between what one might be worthy of and what one receives). The sensitivities of commodity culture, the desires, the visceral affects, the intensities index the deprivation of sense (sensation, sensuality, experience, possibility, plenitude) for the majority of human beings. On a worldwide scale, the living hell for most in the form of near-starvation and dollar-a-day wages, brings such joy, or the self-image thereof, to the few. Capital forces a redistribution of sensation that at once delimits sensibility (what can be thought and felt) and provides a disproportionate amount of commodified sensation to the first-world rich. Unmarketable but all-too-necessary excesses, such as the experience rather than the spectacle of pain, of hard labor, of malnutrition, inadequate health care, governmental brutality, and imperialist wars are reserved for the subaltern. It is clear that images do not bring to us the transparency of society and the immediacy of democratic opinion as they were to have done with *cinéma vérité* and Dziga Vertov's kino-eye. Cinema does not bring about the "spontaneous reactualization of the social contract," at least in Rousseau's sense of it.[9] The contract they realize is in fact antithetical to Rousseau's: Adorno and Horkheimer's "enlightenment as mass deception."

Bio-Power/Image

A warning from Marx regarding the cinema: "Though private property appears to be the source, the cause of alienated labor, it is really its consequence, just as the gods in the beginning are not the cause but the effect of man's intellectual confusion."[10] This self-same relation is paramount in the formation and power of images. Though today it may appear that images are the cause of "man's intellectual confusion," the alienation of our senses; they are really its consequence. Such is the reason, for example, that Americans do not know or did not see or did not feel the deaths of all those Iraqis, do not dwell on the poverty and prostitution of Asia, do not rise up to help ameliorate the disease and famine imposed upon Africa, do not reckon the consequences of their intervention in Latin America. Images are the alienated, objectified sensuality of humanity becoming conscious for itself through the organization of consciousness and sense. They are an intensification of separation, capital's consciousness, that is, human consciousness (accumulated subjective practices) that now belongs to capital. The answer to whether or not computers have consciousness is easy. They do: ours. And because our senses don't belong to us, images are not conscious *for* us. Or rather, they are conscious "for us" in another sense, that is, they are conscious in place of us. Which is to say that capitalized images constitute the experiential domain that it is the role of language to process. As the consciousness-machine of the world system, these new sites of sensuous production serve someone or something else—the myriad algorithms of capital. Entering through the eyes, images envelop their hosts, positing worlds, bodily configurations, and aspirations, utilizing the bio-power of concrete individuals to confer upon their propositions the aspect of reality. In realizing the image, spectators create the world.

In my discussion above of the continuity between objects and images in capitalist circulation, it was implied that exchange-value is the spectre in manufactured objects; their abstract equivalence in money as price is a proto-image. When a quantity of money is given for an object, the object is in effect photo-graphed, its impression is taken in the abstract medium of money. What is received in return for money is not, at the moment of exchange, the object itself but the commodity with its fetish-character, its affective, qualitative image component that corresponds to that quantity known as price. We have money given for affect, affect for money.

This system functions by virtue of the conversion of labor time to exchange value (by capital), and the corresponding conversion of money into productive power (by the consumer). Exchange-value is sensuous labor, subjectivity, shunted into an alien(ating) system. When humans' production is alienated production, that is, when their product is produced for exchange and taken away from them at a socially leveraged discount, work becomes not a satisfaction of workers' needs but a *means* to their satisfaction. Marx told us that labor's "alien character emerges clearly in the fact that as soon as no physical or other compulsion exists, labor is shunned like the plague."[11] To properly understand visual culture, the "other compulsions" not specified by Marx necessarily must be part of our investigations. Why do we want to watch TV or be on the computer? In what sense are these compulsory? If the image is a development in the relations of production, a new site of dyssemmetrical exchange between "labor" and "capital" and therefore a machine for the production of value itself, how do we explain the hold, that is the entrenchment, of the image? Put another way, how is the desire for television a development in expression of the desire for money? The desire of money?

Dialectical Expansion of the Image

In the previous chapter, we saw that cinema marks capital's necessary extension of the working day via that cybernetic relation known as the image in order to counter the falling rate of profit. Indeed, as soon as human beings produce for exchange and when exchange-value glows in the pit of each and every commodity, all things are ready to become images. To a large extent, they already have become images, in at least as much as they may be grasped as exchange-value. When all things are ready to become images, when each new object exhibits its shining forth, consciousness itself becomes cinematic. The modality of this consciousness is precisely its organization of circulating image-objects. We are first posited as cameras in a universe of fetish-objects, and then in the postmodern we are absorbed in simulation—effectively positioned as cameras in a world of ambient images. Consciousness, now a cybernetic relation between flesh and the materiality of production, is driven by the continuous abstraction of concrete materials according to the laws of exchange. To reiterate, commodities as proto-images induce consciousness as proto-cinema. When necessary, that older, (pre-capitalist?) medium known as language provides a sound track. Often as not, most of what counts takes place in the ellipses and picnoleptic moments.

Cinema proper develops as a technology of consciousness, in effect achieving a higher level of abstraction and dematerialization of the entire assembly-line process (montage) and thus a more efficient modulation of the consciousness of commodities. The amount of material substrate (objectified human labor time) necessary to induce forms of consciousness decreases. The consciousness of commodities, that is the thought of money, emerges directly out of industrial process. This imaginal consciousness (imaginary domain) is attendant to the circulation of mass-produced commodities, and marks a qualitative shift in perception due to an ever-increasing quantity of alienated sensuality. In chapter 4, I linked the emergence of cinema to the falling rate of profit and thus to the need to increase the proportion of value extraction in relation to labor time from worker/spectators. We can understand the spread of cinema here as the increasing capacity of capital to capture corporeal function, that is, to increase the leverage of capital over worker/spectators. Thus, *cinema is an alienation effect*, a result of the increasing quantity of historically sedimented labor creating a shift in the quality of capital itself. Sedimented human labor, that is, the objectification of the species, dead labor made to function as capital, demands a new order of service from the living. Mediations that formerly appeared as ontological (seeing, desiring) now appear as technological (viewing, producing). The shift in quantity that leads to a dialectical shift in quality, that is, the shift in the quantity of capital that leads to a shift in the quality of capital as cinema, gives rise to what Debord ascerbically calls the "humanism of the commodity," and indicates the new modalities for capital's valorization. By flattering you with personhood, capital has its way with you. Where necessary, capital treats you with subtlety and respect in order that it can continue to work its barbarous violences. This "false" humanism is another production cost, one that can be produced for almost nothing. Phone-free recordings become more polite and reserved capital smiles while it fleeces us. This new modality of capitalism in which we participate culturally and socially vis-à-vis the senses in the production of our own impoverishment and liquidation has been misunderstood most banally as "consumerism."

Cinema's particular administration of sensuality derives not merely from the fact that it is an historical amalgamation of sensuous labor, but sensuous labor alienated from the species on a higher order of magnitude requiring higher speeds of valorization and accumulation. Its penetration of the human organism is increasingly total and totalitarian. The technologized visual, as something like a command-central of consciousness, becomes en toto, like a super-consciousness even as it is folded into the unconscious. Taken as a whole, visual technologies become a world wide web of management protocols for visual production. The technologized visual is therefore at once above and beneath discourse, the outside expanse that feels like interior depth, and it is indeed the möbius-like folding into itself of this spatial dynamic that produces the famous flattening out of the postmodern. Famously, the outside is the inside. Mouth, stomach, anus. Like microorganisms clinging to one another in a ring in an ocean of images, words desperately strive to impose order on the liquid visible by creating small enclosures of the known. As they become more marginal, time gives way to space, consciousness to unconsciousness. As in *Liquid Sky,* what appears as consciousness is only a computer-generated and corporately managed dream—the aftermath of the death of the subject. All of this unconscious "consciousness" is structured and organized by the development of capital—indeed it *is* the development of capital. Your thought is money thinking in the world—the consciousness of computers.

Such a claim would dramatize the relationship between capital expansion, visuality, discourse, consciousness, and the unconscious in a dynamic way. Narrative is unable to cope with the intensity and pressure of images. The figure for the generalization of this process by which visuality overwhelms language is best apprehended in and as the cinema itself, in which, following the analysis of Metz, spectatorship is built right into the apparatus as one of its essential moments of valorization but, from an organizational point of view, a lower level function.

Such a figure for the situation of narratives among the images clearly should have an impact on cinematic texts. Indeed, in my work, I often have said that images of cyborgs are paradigmatically the cybernetic interface it-self—if not a moment of self-consciousness exactly, then a moment of symptomatic hysteria. The gyroscopic space-time-machine that appears in Carl Sagan and Jodie Foster's film *Contact*—a film that I analyze below—supplies another concise image from the repertoire of popular culture for the new alienation effects that are driven by the accelerating cycles of cap-ital. This claim, or for that matter any other that argues that cinematic texts bear the mark of a new order of capital, should not be cause for undue sur-prise. Given that the falling rate of profit drives the intensification of capi-talist production in and through image culture in order to multiply the sites and increase the duration of value extracation, we should not be over-awed if contemporary images contain the algorithms of the cinematic mode of production. The trace of the potter's hand in the pot, which for Benjamin provided the pot's link to the artisanal mode of production, has become the image of the spectator's activity in the mise-en-scène.

Here's how such an algorithm is manifest in *Contact*: Ellie Arroway (Jodie Foster) is a rational and thus atheist scientist seeking contact with alien life. Using a radio telescope, Arroway picks up a signal from an alien source, a pulsar twenty-six light-years away. Under what is first perceived to be an electronic pulsing of the prime numbers between 1 and 101, the signal is decoded to reveal that it contains a retransmission of a video-image of Hitler's visage from the first television broadcast of the opening of the 1936 Olympic games. This astonishing signal contains an image that apparently has been picked up and beamed back at Earth by intelligent life elsewhere in the universe. Further decodification reveals that *under or internal to the image,* the signal contains the blueprints for a space-time ma-chine. The plans show Arroway how it will be possible to build some un-imagined machine with existing technologies that uncannily resembles an early cinematic apparatus: a tremendous phenokinetescope intersecting in a sphere with two more of the same. No explanation is given regarding the purpose of this machine, but the plot makes us aware that neither the detection of the signal nor its decodification would have occurred without Arroway's haunted drive for some sort of contact.

The machine, built with public funds at the cost of billions of dollars, consists of three interlocking off-axis rings with a pod in the center. As it turns out, with increasing acceleration of its cycles, this spinning machine (which also resembles the great spinning wheels of Vertov's *Man with a Movie Camera)* creates a wormhole in space-time. For Arroway and for the spectator, this pathway opens onto a profound alien contact, onto pleni-tude, the spiritual itself, and as Arroway's post-trip conversion from a purely rational, atheistic scientist to a spriritual being brimming with be-lief testifies, the pathway opened by the machine opens to belief itself. Be-lief is precisely what the cinema creates, as Deleuze says. Belief is what the cinema films: "belief in this world, our only link."[12] As an audience, we be-hold that with enough cyclical speed and state-sponsorship, a change in the spatial and temporal consistency of the universe appears. Such is the result of the evolution of technologies of mediation: the disruption of space-time and a new order of belief.

But similar to what we saw with Beavis and Butt-head, the journey out-ward is also a journey inward. As a result of the movement of a cyclical space-time machine, Arroway travels thousands of light-years to the tropi-cal beach of her dreams and encounters alien life in the form of her de-ceased father whom she lost in childhood. Significantly, the encounter with alien presence is an encounter with her most profound desires, her child-hood, her past, and her lost dreams and her future hopes. She has passed through a lifetime of scientific rationality to transcend alienation and attain a plane of immanence. Somewhere out in the cosmos, her extruded past and spirituality is to be found—the primordial intimate link to cosmic truth is to be found outside in the realm of an alien that is hauntingly familiar. This cinematic machine, designed by aliens (alienation), and grafted onto the forms of her past, provides the key link to an inside that is outside.

When Ellie returns to Earth, the perception is simply that her space-pod dropped directly through the rings into the ocean below—the rationalists at NASA and the Pentagon say she went nowhere. But in spite of the facts and the evidence, Arroway *knows* that she did. Thus her rational investiga-tions lead her to affirm the primacy of her experience as faith. Mathemati-cally stated, reason (science) plus mediation (cinema/technology) produces faith. Just as in a previous scene Arroway was not able to "prove" that she loved her deceased father, she cannot prove the truth of her contact with in-telligent life in the cosmos. But still something transformational happened to her in that big space-time machine that we might call the cinema.

Contact is a utopian narrative about technology making its progressive way through the cynicism and evil in the world. It suggests that in spite of human foibles, cosmic destiny will manifest itself through the individual. The film's Hegelian recapitulation in a quasi-historical fashion of the evo-lution of technology, from rudimentary mathematical electronic code, to the repetitive and iconic utilization of programmatic images that gave rise to fascism, to digitized images capable of encrypting liberatory plans, to actuating a kind of spiritual repletion that inspires in its protagonist an apparent transcendence of the social, is also a narrative about the increasing externalization and simultaneous dematerialization of human power. Put another way, the salvation of the species lies in contact with and recuperation of humanistic aspirations alienated in techno-capitalism. The objectification of the species is part of a universal plan. The organization of materiality, in the form of technology, demographics, the built environment, computation, has its *telos* in the transcendence of space-time and matter. *Contact* responds to the call that all the humanity, species being, world spirit, or divinity that has been transmitted forth (expropriated) and is now part of the historical legacy somehow must be recuperated and redeemed. The socialist longings that underpinned certain dimensions of fascism, the unprovable love for the father that informs Arroway's science, must be separated out from the corruption of state power, big business, and Nazi genocide. Alienation must be overcome. The forces that humans have released that have been taken up by capital, and that "confront us as something hostile and alien" while simultaneously modifying the very warp and woof of the universe, must also, in all their modernity, deliver the promise of contact with what is most us, most universal—here figured as extraterrestrial life as the embodiment of wisdom, cosmic destiny, and life itself—if living in the present is to be at all justifiable. However, one ought to come down from the clouds here and see in the figuration of this space-time machine as cipher of cosmic destiny an allegory of television and the cinema as a spiritual recompense amidst the bankruptcy of a totalitarian capitalism. The Hitler broadcast is returned to us as a sign of a greater intelligence— an endemic intelligence whose destiny-shaping potential exceeded our understanding and that holds our fate. The footage of Hitler is at once a reprimand and a promise. Yes, the film seems to say, on the way to truth humans have done awful things, but this growth process that in spite of all its pain includes the growth of technology—this growth can and shall be redeemed. What is not said and cannot be said for the film to work its magic, is that this exchange of living labor for spiritual cinema, of life for faith, of the particularities of genocides for the universal manifestation of truth, is also, itself, the new technology of exploitation. Belief in the world as the diplomatic presentation of hierarchical society to itself. To the film's credit, however, *Contact* does register fitfully the calculating instrumentality of governments and multinationals to co-opt this alien force (of cinematic technologies) according to their diabolical interests. Indeed, contact with originary plenitude made possible by the new technology becomes within the film's narrative the central point of contention for state regulation, legislation, and funding, and the desire for such plenitude, for a radical disalienation, becomes a key political and pedagogical game-piece.

Appropriately, *Contact* also registers the possibility that science and its effects are only the outward appearance of a deeply internalized relation. The opening scene in which a camera backs up from Earth, through the solar system, and into deep space while the sound track, utilizing recognizable radio signals from farther and farther back in time, culminates by passing from stellar fields, into a black hole, and out of the young Ellie Arroway's eye. The implication that whatever is out there is also somehow inside shows that there is a cosmic destiny at work. It is as if the other is already inside us and is shaping our path in ways we do not understand. Arroway's encounter with her father on the paradisiacal beach at the end of the universe is an echo of her time with her father as an eight year old. When he puts her to bed early in the film, the eight-year-old Ellie, who is still mourning the death of her mother, asks her father about the possibility of other life elsewhere in the universe. As he says goodnight, we see a child's drawing of a beach on her bulletin board. The narrative reinforces this sense of predestination. Throughout the film, the right people die and others propitiously intervene even if for the wrong reasons to make sure that Arroway achieves contact. At some level, the message of the film is that the cosmos, alienated through a rationality that is interior to capital, somehow can be reappropriated through belief restored via cinema. In fact, *Contact* is quite clear on this fact that the image, however tenuous or unresolved, is our only link to the world: The single shred of evidence that scientifically supports Arroway's claim to have actually escaped the reality principle of Earth and made contact with aliens, is that her video camera headset recorded eighteen hours of static during the split second of Earth time when the capsule dropped and she lost radio contact with mission control. It is that evidence, containing no specific image, but marking pure duration, that is suppressed by the national security advisor and a White House aide. What is at stake in the organization of the image is nothing less than national security, which in the U.S. context means capitalism as we know it.

Although *Contact* is clear on the inevitable struggles within the larger framework of media-capitalism, it affirms the socio-political totality as being somehow one with cosmic destiny in such a way the precludes a whole set of questions regarding the uses of technology, to say nothing of its conditions of possibility. The technological as we know it is not separable from the catastrophic character of history—these are mutually constituting. In a world-historical moment in which, as Fredric Jameson has pointed out, we can more easily imagine the total destruction of life by military or environmental catastrophe than we can imagine the end of capitalism, we must mark here that despite its aspirations to transcend this historical moment, *Contact* shares the catastrophic limits that the capitalist command of the social totality would place upon our imagination.

From the origins of capitalism onward, exchange-value, the pre-eminent abstraction informing the development of contemporary technology, has become ever more eloquent both as an organizational force and as a site of libidinal cathexis. The price inside an object that pleads with every observer to restore the object to its rightful owner (you) finds ever more complex and subtle methods of asserting its claim on us, until, finally it is, as in *Contact*, the cosmic other. Collective alienation requires collective reappropriation. Simmel already shows how money structures thought; cinema is the movement of money as experience and belief. The well-known phrase "money talks" means only that exchange-value has indeed learned to speak, first through the subject-form and then through the machine (*Grundrisse*, 131–32).[13] And it speaks as if it were a God. Money talks because objectified humanity is not a metaphor in Marx, but the conversion of human sensuality into material reality—objectified humanity speaks to, through, and as bodies. This is the phenomenon that Paul Virilio refers to in *Speed and Politics* as "the habitation of metabolic vehicles," in which alien, collective logics overcode and administer individual bodies. However, in and as commercial cinema, money speaks not in our favor, but, taken as a whole, against us, for humanity objectified under capital is, in the old language, an alienated humanity. Those who speak on behalf of capital speak as prophets of a false god in a mode no less theological than any other so-called fundamentalism. As loudly as our alienated senses call for their restoration in the bloody television wars or the heroic struggles of Hollywood personalities, as loudly as the shadows rattle their chains against servitude in the framework of the Hollywood script, their very alienation ensures that this call is not heard as a real cry for justice, but as pure simulation, the ecstasy of communication, entertainment, or what have you. The sensual labor that receives and processes the alienated cries of humanity is itself alienated, the result being that the entire bio-sociality of questions from justice to metaphysics is shunted back into the circuitry of capital and remains unable to stand in opposition to it. The crisis of humanity, which is rightfully ours, is itself made to exist for another. It is one media event after another belonging to the god, Capital. Short of a total transformation of social life through what Debord calls "an onslaught on the machinery of permitted consumption," we consume our own privation as a spiritual exercise that continues to produce it.[14]

But simulation, despite its saturating and subsumptive character, is at the same time a pouring forth of the Real. In as much as consciousness and the senses are alienated, in as much as immediacy has to pass through a material-consciousness that has required the history of the capitalist world to achieve its cinematicity, Benjamin's "orchid in the land of technology" (the image that in the cinema appears as if naturally, as if there were no technological apparatus) is the Real. Yes, it is not what it seems— the mechanically reproduced object appearing without any of its mechanical appurtenances and becoming visible in itself, is not the object itself. However, the fact of its *seeming*, its hyper-reality, is indeed a spilling forth of the Real. "In a world which really is topsy-turvy, the true is a moment of the false."[15] The seeming itself, the very workings of capital, that which eludes symbolization, is that which must be analyzed. The image is a hammer, a blade, an avalanche. All those televised screams, rapes, murders, and wars express the real. It may not be *that* rape, *that* scream, *that* murder, or *that* war, which is shown that is the referent of a particular image, but the general condition of rape, brutality, and warfare expresses itself in the media-imaginary. These are indeed our images. Therefore, the bouquet of orchids, the truths, the histories, the personalities, and the intensities of cinema and television are the eloquent testimony to our non-being for ourselves: contact, in short, an encounter with the Real. These after-images of a work process centuries in the making are the expression of our alienation. Our consumption of them is also the performance of a labor that allows us continually to develop a lived relation to our alienation, that is, the alienation of our social product from our will, that is, our lack. As with those early gods, media images are not the cause but the symptom of our confusion. Later the relationship becomes reciprocal.

Dialectics of Alienation

To say that media, that is, capitalist mediations, are an effect of alienation is neither to indulge a Luddite fantasy of a return to a prior state of plenitude, nor to dismiss the possibilities inherent in technological development, but an elaborate, even painful endeavor to imagine a world in which the dead and the dying still mattered. What are *Contact*'s Vegans to those who died in the Holocaust, in Vietnam, in East Timor, in Rwanda, and in hundreds of thousands of other crimes against humanity? Are the living so eager to forget the dead who have made them possible? As objects started to spiral more quickly in capital's gravitational vortex, and prices began to circulate more widely in space and time, they began to whisper the news of the death of traditional society.

Money, though itself without qualities, could, if it had the price, extract the qualities from the commodity even if the commodity were a human being. All of the West's literary images of worn-out humans from Stendhal to Burroughs testify to this process. Humanity was being hollowed out, consumed, eaten alive. This abstraction of humanity is precisely the logic of the image (and I use the term "humanity" advisedly as the strategic antithesis of the image)—the image proper is the extraction and realization of human qualities in exchange-value. The commodity begins to be truly image when the material itself becomes only a medium for exchange-values now capable of circulating as qualities—qualities that have become abstract, and are general social currency and thus always tied to economistic relations. The material of the image, its substrate, supplies only the smallest piece of grit (a little celluloid, a few atoms of silicon), upon which the opalescent fetish will be cultivated—the new qualities of exchange-value, the new media of abstract human labor-time. On mere inanimate matter is encrypted all the subjective pyrotechnics and visceral intensities "belonging" to humanity. Beyond the image —that capitalized imaginary— little is left but the husk, the impoverished object. The correlative conversion of people into instruments (means) of exchange meant first that they became (for the symbolic of capital) pure corporeality (slavery, existentialism/ statistics), and then, pure sign-image (racism, objectification/hyper-reality). From the perspective of capital, people first were deprived of subjectivity, and later, as in the case of the diasporas of third-world prostitutes and domestic workers, of body as well.[16] When subjective affects and embodiment become the exclusive domain of image-culture, then and only then do humans fully become the vehicles of images, their energy substrate.

Imaginary War

Just as the vicissitudes of the money economy cause, simultaneously with the development of production, the emergence of ever more complex monetary technologies and properties (from gold to paper money, to debt and credit, to stocks, bonds, options, and derivatives), the visual economy develops its own form of visual technologies and properties: tablets, coins, paintings, lithographs, photographs, films, video, computers. Each successive innovation in the technology of mediation allows for new social functions that at once provide for and force increasing individualization. Credit cards create individual money to be paid by the bearer whereas money was general credit, to be paid (in labor, commodity, or any other exchange-value) by anyone. Video allows us to create our own images so that we might more completely transpose ourselves and our perceptions in accord with the logic of cinema. Each allows for the naturalization/institutionalization of the dialectically prior medium. But just as credit shows that money is a commodity, video shows that filmic perception and duration is a commodity. Each of these developments signifies a (spatio-temporal) crisis for the previous technology—credit, for example, before becoming an entity to be bought and sold by brokerage firms, arises from a shortage of money. Just as (to an extent) credit is the image of paper money, and paper money is the image of gold, and gold (perhaps the first genuine image) is the image of exchange value, video is the image of film, film is the image of photography, and photography is the image of sketching (writing?, the sign?). To a certain extent, the visual technologies mentioned would allow for an accounting of the social activities historically indexed by their money-form analogs. These separate strains coalesce in and as the computers that second by second image (with interest) the business of the world (finance capital), on Wall Street, in Hollywood, and around the world.

Cinema (the history of cinema as not merely the history of its institutions but as the history of the visual economy, its "open book") is the spectacle of exchange accelerating its own logic; it is exchange as spectacle and the corollary effects of exchange as spectacle. The corollary effects—including the actual circulation of image-commodities and the affective results of this circulation—are necessary for capital's valorization. Of course, we are not just talking about the spectatorial buzz generated by CGI or the paid product placement solicited by studios in the making of their films, but the whole function of the cinema-industrial complex. For the moment, cinema thus understood is the crucial juncture because it spans the gamut of the different scales of production, from the simulation of a globe (as "the global"), to representing and being the representative of multinational corporations and the military-industrial complex, as well as the grit of the world, and whatever remains of the subject along with its interiorities, visceralities, and intensities, as well as the" far-flung" global population of those whose existence exceeds the purview of the spectacle. For cinema means the techno-industrial coordination of all of these elements for capital, via the command and control of the image.

As previously noted, cinema historically is posited first by exchange as the circulation of prices and then, today, presupposed by exchange. The commodity is designed as an image by the architecture of capital. In becoming an industry unto itself, cinema moves political economy to a new level of organization. "The spectacle is *capital* to such a degree of accumulation that it becomes an image."[17] Cinema valorizes this higher order of capital—it is the organization and extension of the spectacle. Although we have said that the image is productive in two distinct ways: 1) through the labor of looking—images become more valuable the more they are looked at; and 2) through the self-modification embarked upon by spectators as they retool themselves, the complete political economy of this image, remains to be written.

What began with Lumiere and Edison as a speculator's novelty became an attraction, then became a montage of attractions, and, at present, has become the main attraction, in some cases, the only attraction. The moving image emerges first as an apparent spin-off from industry at a moment when its conditions already were given by the growing industrial revolution as the movement of price. Cinema as the abstraction of the assembly-line process and enhancement of the sensual pyrotechnics of the commodity brings the industrial revolution to the eye. Let us listen to Guy Debord:

The commodity's domination was at first exerted over the economy in an occult manner; the economy itself, the material basis of social life, remained unperceived and not understood, like the familiar which is not necessarily known. In a society where the concrete commodity is rare or unusual, money, apparently dominant, presents itself as an emissary armed with full powers who speaks in the name of an unknown force. With the industrial revolution, the division of labor in manufactures, and mass production for the world market, the commodity appears in fact as a power which comes to *occupy* social life. It is then that political economy takes shape, as the dominant science and the science of domination.

The spectacle is the moment when the commodity has attained the *total occupation* of social life. Not only is the relation to the commodity visible but it is all one sees: the world one sees is its world. Modern economic production extends its dictatorship extensively and intensively.

In the least industrialized places, its reign is already attested by a few star commodities and by the imperialist domination imposed by regions which are ahead in the development of productivity. In the advanced regions, social space is invaded by a continuous superimposition of geological layers of commodities. At this point in the "second industrial revolution," alienated consumption becomes for the masses a duty supplementary to alienated production. It is *all the sold labor* of a society which globally becomes the *total commodity* for which the cycle must be continued. For this to be done, the total commodity has to return as a fragment to the fragmented individual, absolutely separated from the productive forces operating as a whole. Thus it is here that the specialized science of domination must in turn specialize: it fragments itself into sociology, psychology, cybernetics, semiology, etc., watching over the self-regulation of every level of the process.[18]

When the commodity becomes "all one sees," cinema emerges as a machine—the crystallization of an extant social logic—to regulate the expression of commodities. The academic disciplines are the necessary substrata of image processing. In chapter 3, I discussed the emergence of psychoanalysis and to a lesseer extent of semiotics as subroutines of image-capitalism. Additionally, cinema emerges as the development and the intensification of the form of consciousness necessary to the increased mobilization of objects as commodities. What Debord refers to as "the second industrial revolution" develops as a strategy for the production of and control over what Benjamin refers to in his writing as "second nature," that is, the techno-mechanical world. The movement of commodities appear as a complex of natural forces whose rules must be learned. As Benjamin puts it, "To make this whole enormous technological apparatus of our time into the object of human interiorization and appropriation [Innervation]—that is the historic task in whose service film has its true meaning."[19] The expressive power of the system of production and circulation of commodities develops a conviction in the spectator/consumer/worker of the all-pervasive power of the world of objects and of the objective world, or more precisely, of their images. Such subjective experience of the force of objects and of objective organization as cinema (as the cinematic aspect of society) is the other side of the "science" of political economy, of psychology, of anthropology, the affective side. To paraphrase Simmel, the exact engineering of (second) nature is the practical counterpart to the institution of money. The calculus of the image means then, the production of meaning and affect in accord with the requisites of capital valorization. As natural philosophy, media programming, because of its high degree of mathematical calculability—the statistical process that can be utilized to predict the affectivity of the image—approaches the Kantian criteria for science invoked by Simmel. If the world is conceived as a huge arithmetical problem, then it is clear that efforts to image this world most often result in the mathematical sublime (think all those pods full of bodies in *The Matrix*).

So. Everyone knows that it is the development of technology that makes possible all those great stories, all those new styles, all those new fetish objects that accompany the age of cinema, but so-called representational technologies do not only train us to cope with the conditions attendant to a particular historical moment's circulation of value. The "duty" of alienated consumption mentioned above by Debord is a form of *dressage* for the senses—it is a productive activity—a ritual practice of those "other compulsions" to labor mentioned above by Marx. Neither does the emergence of the spectacle as "the total occupation of life by commodities" limit itself to the inauguration of science-fragments such as sociology, psychology, cultural studies, and the like (and their attendant "star systems"), which are cognition machines for particular constellations of corporeal phenomenon and social organization, which are at base economic—the survival of disciplines depends upon their economic productivity, that is, their productive engagement with new types of images.

The spectacle begins to emerge from the money-form as we have known it—not only in the production of codes on computer screens for statistically evaluating complex options packages on Wall Street (these codes *are* money) but in the commonplace conventions of social codes: screened "representations" and "programming." The disciplines mentioned above might be taken as the catalogues of phenomena that, like Marx's extensive tabulation of prices, could be considered empirical data for a political economy of culture: Psychoanalysis, for example, as the science of a new set of phenomena emerging from the intensification of the interruption of language function by the image (recall, Lacan's *objet petit a* taken as the image itself). The inflation and eventual devaluation of the psyche and psychoanalysis (its migration from medicine to advertising), or the cycle of boom and bust in semiotics, are historical shifts indexing the overall saturation of consciousness by images (where the unconscious [surrealism], meaning [semiotics], and postmodern depthlessness [simulation] become something like three stages of the image). As well, there is the production of consciousness itself, as a screen (in Lacan's terminology), a machine that affects the same presentation and filtration practices as attend to moving images and circulating commodities. Behind the shine of the scene on the screen, knowledge of the production process is left on the cutting-room floor, along with those with whose blood the image was made. The repression of history and of the perpetual violence that today underpins the constitution of all Western subjects is displaced by the total occupation of life by the spectacle. Thus the spectacle and the attendant emergence of disciplinary and industrial specializations as sciences of the particular dimensions of the human interface with the objectified world show that all interactive sites are now potentially productive sites—sites of capital investment and exploitation, but also (and here is the as-yet unwritten accompaniment to this map of domination) sites of struggle.

We have heard that in the postmodern struggle occurs over representation, not in the modern sense of political representation (which today seems to be but a marginal subroutine of the overarching capitalist program) but over representations: style politics, performativity, "articulation," spin-doctoring. Representation, presentation, performance are forms of currency that confer buying power. Televisual *currency*, for example, produces competence in social codes, that is, *socially necessary codes* (in the sense of socially necessary labor time) that translate into access to power, among other things. That is why everyone wants to know the news, be the fashion, talk the talk, and surf the web. In the most pernicious (widespread) forms of postmodern media-culture, democracy is everywhere proclaimed and class struggle everywhere submerged because the representatives of representation claim (under their breath) a partial truth as total truth: Representation is not about money, representation is style, representation is freedom of choice, and anyone can have that. Yet, in the manner of Baudrillard's *For a Critique of the Political Economy of the Sign*, the codes within representation provide access to money—*and vice-versa*. What we consume is the process of commodification as culture, what we produce is ourselves as commodities. One thinks here of Benjamin's description of fascist aesthetics in which we are invited to consume our own destruction as an aesthetic pleasure of the highest order.

The fact that so many wannabe citizens of capital today invest in style shows only what we think we already know and understand: that style has, in the postmodern, become a privileged realm of struggle. However, the play of struggle in style (which has genuinely uplifting as well as devastating effects) produces socially cooperative subjects and rarely disturbs the overall organization of cinematic society with its absolute dependence upon and nonrepresentation of third-world labor. In this view, "style" is a death mask for any revolutionary culture, for once it partakes of the logic of style it is a subroutine of capital. Indeed, style-politics may be gleaned as part of the so-called cultural turn that at once marks the economicization of sensuality, and characterizes the current "liberal" multicultural de-essentialization of terrorists. Communists, Orientals, Africans, African-Americans, Latin Americans, and Arabs who were formerly terrorists by virtue of race and/or nation, are now such only because of their flawed, fundamentalist, extremist cultures. Terrorism is not an identity, it is a performance that is only statistically more likely among certain peoples of color. Or so goes the mainstream rationalism in the *USA Today* and Fox News. Whoever agrees with and thrives under the violent hierarchical regime betokened by the infinitely hypocritical liberal values of late capitalism, is fine, as good as white for the most part; and, as far as the regime of capitalist culture is concerned, whoever protests is a terrorist (spelled with an "n"). Thus, the economicization of perception results in a world-scale transcoding of racism and capitalism as matters of culturalism ("the Muslim world"), while allowing all the virulence of racism and economic exploitation to continue to wreak its violence on the world. This is how racism has been grafted so directly onto nationalism. As a necessary part of the process, the Pentagon reconfigures nuclear bombs, annexes huge allocations of human value (cash), continues its murderous presence on every continent, and broadcasts a mise-en-scène of fear fostered by ignorance. Not a pretty picture, but it's ours, or rather, of us. Let us work to retransmit it not to inspire an imaginary transcendence, but rather such that all can taste the blood inherent in each pixel and be impelled to make the world anew.

NOTES

1. Georg Simmel, *The Philosophy of Money*, 2nd ed., ed. David Frisby, trans. Tom Bottomore and David Frisby (New York and London: Routledge, 1990), 443–44.

2. Ibid., 444.

3. Ibid., 444, 446.

4. Ibid., 442.

5. Ibid., 450.

6. Gilles Deleuze, *Cinema 2: The Time-Image*, trans. Hugh Tomlinson and Robert Galeta (Minneapolis: University of Minnesota Press, 1989), 77.

7. Karl Marx and Friedrich Engels, *Economic and Philosocical Manuscripts of 1844*, in *The Marx-Engels Reader*, ed. Robert C. Tucker (New York: Norton, 1978), 87–88.

8. Compare ibid., 96.

9. Michel Foucault, "The Eye of Power: A Conversation with Jean-Pierre Barou and Michelle Perrot," in *Power/Knowledge* (New York: Pantheon, 1980), 161.

10. Marx and Engels, *Economic and Philosophical Manuscripts,* 79.

11. Ibid., 74.

12. Deleuze, *Cinema 2,* 172.

13. Compare Louis Althusser, "Ideology and Ideological State Apparatuses: Notes towards an Investigation," in *Lenin and Philosophy* (New York: Monthly Review Press, 1971).

14. Guy Debord, *The Society of the Spectacle* (Detroit: Red and Block, 1983), 15.

15. Ibid., 9.

16. See my essay "Third Cinema in a Global Frame: Curacha, Yahoo! and Manila By Night," in *positions* 9, no. 42 (Fall 2001): 331–68.

17. Ibid., 34.

18. Ibid., 21.

19. Walter Benjamin, "The Work of Art in the Age of Mechanical Reproduction," in *Illuminations,* ed. Hannah Arendt (New York: Schocken Books, 1969).

Chapter 6
Proprioception
Killer-Eye, Killer World:
The Media-Environment
for *Natural Born Killers*

The spectacle erases the dividing line between self and world, in that the self, under siege by the presence/absence of the world, is eventually overwhelmed; it likewise erases the dividing line between true and false, repressing all directly lived truth beneath the real presence of the falsehood maintained by the organization of appearances. The individual, though condemned to the passive acceptance of an alien everyday reality, is thus driven into a form of madness in which, by resorting to magical devices, he entertains the illusion that he is reacting to his fate. The recognition and consumption of commodities are at the core of this pseudo-response to a communication to which no response is possible. The need to imitate that the consumer experiences is indeed a truly infantile need, one determined by every aspect of his fundamental dispossession. In terms used by Gabel to describe quite another level of pathology, "the abnormal need for representation here compensates for a torturing feeling of being at the margin of existence." —Guy Debord, Society of the Spectacle, #219*

Kino-I, Kino-World

The development of a media-environment that functions as the mise-en-scène for capitalist production via social cooperation—engineered both culturally and by the deployment of military hardware—short circuits, as it were, traditional forms of subjectivity (experience) and of objectivity (events, collective knowledge, reality).[1] In other words, the experiential transformations detailed in the previous chapter have their subjective and discursive corollaries in what from a modern point of view could appear as a form of psychopathology. The disintegration of the subject that occurs as the sensorium takes its cues from a capitalized media-environment begins to offer an historical periodization of poststructuralism and deconstruction, because it links the crisis of subjectivity and of metaphysics (deconstruction, but also identity politics) to the technological and the economic determinants of social life. The consequences of what I call the media-environment therefore are not limited only to the spatio-temporal conceptions of the subject's location as effected through re-presentation (TV, VR, computers, commercial narrative, in short, "culture"), or, equally, the subsequent reconstruction of the built environment as a "space of flows."[2] In the media environment, the subject itself is reconceived.

One can grasp how in tele-visual warfare the spectacular intensity of destruction as well as the illusion of its collective sanction creates certain subjective effects—a sense of agency and power via the technological prosthesis that compensates for the generalized lack of these in daily life.[3] The word "America" still can be made to function in this way. The prerequisite for the full realization of this tendency, however, is that the so-called other whom the self is defined in relation to, completes the motion, already visible in the psychoanalytic work of Jacques Lacan, toward becoming pure image. Such is the final effect when one sees through the eyes of capital. Both the frequency of others (their number and appearance) as well as their depth are effected. Existential loneliness and inhumane brutality, meaninglessness and socio-pathology, appear as obverse and reverse of this postmodern coinage—and the coins get thinner and thinner.

Steadfastly guarding against the tendency of the other to become pure surface, Lacan, in *The Four Fundamental Concepts of Psychoanalysis*, makes a critique of the solipsistic character of idealism. "The mode of my presence in the world is the subject in so far as by reducing itself solely to this certainty of being a subject it becomes active annihilation" (*FFCP*, 81). For Lacan, this statement describes the inordinate self-privileging of the subject caught up in "the immanence of the *I see myself seeing myself*" (*FFCP*, 81). As he says, "The privilege of the subject seems to be established here from that bipolar reflexive relation by which, as soon as I perceive, my representations belong to me" (*FFCP* 81). Such a conceit, says Lacan, belongs to an idealism intent upon doing away with the material. "This is the irreducible method of Bishop Berkeley, about whose subjective position much might be said—including something that may have eluded you in passing, namely, this *belong to me* aspect of representations, so reminiscent of private property. When carried to the limit, the process of this meditation, of this reflecting reflection, goes so far as to reduce the subject apprehended by the Cartesian meditation to a power of annihilation" (*FFCP*, 81). When the world becomes pure image, the subject-function is active annihilation.

In order to explore this relation among subjects further—a relation that is at once ordained by private property and developed to new and extraordinary levels of productivity by cinema and television—I would like to turn here to Oliver Stone's *Natural Born Killers*. Here characters do not spend time doubting that it is their hands they see in front of the faces but rather they become almost utterly indifferent to the fact that it is other people they see before their eyes. *Natural Born Killers* provides a description of the interactivity of subjects and media in the general constitution of a capitalized media-environment. With a high degree of success, it has abstracted a matrix of the dominant social relations informing the totality of postmodern society. However, despite the critical attention it has received, the ultimate implications of its form have not been drawn.

Born in the contemporary United States, *Natural Born Killers* is a *blitz-krieg* narration of the life and love of mass murderers Micky and Mallory. The film stalks the ebullient brutality of Micky (Woody Harrelson) and Mallory (Juliet Lewis) from the time that they slaughter Mallory's abusive parents through the remainder of fifty-two murders. From there, *Natural Born Killers* chronicles Micky and Mallory's subsequent incarceration, and eventual escape. The surface of the screen seethes with a veritable *jouissance* of killing as well as with, in the phrase of Jean Baudrillard, "the ecstasy of communication."[4]

It is important to note that the mise-en-scène of the film is always *represented* as belonging to different film genres and to the media itself (during the opening credits, for example, the characters drive their automobile through a rush of images). In short, the mise-en-scène is a media-scape that is on a continuum with the one that has been described as the scene for the production of the first Gulf War.[5] In *Natural Born Killers*, changes in film and video stocks occur every few seconds, including hundreds of insert edits of fragments from film and television history, bizarre superimpositions, and an eclectic blood-pumping sound track. These elements are at once diegetic and extra-diegetic, sometimes seen by the characters and sometimes merely playing on the surface of buildings or on the screen— expressive but unrecognized—as if part of a postmodern Faulknerian world in which history, consciousness and the unconscious were blended together in a visuo-cinematic heteroglossia.

Though offhand dismissals of the film as excessive, simplistic, exploitative, and hypocritical contain in germinal form genuine concerns, most often these easy dismissals mean something else.[6] Although certainly not an embodiment of every progressive agenda, the film is in fact a detailed and subtle *analysis* of the predication of identity-formation and consciousness on violence in contemporary capitalist society, that is, an analysis of the subject-function as "active annihilation."

I would suggest that the misunderstanding of Stone's "critique," in the American press and elsewhere, is driven by a certain self-interested necessity. In popular reviews, the idea that "Stone uses, in *NBK*, exactly the same elements and dynamics that he is criticizing," that is, that he criticizes violence with violence, was reiterated endlessly. Of course, what the substance of Stone's criticism is, according to these detractors, we are most often left only to imagine, but it is perhaps something of the order that "television glorifies violence and this is bad." Stone, we are told, finds it necessary to use the appeal of violence in order to critique it, when there ought to be more dignified ways.

Why this exigency is taken as an indictment of Stone and not of the entire environment in which films are made and seen, I am not entirely sure, especially since it is built into the structure of the film that violence or the threat of violence is precisely the *language* of intervention in contemporary society. Although Stone is condemned for showing the same violence that exists everywhere, which indeed he does, his presentation is no mere repetition. Rather, violence for him is the prerequisite for social visibility, while peacefulness is, in the present environment, tantamount to disappearance. Better to say then that *Natural Born Killers* takes violence as the condition of representation in contemporary society.

The root of the Orwellian doublethink ("the holding of two contradictory ideas in one's head simultaneously and believing them both to be true"), which enables the easy dismissals of *Natural Born Killers*, can be discovered in Stone's own analysis of the production of personality. In the spirit of Debord that "when analyzing the spectacle one speaks, to some extent, the language of the spectacular itself in the sense that one moves through the methodological terrain of the very society which expresses itself in the spectacle," Stone galvanizes the language-function of media violence itself to checkmate the assumptions of the culture that takes the spectacle as its legitimate expression.[7]

The story of Micky and Mallory Knocks, littered with murders in every frame, passes not only through numerous stock narrative devices but through various television genres as if the story itself were a composite of media forms. Though the film is held together tightly by the storyline, it is riddled with jarring discontinuities and violent outbursts of action and images that are taken from elsewhere, from spaces other than the immediate mise-en-scène of the narrative. The noise of other mediations, other hyped intensities, puts pressure on nearly every scene. This media overflow, which gives cultural formations beyond the immediate narrative line the stature of hallucination, extends the effect to the peripheral characters within the narrative, that is, the victims. Because the camera enters the lives and the romantic love of the protagonists, while leaving their victims more or less as caricatures or anonymous, Micky and Mallory appear as subjects; those whom they kill do not. The couple's nameless victims are for the most part targets in the landscape, hallucinatory apparitions, perceptual effects without personality. As the gratuitous shotgun killing of the roadside cyclist illustrates, the victims are mere "target practice" because they are not represented as anything other than the statistics or extras which, in this love story, they are. They are extra people—there to be killed. Micky and Mallory become subjects not only because they hold the interest of Stone's camera, or because they assert themselves through violence, but because they accumulate momentum through the liquidation of others. This is central to their subjective agency. Equally important, their form of self-expression is marketed to other anonymous people who, like Micky and Mallory's victims, are also extras—without personality in the sense that Micky and Mallory eventually achieve it. *Natural Born Killers* investigates this social relation in which nobodies pay to be in the proximity of somebodies who appear as somebodies by annihilating nobodies. They achieve a fascistic celebrity through the sublime abjection of their followers. And we don't need too many more Columbine High School incidents to realize that this is how it works.

The marketability of violence, along with the *subjective* and *economic* gradients produced by it, is not a mere accusation launched by Oliver Stone against the media industry; rather, it is an economic hypothesis acted upon and therefore validated daily by mass media. The dialectic of celebrity and abjection is a structural formation. As Stone's episodic construction of the film through forms from nearly every television genre argues, Mickies and Mallories are starring everywhere, from cartoons to television news. The film argues that violence as a product (as a commodity) produces *interest*, in both the visceral and financial senses of the word (even if it doesn't produce much analysis by anyone other than media *commandants*, that is, media producers). This lack of an analysis of violence by those who consume it, coupled to the intensive development in the marketing and sale of violence by people with advanced degrees and six-figure incomes, produces the contradiction in the public sphere that violence is interesting and violence is banal, that violence is central and violence is marginal.

Violence appeals to the unconscious as a type of fetish because of its proximity to the generalized organization of society even as it is consciously dismissed. This semiconscious attraction of violence draws precisely on our semiconscious *participation* in rituals of violence. Because those who broadcast violence become personalities and because those who receive violence remain statistics, known to television producers *and to each other* only as ratings, such a division suggests that personalities are constituted through the annihilation of other persons. Therefore our social relations are mediated by violence on which the identities of personalities are built. As the consumers of these identities, we participate in their construction—we ratify the terms of personality. Our consumption of violence is in effect an expression of our relations with each other. The less we are as audience, the more they are as stars, as if their personalities were vacuum bags that evaluated and collected our identities until we were flat. Such a form is analogous to that of the global United States as subjective agent in the world, hell-bent on a romance with democracy.

This formula for the mediatic production of personality precisely reproduces that of other structures that create subjective agency by utilizing the leveraged pyramid of capital. A corporate head who exists intellectually and socially thanks to the labor of nameless workers in the sweatshops of Malaysia or Mexico, exists through a similar annihilation of persons. So too does the owner of bonds and mutual funds. Those who command capital are subjects, those who do not, exist below the threshold of social subjectivity. The workers' sensual labor, their subjective potential, is extracted by capital and confronts them as something alien. The construction of personality through violence is not just another form of "free enterprise" (free enterprise at a higher level, an abstraction of free enterprise), it is the truth of free enterprise. The value that accrues to the likes of media icons such as Micky and Mallory, occurs via an economy that prevents other people from achieving personality, that is, from achieving power and status as subjects. Indeed, the very personality and subjectivity of victims and consumers alike accrues, in the film, to Micky and Mallory. The more Micky and Mallory kill, the more adored they are. The more adored they are, the greater the violence they have license to effect. They are the sum total of their victims—the collecting of victims is the creation of personality and the creation of personality is a mode of production.

If mid-twentieth-century existentialism held that subjectivity is at base a kind of violence, it was because, historically speaking, violence was slowly becoming the condition of existence, the condition of saying anything at all. With the decay of traditional societies, to exist for others, to speak to others, to demand a place in the consciousness of others becomes a violent act. Stone develops the idea of *Natural Born Killers* through violence not because violence among humans is ontologically given (the infinitely mediated presentation of nature in the film argues that the "nature" of *Natural Born Killers* always is mediated by culture and technology and therefore can be only a question, never a fact), but rather because *historically*, in the war of each against all, it has become the language of the times. Nature and history appear as they do through the *lens* of contemporary violence. The new pre-eminence of violence and the appearance of nature as violence is not merely a matter of fashion or trend, but an historical and economic eruption. Careers, fortunes, and nations are built on violence and increasingly, since the Cold War, the threat and the spectacle of violence.[8] Violation has its immediate effects and its affective effects; it is productive both as event and as representation. However, the increased frequency of both of these conditions makes them merge into a unified productive process. At an international level, this violence at once derives from and endeavors to ensure the continued exploitation of proletarian and third-world–style labor and third-world–style polities. At a personal level, it derives from the taking of others as means. Wealth, political, and military power are increasingly the conditions of subjectivity, the conditions of articulating anything, at any and all levels of society.

As few as one hundred years ago, it was perhaps unnecessary to be on television in order to really exist. Today, only those who command the most attention are genuine personalities. Those who have nothing (the indigent, the homeless, the planet's impoverished majority) cannot speak, and those who have little speak through their consumer practices. One of the things we (those of us who have little) buy are images (enabling) of personality. The consumption of these personalities helps us to imagine what it would be like to actually have one. That action, which in its own meager way realizes a desire for individuality, is necessary because if we did not believe in the possibility of eventually having a personality we might not believe in individuality, which means we might not believe in "representative" democracy, or in America, or in that Truth among truths: humanity's social nature itself—capitalism. If we doubted more rigorously the moral rectitude of capitalism, its truth as an expression of human nature, its incontestable force of destining the world, we might become more imaginative. In valorizing the closed circuit that constructs personality at our own expense, we consume and internalize the very relation that negates us. We pay, we give our all, to retain our faith in the system that denies us precisely what we desire: agency. This is the rationale of consumerism, which finds its homology in the fascist aesthetics noted previously in which we consume our own destruction as an aesthetic pleasure. In consumer society, we renounce our own agency for the myth of agency. This is the nature of representative or, better, representational democracy in capitalism. It need not be added that this mediated flattening out cum crushing of human agency in "democratic capitalism" is necessary to the function of capitalism precisely because democracy and capitalism are oxymorons. Structural inequality is the direct contradiction of egalitarianism. The consumption of one's structural privation is the mediation that sustains this contradiction and renders it as nearly as possible unconscious.

Thus the sublime proportions of Micky and Mallory's agency puts us all in our places; indeed, these figures exist in place of us. We are their abject, that which they must cast out if they are to constitute themselves as agents, subjects, personalities, media-icons. It is *their* "lifestyle" that is represented and we who quietly pay to see it. Our payment, it must be emphasized, is not rendered in the single act of trading money for admission to a theater or for video rental, but is our valorization of the affective complex generated and objectified in our viewing of film and TV in general. What is unusual about *Natural Born Killers* is that the film provides us with an opportunity to see what we have made. We are forced to reckon with what our participation, our activity, and our aspirations generate. To claim exemption from this economy is, in short, to lie. Micky and Mallory's existence is not based only upon the liquidation of their immediate victims, but on the liquidation of us all. Additionally and at the same time, they murder so that we don't have to. Their personalities, acquired through killing, sustain our (necessary) belief in the possibility of subjective agency, since we exercise so little of our own. Micky and Mallory's murderous escapades help us to affirm our own existence as subjects, an existence that in the environment of capital we might realize fully only through the very same means that they employ. In fact, the extent of our agency in capitalism is a fairly reliable index of the extent of our complicity with murder. Through murder, Micky and Mallory become personalities and personalities become our role models. Should we desire to become anyone, there is the path of the star system: Micky and Mallory, or the subject "America" in the Gulf War. It is this aesthetico-political structure in which the agency of a celebrity, a president, or a superpower, provides a compensatory and illusory agency for an impotent subject that is characteristic of fascism. Because this logic is both ideological and material, and because it is hegemonic in the realm not only of economics but also of representation, if we are to claim a stake in existence under these terms, we either worship the killers or become them.

As the driving scenes in *Natural Born Killers* beautifully assert (Micky and Mallory drive through a road of moving images), it is media finally that is the mise-en-scène of the film: The media is the environment, at once the space where power, capital, and murder are negotiated and the very possibility of their negotiation. Television is an essential component of global organization; it provides the environment for the perpetuation of everything. Micky and Mallory travel through a world of images. This is not to say that the media landscape is nature, but that it has replaced nature. It is a second nature made possible through the intensive logic of capital. The environment, everywhere penetrated by technology, capitalized by technologies for the reorganization of space, matter, consciousness, and the genetic code, overdetermines the terms of appearance and action for concrete individuals, their meanings, and their possibilities. "The spectacle is the accumulation of capital to such a degree that it becomes an image";[9] the image's mediation of the environment and all it encompasses, is capital's mediation of the same. Exchange-value, first posited then presupposed as the universal systems language, mediates all matter in and as image. All that matters appears on a screen, or it is of no matter. Such a media-world selects for Mickies and Mallories, as the Darwinians might say, and in this world they too select their prey according to the rules of the media environment. The *nature* of Stone's killers derives from capitalist mediation— they are subjects who embody the logic of the media economy. In short, they are *forms* of capital.

Stone does not so much offer a critique of media society as provide a text with which its contradictions can be thought. In my opinion, most of the angry dismissals of *Natural Born Killers* occur at the moment when the logic of the consumption of violence begins *at a semiconscious level* to indict the liberal ideologies informing the intellectual positions and practices of free-market liberals, that is, at the moment when violence begins to appear as the *necessary* underside of the free market. Thus, the hasty condemnation of *Natural Born Killers* is, in the Orwellian vocabulary, an example of "crimestop," the refusal to continue a line of reasoning that might lead to "thoughtcrime," or unorthodoxy punishable by nonexistence. In order to maintain that the free market is the bastion of individual freedom, human possibility, and collective achievement, violence must be relegated to the status of a mere accident, exception, or moral failing, and must not appear endemic or systematic, that is, it must not appear to be directly *produced* by the free market. To praise the free market and to condemn violence must not erupt in liberal consciousness as an essential contradiction, that is, as a form of nonsense or a lie. The Persian Gulf Wars must remain justified correctives to a violent Iraq, not a violent act of neo-imperialism, necessary both for the destruction of surplus (in order not to return it to the general population and subvert the wage structure) and the production of pro-corporate America affects. East Timor must remain invisible, or shed so much blood for so long that the stain cannot be hidden. We must believe that dictators and so-called terrorists, inasmuch as they feed off of the lives of others, are immoral actors, not *products* of the free market responding to it *as subjects* in accordance with its own logic. America, the subject of history, cannot maintain its essential innocence if violence emerges as its basic premise. *Forrest Gump* got one thing right: America can imagine itself innocent only on the condition that it remain as stupid as the film's central character.

The differences between Micky and Mallory and most of the rest of us are twofold. First, they are celebrities and we are not—they do capitalism better than we do. Second, they do capitalism so well because they have fully internalized the logic of television—they produce according to the protocols of television. Its properties are their environment. During their predatory escapades atom bombs explode, the walls of buildings screen images of flame, the entire world is a screen on which is projected their momentary thoughts and feelings. Their emotions and hopes, their moods and affectations are not only *signified* televisually, they *are* televisual images, historical fragments of decontextualized moving pictures summoned up by who knows what. In short, Micky and Mallory *have* tele-vision and therefore *treat people as images.* By treating others as images, they become icons. Their relationship to the world and to others is in fact not subject/object, but rather subjective/image, or better, *god/image.* They see their entire lives *through* television and televisual conventions, hence they "naturally" select victims the way we would images, wiping them out by remote control when they tire of them. Capitalism turns empathy into television and humans into images.

Materiality and Dematerialization

As argued in the first two chapters of this volume, revolutionary Soviet filmmakers including Dziga Vertov and Sergei Eisenstein were painfully aware of capital's encroachment on the visual, precisely because they fought capital on its most advanced front. These directors went directly to the evolving properties of the visual to combat capital expansion. Vertov's decodification of commodity reification in *Man with a Movie Camera*, his "communist decoding of the world," tracks the process of industrial assemblage. The image composes itself in such a way that objects become legible as process. At the same time, the image tracks (represents) its own conditions and strategies of production, and effectively reveals that the image is built like a commodity. With *Man with a Movie Camera*, industrial culture attains the visual and cinema is grasped as the necessary medium for the decodification of objectification under capitalism—the rendering of objects and images as social relations.

The easy legibility of this relation between image-objects and the process of their assemblage so carefully articulated by Vertov quickly falls back into the unthought of the image during the course of film history. However, as this book has endeavored to show, the structure of the image thus revealed nonetheless continues to pertain. For his part, Eisenstein, an engineer by training, works with the industrial application of visual technology. He deploys it in accord with the logic of Pavlovian Behaviorism and Taylorization, and takes the image as a technology for "the organization of the audience with organized material," effectively grasping cinema as a social machine for engineering the *socius*. For Eisenstein, a film is "a tractor ploughing over the audience's psyche." Even though not conceived precisely in these terms, in the films of Eisenstein, for the first time, image machines are slated to function for the configuration, extraction, and application of what Marx termed "sensuous labor." The films were to release the necessary energy for the proletariat to continue that labor intensive project called revolution.

Whereas in Vertov, the audience must be shown going to the theater in order to develop a critical relation to ambient images, and in Eisenstein, the director controls the effect of the image on the audience by rigorously controlling their organization according to a plan for sequencing conditioned reflexes, some seventy years later, in *Natural Born Killers*, the images come to viewers higgledy-piggledy. Here the image, rather than a mere outgrowth of industrial society, has folded itself back into the fabric of the *socius* and of the subject. Viewers do not encounter the techno-imaginary only on the screen; its logic is already inside them. This enfolding of the image into the social fabric already was implicit in Vertov; recall that the kino-eye project was to make new films every day and was to be part of the quotidian apprehension of sociality. The spectator saw through the very material of industrial society and film was to forever alter perception in the combinatory dialectic of mind and nature, corporeality and technology. However, in something like an ironic fulfillment of Marxist utopian poetics, *Natural Born Killers* marks the technological realization of this condition of ubiquitous, ambient, instrumental images and the fusion of perception with technology, because the mediations presented in the film, while operating in accord with the two great insights of soviet cinema (the cybernetic extension of perception and the engineering of social praxis), are precisely the mediations of capital. The images do not foster dialectical thinking; rather, they are the raw material of the dialectic itself—the modality of capital's articulation of the viewer. The images are capital's cutting edge. They dream us while we dream through and in them.

With *Natural Born Killers,* we may mark an evolutionary moment in the history of cinema. Instead of merely positing a new order of consciousness mediated by images, as in Vertov, the money-driven image is shown to envelop consciousness. This is consistent with the argument put forth in chapters 3 through 5. In *Natural Born Killers,* the image, through an increase in sheer quantity, achieves a shift in quality, realizing a change of state in which images themselves become the mise-en-scène for action. *Natural Born Killers,* in which two young lovers rescue one another from drudgery and oppression and become mass murderers and then celebrities, is about the conditions of personality formation in such a media-environment. Micky and Mallory drive through a mediascape in which natural landscapes fuse seamlessly with CGI, resulting in hallucinatory shifts in context and scale. This world is not virtual in the sense that it is make-believe or pretend, but virtualized by virtue of becoming bereft of its traditional standards, properties, and proportions, all of which have been geographically, temporally, perceptually, and proprioceptually transformed by media-capital. In this new world, where nature is not nature (but always already mediation) and people are "naturally" born killers, the image of a nuclear explosion or of two open-mouthed hippos having intercourse in a swamp are of the same order: They are pure affect machines. They are on parity here; each exists here as an intensity in an endless series of dematerialized flows. The images come out of the walls and the woodwork and their omnipresence alters the significance, that is, the signification, of each and all forever.

It is the image as the context for action that not only renders ethics virtual but allows Micky and Mallory to accelerate the logic of capital in the creation of their personalities. Instead of stealing the lives of others over an extended period of time, as do plant bosses, plantation owners, and stockholders in order to establish themselves as social agents, Micky and Mallory use weapons to appropriate the value of individual lives all at once. Micky and Mallory see through the media, and having internalized its vision, act out its very logic. They are, in short, higher iterations of capital. Because they have tele-vision (they are television incarnate), that is because their sight is televisual, they see everything as if it were already an image, people included. The depthlessness and ostensible immateriality of others accelerates the rapidity with which others can be liquidated and, somewhat like the worker in *The Strike* whose suicide is the catalyst for the work stoppage but for antithetical purposes, their subjective potential profitably taken. They convert people into spectacle.

As I have noted, such a conversion process depends upon an evacuation of the other and is in accord with an intensification of the constitutive relation in the formation of the subject described by the Lacanian theory of the *objet petit a*. As is the case with *Psycho's* Norman Bates, whose name I long have been convinced is the jump-cut version of the phrase "The Normal Man Masturbates," desire's shortcutting around the social prohibitions that give the Other subjective amplitude, and its unrepressed taking of Others as image-objects, outside the codes prescribed by Western civilization and laid out in psychoanalytic theory, leads to psychosis and murder. Of course, these shortcuts (stealing the money, the knife in the bath) are symptomatic of over-"objectification," otherwise known as castration, and are a cultural tendency of capitalist reification. The person/object is deep-frozen as image and drained of all subjective content. Overcoming that nonexistence involves a desperate and violent act of inflicting it upon another. In *Natural Born Killers*, identity based on mass murder made possible through the taking of the other as image is the logical outcome of the constitutive relation between the subject and the *objet a*, a relation of capital from an earlier social moment, now placed under the pressure of an intensifying capitalism where language can no longer fill in and give amplitude to the troublesome image of the other. Subjects assert themselves in the liquidation of other subjects by taking these others as images. Self is produced and maintained today through an intensification of the annihilating function of the gaze. With the deepening penetration of materiality by media, a process that really means the intensifying mediation of materiality, a dematerialization of the object-world occurs. The more deeply entrenched in material structures capitalist mediation becomes, the more everything tends toward the image. Here is Guy Debord:

> Every given commodity fights for itself, cannot acknowledge the others, and attempts to impose itself everywhere as if it were the only one. The spectacle, then, is the epic poem of this struggle, an epic which cannot be concluded by the fall of any Troy. The spectacle does not sing the praises of men and their weapons, but of commodities and their passions. In this blind struggle every commodity, pursuing its passion, unconsciously realizes something higher: the becoming-world of the commodity, which is also the becoming-commodity of the world. Thus by means of a ruse of commodity logic, what's specific in the commodity wears itself out in the fight while the commodity-form moves toward its absolute realization.[10]

This passage might well be taken as a thesis on the philosophy of cinema history, that is, a meditation on the adventures of the medium par excellence for the epic poem of the commodity. It also provides a chilling image for the struggles of cinematic-cybernetic "subjects": us. For it is finally we ourselves, the kino-I's, who engage in a pathological life and death struggle with/as the commodity form. However, if Debord's attention to the spectacular and the visual as the paramount field of capital exploitation is to be understood properly, then that which he calls "a ruse of commodity logic," which over time allows for the liquidation of the specific materialities of commodities as it brings the commodity-form toward "its absolute realization" (as image), must be shown in its socially productive aspect. The spectacle means not just commodification but production. Psychopathology, of which, if you will excuse me, all of you are guilty, is a means of production, which is to say that you, kino-you, are a means of production.

This is the lay of the land. That old spectre still haunts the house of Hollywood. What *Natural Born Killers* shows most graphically is that massive social formations (a nuclear bomb blast, for example) today are experienced on the same level as a pang of jealousy or a bad mood. The quantity of inequality has induced a qualitative shift in the form of its appearance. For God the spectator, the image of the enormity of the atom bomb persists on the same scale as a momentary subjective impression. Images have taken pre-eminence over what was once known as reality; they have supplanted and thus restructured our experience. In this situation of the gross violation of the law of equivalence, people no longer relate one to one. Human proportions have been annihilated. A few days ago, for example, I read an article in the newspaper that examined how the war in Yugoslavia affected the mindset of shoppers at the mall with respect to their purchases. There has been a terrible shift in scale. One death or thousands or millions of deaths today carry for a viewer-deity the same weight as an emotional twitch. With the inequality of power and representation prevalent in the world, this situation of radical inadequation is not merely theoretical, but real and realized. Hundreds of thousands dead in Iraq, Bosnia, Rwanda, Afghanistan barely perturb: We are powerless in the face of that and hence give it but little thought. At the same time, the whims of the few, be they presidents, political entrepreneurs, drug lords, or financiers, can change the lives of thousands, even millions. If we are natural born killers, then it has taken all the artifice of corporate capital and the history of industrial technologies to help to realize our present nature.

The media-environment that today enfolds the sensorium is not a completely new set of effects. As I have argued in previous chapters, cinema is an extension of the relations of commodities, commodities that have themselves always been mediations. Cinema and now television are machines for the extension of the rationale of objects (which are impacted social relations) into consciousness and viscerality. They express the point of view of the commodity with the same degree of centrifugal variation that is possible in commodity production. The laws of exchange of which object relations were and are their expression shift into the visual environment. The world of alienated objects, in other words, which slowly was perceived to have its own alien will, helped to create new perceptions and was the consequence of new perceptions.

Today the tendrils of the prosthetic body of capital have a grip not only upon objects and therefore upon the relations of production but upon images and therefore upon the senses, a grip that forces the production of new sensations and new sensibilities. Among these new sensibilities are geographical dislocation and the overall conversion of objects (which are always objectified subjectivity and therefore subjects in potentia) into images. Subjectivity, on the other hand, if one chooses to hang on to the term, now achieves, inasmuch as it exists as such, a sort of specialization as spectator-destroyer. Those who see *and are seen seeing*, are seen because they destroy. Recognized subjects are seen because they destroy and because they destroy what they see. Those who merely see have a lot of destroying to do before they might actually be seen seeing.

1. For more on the term "social cooperation," see Antonio Negri, "Twenty Theses on Marx," trans. Michael Hardt, *Polygraph 5: Contesting the New World Order* (Durham, N.C., 1992). "When the capitalist process of production has attained such a high level of development so as to comprehend every even small fraction of social production, one can speak, in Marxian terms, of a "real subsumption" of society in capital" (139). This subsumption of society in capital means that that in principle all human activity is potentially productive labor for capital.

2. See Manuel Castells, *The Informational City: Information Technology, Economic Restructuring and the Urban-Regional Process* (Oxford: Blackwell Publishers, 1989). See also M. Gottdiener, *The Social Production of Urban Space,* 2nd edition (Austin: University of Texas, 1994). As Gottdiener writes, "The process of socio-spatial development associated with the present phase of Late Capitalism is deconcentration, which produces a distinctive form of space—the polynucleated, sprawling metropolitan region" (198). My argument is that in the society of control in which social relations in their entirety have been subsumed by capital, the structure of the built environment is homologous with the structuring of representation and subjectivity.

3. Here of course the Gulf War is the usual example, but one should see this as only a particularly striking example of the generalized war on subsistence and laboring populations being waged politically, culturally, and economically every day.

4. Jean Baudrillard, *The Ecstasy of Communication,* trans. Bernard and Caroline Schutze (New York: Semiotext(e), 1988).

5. See my essay "City of Television: Metropolitan Affects and the New Americanism," *Polygraph 8: New Metropolitan Forms* (Durham, N.C., 1994).

6. Excessive: "More troublesome still about *Natural Born Killers* is the picture's basic fascination with its subject. Of course it is difficult to analyze something without in some way representing it, but the joyride aspect of this movie makes it less than the coolheaded and sardonic critique of media culture that the film at first affects." Christopher Sharrett, "Movies vs. the Media," *USA Today* 123 no. 2598 (March 1995): 37.

Simplistic: "*NBK*... certainly represents some kind of breakthrough in terms of the speed and intensity with which it marshals its images, but it does so without any rhetorical complexity. By throwing enough extreme images at us, it proves we live in an extreme world.... *NBK* is a clumsy, stupid, extremely tiring film that leaves you numbed and disinclined to form any complex judgments," Jonathan Romney, "Virtual Violence," *New Statesman and Society* 8, no. 341 (February 24, 1995): 49.

Senselessly Exploitative: "For no apparent reason, Mr. Stone's camera spins around in all directions and angles, and goes back and forth from colour to black-and-white. The picture ends with glimpses of two real-life killers: the Menendez brothers.... Other examples of real-life-murderers-as-popular-heroes appear on Mr. Stone's screen along with the final credits. No justice is seen to be done but a lot of money is being raked in at the box-office." *The Economist* 333, no. 7885 (October 15, 1994): 119.

Hypocritical: "How lamentable . . . is Oliver Stone's latest and most horrible film, *Natural Born Killers*, from a story by another current hotshot, Quentin Tarantino. Mr. Stone's narcissism and megalomania, like badly driven horses, run away with this gross, pretentious, and ultimately senseless movie. Purporting to show how crime appeals to the American public, and how the media exploit it for their self-promotion and the public's cretinization, it is manifestly far too enamored of what it pretends to satirize, even if it knew how to do it. . . . *Natural Born Killers* is neither wise nor witty enough for a satire, and displays only the depraved unhingedness of a hypertrophic ego." John Simon, *National Review* 46, no. 18 (September 26, 1994): 72.

Hypocritical (again): "*Natural Born Killers* is like bad sex and a bad drug trip combined. It's an ejaculatory farce, but without satiation or rest. Stone pushes well beyond plausibility, yet we are meant to take the movie seriously as the essential, rabid truth of our times—we are meant to take it as satire. Stone can't successfully satirize anything, however, because he can't distance himself from his subjects. He's driven by the logic of what he hates, or what he claims to hate." David Denby, *New York* 27, no. 35 (September 5, 1994): 46.

7. Guy Debord, *The Society of the Spectacle* (Detroit: Red and Black, 1977), #11.

8. Weapons no longer have to fire but have to seem to be able to destroy. See Paul Virilio, *Speed and Politics: An Essay on Dromology*, trans. Mark Polizzoti (New York: Semiotext(e), 1986). See also his more recent work, *The Vision Machine*, trans. Julie Rose (London: BFI, 1994).

9. Debord, *Society of the Spectacle*, #34.

10. Ibid., #66.

Epilogue
Paying Attention

And ale does more than Milton can
To justify God's ways to man.
—A. E. Houseman

Since the major part of each of the chapters that make up this book were first drafted in the early to mid-nineties, much has transpired to make the *Cinematic Mode of Production* along with the attention theory of value seem even more necessary to an understanding of the present moment. The question, "what is the relationship between media, social organization, and production?" is more urgent than ever—having become central not only in the unthought of the logistics of globalization, but central in current economic thinking as well. In the screen/society how can we think simultaneously the systemic imbrication of mass media (from cinema to cell phones), the politico-economic (including neo-imperialism and war), and consciousness (from the quotidian to the outer limits of philosophy and fantasy)?

The internet came into being, along with the explosion of the stock market and a new set of billionaires and business models. In one way or another, these transformations perceived, acted upon, and realized the transformed situation of media pathways and their attendant bodies. Michael Hardt (who read an earlier version of this book with his graduate students at Duke in 1995 when it was my dissertation) wrote *Empire* with Antonio Negri, and together they later developed the concept of affective labor from their prior concepts of social cooperation and what, in *Labor of Dionysus*, they called the factory-society. For them, and now for a reviving Marxism, media played a larger role in capitalist mediation. Jonathan Crary wrote *Suspensions of Perception: Attention, Spectacle and Modern Culture*, which understood the organization of attention as central to the development of visual forms and technologies. September 11, the spectacle, happened, resulting in wars in Afghanistan and Iraq. These wars, though now admitted even by government to be based upon "faulty intelligence" (a further breakdown of sign function?)—as if there were ever any doubt, have served not only as vehicles of imperialist control, but also to underscore the continuous calibration of social relations embarked upon by the state. But it is perhaps only now in 2005, with the full blown emergence of what is being called the attention economy, that the significance of the convergence of media and society are becoming fully apparent.

In my own view, the academic left still has some catching up to do to the shifts in mediatic function. On October 29, 2005, I attended a forum on the Geopolitics of Contemporary Capitalism at the University of California–Santa Cruz that was organized by *New Left Review* editor Gopal Balakrishnan and focused on the recent book by members of the Retort Collective, Iain Boal, T. J. Clarke, Joseph Matthews, and Michael Watts entitled *Afflicted Powers: Capital and Spectacle in a New Age of War.* Balakrishnan, these authors, and economist/theorist Bob Brenner were on the panel. While raising important issues, this discussion helped me to pinpoint what aspects of media theory still need to be internalized by "the left" in the United States.

In an assertion that I largely would agree with, the authors of *Afflicted Powers* write:

The deeper and deeper involvement of the state in the day-to-day instrumentation of consumer obedience meant that increasingly it came to live or die by its investment in, and control of, the field of images—the alternative world conjured up by the new battery of "perpetual emotion machines," of which TV was the dim pioneer and which now beckons the citizen every waking minute. This world of images had long been a structural necessity of a capitalism oriented toward the overproduction of commodities, and therefore the constant manufacture of desire for them; but by the late twentieth century it had given rise to a new polity."[1]

This assessment is correct in its broad outlines; however, the enormity of this transformation somehow escapes Retort when it comes both to the collectives own strategies of representation and analysis, and to its understanding of the relationship between media and what the collective calls "primitive accumulation." In an effort to register the ever-more-dynamic field of signification/signalization, Retort has written that, "the modern state . . . has come to need weak citizenship."[2] Weak citizenship "but for that very reason the object of the state's constant, anxious attention, an unstoppable barrage of idiot fashions and panics and image-motifs, all aimed at sewing the citizen back (unobtrusively, "individually") into a deadly simulation of society."[3] Readers of The Cinematic Mode of Production will recognize the necessary daily calibration of spectators here as well as the transformed proprioception of subjects. However, for Retort, 9/11 represents a huge blow to the state's control and organization of the spectacle that left the state anxious and afraid and feeling vulnerable (don't you feel sorry for it?). Retort's account of the emotional and psychological condition of the state in the current political situation stems from their view that images of 9/11 represented a crisis for the state—a defeat. "The spectacular state . . . is obliged to devise an answer to the defeat of September 11th."[4] Thus, for Retort, the war and all the hoopla in Iraq is a quasi-hysterical endeavor to overcome this defeat in the spectacle.

At the conference, Retort defended this "Miltonian" view of 9/11 and the paroxysms of the "afflicted powers," and, in accord with their own political seriousness, took the spectacle seriously on its own terms, as it were, eschewing a kind of bread and circuses understanding of its fevered inanity. For Retort, the situation of afflicted powers results in a "military neoliberalism" that they defined there as "violent accumulation under conditions of the spectacle." This idea leads them to theorize an emergent condition of permanent war, not too different from that argued for by Agamben in State of Exception, but surprising to hear without any mention of George Orwell's ideas on the topic from the mid-1940s.[5] What is noteworthy here is that Retort considers this state of permanent war to be a consequence of the defeat dealt to the U.S. superstate in the spectacle, and that furthermore, this defeat plunges the United States back into a kind of primitive accumulation through warfare. However, this idea that the Bush regime is purely reactionary misses the pro-active, indeed pre-emptive, character of contemporary state power. One does not even have to believe that "Bush did it," as the theory ran, to see that the current U.S. regime and those who are close to it have been the real beneficiaries of 9/11.

Bob Brenner, for his part, did not see 9/11 as a defeat for the current U.S. regime, but rather as an opportunity, a step forward in some respects, a necessary condition for an ultra-right-wing power grab that set out not to make the world safe for capitalism, but to enrich a particular domestic coterie of neo-conservative capitalists. Indeed, according to Brenner, the pay-off of 9/11 for the neo-conservatives has been the unfettered implementation of their "ultra-capitalist domestic policy." Interestingly, Brenner does not see the Bush regime as a sheer, or even a creeping coup, but notes almost in passing that the religious right had been building grassroots support for itself for many years.

Gopal Balakrishnan, who asked the provocative question "why put twenty-five years of good business at risk?" with reference to the invasion of Iraq and the global war on terror, spoke of the "erosion of the field of intelligibility of the intrastate system," saying that the intentions of nations were no longer legible. Systems and sub-systems including militaries, corporations, juridical institutions, and national agencies were all behaving as if they were semi-autonomous. Thus, they spin out their own often contradictory logics, thereby creating a crisis in the categories of geopolitical rationality.

The erosion, or perhaps we should say implosion of the field of intelligibility, voiced by Balakrishnan, is also characteristic of Giorgio Agamben's learned and meticulous long deconstruction of sovereignty in *State of Exception*. Agamben shows that the juridical inclusion of the extrajuridical suspension of juridical powers by the sovereign or sovereign state—its effort to include powers that by definition are excluded from the legal exercise of is sovereignty—is the very condition of sovereignty and has been since the Roman Empire.[6] Likewise, Jacques Derrida in *Rogues* argues in the first long essay, "The Reason of the Strongest (Are There Rogue States?)" that the state of permanent war has produced an erosion in the legibility of social, juridical, and national movements/modes of governance.[7] His inquiry into questions of sovereignty, subjectivity, democracy, and freedom, cleanses the common and even the philosophical categories of the understanding of these phenomena of their use, and splits philosophical hairs in search of the event.

In spite of the fact that Derrida concludes that "there is something of the Rogue state in every state," *Rogues* does not have much encouragement for the activist.[8] Furthermore, in *Rogues*, one cannot easily identify, as it were, the agents of history. This leaves, for the second essay, the question of reason and the effort to "save the honor of reason" as a kind of necessity given the absence of other identifiable agents and the effective autonomization of rationalities. Without getting lost in the mire of Derrida's two essays in *Rogues*, the first of which seems to say that "when it comes to politics, if you think you know than you're a fascist," and the second of which seems to say, "it may be impossible but let's make reason reasonable," the question of history and periodization seems paramount. At one point toward the end of the first essay, Derrida engages in plainspeak and seems to imply that his descriptions of the deconstruction of democracy on the one hand and of reason on the other are not a mere philosophical exercise carried out at the highest levels of abstraction, but are informed by a kind of historico-material exigency: "such a questioning of sovereignty is not simply some formal or academic necessity for a kind of speculation in political philosophy, or else a form of genealogical, or perhaps even deconstructive, vigilance. It is already under way. It is at work today; it is what's *coming*, what's *happening*."[9] Thus, what at first appears in his text as a kind of ontology of "democracy" and "reason" (that is, their necessary conditions of non-being) is cast into a historical periodicity, if not narrative—one that is not exactly told but nonetheless haunts the text as the only possible, or rather ultimate explanation for its occasion—the deconstruction of the categories of sovereignty is "what's *happening*." Thus the "real referent" of *Rogues* is History. With different emphasis, Agamben's book *State of Exception* traces the fact, if you will, that extrajuridical powers, in/as the state of exception, are the very condition of sovereignty at least since the Roman Empire. Thus, even though Agamben points out that today many so-called democracies are regularly if not permanently calling upon their exceptional powers to maintain rule, he shows that this exceptionalism, recognized either partially or, in Schmitt, clearly, has been the historical condition of sovereignty since it has been theorized.

With respect to Derrida and Agamben, the question arises, why now? Why do these works about the crisis of reason, democracy, and law appear as we approach a condition where exceptionalism and roguery are exercised regularly rather than lurking at the deconstructible edges of the closure of the juridical (even though Agamben shows numerous historical examples of the exercise of the state of exception)? Rather, why do these quasi-ontological works, which strive to show that (now) it has never been the case that democracy, sovereignty, and reason have been fully present, appear at *this* historical juncture? If such has always been so, what is different about the present moment that calls forth the articulation of this now quasi-ontological situation?

The Retort Collective, too, writes at length about a condition they call permanent war, which results in a kind of collapse of the thinkability of war itself. Orwell, though none of the abovementioned seem to think he is worth invoking, theorized this as early as 1948 under the rubric of Newspeak and its annihilation of thought (War is Peace). Orwell did so not in the rarefied atmosphere of high philosophy but rather in the fairly realist-driven language of sociology and dystopian social realist fictional narrative. Significant here is that Orwell showed that the conditions of permanent war emerged as a strategy of accumulation and *simultaneously* as a strategy of thought control designed for the preservation of hierarchical society. War, while driving the engines of production more and more furiously, provides a psychologically satisfying rational for both the appropriation and destruction of the social surplus. Furthermore, and this seems key, this systematic is inseparable from the effective collapse of language by what he somewhat heavy handedly though no less deftly for all that saw as the necessary thought control exercised through the utilization of media (linguistic and visual) as an assault on the intelligence and thus upon the physical life of the population. The conscious dimension of this systematic that had to deny even to itself the function and implementation of its own agenda, Orwell famously called "doublethink." Doublethink, or the ability to hold two contradictory ideas in one's head simultaneously and believe them both to be true, was, in 1984, characteristic of all aspects of social life (recall the party slogans: War is Peace; Freedom is Slavery; Ignorance is Strength) and as such represented the collapse of any dialectical thought by the real, practical imposition of what he already had glimpsed as the end of history—the eternal domination of humanity by an immortal, relatively static, and ultimately unconceptualizeable totalitarian society.

For me, after briefly surveying this field of inquiry into political sovereignty, characterized by this erosion of the field of intelligiblity, what all of the commentaries discussed above have in common is that they represent various takes on the crisis of representation, to borrow a phrase from poststructuralism. Retort sees a media environment in which 9/11 itself induces a crisis in the spectacle that threatens and panics state power. Brenner mentions in passing that 9/11 has something to do with the strange ability of the right to convince Americans that it represented their interests, and Balakrishnan sees the erosion of the field of intelligibility of the interstate system. Likewise, Agamben and Derrida, themselves explicitly plying the deconstructive möbius strip (Agamben works on one large one while Derrida moves into its fractal structure), are concerned with the impossibility of a correct notion of sovereignty and thus of freedom. Given this shared symptom of the crisis of representation, is it too much to ask the following: Might it be that the intensification of the penetration of visual technologies—of cinematic ale—into the discursive sphere of civil society and geopolitical rationality offers a point of connection for these partially divergent takes on contemporary globalization? Again, does political theory need to become film theory, or media theory?

In previous chapters, I already have mentioned how visual technologies scramble language-function and indeed I have suggested that linguistics, psychoanalysis, structuralism, and post-structuralism might, like so many architectural styles, all be taken as periodizing markers for intensification of the operation of machines of the visual—spitting out their particular analytics and thus their particular objects at different moments of the reorganization of the graphosphere by the mediasphere. Skipping a few steps here and leaving out the "somes," "mays," and "mosts" that liberals like to see in claims so qualified that they offend no one but the "unreasonable," let me say directly here that such a thesis places the intersection of political economy and culture at the center of all humanistic inquiry. The media are not merely engines of representation, they are economic engines, which as they represent also monetize. Therefore, what I find missing from all of the above accounts of the war in Iraq and the direction of the U.S. superstate is precisely this question of culture, more particularly even, the question of the culture *industry*.

It seems to me that the work of Adorno and Horkheimer (long dismissed as being too overdetermining and illiberal), who see the culture industry as an essential component in the processing of the masses to make them fit to return to work, as well as that of Althusser, who understands ideological state apparatuses such as "the school," "the church," and "the media" as implements for the production and reproduction of subjects "who work," and also of Foucault, who understands the articulation of various subject-formations and those of power to be inseparable (as in one and the same), were missing from the discussion of Retort's work on that day and that their lessons, along with the lessons of feminist work on domestic and informal labor, have been all too quickly forgotten. It is as if what were really most radical about the sixties and seventies had fallen away, and the New Left had all of a sudden become the Old Left. Let us hope that work such as Angela Davis's *Are Prisons Obsolete?*, which shows that not only is the prison-industrial complex a state and corporate system directly tied to the legacy of slavery, but also an ideological institution that naturalizes many other normative social impositions regarding not just punishment and crime but also race, class, gender, justice, human possibility, and humanity itself, will not meet the same fate.[10] I bring up Davis's work here because not only is it an intervention in a field of relative invisibility (since prisons are for-profit institutions that claim to disappear problems of to-day's for-profit society), but because it shows important aspects of the rela-tionship between institutional and cultural hegemony and the prevention of revolutionary progressive social change. The crisis of representation (in every sense of the word) of the incarcerated is linked directly to the socio-political, the historic, and the economic, all of which are registered in the cultural. Davis's work, however, shows where the profit-making and taking occur, and offers numerous sites of struggle. It points toward the politico-economic organization of race, gender, class, nation, and sexuality. She points out that before the abolition of slavery many people could not imagine its end, just as today many cannot imagine the abolition of the prison. Davis shows that the questions of punishment and social justice are also questions of culture, and more particularly of the economiciza-tion of culture.

The multiplicity of the cultural (not to say of the multitudes) leads Davis to the introduction of complexity without the aporia of abstract philosophy itself becoming a stultifying burden. In deconstructing the single libera-tory solution, we move toward, the people. In some ways, Davis' discussion of the prison-industrial complex and Derrida's discussion of sovereignty are moving in the same direction. However, there are more and less effec-tive ways to displace the unitary ideals of sovereignty and make such a move toward the masses. Derrida writes, "For wherever the name of God would allow us to think something else, for example a vulnerable nonsov-ereignty, one that suffers and is divisible, one that is mortal even, capable of contradicting itself or of repenting (a thought that is neither impossible nor without example), it would be a completely different story [different from that of the unitary soverign God], perhaps even the story of a god who deconstructs himself in his ipseity."[11] But Davis writes, "It is true that if we focus myopically on the existing system [of crime and punishment] . . . it is very hard to imagine a structurally similar system capable of handling such a vast population of lawbreakers. If, however, we shift our attention from the prison, perceived as an isolated institution, to the set of relation-ships that comprise the prison industrial complex, it may be easier to think about alternatives. In other words, a more complicated framework may yield more options than if we simply attempt to discover a single substitute for the prison system. The first step, then, would be to let go of the desire to discover one single alternative system of punishment that would occupy the same footprint as the prison system."[12]

We are to understand from this juxtaposition that in a society still underpinned by the dialectic of the identity of identity and non-identity, in other words, in a society in which multiplicity is constantly being configured as a moment in the movement from M(1) to M(2) (from money as capital to money as a larger capital), that the unitary formations are the reactionary ones and that the scene of the multiple is where production and struggle occurs. The god who deconstructs himself in his ipseity and the letting go of the desire to discover one single alternative system of punishment both express a will to unravel the unitary, the identitarian. This deconstruction indicates a movement by (the) people beyond the normative modes of capitals' valorization, and while capital must hasten to capture the always-expanding envelope of revolutionary innovation, the increasing complexity of society is driven by the masses and this complexity is a result of struggle. However, it may be that in the current moment the less abstract and the more concrete the referent of theory, the closer it might get to various forms of struggle. Because *The Cinematic Mode of Production* is a work that traces the trajectories of abstraction and capitalization of concrete social practices of spectatorship and attention, it is important to say here that once the new architectonics of social domination are grasped, a turn to the particularities of struggles against the logic of the spectacle is essential. It is for that reason that the companion text for this volume is my book *Acquiring Eyes: Philippine Visuality, Nationalism, and the World-Media System*, which examines the struggle with the spectacle from the standpoint of activist-artists and revolutionaries in the postcolonial Philippines.[13] It also explains why the imagination, which in Adorno and Herkheimer's paradigm of the culture industry "withers away" and in *The Cinematic Mode of Production* is shown to undergo continuous assault, is the terrain on which many anti-racist feminist Marxists today place their hopes and stake their claims.

To continue to make the case for culture and for the specificity of culture in the context of this political economy of culture in stacatto form: What an analysis of the current situation requires is what Althusser called "the standpoint of the production and reproduction of the relations of production," which took into consideration not only the replacement of used-up materials at the factory, but the replacement, whether daily or generationally, of laborers. For Althusser, the question of politics involved the question of the production and reproduction of subjects, not only through wage labor and the necessities that could be purchased with the wage, but psychologically, as it were, through a process he called interpellation—the calling of the worker-subject into being by ideological apparatuses. These were exemplified in his work by the "Hey you" of ideology, in the mouth of the police officer, or of God (to Moses), but generally also uttered by licensing boards, politicians, television—all of the techno-material structures that daily produced and reproduced the subject through various modes of instantiation. Not only is ideology "omnipresent" (Althusser) and practice always already "ideological" (as Zizek has shown) but any clear sustainable distinction between ideology and materiality in the society of the spectacle has collapsed.

Today, with the "death of the subject," its shattering, the matter is more complex. Thus, in calling for the abolition of the prison, Davis takes into consideration not only media representations of criminality, but also the strong links of the institution of the prison to slavery, the privatization of prisons and the sale of prison labor, the exponential growth of prisons over the past three decades, the ideology of security, multinational capitalism, U.S. imperialism, and third-world labor, among other factors. She writes, "if we are willing to take seriously the consequences of a racist and class-biased justice system, we will reach the conclusion that enormous numbers of people are in prisons simply because they are, for example, black, Chicano, Vietnamese, Native American or poor, regardless of their ethnic background. They are sent to prison not so much because of crimes committed [Davis has pointed out that most of us have broken the law at one time or another], but largely because their communities have been criminalized. Thus programs for decriminalization will not only have to address specific activities that have been criminalized—such as drug use and sex work—but also criminalized populations and communities."[14] In short, the prison industrial complex depends upon the coordination of multiple vectors of social practice spanning the representational, the subjective, the psychological, and the economic. It is a particular formation, constructing its subjects and its objects, as well as its partial subjects, it's intensities, and it's systemics, that results from an amalgamation of a variety of racist, sexist, nationalist, capitalist practices—all of which are negotiated and renegotiated at the cultural level. For Davis, it would seem that the prison is everywhere, a fundamental presupposition of U.S. society—an institution, but also an ideology and a philosophy, a material structure and a structure of feeling, in short, a set of practices that underpins daily life in both conscious and unconscious ways. As I mentioned earlier, because the arguments against prison abolition are so entrenched that they are presuppositions, Davis must remind us that only a short time ago the abolition of slavery for many—including many slaves themselves—was unimaginable. In making an argument that suggests not only that prisons are the legacy of slavery (where Black Codes, chain gangs, and prison labor constitute slavery by other means) but also that the exponential growth of the prison industrial complex from the 1970s forward is effectively one Postmodern equivalent of enslavement, Davis demonstrates that the various avatars of incarceration (racism, misogyny, capitalist production of its human detritus, ideologies of crime and punishment, and "security") require mobilization, maintenance, development, and constant redeployment in order to do the work of supporting and increasing the scope of the prison industrial complex. Concealed as the prison system, these avators function to disappear human and social problems, creating a zone of unrepresentability, a kind of anti-spectacle that is part of the other side, the unseen of the spectacle. Now, in the current moment of the "post-human," these processes, along with other similarly mobilized avatars of domination, are chunked and microchunked—endlessly fragmenting and differentiable, but nonetheless functional and functionalized. What one needs is a dialectics of multiplicity, of visibility, of representation—a dialectics of the utterance.

Since we now have the production of subjectivity (or post-subjective affects and intensities) in the equation, we also have the situation of the spectator, or what, in a different and more utopian context, Alvin Toffler once called the prosumer. As I have been arguing throughout *The Cinematic Mode of Production*, this prosumer finds his/her first incarnation as a spectator, who produces and reproduces him/herself by exercising the "freedom reflex," desire, intention, the unconscious, what-have-you, while valorizing the media pathways; s/he produces value for capital through attention—both as a commodity that is bought and sold in advertising, is speculated on via the promotional budgets of blockbusters, and as a medium that remakes, reconfigures various corporeal-mental-chemical structures that allow him or her to go back to work in a situation of hyperflexible accumulation. Deleuze called this arrangement "desiring-production," but I have endeavored to give these assemblages a strict economic meaning that accompanies its other personal, cultural, collective significances. Clearly then, if the spectator works and cinema brings the industrial revolution to the eye, not only has the situation of production been transformed because the form of labor has undergone a profound modification in its interface with technology, but in the dialectics of visibility and invisibility the commodity form itself has also been altered and with it, the form of value. I have tried to show how these transformations can be conceptualized in the cinematic century in and through that relation known as the image. It now seems more obvious than ever that the present moment is going to produce a new set of interfaces in which a shift in the quantity of attention being expropriated will result in yet another shift in the quality of social relations themselves.

What we are party to (and in this I am close to the Retort project and their embrace of the work of Karl Polanyi) is the continuing enclosure (or capture) and thus expropriation of the commons, not only of water, air, federal lands, DNA, and nature, but of all of the objective and subjective resources that have to date constituted the "human" in humanity. In the twenty-first century "the human" will return as a spectre, a haunting. Indeed, "our" vestigal humanism haunts a planet where billions of human beings do not have the luxury to indulge in the richness of such a conceit. Because the expropriated commons includes not just shared social spaces or "natural" resources but the historically produced and won realms of freedom and creativity that have been considered the inalienable characteristics of human beings—thought, imagination, proprioception, aesthetics, faith—in short, all those zones of creativity that traditionally functioned in a relation of relative autonomy to capitalism, we are in a position to discern that Retort's idea that capital has moved to a strategy of primitive accumulation through warfare is incomplete in significant ways. Not only because war, and particularly imperialist warfare has been characteristic of the United States for more than one hundred years, but because all of the indicated human qualities, our common humanity, are now being brought online to feed the beast. We must understand that primitive accumulation, if it means the violent robbing of the wealth of people without payment, is not, as Retort acknowledges, only or even mostly about oil. And it is not even about permanent war, although, as noted, war is an important component inasmuch as it serves to concentrate production while giving the minimal return of socially produced general wealth to the general population—and as such is not just an economic but also a *cultural* endeavor. Primitive accumulation is now about mounting a belligerent campaign against the source of all value—human creativity itself, now located not just in the body of the worker, but in the mind of all: content producers, weak citizens, janitors and professors, natives, overseas contract workers, whores of all stripes—the general intellect. Wage labor, the exchange of money for subjective power, is not the only mode of exploitation—what falls outside of it and yet still enriches capital is primitive accumulation.

Primitive accumulation is not simply the annexing of lands and resources, nor the environmental devastation wrought by corporations, nor the usual privatizations of public trusts demanded by the World Bank, the IMF, and now the WTO. All of the unpaid work of social cooperation, of attention, is also the active expropriation of the commons—part of the real costs of production, paid for with the living labor/life of disenfranchised masses. *The Cinematic Mode of Production* lays out the nascent architecture of normalization for this form of primitive accumulation that is even now being legitimated and set in place in the official economic policies of capitalism. Along with life and labor, the very consciousness of our bodies has been and is being expropriated. For this we have become not just spectators, but specters. The only way out, short of a complete expropriation of the expropriators, a radical redistribution of wealth and a complete overhaul of the human network (whatever that would look like), is to drop out completely, that is, for all practical purposes, to cease to exist, to cease to speak, write or be written as the discourse of the spectacle. Otherwise, you (or at least chunks of you) are working for the man. Sorry, Jim, but that's how it is.

Of course, this spectacular mode of accumulation, which announces a transformation if not a superceding of the money form, shows that there is nothing primitive about contemporary primitive accumulation. It is accumulative hoarding under capitalism by means other than the wage, but these means and the economies of spectacularity and spectrality that they imply are composed of the very latest methods for the reduction of massive populations to the most "primitve" forms of suffering and bare life.

In a remarkable book, which only recently came to my attention, Paolo Virno in *A Grammar of the Multitude* makes the case that it is precisely the general intellect that has be subsumed by postmodern capitalism—the cognitive-linguistic abilities of the species have been harnessed by capital as an engine of production. Arguing that "*productive* labor in its totality appropriates the special characteristics of the performing artist," Virno understands virtuosity as the paradigmatic operation of production.[15] "Each one of us is, and has always been, a virtuoso, a performing artist at times mediocre or awkward but, in any event, a virtuoso. In fact the fundamental model of virtuosity . . . is the activity of the speaker."[16]

Virno asks the following question, "If the entirety of post-Fordist labor is productive (of surplus-value) labor precisely because it functions in a political-virtuosic manner, then the question to ask is this: what is the *score* which the virtuosos-workers perform?"[17] He answers as follows: "I maintain without too many reservations that the score performed by the multi-

tude in the post-Ford era is the Intellect, intellect as generic human faculty . . . . [T]he score of modern virtuosos is the *general intellect,* the general
intellect of society, abstract thought which has become the pillar of social
production."[18]

As I have argued throughout *The Cinematic Mode of Production,* the cinematic organization of society has led to the restructuring of perception,
consciousness, and therefore of production. Furthermore, this production
vis-à-vis the cinematicization of society has become increasingly dematerialized, increasingly sensual and abstract, to the point that it occupies the
activities of perception and thought itself. While not actually exploring the
techno-visual history of capital that leads up to the colonization of the sensorium and the expropriation of the senses and the intellect, Virno's work
complements the work of *The Cinematic Mode of Production* by theorizing
the performative dimensions of consciousness-production in relation to
capital. He writes: "The *general intellect* manifests itself today, above all, as
the communication, abstraction, self-reflection of living subjects. It seems
legitimate to maintain that, according to the very logic of economic development, it is necessary that a part of the *general intellect* not congeal as fixed
capital but unfold in communicative interaction under the guise of epistemic paradigms, dialogical performances, linguistic games. In other words,
public intellect is one and the same as cooperation, the acting in concert of
human labor, the communicative competence of individuals."[19] "The general intellect manifests itself, today, as a perpetuation of wage labor, as a hierarchical system, as a pillar of the production of surplus-value."[20]

Virno further elaborates:

> The general intellect is social knowledge turned into the principal pro-
> ductive force; it is the complex of cognitive paradigms, artificial lan-
> guages, and conceptual clusters which animate social communication
> and forms of life. The general intellect distinguishes itself form the
> "real abstractions" typical of modernity, which are all anchored to the
> principle of equivalence. Real abstraction is above all money, which rep-
> resents the commensurability of labor, of products, of subjects. Thus,
> the general intellect has nothing to do with the principle of equivalence.
> The models of social knowledge are not units of measurement; instead,
> they constitute the premise for operative heterogeneous possibilities.
> Techno-scientific codes and paradigms present themselves as an "im-
> mediate productive force," as constructive principles. They do not equal-
> ize anything, instead they act as a premise to every type of action.[21]

Which is like saying that the materials of thought have become the hammer, nails, and bulldozers of contemporary social production (but to my mind nonetheless implies that these tools operate within a larger field of equivalences and are organized accordingly). However, what is important here is that in a way that significantly modifies the supplementarity of ideology, Virno understands cognitive-linguistic function as having become directly productive of (surplus) value. As Virno sums it up, "the primary productive resource for contemporary capitalism lies in the linguistic-relational abilities of humankind, in the complex communicative and cognitive faculties (*dynameis*, powers) which distinguish humans."[22]

So if one thinks of the general intellect as a new order of fixed capital (infrastructure) and virtuosity (performance), as a new paradigm of labor, then what of cinema and attention? For me, a choice between the sets of terms is at present undecideable. Each term provides a figure for the transformed ground of production and productive activity. "The general intellect" has the virtue of invoking the sedimented thought of human history and its material overdetermination but leaves out the decisive character of the visual turn. "Cinema" underscores the historico-material shattering of the linguistic alongside the rise of the visual, the displacement of ontological categories, and the reconfiguration of the imaginary and the subject in the logistics of spectacle. "Virtuosity," articulates the dynamic between performance and score, emphasizing the creative mediations of subjective activity (labor). Attention makes clear the baseline functioning of consciousness/bodies (labor) in relation to all forms of social machinery, and allows for a consideration of input, output, and throughput at intellectual and corporeal levels. The struggle over the future will undoubtedly refine these terms.

For the moment however, we might note once again that if, as Lacan says, the unconscious is structured like a language, and, as Virno's work implies, language is structured like the factory, then the unconscious too is an engine of production. This takes on a kind of thickness, if we understand the operations of the unconscious, in addition to dream-work and to the effect it exercises on the organization of the signifier, in terms of the political unconscious. In a previous chapter I argued in a somewhat ontological vein that cinema is the unconscious of the unconscious, and while I would still hold out for the encroachment of capital on the visual as the fundamental historical shift that inaugurates the discourse of the unconscious, it is also important here to see that the prison industrial-complex, the third world, and the invisibility of production in general are also concrete formations, the excluded formations of the spectacle's "epic poems of commodities"—each and all formations for which the set of operations identified with the unconscious are symptoms.

In the organization of the visible world, cinema, or what elsewhere I have called "the world media-system," simultaneously creates huge swaths of functional invisibility. Such a conception, in which human activity (aesthetic form, political ideology, identity, desire, sexuality, reproduction, old-fashioned work, utterance, etc.) is spawned in some determinate relation to the world-system, is therefore mediated by and mediating the dialectics of visibility and invisibility. Indeed the apocalyptic themes of mid-century, themes that include the fundamental irrationality of the rational (Horkheimer's "End of Reason" and Adorno and Horkheimer's "Enlightenment as Mass Deception"), the evacuation of being not only from the sign, but from writing understood as the situation of all representation (Derrida), and the foreclosure of representation itself (Debord) function as a kind of barometer, charting the tidal rise of an unconscious that swallows up what may now be glimpsed as the relatively small islands of intelligibility that formerly seemed to contain All. The irrationality of capital's rational accumulation, its constant humanization of an anti-human agenda was, in the onslaught of its expansion, understood to require profound structural shifts in the operation of mediation in order to adequately distort the field of intelligibility and operationalize it in accord with its deeper though unrepresentable logic. In fact, Virno's insight into the capture of speech itself by capital was already audible in the following passage from Derrida in 1967:

It is therefore as if what we call language could have been in its origin and in its end only a moment, an essential but determined mode, a phenomenon, an aspect, a species of writing. And as if it had succeeded in making us forget this, and *in willfully misleading us,* only in the course of an adventure: as that adventure itself. All in all a short enough adventure. It merges with the history that has associated technics and logocentric metaphysics for nearly three millennia. And it now seems to be approaching what is really its own *exhaustion;* under the circumstances— and this is no more than one example among others—of this death of the civilization of the book, of which so much is said and which manifests itself particularly through a convulsive proliferation of libraries. All appearances to the contrary, this death of the book undoubtedly announces (and in a certain sense has always announced) nothing but a death of speech (of a so-called full speech) and a new mutation in the history of writing, in history as writing. Announces it at a distance of a few centuries. It is on that scale that we must reckon it here, being careful not to neglect the quality of a very heterogeneous historical duration: the acceleration is such, and such its qualitative meaning, that one would be equally wrong in making a careful evaluation of past rhythms. "Death of speech" is of course a metaphor here: before we speak of disappearance, we must think of a new situation for speech, of its subordination within a structure of which it will no longer be the archon.[23]

For Derrida, this structure is to be called "writing," and he sums it up, in one of those formulations that shatters the glass through which, without realizing it, many of us formerly viewed the world: "The 'rationality'—but perhaps that word should be abandoned for reasons that will appear at the end of this sentence—of a writing thus enlarged and radicalized no longer issues from a logos."[24] It would appear that for Derrida, this shift away from the linguistic ground of rationality is a response to a moment of "economy" just as was the epoch of phonologocentrism:

> The privilege of the *phonè* does not depend upon a choice that could have been avoided. It responds to a moment of *economy* (let us say as the "life" of "history" or of "being as self-relationship"). The system of "hearing (understanding)-oneself-speak" through the phonic substance— which *presents itself* as the nonexterior nonmundane, therefore nonempirical or noncontingent signifier—has necessarily dominated the history of the world during an entire epoch, and has even produced the idea of the world, the idea of world-origin, that arises from the difference between the worldly and the non-worldly, the outside and the inside, ideality and nonideality, universal and nonuniversal, transcendental and empirical, etc.[25]

Now it is the optico-visual dimensions of the emerging visual economy that displaces phonologocentrism and some of the mechanics by which its economics organize the imaginary and displace not just the signifier but signification.

In setting out such a genealogy of cinema, of capitalized visuality's displacement of the sign, as a consequence of the continuation of the institution of private property (not the cause but the effect of alienated labor as Marx says), it is correct to recall that the transformed situation of speech and of the sign implied by the cinematic mode of production also received rigorous treatment by Jean Baudrillard in *For a Critique of the Political Economy of the Sign*.

Noting that "the operation of the sign, the separation of signs, is something as fundamental, as profoundly political, as the division of labor,"[26] Baudrillard writes:

> 1. It is because *the logic of the commodity and of political economy is at the very heart of the sign*, in the abstract equation of signifier and signified, in the differential combinatory of signs, that signs can function as exchange value (the discourse of communication) and as use value (rational decoding and distinctive social use).
>
> 2. It is because *the structure of the sign is at the very heart of the commodity form* that the commodity can take on, immediately, the effect of signification—not epiphenomenally, in excess of itself, as "message" or connotation—but because its very form establishes it as a total medium, as a system of communication administering all social exchange. Like the sign form, the commodity is a code managing the exchange of values. It makes little difference whether the contents of material production or the immaterial contents of signification are involved; it is the code that is determinant: the rules of the interplay of signifiers and exchange value.[27]

Baudrillard's analysis of the homologous logics of signification and commodification is symptomatic of the subsumption of the code by the laws of exchange, *its financialization*. This financialization must now be understood as part of the effect of the cinematization of social relations. The fusion of industrialization and signification brought about by cinema gives rise to what today is becoming known as the attention economy. The early organization of sensual labor by the circulation of commodity-images from the factory, and then through relationships of what became known as spectatorship, brings about the fundamental cyberneticization of "the code"—the radical and irreversible denaturing of language as machine-language, its "inhuman" (that is machinic and economic) dimension, and its imbrication with the capitalist-imaginary. Thus we can see that it is not because of the ontology of the image that the metaphysical ground of signification is shattered, but rather, it is shattered (sublated) through the historico-material operations of the *capitalized* image, itself a social relation, a product of social praxis and a technology of production.

Throughout this book, I have made an argument for the increasing inadequacy of consciousness to cinematic society and now to media society—

to a society that functions through visual and other media and the organization of affect. Jameson's cognitive mapping provided one (heroic) strategy for producing propaedeutic crutches for a failing consciousness, but this strategy was also an aesthetic—in a worst case scenario a *Brazil*-like exercise in the imaginary triumph of conscious will over the sublime of a world-system with no outside (for us). In mapping the architecture of the dynamic cage, consciousness increasingly becomes understandable for what it is—a subroutine of global organizational vectors—while the unconscious is revealed to us as the dream-life of the world-system, a dream-life that is first instantiated, formalized and then tapped to harness the living creative power of human tissue, a source of dream-work, of living labor slated to digitize, objectify, and capitalize its productions. The primitive accumulation at these final frontiers—which in my own worst case scenario makes me think thoughts such as, "as soon as you know it's too late" (wherever you look, capital is there), and, "if there is hope, it's in the body" (hence the resurgence of martial arts films)—has resulted in a new set of business models that amount to the foreclosure of humanity. These models, which I will discuss at the end of this chapter, ready a formalization and, therefore, a routinization and legalization, in short, a monetization of these being-expropriated bio-psychic processes that finally will be as inescapable as the air we (will soon pay to) breathe if left to continue on their current trajectory.

The media is the message, or rather, in a dramatic reversal, the message (all of them) is the media . . . of capitalization. Not surprisingly, then, we are living in a time of the hyper-valuation of media, of which the military is but one. The war in Iraq is symbolic violence—it being understood, of course, that symbolic violence (at the level of the bomb or the letter) implies real murder (words of Richard Dienst: not just Television is War by other means, but War is Television by other means). What we must do, what is being done, is to embark upon the general expansion of the whole concept of mediation, such that one can grasp the multiple and interlaced vectors of mediation (of the network of particulars) and simultaneously figure capital as the ur-medium: the genetic material of first proto- and now actually existing digital culture. Today, de-reification means grasping all objects, images and entities (all ontological catagories and their referents) as mediations. This would imply that most unitary formations confronting us today might best be viewed as a collection of software programs for the organization and representation of data: from the various Islams, to "America," to Israel, to White. Each of these has an ability to image data and create screens of actuation that enable operators to operate and be operated. These various "world-views" now can be understood as the abstract machines that opened up the social space for the concrete machines that are the various screens and page-views now attended to with ever more fervor and regularity. And just as Marx's phrase "the anatomy of man is the key to the anatomy of the ape" is a formulation that while correctly giving priority to the most advanced evolutionary iteration of a series, changes forever the situation of the ape, so too with the ideologies of yesteryear. They continue to function, but now they must make their way in a "man's" world, it being understood of course that today's "man," whatever her race, gender, class, and nationality, and whether she has access to a computer or not, is also a computerized cyborg running the Pavlovian programs of capital. In Christian Metz's words, "We watch and we help."

To conclude then, I would like to take a final chunk of your attention to look at current industry discourse on the attention economy. With apologies for the metallic cheer in some of the language, below follows a post by one Mitch Wagner on Google:

> Google's latest surprise is that it's now offering enterprise-class Web analytics for free. Why would they do such a thing? They've decided that licensing fees are worth less money than the opportunity to find out what pages people are visiting, how long they're staying there, where they're coming from, and where they're going to next. Google Analytics is another microscope Google can use to peer into what people are paying attention to.
>
> It's just an extension of the real business that Google is in, which isn't search, or e-mail, or maps, or even advertising. Rather, Google is in the attention business.
>
> Most of us are in the attention business in one way or another. Most jobs consist of large amounts of getting other people to do what you want them to do. But before you can convince someone else to do things your way, you have to get their attention. You need to get some time on the boss's calendar, or to lure the potential customer into the store. Sometimes you need to hire a lawyer or call the cops just to get the other guy's attention.
>
> The advertising business is the business of buying and selling attention in bulk quantities. Media outlets such as newspapers, TV, radio shows and online periodicals get you to pay attention by giving you in-

formation you want. Then the media outlets turn around to the advertisers and say, "We have all these people paying attention to us. Give us some money and we'll slip your message in front of them."

Whereas the rest of us are trying to get other people to pay attention to us, Google seeks to find out what people are already paying attention to and get in front of them for a moment. That's how AdWords works; Google displays its advertising based on keywords in searches. Search Google for the word "golf," and you'll see ads for golf equipment, services, and resorts.

For Google, being in the attention business means it's of utmost importance for Google to find out what people are paying attention to. To do that, Google has made a history of giving away services that other companies charge an arm and a leg for. Even more amazingly, the service that Google gives away is usually better than the services that other people are charging for. GMail is a great mail client with 2 gigabytes of free storage. Likewise, Google Maps, Google Desktop search, and the Picasa desktop photo-organizer are first rate implementations of what they do.

In exchange for that free service and software, Google wants to look over your shoulder and take notes on what you're paying attention to and what you're ignoring.

Right now, Google uses the attention information for one purpose: Ads. It seems to me that attention is a valuable commodity that can be sold in many other ways other than advertising—but I guess I'm too stuck in 20th Century thinking to come up with any ideas. How else might Google make money, other than by selling ads? What other ways are there for an Internet business to make money by selling its users' attention?[28]

This inquiry into the profitable stripping of attention seems to be the key question for the current generation of venture capitalists. How can the whole attention economy take off? While the hyper-capitalization of Google has the company developing numerous practical means for the tracking, bundling, and selling of attention, the clearest financial analysis that I have found to date is that of Seth Goldstein, an entrepreneur. Interestingly, Goldstein approaches the dynamics between attention and capital from two diametrically opposed perspectives: that of the attention provider and that of the capitalist.

Palo Altoan Susan Mernitt, on her blog, writes and quotes the following from Goldstein:

Seth defines attention as a valuable commodity and posits that we can manage it like other assets (I think).

He writes: "Our challenge as consumers in the age of paid search and performance marketing, therefore, is whether/how to wrest control back from the machine that has begun to anticipate our intentions for its proprietary gain."

And

"The choruses of attention, data, privacy and identity are all converging in one giant conceptual mashup, which stretches from Web 2.0 pundits to members of Congress grappling with identity theft regulation. Lost at times are the basic rights we are fighting for, which I understand to be:

- You have the right to yourself.
- You have the right to your gestures.
- You have the right to your words.
- You have the right to your interests.
- You have the right to your attention.
- You have the right to your intentions."[29]

Clearly here, these rights are imagined in terms of proprietary rights, but interestingly do not extend beyond the parameters defined up to but not including our outer skins. The vestigial space of interiority is to be preserved, for now, but our images, it seems, are up for grabs in the proprietary world. Witness the emerging legal contest between athletes and celebrities, who claim that they own all images of themselves, and sports photographers and paparazzi—but the smart money is with the photographers and the media who employ them. Or the satellites—everytime they take a picture of you, who owns that? I haven't signed any release forms for outer-space photography lately.

So it seems that there is a distinction to be made between physical presence and practices on the one hand—ATM and parking lot security systems photograph us, John Poindexter's Total Information Awareness System, which was to be built for the Pentagon and for all we know still is being built, might in principle track our movements throughout the urban landscape, correlate it with the books we read and the spices we buy to decide if we are terrorists—and our intentions or attention, on the other hand, attention being the more readily quantifiable of the two (since intention is thus far only legible as it manifests itself). It is now being presupposed that attention, like labor, belongs to a juridical subject, that is, a proprietor who has the right to bring it to market. Goldstein has founded what he calls an Attention Trust, where web users can track their web usage—every click a user makes is recorded. While in certain respects this trust exists to document and therefore give a kind of heft (economic reality) to attentional practices by converting them systematically into data, it might also serve as the foundation of a new market, which is to say, it is one potential model for the increasingly organized tracking of attentional practices.

While ostensibly the attention trust exists in part to help consumers realize and protect the value of their attention (this cannot, ultimately, mean here anything but the financialization of their attention), it also serves as a strategy to bring attention online with a higher degree of informational quality and therefore of calculability. In his brilliant if chilling essay "Media Futures: From Theory to Practice" on his *Transparent Bundles* website, Goldstein writes about the securitization of attention—a process through which attentional practices are to be bundled and resold. This securitization is not a thought experiment, despite the fact that the essay appears with a sidebar of recommended readings that includes Georg Simmel, Norbert Weiner, and Walter Benjamin. Goldstein has hooked up with Lewis Ranieri, formerly of Solomon Brothers, to put the securitization of attention into practice. In Goldstein's words, securitization works as follows:

> If you consider the housing market in the 1970s and early 1980s, you will recall that the process of obtaining a mortgage was considerably more arduous than it is today and therefore far fewer people as a percentage of the population owned their own home. In each instance of a borrower asking the bank for a loan, the bank had to independently vet the risk that the borrower might default on the loan. The breakthrough idea was to consider a mortgage as simply a "promise to pay." Such an individual promise held risks for default and pre-payment, but could be combined with other mortgages to create a pool of mortgage-backed securities that could be priced in the aggregate. The local bank, therefore, when presented with certain consumer borrowing variables, could check in with the "market" and provide the risk-adjusted rate almost immediately. In attention computing terms, the physical gesture (i.e., applying for a mortgage) became mapped to an electronic signal (i.e., a series of personal data fields), which could then be priced, traded, and optimized. Once freely tradeable by investors, consumers in turn benefited from faster response times, better rates, and clear access to home ownership.

This process has a name:

Securitization is a financial technique that pools assets and, in effect, turns them into a tradeable security. Financial institutions and businesses use securitization to immediately realize the value of a cash-producing asset. Securitization has evolved from its beginnings in the 1970s to a total aggregate outstanding (as of the second quarter of 2003) estimated to be $6.6 trillion. This technique comes under the umbrella of structured finance. (from Wikipedia)

The person most responsible for inventing securitization was a legendary Wall Street maverick named Lew Ranieri forever immortalized in Michael Lewis's classic *Liar's Poker.* In the 1970s, from his perch at the Salomon Brothers trading desk, Ranieri famously applied securitization to the mortgage market, creating what is now referred to as MBSs (mortgage backed securities) and CMOs (collateralized mortgage obligations). This application has enabled (1) millions of consumers to more easily become homeowners by (2) transferring credit risk away from banks and thrifts to independent financial investors in the bond markets.[30]

Goldstein and Ranieri together run a company called /ROOT Markets, which is committed to creating a market for attention. Consumers (i.e., attention producers/providers) will be linked to marketers (advertisers) in such a way that the aggregated attention not only can be bought and sold but turned into a financial instrument subject to the laws of markets, that is, speculation. Clearly this project requires a new business model, as well as the development of new technologies. However, what is significant in the context of the discussion of *The Cinematic Mode of Production* is that what is being captured and formalized is the historical production and isolation of attention as the general form of socially productive labor. Before I discuss this paradigm shift further, a little more from Goldstein:

In the same way that the mortgage security market transferred credit risk away from the balance sheet of operators and into the portfolios of professional investors, a media futures market will enable non-advertisers (aka speculators) to take on the risk from the balance sheets of publishers. Publishers will be happy to hedge out their inventory, limit earnings volatility, and focus entirely on creating value-added programming; rather than spending their time speculating whether CPMs are going up or down.

Similarly, companies (i.e., the buy-side) can concentrate entirely on developing better products and service. Their marketing groups can focus on creating and communicating their brand images, while their sales organizations can simply specify the kinds of customers they are looking for and the prices they are willing to pay; the Media Futures market will take care of the rest.

Within these new markets enabled by Internet arbitrageurs, there are billions of micro markets where a query or a unique user path comes into contact with one or more targeted advertisements. A constructive tension emerges between the user who intends to find or do something and the sponsor of the link who is trying to lure her into the sponsor's particular commercial environment. Each one of these tiny interactions feature a buyer (advertiser), seller (publisher) and asset (consumer attention) financed by an arbitrageur (investor).

Our goal at /ROOT Markets is to maintain liquidity across all of these tiny markets. This is no small task, especially against the backdrops of apathy. Consumers are generally apathetic about the value of their attention data. Advertisers and publishers are apathetic about the cost of taking consumer attention. Investors are apathetic about consumer attention as a tradeable commodity. By educating the market about the value of attention, and enabling it to be traded (in the form of leads), we can continually feed back better and better information in terms of price, quality and yield on attention. While this may not create new attention, it may indeed help reduce our significant attention deficit.[31]

/ROOT Markets, it should be noted, has one type of proposal for the creating of an attention market similar to a stock exchange. A pressing question, of course, is what motivation web users might have to make their attentional practices more legible (and therefore more amenable to the instrumental calculus of capital) than these practices already are. In a recent conversation with Goldstein (who, for the record is a genuinely brilliant individual), I suggested that the only real motivation for users to open their private computing practices more fully to capital would be something like a proprietary stake in the process. That is, if the trust were to be owned like a collective such that its profitability were shared with attention providers, there would be motiviation to "work" in such an operation. Goldstein told me that their board had been "talking about this this morning." Because of the nature of the valuation of these economies, those who get in earlier do better than latecomers who, at the extreme, end up working in new economy companies for what is effectively only a wage. The general model will tend toward that relation, where users work in the attention factories for something like a wage, and over time we might expect this relationship to computers and information flow generally to be more and more unavoidable—as if an information proletariat is currently under construction, such that if you do not work for the information industry you will have no access to the general form of social wealth. Humans will have to make themselves increasingly porous to data chains, such that not only their (I mean "our") interests in cars and digital cameras are legible, but eventually their medical requirements, food preferences, psychopathologies, and erections will be subject to the laws of informatics and monetization. We will not only create information, we will be /ROOT Market's information.

It should be added here that, at least as it appears from the Attention Trust, an opt-in model is not the only model for the capture of attention and in the end may not be the successful one. Google is currently looking into acquiring a browser in order to do away with "www" headings altogether and track every user action; and Yahoo! and Google are currently figuring out ways to "meld" television and internet. No doubt by the time these sentences see the light of day more innovations will be afoot. We may be sure that these advances will ever more completely encroach upon the remaining uncaptured activities necessary to us in the pursuit of . . . what? Debord's terms "enhanced survival" and "gilded poverty" come to mind.

However, there are a few basics inadequacies in the new business models that *The Cinematic Mode of Production* allows us to designate, and these are sites not only of speculation but perhaps also of hope, which, in some ideal version, I suppose, is a kind of non-capitalist speculation. First of all, it is to be hoped that even the most elaborate calculus cannot fully render the subtleties of image-function with respect to its incorporation both during the moments of its viewing/legibility and during the aftermath of the instance of incorporation as the image/text enters the living vocabulary/ programming of the subject as well as his/her unconscious/body. In the moment of creation there always exists a possibility to smash the code. The wide literature on divergent reading practices, subcultural endeavors, graph-art, dreamwork, imagination, and social movements is useful to remember here. We are developing new capacities, new possibilities that cause our houses and cars to sprout computers. Are all these refinements and sensual extensions only there to fuel forever an immortal and totalitarian capitalism? Is the spectacle of civilization destined forever to float on a sea of blood?

On the one hand, the fact that viewers channel surf looking for pixilated flesh is registered by advertisers and their networks, and it is true that even generic/iconic body types have been distilled more or less scientifically and represented as formula most likely to succeed. The recent film *Ultraviolet* may be the latest if not the highest testament to and crystallization of this logic of the survival of the fittest image. Yet who can really say how the curve of a particular breast, the plump appeal of a tightly swaddled botoxed labia, or the particular ribbing of depilitated washboard abs really works at the micro-levels of incorporation? Equally elusive here are reading practices, with all of their idiosyncratic interpretations and ideolectical resultants. What about all the intimations of misery—personal and collective—percolating through myriad pores and pixels of daily life. And these divergent vectors can be extruded not only along a particular square inch of flesh or in relation to a single phrase or still image, but also across a broader range of these types of texts, which despite their grammatological programs and intentions and their statistical calibrations, are everywhere open to variance, aberration, *differance*. And while we know that variation is everywhere open to further statistical analysis and data crunching of all types via flowcharts, algorithms, and electronic machines, we also believe (those of us who have ever been a statistic of any kind) that after all the expropriation, deconstruction, and slaughter there is a certain excess there, a voice, a thought, an experience, a will, or a spirit, that does not resolve itself in the mathematical of the now. Isn't there a leftover presence, a haunting, that is mathematically, linguistically, visually, and politically irresolvable? And who is that? A mere ideological after-effect, a protesting ghost, a reason to write or speak?

Evidence of variation and anti-systemic excess, new types of attention-getting virtuosity, may be found many places, outside and in. Here's one from "The Poverty of Philosophy" by spoken-word/hip-hop artist Immortal Technique:

> I'm quite sure that people will look upon my attitude and sentiments and look for hypocrisy and hatred in my words. My revolution is born out of love for my people, not hatred for others.
>
> You see, most of Latinos are here because of the great inflation that was caused by American companies in Latin America. Aside from that, many are seeking a life away from the puppet democracies that were funded by the United States; places like El Salvador, Guatemala, Peru, Columbia, Nicaragua, Ecuador and Republica Dominicana, and not just Spanish-speaking countries either, but Haiti and Jamaica as well.

As different as we have been taught to look at each other by colonial society, we are in the same struggle and until we realize that, we'll be fighting for scraps from the table of a system that has kept us subservient instead of being self-determined. And that's why we have no control over when the embargo will stop in Cuba, or when the bombs will stop dropping in Vieques.

But you see, here in America the attitude that is fed to us is that outside of America there live lesser people. "Fuck them, let them fend for themselves." No, *fuck you,* they *are* you. No matter how much you want to dye your hair blonde and put fake eyes in, or follow an anorexic standard of beauty, or no matter how many diamonds you buy from people who exploit your own brutally to get them, no matter what kind of car you drive or what kind of fancy clothes you put on, *you will never be them.* They're always gonna look at you as nothing but a little monkey. I'd rather be proud of what I am, rather than desperately try to be something I'm really not, just to fit in. And whether we want to accept it or not, that's what this culture or lack of culture is feeding us.

I want a better life for my family and for my children, but it doesn't have to be at the expense of millions of lives in my homeland. We're given the idea that if we didn't have these people to exploit then America wouldn't be rich enough to let us have these little petty material things in our lives and basic standards of living. No, that's wrong. It's the business giants and the government officials who make all the real money. We have whatever they kick down to us. My enemy is not the average white man, it's not the kid down the block or the kids I see on the street; my enemy is the white man I don't see: the people in the white house, the corporate monopoly owners, fake liberal politicians—those are my enemies. The generals of the armies that are mostly conservatives—those are the real mother-fuckers that I need to bring it to, not the poor, broke country-ass soldier that's too stupid to know shit about the way things are set up.

In fact, I have more in common with most working and middle-class white people than I do with most rich black and Latino people. As much as racism bleeds America, we need to understand that classism is the real issue. Many of us are in the same boat and it's sinking, while these bourgeois mother-fuckers ride on a luxury liner, and as long as we keep fighting over kicking people out of the little boat we're all in, we're gonna miss an opportunity to gain a better standard of living as a whole.

In other words, I don't want to escape the plantation—I want to come back, free all my people, hang the mother-fucker that kept me there and burn the house to the god damn ground. I want to take over the enco-mienda and give it back to the people who work the land.

You cannot change the past but you can make the future, and any-one who tells you different is a fucking lethargic devil. I don't look at a few token Latinos and black people in the public eye as some type of achievement for my people as a whole. Most of those successful indi-viduals are sell-outs and house Negroes.[32]

Part history lesson, part class analysis, part critique of collaboration, indi-vidualism, consumer culture and white supremacy, these lines as a re-cording are an example of another kind of machine: cognitive-linguistic, musical, affective. They provide an occasion for us to shape our thought even in their contradictions. As a performance, these lines are a reclama-tion of the voice, varying the score of the general intellect in ways intended (in part at least) to be fatal to its current dispensation. It steals the voice to perform a call to community—a formation of community that makes for an uncomfortable fit with capitalist domination, white supremacy, and U.S. Empire. Those of us who attend to these lines may also begin or deepen our affiliation with the anti-capitalist, anti-white–supremacist col-lective they invoke through the organization of our sensual capacities, our structures of feeling, and our discursive production in relation to not just the message here encoded, but to the histories, the possibilities and the affects transmitted here. This transmission takes place via the words and rhythm, accents and inflections of the voice, but also in its activation of prior, similar transmissions that are part of collective/mass culture, mem-ory, history.

As with many things, this relating to this mediation, does not propose a slavish accession to its imperatives, but rather an internalization and then a re-mediation of the life and the life-world it proposes and calls into being. Thus, Immortal Technique's "The Poverty of Philosophy" is another tech-nology for the bundling of attention, but its method of operation, it's ra-tional and its rationalizations are markedly different than the internet models. This bundling is not undertaken (exclusively, anyway) to be parsed and resold. It activates other systems of account. First, "The Poverty of Phi-losophy" calls upon the various modes of attending we have developed his-torically and assembles them to create its aesthetic/intellectual/communi-tarian experience (be it tinged with fervor, beauty, love, or panic), and it bundles the attention required both to produce the piece for the artist (the reservoir of past forms and learning, Marxism, decolonization, anti-racist struggle, rap) and for the audience (the collective modes of relating both to the piece and to one another). While not exactly cinema, it is cinema and things cinematic that has brought the contest between labor and capital to a new stage—a stage where the organization of attention, perception, and of voice may be decisive. In this process—the machinations of a movement that re-presents the poverty of philosophy and the philosophy (as praxis) of poverty—there may be less transparency (and thus a deeper poetics) than that required or even allowed by the emergent data-sphere in its capacity as a medium of capitalization. Binary code may transmit the mp3 files that disseminate "The Poverty of Philosophy" and thousands if not millions of similar encodings, but running the program requires wetware and organizes zones that are beyond the reach of the project and projection of capital. Or so we must assume. And, perhaps, it is there in the shadows, that the poverty of philosophy may be seen to expresses Our new power. This time, here, now, it is capital that will have to catch up or fizzle out. Either way, there will be blood.

NOTES

1. The Retort Collective, *Afflicted Powers: Capital and Spectacle in a New Age of War* (London and New York: Verso, 2005), 21. The phrase "Perpetual emotion machines" is taken from Perry Anderson, *The Origius of Postmodernity* (London, 1998), 89.

2. Ibid.

3. Ibid.

4. Ibid., 34.

5. See my short essay, "Military Industrial Complex," in *Shock and Awe* (2004).

6. Giorgio Agamben, *State of Exception*, trans. Kevin Attell (Chicago and London: University of Chicago Press, 2005).

7. Jacques Derrida, *Rogues: Two Essays on Reason*, trans. Pascale-Anne Brault and Michael Naas (Stanford: Stanford University Press, 2005).

8. Ibid., 156.

9. Ibid., 157.

10. Angela Davis, *Are Prisons Obsolete?* (New York: Seven Stories Press, 2003).

11. Derrida, *Rogues*, 157.

12. Davis, *Are Prisons Obsolete?*, 106.

13. Jonathan L. Beller, *Acquiring Eyes: Philippine Visuality, Nationalism, and the World-Media System* (Manila: Ateneo de Manila University Press, 2006).

14. Davis, *Are Prisons Obsolete?*, 113.

15. Paolo Virno, *A Grammar of the Multitudes*, trans. Isabella Bertoletti, James Cas-

caito, and Andrea Casson (New York and Los Angeles: Semiotext(e) Foreign Agent Series, 2004), 54.

16. Ibid., 55.

17. Ibid., 63.

18. Ibid., 63.

19. Ibid., 65.

20. Ibid., 66.

21. Ibid., 87.

22. Ibid., 98.

23. Jacques Derrida, *Of Grammatology,* trans., Gayatri Chakravorty Spivak (Baltimore and London: The Johns Hopkins Press, 1976, 1982), 8. Originally published in France as *De la Grammatologie,* Les Editions de minuit, 1967.

24. Ibid., 10.

25. Ibid., 7–8.

26. Jean Baudrillard, *For a Critique of the Political Economy of the Sign,* trans., Charles Levin (St. Louis: Telos Press, 1981), 189.

27. Jean Baudrillard, *For a Critique of the Political Economy of the Sign,* trans., Charles Levin (St. Louis: Telos Press, 1981), 146–147.

28. Posted by Mitch Wagner on November 15, 2005, at 5:39 PM, http://www.informationweek.com/blog/main/archives/2005/11/google_wants_yo.html.

29. Susan Mernitt, http://www.informationweek.com/blog/main/archives/search/index.html.

30. Seth Goldstein, "Transparent Bundles," http://majestic.typepad.com/seth/. I thank Renu Bora for bringing Goldstein's work to my attention.

31. Ibid.

32. Immortal Technique, "The Poverty of Philosophy," from the album *Revolutionary,* Nature Sounds.

INDEX

abstract universal labor time, 234,
236n14

Acquiring Eyes (Beller), 291

Adorno, Theodor: on amusement, 76;
critique of the culture industry, 18,
27, 33n50, 86n44, 246, 247, 289–91;
on rationality, 298; on the surfacing
of signification, 239–40n34

advertising, 6–7, 184n6, 207, 234–35,
302–4

Agamben, Giorgio, 285–86, 288

agency. *See* individualism; subjectivity

alienation: cinematic appropriation of
the *logos* and, 161–62, 187n26; collective alienation, 29, 253–56; of consciousness, 15; of consumption,
259–61; dialectics of, 256–57;
fetishized objects and, 21–22,
216–17; image-commodities and,
199–200; labor theory of value and,
15, 44, 8in10, 135, 203–4, 229;
private property and, 111; of sensual
labor, 21, 23, 114; vel of alienation
(Lacan), 240n35; of vision, 7–8;
voracious eye of capital and, 169–70,
189n46

Althusser, Louis: on ideological state apparatuses, 289; on the imaginary, 10,
25; on overdetermined structures,
121; on the production/reproduction
of subjects, 291–92; on the Real as
mode of production, 110; theory of
subjectivity, 11, 174–75, 230

Amazon.com, 5, 235

Americanism, 124, 147–48n69, 187n25,
232–33, 241n44, 266

Amin, Samir, 88

Anderson, Benedict, 5–6

Antonioni, Michelangelo, 153

aphanisis (Lacan), 221–22

Appadurai, Arjun, 32n44

Arabian Nights (Pasolini), 141n9

art: aura of cinematic perception and,
210–13, 215–16, 237n25; disinterestedness and, 63; fetishization of, 23;
futurism, 109; layering of subjectivity
in, 181; painting as cinematic gaze,
171–73, 177–81; surrealist montage,
156–57

attention theory of value: abstract universal labor time and, 234, 236n14; accumulated attention as value, 181–82;
attention as commodity, 302–8; capitalization of aesthetic faculties, 14;
defined, 4–5, 201–2; in Eisenstein
vs. Vertov, 69–70; entertainment
and, 138–39; fetishization of art and,
23–24; labor theory of value and, 28;
opt-in vs. opt-out models, 308; postmodern capitalism and, 8; productive
value of attention, 107–8; sensual
labor and, 74–75, 248–50; types of
image value, 207–8; violence and,
269–71. *See also* spectatorship;
visuality

Attention Trust, 304–5, 308

attractions (Eisenstein), 45, 69, 96

audiences. *See* spectatorship

Augustine, St., 180–81

aura (Benjamin), 210–17, 237n25,
238–39n30–31

authenticity, 215

autism, 151, 153, 155

Balakrishnan, Gopal, 284–86, 288

Barthes, Roland, 101, 103

Barton Fink (Coen brothers), 193–97

base/superstructure dichotomy, 56, 174

Baudelaire, Charles, 107

Baudrillard, Jean: cinematic reading of, 10; on the circulation of mediators, 115; on the consumption of culture, 262; on the "ecstasy of communication," 16, 267; end-of-representation argument and, 219; on the political economy of the sign, 300; on revolutionary discourse, 93; on seduction, 69; on semiotic codification, 243; on simulation, 21, 211–12, 238–39n31

Beavis and Butt-head Do America (Judge and Kaplan), 151–55, 175–76, 220–21, 252

belief, 252

Beniger, Jim, 147n65

Benjamin, Walter: on the aestheticization of the political, 63–64, 262; on the aura, 210–15, 237n25, 238–39n30–31, 251; on the cinematic image mechanism, 18, 70–71; on connoisseurs, 2; on the decline of experience, 163, 196, 213, 235n8, 237n27; on information, 213; on the kaleidoscopic sensorium, 107; "orchid in the land of technology" reference, 18, 94–95, 114, 256; precinematic technologies discussed by, 209–12; on the "second nature" of the techno-mechanical world, 260; Seth Goldstein on, 305; on the shock characteristic of modern life, 147–48n69; on surgical cinema, 43–44, 131–32

Bentham, Jeremy, 84n23

Berger, John, 211, 238–39n31

Berkeley, George, 266

Bezos, Jeff, 5

biopower, 4–5, 6–7

blindness, 217–18

Bloch, Ernst, 53

Blue Planet (Burtt), 229–30

Boal, Iain, 284–85

body: adaptation to visual technology, 231; agency as spectral haunting, 139; cinematic extraction of value from, 6, 13, 65, 108, 116–17, 200–201, 205–7, 236n12, 257; globalization of capital and, 198–99, 202; pain as discourse, 132; as productive force in capitalism, 20, 72–73; reflexology and, 120, 122–24, 136, 137, 148n73; revolutionary movement as reclaiming humanity, 101–2. *See also* movement

Borges, Jorge Luis, 165

Boulez, Pierre, 1

bourgeois economic, 181

Brazil (Gilliam), 301

Brenner, Bob, 284–86

Bresson, Robert, 105

Burch, Noel, 2–3

Bush, George W., 286

Can Xue, 221

capital: abstraction of, 95–96, 243–44; attention theory and, 4–5, 7–8; cinema as reassembled unity of, 134; cinematic critique of, 46–47; cinematic experience as, 104–5; coordination of nonsynchronicities, 53; dehiscence as repressed violence, 63–64; dematerialization of the commodity, 20–21, 87n48; double unconscious and, 155–56; entrepreneurship and, 170, 187–88n29; expansion of, 201–2, 204–6; falling-rate-of-profit crisis and, 12, 122, 201–2, 205–6; forms of production and, 105, 143n23; fragmentation of the subject and, 8–9; gaze as, 169–70, 174–76, 188n35; human agency and, 101–3; industrial production of objects and, 47–48; industrial vs. consumer capital, 56; market interventions, 68; primitive accumulation and, 284–85, 294–95; rationality of, 93, 134–35, 275–76;

subsumption of culture/society to, 10, 24–25, 26–27, 280n1; three machines of capitalism, 19; transformation of the value form, 208, 233–34; valorization gap, 78, 87n46; violence and, 273–74, 277; Wurzer "filming" thesis and, 62–64. *See also* circulation; exchange-value; money; production; surplus-value

Capital Cinema (Coen brothers), 193–97, 216

Carlyle, Thomas, 8

Castoriadis, Cornelius, 10

celebrities, 200, 239–40n34

Cezanne, Paul, 171–72

Chaplain, Charles, 125, 199

Chomsky, Noam, 107, 147n65

Chow, Rey, 6

cinema: capital circulation and, 52–53, 58–59, 64–69, 72–73, 76–77, 129–30, 199–200; cinema-as-cinema vs. cinema-as-capital, 111; defined, 29; "film" distinguished from, 22, 58; image production and, 9–10, 58, 137; language compared with, 31n26; role of the symbolic in, 116; as spectacle of exchange, 258–59

cinematic images. *See* images

cinematic industrial complex, 55, 193–97

cinematic mode of production (CMP): appropriation of consciousness in, 196–97; circulation of value in, 200; commoditization of the visual realm and, 12–13; defined, 1–2, 14; depicted in *Man with a Movie Camera*, 32n37, 40–41; depicted in *The Strike*, 98–99; freedom as specter of, 139; as general theory of capitalized sensorium, 106; Lacanian psychoanalysis and, 157; Metz "second machine" of cinema and, 111–12; spectator labor

and, 176–77; table of comparison with Marxism and Psychoanalysis, 183t; technology of cinema and, 19, 32n37; two dialectical hypotheses of, 199–200

cinematic techniques: abstraction of the sensual by, 243–45; acted cinema, 72, 86n40, 147n66; coordination of nonsynchronicities, 53–54; cutting as industrial process, 41, 133–36, 208–9, 236n17; cutting as vivisection, 136–37, 149n74; empathy with the blind and, 217–18; illusion of movement in cinema, 156; precinematic technologies, 209–10; reflexive chains (Eisenstein), 125; shooting scripts, 96; split images, 42; surgical cinema (Benjamin), 43–44, 131–32; video, 217–19, 222–25, 258; violent media-scape of *Natural Born Killers*, 267–68, 273, 276–77, 280–81n6; Wurzer "filming" thesis and, 61. *See also* kino-eye; montage; technology

circulation: capital circulation as "abstract machine," 52–53; cinema as, 64–69, 76–77, 129–30, 258–59; as cutting, 208–9, 236n17; exchange-value and, 54, 87n48; of images, 49–52, 58–59, 72–73, 77, 199–200, 231; labor theory of value and, 113–14, 202–4; media pathways and, 13, 114, 213; transnational circulation of capital, 198–99, 236n11, 241–42n46.
See also capital; exchange-value; production; surplus-value

Clarke, T. J., 284–85

class. *See* society; subaltern society

CMP. *See* cinematic mode of production (CMP)

CNN, 24

Coen brothers, 193–97, 216

commodification: as abstraction process, 243–45; afterlife of commodities, 32n44; automobile as paradigmatic of, 33n50; capital circulation and, 97; commodity fetishism, 9, 21–22, 180–82, 215–16, 284–85; commodity-object vs. image-object, 75–77, 114–15; dematerialization of the commodity, 20–21, 75–76, 87n48, 180, 278; Marx on, 7–8, 67–69; monetization of web content, 234–35; property and, 66–68; of the public sphere, 113; "secret" of the commodity-form, 158, 185n11; of violence, 269–71; visuality and, 12–13; Warhol treatment of, 22–23. *See also* image-commodities; materiality

Commoli, Jean-Louis, 11

commons, 294–95

communism, 72, 74, 84n22, 121

computers: deterritorialization of work and, 1, 74, 112; FreePC, 4; Microsoft, 68–69; programming as movie-making, 132, 144n39, 230. *See also* Internet

consciousness: absence in reflexology theory, 135–36; cinematic creation of the unconscious, 18, 26, 40, 70–71, 79, 97, 174–75; of cinematic images, 47, 50, 82n15, 247–49; commodification of, 106, 217–22; discontinuity as appearance of unconscious, 156–58, 163–65, 182; double unconscious, 151, 155; Eisenstein approach to, 93, 99; image as condensation, 14–15; labor theory of value and, 176–77; managerial consciousness (Lacan), 170; Marx on, 82n14; materialization/dematerialization of, 44–46, 55, 94–95; money as, 144n37; montage as reflective of, 39; perception and, 144n37; production and, 30–31n21, 110, 196–97, 235–36n9; pulsative

function of the unconscious (Lacan), 182; quantity of the unconscious, 161–64; relation to totality, 51; repression of reality and, 195–96; as response to cinematic society, 300–301; revolutionary discourse and, 225–26; scopic derivation of the unconscious, 165–73; "second nature" (Benjamin), 70–71; self-consciousness of the proletariat, 73–74; split-image technique and, 42; sublimation, 152, 179; Vertov concern with, 50, 57, 70–72, 79; Wurzer "filming" thesis and, 63. *See also* Freud, Sigmund; psychoanalysis; subjectivity

consumption: alienation of, 259–61; Baudrillard on, 262; consumerism, 250; Marx on, 234; of media personalities, 271–72; prosumers (Toffler), 293; spectatorship as consumption vs. production, 112, 232–33, 261

Contact (Zemeckis), 251–55, 257

correlation, 131

Crary, Jonathan, 3–4, 283–84

credit, 258

Cubitt, Sean, 6

culture: abstraction of capital and, 95–96; cultural forms as social machines, 207; cultural value, 208, 233–34; culture industry, 27, 33n50, 86n44, 176, 288–91; expropriation of the commons and, 294–95; Iraq War and, 288; multiculturalism, 263

cutting. *See* cinematic techniques; montage

cybernetics, 141n9

cybertime, 6

Dalton, Kevin, 185n14

Darwin, Charles, 134

Davis, Angela, 289–92

Debord, Guy: on alienation in commodities, 22; on the cinematization of the subject, 26; on the consciousness of commodities, 106, 249; on domination by the commodity, 259–61, 278; on the "epic poem" of the commodity, 58, 297–98; on intellectual autism, 155; on representation, 298; on the repression of reality by the spectacle, 195; on revolutionary discourse, 256; on the spectacle, 180, 211, 217, 227, 268, 308

Debray, Regis, 11–12, 30–31n21, 93

deconstruction: cinematic critique of, 16; of God as unity, 291; of presence, 172; of sovereignty, 286–87; subjectivity and, 266; Wurzer "filming" thesis as, 61–62

Deleuze, Gilles: on capital circulation, 53; on consciousness, 162, 225–26; on desiring-production, 152, 293; on the deterritorialization of the image, 105, 246; on the mediation of belief, 252; money as the obverse of images, 106, 245; on the movement-image vs. time-image, 229–30, 235n1; on the organization of movement, 141n9; on simulation, 237n21; on the "society of control," 139

de-linking, 88

democracy, 132, 241–42n46, 271–72, 286–87

Denby, David, 28n6

Derrida, Jacques: on "Marx's injunction," 88–89, 140n2; on national governance, 286–88; on presence, 172; on sovereignty, 290; on the trace, 240n35; on writing, 298–99

Descartes, René, 67, 148n72, 245, 266–67

desire: cinematic desire, 3; for commodities, 284–85; desire of the Other, 170–71, 181, 276–77; drive (Lacan), 156–60, 184n9, 221–22; emergence of the imaginary from, 17; envy, 180–81, 189nn45–46; exchange-value as abstraction of, 255; libido as "desiring-production" (Deleuze), 152; mediation by capital, 217–19; photographic objects and, 168–70; for restored commodity wholeness, 22; "secondary gratification" of the fetish and, 180; sensual labor and, 248–50; surplus-enjoyment and, 173–74. *See also* sexuality

deterritorialization: of cinematic images, 74–75, 105–6, 246; of consciousness, 94; "deterritorialized factory," 10, 13–14, 29, 79, 112–15; of intentionality, 161–62; sites of spectator-labor and, 201; spatial deconcentration, 280n2; Taylorization and, 132

dialectics: of alienation, 256–57; base/superstructure dichotomy, 56, 174; of CMP, 182–83; collapsed dialectic of *Natural Born Killers*, 276; dialectical image presentation in Vertov, 48–49, 51; negative dialectics, 27–28

Dienst, Richard, 301

Dirlik, Arif, 236n11

discontinuity, 156–61, 163–64, 182, 184n9, 185n12, 185n14

disinterestedness, 63

Disney, 68–69, 120

distance (Benjamin), 237n25

doublethink (Orwell), 288

double unconscious, 151, 155

dreams, 157, 159–60, 168, 184n6, 185n15, 185n17

Eagleton, Terry, 110

Edison, Thomas, 19, 60, 259

editing. *See* cinematic techniques; montage

Eisenstein, Sergei: animal/human dichotomy in, 101–2, 122, 126–27, 136; Barthes on, 103; cinema as social production for, 20, 66, 72, 86nn37–38, 93, 107–8, 112–13, 118; dematerialization of industrial process, 95; engineering approach of, 68–69, 122, 124–25, 130–31, 149n74, 275; film career of, 139; on the ideology of form, 121, 146n55, 146n56; "manufacturing logic" principle of, 97–98, 109; montage-of-attractions technique, 45, 69, 96, 131, 133, 139; on movement, 124–25; Pavlov and Taylor compared with, 133t; rationality and, 125–35, 137, 148n72; representation vs. presentation in, 109, 118, 125; resistance to the capitalist cinematic sensorium, 106; Vertov compared with, 50, 66, 83nn20–21, 86n38, 99, 129–31. See also *Strike, The*

email, 13, 76

Engels, Friedrich, 85n32

entertainment/enjoyment. *See* pleasure; spectatorship

entrepreneurship, 170, 187–88n29

envy, 180–81, 189nn45–46

evolution, 134

exceptionalism, 286–87

exchange-value: aura as, 238n30; bourgeois economic and, 181; cinematic experience as, 104–5, 110, 214; of images, 76, 245, 248–49; money and, 66–68; signifier as, 220–21; as site of cathexis, 255. *See also* circulation; labor theory of value; surplus-value

existentialism, 271

Faulkner, William, 226, 267

feminism. *See* gender

fetishization: of artistic works, 23–24, 180, 212–13, 237n24; of commodi-

ties, 9, 21–22, 175–76, 215–16; de-fetishization capacity of film, 44; as invisible labor, 114–15; labor theory of value and, 47; simulation and, 239n32

film: "cinema" distinguished from, 22, 58; as money, 58, 66–67, 77, 85n32, 86–87n45. *See also* cinema

"filmic" encounters (Barthes), 103

"filming" (Wurzer), 59–65

film-language, 17–18, 162

financialization of the sign (Baudrillard), 300

Fordism, 110, 122, 147–48n69, 149n77, 208–9

Forrest Gump (Zemeckis)1, 274

Foucault, Michel, 84n23, 132, 289

frames, 42, 58, 77, 86–87n45, 105–6

freedom: freedom reflex (Pavlov), 119, 136, 139–40, 145n50, 293; market capitalism as, 273–74; programming and, 132; recuperated as alienated capitalist productivity, 27–29; as specter of capital, 139

FreePC, 4

Freud, Sigmund: on condensation, 15; on dreamwork, 157, 160, 167–68, 185–87nn17–18; on fetishes, 21; on parapraxis, 18; on the pleasure principle, 8, 195; on repression as "cutting," 196; role of language in, 187n26; sublimation concept, 152, 179; theory of the unconscious, 17–18, 165–66

Friedberg, Anne, 184n6

Gabel, Joseph, 155

gaze, 166–81, 188n35, 210

gender: of capital and labor, 188–89nn37; feminist critique of subjectivity, 224–25, 241n38; informal economy and, 242n52; male desire as origin of the imaginary, 17; in *Man with a*

Movie Camera, 70; pre-oedipal consciousness and, 221–22, 225; Taylor worker screening process, 146n61; in *Until the End of the World*, 221–22

general intellect, 295–96

globalization: of capital, 24, 198; deterritorialization and, 74–75; globe as image, 230; national borders and, 236n11; transnational capital, 241–42n46

global warming, 164, 229–30

Godard, Jean-Luc, 82n15, 84n24, 115

Godzich, Wlad: on the breakdown of language by images, 15, 18, 150–51, 161, 162–63; on postmodernism, 153; on the temporal fallout of the image, 183–84n1

Goebbels, Joseph, 81n5

Goldstein, Seth, 303–7

Google, 68–69, 234–35, 302–3, 308

Gorky, Maxim, 127

Gottdiener, Mark, 280n2

Goux, Jean-Joseph, 10, 25–26

Gramsci, Antonio: on Americanism, 241n44; on Fordist manufacturing, 110, 122, 147–48n69; on repetition in labor, 148n73; on sensation/movement severance, 228, 241n44

graphosphere, 11–12

Guattari, Félix, 152, 162, 225–26

Gulf War of 1990, 198, 267, 280n3

Gynesis (Jardine), 222, 241n37

Hardt, Michael, 149n77, 283

Heath, Stephen, 12, 17

Hegel, Georg Wilhelm Friedrich, 94, 140–41n6, 240n35

Heidegger, Martin, 10, 60, 63–64

Herman, Edward S., 147n65

history, 97–98, 109, 123, 214

Hitchcock, Alfred, 17, 178

Hollywood: attention theory and, 181–82; business structure of, 32n37,

209; depicted in *Barton Fink*, 193–94; Eisenstein compared with, 68–69; globalization and, 24; as important industry, 3; television compared with, 152–53

Horkheimer, Max: on amusement, 76; critique of the culture industry, 27, 33n50, 86n44, 247, 289–91; on rationality, 228, 298; on the the surfacing of signification, 239–40n34

Hughes, Langston, 226

humanity: abstracted humanity in *Contact*, 255–56; collective agency in Eisenstein, 101, 127; commons as constitutive of, 294–95; consciousness of human achievement as resistance, 41; human/animal dichotomy, 101–2, 120–22, 126–27, 134–36, 146n63; machine-human continuum in Vertov, 46, 49; movement and, 125; as site of resistance, 29. *See also* society

idealism, 266

ideology: Althusser on, 10, 30n16, 291–92; Eisenstein approach to, 50; form and, 121, 146n55; interpellation, 291–92; pedagogical value of film, 81n5; psyche of modern capital as, 174–76, 188–89nn36–37; simulation and, 214; technology and, 12, 30–31n21; Vertov principle of abstraction and, 50–52

image-commodities: abstraction of, 245; cinematic technology and, 47, 236n17; commodity-object vs. image-object, 75–78, 114–15; cultural value of, 233–34; image-commodity in Vertov, 40, 42–46, 66–67; images as fetishized commodities, 9–10; Media Futures market, 306–8; mediation of capital and, 276; science of, 260–61. *See also* commodification; images

images: abstraction of capital and, 95–96; appropriation of attention by, 4–5; breakdown of the *logos* by, 18, 150–51, 161–63; as cinematic technology, 10–11; consciousness and, 71–72, 247–49; desire as origin of, 17; economic production and, 24–25, 47–48, 75–76; of humanity, 257; language compared with, 15, 31n26, 71–72, 73; of money, 257–58; as paradigmatic social relation, 56; representation-unconscious-commodity convergence in, 217–23; semiotics of, 114–15, 160–61, 171–72, 185–87n18; social investment as, 232–33; speed of, 150–51, 165. *See also* image-commodities

Immortal Technique, 309–12

imperialism, 102, 112, 134–35, 198, 200, 236n11

indexicality, 19–20

individualism: commodities and, 44–45; individual agency, 131, 161–62, 266–67, 270–71; individual as locus of society (Marx), 81n11; individual experience, 240–41n36; particularization of surplus-value oppression and, 65; personal names, 239–40n34. *See also* subjectivity

infantilization, 241n38

informal economy, 231, 242n52

information, 213–14, 230, 237–38nn27–28

intention. *See* individualism; subjectivity

Internet: anti-capitalist discourse and, 311–12; attention-based business models, 305–8; attention theory and, 5; as cinematic technology, 13, 76, 106; email, 13, 76; general transformation of media pathways and, 283; Google, 68–69, 234–35, 302–3, 308; monetization of content,

234–35; as site of spectator-labor, 201; Yahoo!, 5, 308. *See also* computers

interpellation (Althusser), 291–92

intervals, 39, 45, 49, 51, 80–81n3. *See also* cinematic techniques; montage

Iraq War, 198, 274, 279, 301

Irigaray, Luce, 225–26

Island of Dr. Moreau (Wells), 102, 134

Jameson, Fredric: cinematic theory and, 16–17; on cognitive mapping, 301; on dreams, 185n15; on history, 109; on the production of visual capital, 24–25; on the totality of capitalism, 255

Jardine, Alice, 222, 225–26, 241n37

Jaws (Spielberg), 96

Jay, Martin, 161

Kant, Immanuel, 60, 243

Keynesian economic paradigm, 149n77

kino-eye (Vertov): acted cinema and, 147n66; capital circulation and, 46–47; communism as, 72; defined, 38, 43; Eisenstein on, 86n37, 131; Marxist principles in, 51–52, 85n26; montage and, 80n2; *Natural Born Killers* compared with, 276; production of consciousness in, 48–49, 57, 247; seeing-eye principle of, 46, 54, 79, 81n13, 82n19

labor: attention theory and, 28–29; capital and, 138; cinematic consciousness and, 110; cottage industries, 13, 112; Eisenstein depiction of, 101–2, 122, 126–27, 136; human agency and, 101–3, 131, 136; informal economy, 231, 242n52; mental vs. manual labor, 82n14, 89; necessary vs. surplus labor, 113, 202–3; as product of capi-

Man with a Movie Camera (Vertov):
cinematic technology in, 41–45;
circulation of image-value and,
199–200; consciousness as concern
of, 82n14, 217; overview, 37–38,
39–40; political economy depicted
in, 24, 48–49, 53, 68, 78, 275;
resemblances in *Contact*, 251.
See also Vertov, Dziga

Marx, Karl: on abstract universal labor
time, 234, 236n14; on alienation by
wage-labor, 15, 44, 81n10, 247–48;
animal/human dichotomy in, 101–2,
302; cinematic aspects of, 24, 105; on
the circulation of capital, 113–14,
203–4; on commodification, 7–8,
67–69, 243; on commodity fetishism, 21–22; on consciousness, 74,
82n14, 176–77, 245; Derrida on
"Marx's injunction," 88–89, 140n2;
on forms of production, 48, 75,
143n23; on the historical production
of the present, 8, 98; on ideology,
174, 188–89nn36–37; on the individual as the social being, 81n11; on the
limited expansion of capital, 201–2,
204; materialist principles of, 94; on
money, 4, 57–58, 66, 85n32, 87n46,
144n37, 197, 255; on necessary labor,
113, 202–3; Negri on, 27; on overdetermination, 185–87n18; principle
of abstraction in, 51–52, 59, 243; on
private property, 111, 247, 299–300;
production-consumption relationship
and, 234; repressive hypothesis in,
63–64; on ruling ideas, 85–86n35,
176; on the "secret" of the value of
commodities, 158, 185n11; on the
senses, 85n26, 169; on sensuous
labor, 89, 144–45nn41–42; on the
subjectification of capital, 174; theory
of sexuality, 84n24; Vertov references
to, 38–39, 51–52; on workers as pro-

ducts, 134. *See also* labor theory of
value; Marxism; sensual labor

Marxism: as active dialectical critique,
115; dreamwork and, 168, 184n6; invasion of consciousness and, 97; as
revolutionary discourse, 173; table of
comparison with Psychoanalysis and
Cinematics, 183t. *See also* Marx, Karl

mass media: as a deterritorialized factory, 10, 13–14, 29, 79, 112–15; media
bytes, 213–15; media-ocracy, 16–17;
media pathways, 13, 114, 213; media
studies, 223; models of signification,
225; videosphere, 11–12

materiality: of cinematic bodies, 65;
dematerialization of material movement, 97–98, 103; dematerialization
of the commodity, 20–21, 75–76,
87n48, 180; of the Lacanian "montage of the drive," 158, 184n9; Lacanian *objet a* and, 166–69; Marxist
materialism, 94; metaphysics as genealogy of "filming," 59; Vertov depiction of, 37–38; of visuality, 16–17,
55. *See also* commodification; metaphysics

Matisse, Henri, 171–72

Matrix, The (Wachowski brothers), 7,
160, 199, 261

Matthews, Joseph, 284–85

McLuhan, Marshall, 214, 231

Mechanics of the Brain (Pudovkin),
148n72

media. *See* mass media

mediation: abstraction ("vanishing mediators"), 59, 76, 138–39, 182; cinema
as remediation of objects, 45–46, 51,
80, 84n24; circulation and, 114; of
commodities by money, 57–58; deterritorialization of work and, 112–15;
film as money of cinema, 58, 66,
85n32; Goux on the imaginary in economic production, 24–26; images as

capital-media, 276; as key to resistance, 301–2; Lacanian screen and, 170–73; as manufactured continuity, 158–59, 185n13; media as prosthesis for human agency, 266–67, 270–71; media pathways, 13, 114, 213; money as proto-image, 106, 245, 248; Money-Commodity-Money formula, 78; of pain, 132; self-conscious vs. functional mediation, 238n28; technology and, 11–12; transnational capitalism and, 198–99; of value in image-commodities, 57. *See also* money

Merleau-Ponty, Maurice, 166, 171, 181, 183

Mernitt, Susan, 303–4

metaphysics, 59, 61. *See also* materiality

Metropolis (Lang), 199

La Mettrie, Julien Offray de, 148n72

Metz, Christian: on cinema as technology of the real, 109–10, 137; on filmic pleasure, 11, 115–16; on film theory, 16; on "financial feedback," 244; psychoanalytic investigation of capitalist cinema, 104, 108; on spectatorship, 250, 302; on the three machines of cinema, 10–11, 111–12, 144n38

Meyerhold, Vsevolod, 148n72

Michelson, Annette, 38, 68, 85n26, 148n72

Microsoft, 68–69

Mirzeoff, Nicholas, 8

modernism: human/animal dichotomy and, 126, 134–35, 146n63; montage as fundamental technique for, 132–34, 147–48n69; psychoanalysis and, 165; as transformation of traditional society, 125, 134–35

Modern Times (Chaplain), 125, 199

money, 4; as abstract "vanishing mediator," 76, 182, 245; commodities relation to, 33n48, 258; coordination of

nonsynchronicities and, 53; exchange-value of images and, 76–79, 87n48, 245, 248; film as, 58, 66–67, 85n32, 86–87n45; forms of, 112, 257–58, 261; mediation process in, 22, 46, 57–58, 76, 144n37; money-image, 217–18, 227; mortgage loans and, 305–6; as the obverse of images, 106, 245; photography and, 4; price and, 58, 77–78; reification and, 44–47; thinking money, 196–97, 214, 245; transformation of traditional society and, 135. *See also* capital; mediation

Money-Commodity-Money formula, 78

montage: assembly-line logic in, 9, 45, 132–34, 147–48n69, 208–9; capital circulation and, 53–54; cutting as discontinuity, 156–60, 184n9, 196, 235–36n9; Eisenstein montage of attractions, 45, 69, 96, 131, 133, 139; intervals and, 39, 45, 80–81n3; Marxist labor theory and, 38–42; montage of the drive (Lacan), 156–60, 184n9. *See also* cinematic techniques; intervals

Morin, Edgar, 3

movement: cinema as transformation of, 108, 141n9; as fundamental to Eisenstein, 96–97, 124–25; illusion of movement in cinema, 156; movement-image vs. time-image, 235n1; programming of, 132; strikes and, 101–3. *See also* body

Mulvey, Laura, 17

Munier, Roger, 15, 31n26

murder, 8–9

Mypoints.com, 5

Myspace.com, 235

names, 239–40n34

narcissism, 217–19

narrative, 152–53, 213, 237n27, 238n30. *See also* storytelling

Natural Born Killers (Stone), 267–79, 280–81n6

negative dialectics, 27–28

Negri, Antonio: on affective labor, 283; on antagonism as capitalist process, 72; on cinematic totalitarianism, 108; on labor, 89; on postmodern capitalism, 26–27; on social cooperation, 8; on social-workers, 199; on the subsumption of society in capital, 280n1

Nelson, Theodor, 144n39

New Criticism, 160

New World Order, 140, 176

Nielsen ratings, 114, 270

Nietzsche, Friedrich, 60

9/11 (World Trade Center destruction), 284, 285, 288

objet a (Lacan), 166–69, 173–74, 176–77, 179, 181, 261, 277

Orwell, George, 219, 221, 268, 285–87

other, the, 161, 176, 266, 276–77

overdetermination, 121, 157, 185–87n18

painting. *See* art

Pascal, Blaise, 175

Pasolini, Pier Paolo, 96, 141n9, 162

Pavlov, I. P.: animal/human dichotomy and, 102, 122, 126, 134–35; Eisenstein and, 69, 117, 133t; evolution and, 134–35; freedom vs. food reflex, 27, 119, 136, 139–40, 145n50; population control as legacy of, 131–32; reflexology theory of, 121–23, 126, 127–28, 137; signalization, 109, 133, 224; Taylor and, 133t

Perry, W. J., 142n11

perverse, the, 221–22, 225

photography: as discourse, 15; language compared with, 31n26; political economy of visuality and, 4; scopic objects and, 168–73, 178–79; still frames in Vertov and, 42

Piaget, Jean, 224–25

plasticity, 2–3

Plato, 60, 178, 237n21

pleasure: as aim of cinematic production, 115–16; control of affect (Pavlov), 119; entertainment as labor, 138–39, 201; of fetishized objects, 22; recuperated as alienated capitalist productivity, 27–28, 76; sensual labor and, 74–75, 248–50; social investment and, 232–33; surplus-value and, 173–74; visual pleasure as murder, 8–9

Poe, Edgar Allan, 107

poetry, 94

Poindexter, John, 304

Polan, Dana, 3

Polanyi, Karl, 294

pornography, 213, 309

postcolonialism, 198, 236n11

postmodernism: art as second-order commodification, 23; domination of the unconscious in, 164; fragmentation of the subject, 8–9, 106–7; gender and, 222; history and, 123; identification with violence, 267–71; Jameson on, 16–17; redistribution of sense, 246–47; simulation as fundamental for, 105, 239n32; subsumption of culture/society to capital, 24–25, 26–27, 280n1; transformation of signification in, 219–21; visual economy role in, 24–25

Potemkin (Eisenstein), 121, 149n74

practice, 175–76

price, 58, 77–78

primitive accumulation, 284–85, 294–95

print technology, 5–6

prisons, 289–92

production: capitalist obscurity of production, 74, 270; circulation and, 114; consciousness and, 30–31n21, 110,

151, 159–60; fetishization as, 212–16, 237n24; Marx on, 48, 102, 143n23; as montage, 235–36n9; pain and, 132; productive value of attention, 108; prosumers (Toffler), 293; sentience of objects of production, 169; social production in Eisenstein, 98–99; social production in Marx, 204; social production in Vertov, 48–49; social production vs. image production, 52. *See also* capital; circulation

programming, 132, 144n39

property: alienation and, 111, 247; capitalized visuality and, 299–300; celebrities and, 200; commodification of the public sphere, 113; commons, 294–95; gaze and, 181; individual proprietary rights, 304–5; intellectual property, 234–35; money economy and, 66–67; representation and, 266–67

prosumers (Toffler), 293

Proust, Marcel, 238n30

Psycho (Hitchcock), 277

psychoanalysis: cinematic machine and, 10–11; cinematic unconscious and, 171–73; discontinuity and, 156–60, 163–65, 184n9; discourse-of-the-Other and, 161, 176, 266, 276–77; knowledge of practice in, 175–76; Metz approach to capitalist cinema, 104, 108; origin of the cinematic imaginary and, 17–19; phallogocentric subjectivity in Wenders, 221–22; Shaviro approach to cinematic subjectivity and, 106; table of comparison with Marxism and Cinematics, 183t. *See also* consciousness

Pudovkin, Vsevoled, 148n72

race, 289–92

Ranieri, Lewis, 305–7

rationality: abstraction process, 243–44;

of capital, 93, 134–35, 298; Eisenstein film theory and, 125–35, 148n72; national sovereignty and, 286–87; Pavlov reflexology and, 135; postmodern "end of reason," 246

reading, 232

reality: cinema as technology of the real, 104, 108–10; cinematic hyper-reality as, 256; enclosure by capital, 10; images/unconscious substituted for, 161–64; marginalization of, 171, 194–96, 235n3, 278–79; Reality-Industrial Complex (Rheingold), 119, 144n39; reality principle (Freud), 194–96; technology-free immediacy of, 10; virtual reality, 7, 230

reflexology, 119–28, 135–36, 145n50

Reich, Robert, 139

reification: dematerialization of the commodity, 20–21, 46–47; general phenomenology of capital and, 109; objectification of the Other, 277; Simmel theory of, 44–45; Warhol treatment of, 22–23

representation: consumption of personalities and, 271–72; end of representation, 217–23, 239–40n34, 288–89; movement-image vs. time-image and, 235n1; prisons and, 292–93; of production in cinema, 118, 125, 137; reflexology and, 109; simulation and, 239n32; stylistic freedom and, 262; the unrepresentable, 220–22. *See also* semiotics

resistance. *See* revolutionary discourse

Retort Collective, 284–88, 294

revolutionary discourse: alienation of, 253–56; attention theory and, 28; capital cooptation of bodies and, 13; capitalization of the resistance to capitalism, 88–89; consciousness as fundamental to, 73–74; discontinuity and, 158, 163–64, 185n12;

305; on tools as forms of consciousness, 40–41

Simon, John, 28n6

simulation: Baudrillard on, 21; Deleuze on, 237n21; as excess of reference, 239n32; postmodernism and, 105; signification-to-simulation paradigm shift, 96; visuality and, 213–17. *See also* representation; semiotics

Smith, Adam, 202

Smith, Barbara Herrnstein, 146n56

Smith, Geoffrey Nowell, 208–9

society: capitalist social production, 204, 270; cinema as organizational paradigm, 111; collective alienation, 253–56; collectivization of production, 44–45; Fordism, 110, 122, 147–48n69, 149n77; fraternal solidarity as revolutionary society, 100–101; growth of bureaucracy, 147n65; inequality vs. asymmetry and, 188–89nn36–37; mediation and, 132; national sovereignty, 236n11, 286–87; participatory social production, 8, 30n15; political economy of social organization, 90; social commons, 294–95; social investment, 232–33; social totality, 45; stability of production and, 143n23; stages of human development (Taylor), 125; television as collective device, 84n22; transparency of, 50, 84n23; weak citizenship, 285. *See also* subaltern society

sovereignty, 236n11, 286–87

spectacle: alienation and, 217; becoming-commodity of the world and, 278; defined, 211; as occupation of life by commodities, 261–62; revolutionary discourse and, 291; simulation and, 214–15; unconscious of, 220–22; of violence, 271, 277; World Trade Center destruction and, 285

spectatorship: audience quality assessment, 28; capital circulation and, 69–70, 76–77; cinematic gaze and, 178–79; cinematic production of audiences, 54–55; cinematic technology and, 11, 230; as consumption vs. production, 112, 232–33, 261; "directed creation," 17; in Eisenstein vs. Vertov, 66, 86n38, 99, 129–30; futurist painting and, 109, 143n32; as labor, 1–4, 11, 14, 181, 200–201, 302–4; reflexology and, 126–27; sensual labor and, 74–75, 248–50; simulacra and, 214–15; valorization gap in, 78. *See also* attention theory of value; visuality

Staiger, Janet, 209

Stalin, Joseph, 118, 147n66

Stalinism, 121

star system, 3

steam technology, 19, 99, 103

Stone, Oliver, 267–79, 280–81n6

storytelling. *See also* narrative, 238n30

Strike, The (Eisenstein): alienated posture of, 121; approach to spectatorship in, 127; depiction of human agency in, 136; as a historical formation, 97–98, 109; immateriality of others in, 277; montage-of-attractions in, 96–97, 149n74; overview, 90–91, 99–101, 142n11; resistance against capital encroachment in, 89, 113. *See also* Eisenstein, Sergei

strikes, 88–89, 98–99, 102–3

subaltern society: disguised wages in, 242n52; global pauperization, 198, 236n11; mediatic violence and, 270; operation of capital in, 257; peasantry as animal worker/spectators, 126–27, 134–35; representation and, 262–63; subjectivity in, 221. *See also* society subjectivity: *aphanisis* (Lacan), 221–22; aura of cinematic perception, 210–17, 237n25, 238–39n30–31; cinematization of, 23–24, 26, 159–60; critical theory as, 223–25; "death of the subject," 292; discontinuity of the subject, 158–61, 185n14; Eisenstein self-privileging and, 146n56; evacuation of the other and, 276–77; gaze and, 167–81; Lacanian screen and, 170–73; layered in the artistic object, 181; media as prosthesis for human agency, 266–67, 270–71; Pavlov experiments and, 119; "Piagetic error" of subjectivity, 224–25; postmodern fragmentation of, 8–9, 106; psycho-social nexus of Fordist manufacturing (Gramsci), 110; reconceptualization of the imaginary and, 10; relation of machines to, 83n20; televisual subjectivity, 274, 277; violence/annihilation as substance of, 267–72, 277–78; voracious eye of capital and, 169–70, 189n46. See also consciousness; individualism

subjugation, 131

sublimation, 152, 179

Surin, Ken, 109, 149n77

surplus-value: attention theory and, 205–6; cinematic technology and, 54–55; circulation and, 114; diminishing rate of, 138, 149n77; expansion of capital and, 204–6; exploitative value extraction and, 112–13, 202; labor as source of, 176–77; repressed violence of capital and, 64–65; surplus-enjoyment and, 173–74. See also capital; circulation; exchange-value; labor theory of value

Tarantino, Quentin, 28n6

Tarkovsky, Andrey, 53, 221

Taylor, Frederick Winslow:

animal/human dichotomy in, 120–22; Eisenstein and, 117, 131, 133t; on film relationship with bodies, 109; industrial design theories of, 119, 137; Pavlov and, 133t; use of montage, 133–34. See also Taylorization

Taylor, Richard, 98, 142n10

Taylorization (scientific management): CMP compared with, 199; effeciency principle of, 122; Eisenstein and, 109, 120, 126, 133t; falling-rate-of-profit crisis and, 205; montage and, 208–9; overview, 123–25; reflexology and, 120, 133t; as socialization, 199; Vertov and, 275; worker screening process, 146n61. See also Taylor, Frederick Winslow

technology: alienation and, 33n50; bureaucracy and, 147n65; consciousness and, 40–41; Eisenstein vs. Chaplain on, 125; equipment-free immediacy and, 93–94; industrial technologies in Vertov, 129; machines as cultural forms, 207; mechanical reproduction of objects, 44; mediation and, 12, 30–31n21; print technology, 5–6; spectatorship and, 11; steam technology, 19, 99, 103; subjectivity and, 83n20; three machines of capitalism (Mandel), 19; three machines of cinema (Metz), 10–11, 111–12, 144n38. See also cinematic techniques

television: attention theory and, 5; cinema as precursor to, 13; as core experience in Beavis and Butt-head, 151–53, 176, 220; deterritorialization of work and, 112–14; narrative as dispensable in, 152–53; spectator-labor and, 206–7; as symbolic violence, 301; televisual subjectivity, 274, 277; Vertov on, 84n22; video, 217–19, 222–25 temporality. *See* time

Terminator film series, 25, 229, 242n48

terrorism, 263

Third World. *See* subaltern society

time: abstract universal labor time, 234, 236n14; cybertime, 6; movement-image vs. time-image, 227–29, 235n1; temporal fallout of images, 183–84n1; temporality, 2–3

Time Machine, The (Wells), 227–28

Toffler, Alvin, 293

Total Information Awareness System, 304

totalitarianism, 2, 19, 74, 108

Towards the Dictatorship (Eisenstein), 97–98, 142n10

Ultraviolet (Wimmer), 309

unconscious, the. *See* consciousness

Until the End of the World (Wenders), 217–28, 241n37

urban sprawl, 280n2

use-value. *See* exchange-value; labor theory of value

utopianism, 121

Valery, Paul, 168, 238n30

valorization gap, 78, 87n46

value. *See* attention theory of value; exchange-value; labor theory of value; surplus-value

Van Gogh, Vincent, 23

Vanilla Sky (2001), 160

vel of alienation (Lacan), 240n35

Vertov, Dziga: on acted cinema, 72, 86n40, 147n66; ambitions for cinematic consciousness, 50, 57, 70–72, 80; critique of money, 45–46; dialectical image presentation in, 48–49; Eisenstein compared with, 50, 66, 83nn20–21, 86n38, 99, 129–31; exposure of commodity production in, 17, 20, 24, 47, 66–69; "factory of facts" approach, 66, 68, 79, 147n66; industrial technologies in, 129; Marxist techniques of, 38–39, 55, 57; montage as fundamental technique for, 39, 80n2, 275–76; remediation of objects, 51, 84n24; seeing-eye principle of, 46, 49, 50, 51, 54, 82n13, 82n19; on television, 84n22; treatment of nonsynchronicity, 53–54; Wenders compared with, 217. *See also* kino-eye; *Man with a Movie Camera*

video, 217–19, 222–25, 258

videosphere, 11–12

violence, 63–65, 267–74, 277, 301

Virilio, Paul, 107, 142n11, 207, 255

Virno, Paolo, 295–98

virtual reality, 7, 230

virtuosity, 295–96

visuality: aura and, 215–17, 238–39n30–31; blindness, 217; commodification and, 12–13, 45–46; distance (Benjamin), 237n25; gaze, 166–81; history of term, 7–8; industrialization of, 9; materiality of, 16–17, 38–42; persistence of vision, 209–10; property and, 181, 189n45, 299–300; violence and, 279; visual capital, 200; visual economy, 19–24; visual fetishes, 231. *See also* attention theory of value; spectatorship

Wagner, Mitch, 302–3

warfare: capitalism and, 273–74, 280n3; permanent war, 287–88; as symbolic violence, 301; as televisual process, 266, 278–79; World Trade Center destruction and, 285

Warhol, Andy, 22–23

Watts, Michael, 284–85